CITY OF HUSTLE

A SIOUX FALLS ANTHOLOGY

MORE CITY ANTHOLOGIES FROM BELT

A Lovely Place, a Fighting Place, a Charmer: The Baltimore Anthology

The Indianapolis Anthology

The Dayton Anthology

The Louisville Anthology

The Gary Anthology

Car Bombs to Cookie Tables: The Youngstown Anthology, Second Edition

The Columbus Anthology

The St. Louis Anthology

Under Purple Skies: The Minneapolis Anthology

The Milwaukee Anthology

Rust Belt Chicago: An Anthology

Grand Rapids Grassroots: An Anthology

Happy Anyway: A Flint Anthology

The Akron Anthology

Right Here, Right Now: The Buffalo Anthology

The Cleveland Anthology, Second Edition

The Pittsburgh Anthology

A Detroit Anthology

The Cincinnati Anthology

CITY OF HUSTLE

A SIOUX FALLS ANTHOLOGY

EDITED BY JON K. LAUCK & PATRICK HICKS

First Edition 2022
ISBN: 9781953368355

Belt Publishing
5322 Fleet Avenue, Cleveland, OH 44105
www.beltpublishing.com

Book design by Meredith Pangrace
Cover by David Wilson

To Harry F. Thompson

for his dedication to this city and this region

CONTENTS

CONTENTS

Preface

PATRICK HICKS

It started at the Paramount. This chic cocktail bar in downtown Sioux Falls had become our place to unwind after work on Fridays and, over a few beers, Jon and I came up with the idea of an anthology about South Dakota's largest city. It was late summer 2019, and as usual, we had the place mostly to ourselves. The bartender was busy slicing lemons and a jazz pianist was setting up for the night.

We knew there were great stories about our city, and we also knew there was a deep reservoir of talented writers who could bring Sioux Falls to life on the page. The more we talked, the more excited we got. We started to write down possible topics on a napkin with a ballpoint pen but quickly switched to a sheet of paper when one idea led to another. Soon, we had a list of essay ideas and we knew we had a book on our hands.

That book is now in your hands.

What makes this anthology unique is not only the variety of voices held between the covers but also the stories that shed greater light on the city. Even though I've lived in Sioux Falls for over twenty years, there were things I didn't know about this place I call home. Thanks to the writers who contributed to this anthology, I can now walk around a little more slowly and consider what makes this place—this vibrant place—special. One of the great joys of coediting this anthology has been seeing Sioux Falls through the eyes of others.

But I'm getting ahead of myself.

Let's get back to the Paramount for a minute.

Jon and I held weekly meetings and the occasional fishing trip to Blue Dog Lake in order to figure out more topics for the book. As time went by, we invited other writers to help us brainstorm. The list grew. Topics were assigned. The table of contents began to take shape. All we needed now was a publisher. It was important to us that the project had a home from the very beginning because we felt we owed that to our contributors. If they were willing to spend time doing research, we wanted them to know from the outset that the book was definitely going to be printed.

It was Jon's idea to contact Belt Publishing. He had mentioned their wildly popular City Anthology Series and suggested that our book would be perfect for their catalog. For several years now, Belt Publishing has been creating anthologies devoted to cities in the Midwest, and they have already published extremely popular collections centered around Cleveland, St. Louis, Minneapolis, Pittsburgh, Detroit, Milwaukee, and many other places. Belt was founded in 2013 by Anne Trubek, and in its nearly ten years of operation, it has produced wonderful books that focus on the Rust Belt and the Midwest. Anne was a professor at Oberlin College from 1997 to 2015, where she taught courses in journalism and rhetoric; she resigned her tenured position in order to start a press that might amplify the literary voices of her community. Belt offers vital space for stories from our region that need to be told, and when Jon suggested that our book aligned with Belt's mission, it was obvious that we should approach Anne. But would she be interested in an anthology about South Dakota's largest city? With a population of nearly 200,000 we would be the smallest city in the series.

Happily, when we contacted Anne, she was interested in the idea and wanted to know more. Emails were sent, questions were asked about marketing, a proposal for launching the book was created, and before too long, we had a contract. We were on our way, and the essays started to roll in.

For a literary project like this, we wanted a wide variety of voices—we wanted to represent the community as best as we could—and we were deliberate in reaching out to those who could speak with authority. It was especially important that we honored Native voices because we wanted to begin with an understanding that the land of Sioux Falls is the ancestral territory of the *Oceti Sakowin* (Seven Council Fires), which was an alliance that consisted of the Santee, Yankton, and Lakota. We were therefore pleased when Avery Jones agreed to write "Hdihunni," which explores language, and George Shurr gave us his excellent essay, "Blood Run." Both are necessary reminders of the rich life existing on this land long before the city of Sioux Falls came into being.

As the book grew, it became obvious that certain topics had to be mentioned. Could there be an anthology of Sioux Falls without, say, an essay on the Big Sioux River or Falls Park? How about John Morrell, the Cathedral of Saint Joseph, the universities, or Phillips Avenue? These things *had* to be in the anthology. We also knew that we needed experts to write about the hospitals and banks that anchor the economy. Other topics came to us almost accidentally when writers approached us with something they wanted to say. This is how we learned about Fenn's Bros., the Nordic Hall, the Pomp Room, the lost history of the wonderfully whimsical Joyland

Park, the incredible life of Joe Foss, and the surprising history of brewing beer in Sioux Falls.

After a year of collecting essays, we began to order the table of contents so that topics were clustered into groups. In this way, writers seemed to be in conversation with each other rather than scattered randomly here and there. For an anthology such as this, however, the table of contents is simply a suggestion for how to read it. Order, of course, is relative. Just because we've placed these essays in a way that makes sense to us as editors, this doesn't mean that you have to follow the pages in sequence. In fact, it's very likely that you'll jump around, reading first one essay that captures your attention and then flipping past fifty pages to read another. This is as it should be. We all see our city differently, so why should reading about Sioux Falls be the same for everyone?

We had a lot of fun turning this idea into a reality, and there are many people who helped us along the way. We want to thank Anne Trubek and everyone at Belt Publishing for believing in the project and giving our anthology a home. We're grateful and delighted that Sioux Falls has joined the City Series. We also want to thank the writers who made this book possible by sharing their expertise, stories, and passion. Without them, we wouldn't have a book at all, and their essays have helped widen the lens of how we view Sioux Falls. The writers in this anthology were generous with their time, they offered suggestions on how we could make the book better, and they quietly taught us more about our city.

But what is a book without readers? We want to thank you for picking this up, sitting down on a comfy sofa or in a coffee shop on Phillips Avenue, and reading this page. In a second or two, you'll flip away from what I'm saying here and move someplace else in the book. Wherever you land—perhaps it will be decades in the past or someplace closer to our present moment—we know that you'll enjoy what you discover about Sioux Falls, this city we call home.

Introduction: Founding a City

JON K. LAUCK

Every city is a product of geography, timing, and its founding settlers. Many early American cities were established adjacent to good harbors and, later, when people moved inland, on navigable rivers. Boston, Philadelphia, and San Francisco were harbor cities, for example, while Louisville and St. Louis were river cities. Their early settlers were also distinct. Boston was settled by dissenting English Congregationalists (the majoritarian Irish came later), Philadelphia by dissenting Quakers, and San Francisco by traders and Spaniards and later by Chinese immigrants and gold miners, who all gave shape and identity and a particular valence to these cities. Boston and Philadelphia are also old by American standards, founded in 1630 and 1682, and so they carry the burdens—and the mystique—of centuries of existence.

The city of Sioux Falls was similarly shaped by place, time, and people. Its founders were drawn in by the presence of a river, the Big Sioux River in this case. The river was not navigable for big boats, but the current was thought to be a source of power for milling and small industry. River navigability was less crucial for Sioux Falls than earlier river cities because by the late 1800s, when Sioux Falls took form, the railroads were disrupting the long-standing riverine dependence of cities. The people who streamed into Sioux Falls were the products of the robust agrarian heartland to the East, the American Midwest, and were joined by immigrants from Scandinavia, Germany, and Ireland. They founded a busy town on the prairie that would blossom into a major American city by the 2020s.

The first crucial step was taken by Iowans and Minnesotans. These midwesterners quickly spotted the big bend in the Big Sioux River and the picturesque falls that would give the future city its name. In 1857, land companies based in Dubuque and St. Paul sent representatives into what would become Dakota Territory to scope out townsites and make claims for what they knew would be a future city, perhaps even a state capital. They were on their guard because of the recent massacre of settlers to the east of Sioux Falls around present-day Lake Okoboji.[1] The few settlers who had trickled into Sioux Falls were completely driven out a few years later,

1 Thomas Teakle, *Spirit Lake Massacre* (Iowa City, IA: State Historical Society of Iowa, 1918).

in 1862, during the Great Sioux Uprising, which saw the death of 700 Minnesota farmers and their families.[2] The paroxysms of the Civil War during the early 1860s further stymied the development of the town.[3]

The 1870s proved to be the formative decade for Sioux Falls. By then, Dakota Territory had been officially created, and its governing structures had started to function. In 1877, the territorial legislature formally created Sioux Falls, which was then home to about 500 people. In those early days, material had to be hauled into Sioux Falls via wagon from the railhead to the east in Worthington, Minnesota.[4] In early 1878, in anticipation of the extension of the railroad from Worthington over to Sioux Falls, the town started to boom. In March 1878, the *Sioux Falls Pantagraph* reported that the "noise of the saw and hammer is heard in all parts of the town from morning till night."[5] Over the previous couple of years, real estate prices had doubled, and the *Pantagraph* said the city had become a "vortex of a whirlpool of immigration."[6] In July 1878, the railroad extension to Sioux Falls was finally finished, and the young city was ready. Eleven hotels and many boardinghouses, which were "crowded continually," had been built to hold the settlers coming in to set up their homesteads on the fertile lands of southeastern Dakota Territory.[7] The federal land office in Sioux Falls, established in 1873, processed over seventy claims a day on average in 1878. Before the young ambitious claimants headed out to their new 160-acre farms, they bought supplies in Sioux Falls at the city's six hardware stores, eleven dry goods stores, fourteen groceries, and six lumberyards (and maybe they even stopped into one of the city's seven saloons).[8] By 1880, Sioux Falls had grown to 2,164 people, and by 1890, to more than 10,000.[9]

Sioux Falls was clearly an *American* city in ways other cities were not. New Orleans and St. Louis were heavily Frenchified, for example, and the Spanish colonial disposition of Albuquerque and Santa Fe persisted for centuries. Early New York was Dutch. Sioux Falls was instead founded in an American republic that was fully formed and stable, nearly a century after the American Revolution. Many of the "urban problems" associated with nineteenth-century cities, such as sewage and fire control, had already

2 Gary Clayton Anderson, *Massacre in Minnesota: The Dakota War of 1862, the Most Violent Ethnic Conflict in American History* (Norman: University of Oklahoma Press, 2019).

3 Harry F. Thompson, ed., *A New History of South Dakota* (Sioux Falls, SD: Center for Western Studies, 2005), 160–66.

4 Gary D. Olson, "A Dakota Boomtown: Sioux Falls, 1877–1880," *Great Plains Quarterly* vol. 24, no. 1 (Winter 2004), 19.

5 Olson, "Dakota Boomtown," 20.

6 Olson, "Dakota Boomtown," 20.

7 Olson, "Dakota Boomtown," 20–21.

8 Olson, "Dakota Boomtown," 21.

9 Olson, "Dakota Boomtown," 18; Timothy R. Mahoney, "The Small City in American History," *Indiana Magazine of History* vol. 99, no. 4 (December 2003), 317, 320.

been debated and addressed, which allowed Sioux Falls to skip over some rough stages of urban development.[10] In the 1790s, for example, Philadelphia was installing public water, and over a hundred other cities installed waterworks before the Civil War.[11] In the early 1820s, Boston was installing gas lighting and sewage systems.[12] When the Civil War ended, New York was installing elevated railways, and San Francisco was installing cable cars.[13] Sioux Falls took shape so late in the process of Western town development that prognosticators such as Frederick Jackson Turner argued that the frontier had already closed.

In recent years, urban historians have argued that it is crucial to get the details of city development correct because, too often, scholars lapse into generic descriptions of city spaces with little regard for specifics.[14] Perhaps the most important detail of urban history is *who* settled a city. Most nineteenth-century immigration and settlement went from east to west, which meant that most of the Americans moving to Sioux Falls were midwesterners, as indicated by the Iowans and Minnesotans who first scoped out the land that became Sioux Falls.[15] During the late 1870s, Harry Corson, the forty-two-year-old owner of the Cataract Hotel (named for the falls of the Big Sioux River, of course) in downtown Sioux Falls, had ten workers who helped run the hotel. These young workers, aged seventeen to twenty-six, had moved in from Iowa, Illinois, Wisconsin, and Norway, an assemblage that reflected the demography of the early city.[16] While 63 percent of the people in Sioux Falls in 1880 were native-born Americans, mostly midwesterners, the other 37 percent were from countries that supplied many of the immigrants to the Midwest, especially to the Dakotas and Minnesota. The largest group came from Norway, as indicated by the worker at the Cataract Hotel, followed by Ireland, Sweden, Germany, and England.[17] Several of the young Norwegians opened businesses in downtown Sioux Falls. Eleven merchants born in

10 Richard C. Wade, "Urban Life in Western America, 1790–1830," *American Historical Review* vol. 64, no. 1 (October 1958), 20–21.

11 Arthur M. Schlesinger, "The City in American History," *Mississippi Valley Historical Review* vol. 27, no. 1 (June 1940), 52.

12 Schlesinger, "City in American History," 52.

13 Schlesinger, "City in American History," 58. On western cities borrowing technological advances from older eastern cities, see Lawrence H. Larsen, *The Urban West at the End of the Frontier* (Lawrence: Regent's Press of Kansas, 1978).

14 James Connolly, "Bringing the City Back In: Space and Place in the Urban History of the Gilded Age and Progressive Era," *Journal of the Gilded Age and Progressive Era* vol. 1, no. 3 (July 2002), 259; Andrew R. L. Cayton, "On the Importance of Place, or, a Plea for Idiosyncrasy," *Journal of Urban History* vol. 24, no. 1 (November 1997), 79–87; James J. Connolly and E. Bruce Geelhoed, "The Small-City Experience in the Midwest: An Introduction," *Indiana Magazine of History* vol. 99, no. 4 (December 2003), 308.

15 John C. Hudson, "Who Was 'Forest Man?' Sources of Migration to the Plains," *Great Plains Quarterly* vol. 6, no. 2 (Spring 1986), 73–74.

16 Olson, "Dakota Boomtown," 26.

17 Olson, "Dakota Boomtown," 26.

Norway, for example, owned grocery, dry goods, furniture, feed, and hardware stores and blacksmith and tailor shops, and they could use their linguistic linkages and easily cater to their immigrant brethren rolling through town on their agrarian quest.[18] On one day in 1878, a visitor from Canton counted twenty-three immigrant wagons passing through Sioux Falls on the way to Dakota farms, and each one of the families in these wagons needed supplies. If they could buy them from a fellow Norskie, all the better.[19] The experience of these Norwegian immigrant farmers was captured by Ole Rolvaag, one of their own, in his books such as *Giants in the Earth*. Rolvaag's writing cabin now sits in Sioux Falls at Augustana University, first founded as a Norwegian Lutheran college. Rolvaag's brethren formed a Sons of Norway lodge in Sioux Falls and built the Nordic Hall downtown.

The falls of the Big Sioux River first drew the attention of prospective settlers, and they would yield the power for a substantial flour mill. The early railroads of Sioux Falls then brought in farmers to settle the surrounding prairie.[20] Both of these steps highlighted the agrarian orientation of Sioux Falls, one which set it apart from some neighboring cities. The Big Sioux River through Sioux Falls was not big in comparison to the Missouri River through Sioux City, for example. The Big Mo drew much steamboat traffic up the river, and that meant a robust outfitting business for youthful Sioux City.[21] By 1857, Sioux City "had emerged as the focal point for commercial traffic moving into and out of the northern Great Plains" and up and down the Missouri River.[22] The development of Sioux Falls, by contrast, was horizontal—the wagons full of settlers, and later the trains, came eastward over land, from the upper Midwest, not via steamboat up the Missouri River. By 1860, when Sioux Falls was still but an imagining, Sioux City numbered about 750 people. Then in March 1868, Sioux City saw the arrival of the railroad from the south, which brought in more supplies to be loaded onto Missouri River steamboats, which were gearing up to serve a burst of gold miners heading to Montana.[23] By 1870, Sioux City grew to 3,400 people, and many of the recent arrivals were immigrants,

18 Olson, "Dakota Boomtown," 27.

19 Olson, "Dakota Boomtown," 22.

20 Olson, "Dakota Boomtown," 17. On the settlement of this area, see Jon K. Lauck, ***Prairie Republic: The Political Culture of Dakota Territory 1879–1889*** (Norman: University of Oklahoma Press, 2010).

21 William Silag, "Gateway to the Grasslands: Sioux City and the Missouri River Frontier," ***Western Historical Quarterly*** vol. 14, no. 4 (October 1983), 397. See also William E. Lass, ***A History of Steamboating on the Upper Missouri River*** (Lincoln, NE: University of Nebraska Press, 1962).

22 Silag, "Gateway to the Grasslands," 399.

23 Silag, "Gateway to the Grasslands," 408–9.

with the largest number from Germany.[24] Similarly, Kansas City grew from the freighting business that shaped the Santa Fe Trail, and Omaha grew by outfitting settlers heading west on the Oregon Trail and then the building of the Union Pacific.[25]

Although late to the urbanization party, the embryonic institutions of Sioux Falls developed quickly. City government took form, the main street filled with stores, parks such as McKennan and Frank Olson were organized, the Masonic Temple was built, the Chamber of Commerce was launched, trolleys began rolling, the country club was established, the Orpheum began hosting vaudeville shows, and the YMCA was constructed. Movie houses like the Olympic, the Dreamland, and the Jewel began rolling films. The Sioux Falls Canaries began playing baseball, and the *Argus Leader* became entrenched as the city's dominant newspaper. Richard Pettigrew began collecting specimens that would develop into a major zoo, spearheaded by the Zoological Society of Sioux Falls. The local architect Wallace Dow designed many downtown landmarks: All Saints School; Booth's Grand Opera House; the Cataract Hotel; the City Auditorium; the First Baptist Church; the First Presbyterian Church; the Grand Army of the Republic Hall (for all the Union Civil War veterans who had moved in, such as Josiah Phillips, for whom the main street was named); the Illinois Central Railroad Depot; Longfellow School; the Rock Island Depot; the School for the Deaf; the state penitentiary; and many private homes in varied Victorian styles.[26]

All throughout its early years, Sioux Falls maintained its agrarian orientation. In 1899, the Sioux Falls Business Men's League brought in the National Buttermaker's Association convention and the national Populist convention was held in Sioux Falls in 1900. A major thoroughfare was named Grange Avenue after the midwestern farmers organization. The agrarian/midwestern tilt of the city could also be found in other early street names: Prairie, Minnesota, Ohio, Indiana. The John Morrell packing plant opened in 1909 and began shipping pork in refrigerated railcars back to the company's mother ship in Ottumwa, Iowa. Soon followed the launch of the Sioux Falls Stockyards and large creameries and dairies such as Terrace Park Dairy.

The Christian geography and architecture of the early city also became

24 Silag, "Gateway to the Grasslands," 410.

25 Silag, "Gateway to the Grasslands," 406; Howard P. Chudacoff, "Where Rolls Down the Dark Missouri," *Nebraska History* vol. 52 (1971), 2.

26 On Mrs. Will H. Booth's work to bring opera to Sioux Falls, see "Sioux Falls Is Smallest City in U.S. to Boast of a Real Grand Opera Season," *Aberdeen Daily News*, November 6, 1921. Mrs. Booth, who was married to a local jeweler, had for five seasons "arranged and promoted a series of concerts and recitals which have, because of the world-wide fame of the artists presented, given Sioux Falls a prominence in the musical world seldom attained by cities of many times its population."

visible. The Episcopalian Calvary Cathedral in the heart of downtown began when Bishop Hobart Hare went to see John Jacob Astor, grandson of the fur magnate, and asked for a donation to build a church.[27] The stone church was built of Sioux Quartzite and its ceiling made from cottonwoods, which once stood along the Big Sioux River through Sioux Falls.[28] The back of the church features a Tiffany window depicting John the Baptist—captioned "Make Straight the Way of the Lord"—and the floor includes stones from the walls of St. Augustine's Abbey, and a cross made of remnants of the rood beam of the Church of the Holy Sepulchre in Jerusalem is fastened on the wall.[29] In 1881, Catholics formed the first parish in the city and some small Catholic churches followed. To the north of the downtown, on a hill overlooking the city, they would build the majestic Cathedral of St. Joseph. Historians have explained how parishes are "inherently spatial institutions," which often "rooted blue-collar Catholics in specific urban spaces," and Sioux Falls followed the pattern.[30] For many decades, Catholics, especially the Irish, were linked to the "North End" of the city.[31] Between the Episcopal and Catholic cathedrals, other Protestant churches soon raised their steeples. The city's many Norwegians met to organize a church in 1877 and acquired a lot downtown, built a house of worship, and then later built the imposing and ornate First Lutheran Church (these winter-bred immigrants also enjoyed snow skiing down the hills on the north side of town).[32] Just north of the Norwegians, the Yankee businessmen of early Sioux Falls used Sioux Quartzite to erect the solid walls of the First Congregational Church. North of there, during the 1880s, thirteen Presbyterians met and formed a congregation that would build First Presbyterian Church of Sioux Falls.[33]

As the early church presence suggests, Sioux Falls was generally an orderly town. In all of 1878, there were zero murders and ten assault charges, and eleven people were charged with drunkenness; for the entire year, there were only forty criminal cases in the wider county, and many

27 David Hein, "Churches on the Prairie II: Calvary Cathedral, Sioux Falls, South Dakota," ***Anglican and Episcopal History*** vol. 59, no. 4 (December 1990), 545–46.

28 Hein, "Churches on the Prairie II," 546.

29 Hein, "Churches on the Prairie II," 547.

30 Connolly, "Bringing the City Back In," 268–69.

31 Tom Dempster and Gary Olson, ***North of Twelfth Street: The Changing Face of Sioux Falls Neighborhoods*** (Pierre: South Dakota State Historical Society Press, 2012).

32 Bruce A. Odenbach, "A History of First Lutheran Church, Sioux Falls, South Dakota" (MA Thesis, University of Nebraska at Omaha, 1970), 6–7; H. A. Ustrud, "Little of Everything," in Iver I. Oien, H. A. Hustrud, M. G. Opsahl, and J. O. Asen, eds., ***Norwegian Pioneers History of Minnehaha County, South Dakota from 1866 to 1896*** (Sioux Falls, SD: Historical Organization's Publication, 1928), 37–38.

33 Donald Dean Parker, ***History of Our County and State*** (privately printed, 1959), 27–29.

of these were outside the city.[34] There was an early miscarriage of justice, however, in the case of the 1882 hanging of Thomas Egan. An Irish immigrant from County Tipperary, Egan was found guilty of murdering his wife, who had brought to the marriage a daughter named Catherine. On her deathbed in Seattle in 1927, Egan's stepdaughter Catherine finally confessed to being her mother's murderer.[35] Egan was only the second person to be executed in what would become South Dakota—the first was Jack McCall, who was put to death in Yankton in 1877 for killing Wild Bill Hickok in Deadwood. The weight and power of the law was represented in the city's impressive new courthouse, completed in March 1890.[36] The courthouse, designed in the Richardsonian Romanesque style by early Sioux Falls architect Wallace Dow, featured rusticated stonework, round arches, towers, turrets, and pointed dormers and was built with local Sioux Quartzite.[37] "Its presence," one architectural historian noted, "is a reminder of the respect and importance once given to county courthouses as symbols of law and justice."[38] When Sioux Falls was smaller and more compact and focused on downtown, the clock on the courthouse tower could be heard around the city.[39]

The great age of building and ordering was not without its setbacks, blemishes, and missed opportunities, of course. An early census found two brothels in Sioux Falls, and a liberal divorce law drew in some wealthy socialites from the East (see Edith Wharton's *Custom of the Country*) who sought liberation from their spouses (local ministers such as Bishop Hare quickly organized to repeal and replace the state's lax divorce statute).[40] Northern Sioux Falls was home to a big brewery, which was popular with immigrant Germans, but which became a flashpoint in the Dakota battles over temperance and prohibition, led by the Women's Christian Temperance Union and its crusading newspaper, the *Gattling Gun*, and supported by some Norwegians and their Scandia Total Abstinence Society.[41] Doubts about the loyalties and activities of the city's Catholics sometimes caused

34 Olson, "Dakota Boomtown," 23.

35 C. John Egan, Jr., *Drop Him Till He Dies: The Twisted Tragedy of Homesteader Thomas Egan* (Sioux Falls: Ex Machina Publishing Company, 1994).

36 Al Larson, "Minnehaha County Temples of Justice: The County Courthouses of Sioux Falls, South Dakota," *Material Culture* vol. 30, no. 1 (Spring 1998), 23–28.

37 Larson, "Minnehaha County Temples of Justice," 25. See also Jennifer Dumke, *W. L. Dow: The Architect Who Shaped Sioux Falls* (Mount Pleasant, South Carolina: The History Press, 2013).

38 Larson, "Minnehaha County Temples of Justice," 23.

39 Larson, "Minnehaha County Temples of Justice," 25.

40 April White, *The Divorce Colony* (forthcoming, Hachette Books, 2022); Olson, "Dakota Boomtown," 23.

41 Charles A. Smith, *A Comprehensive History of Minnehaha County, South Dakota* (Mitchell, SD: Educator Supply Company, 1949), 160; Dana R. Bailey, *History of Minnehaha County, South Dakota* (Sioux Falls, SD: Brown & Saenger, 1899), 409; Chuck Vollan, *Bone Dry: South Dakota's Failed Experiment with Alcohol Prohibition* (forthcoming).

social strains (some would try to keep the impressive football teams of the city's Catholic high school out of postseason play).[42] Sioux Falls missed out on becoming the state capital, depriving it of an added dimension of importance granted to large midwestern cities such as Indianapolis and Des Moines.[43] In a major lapse in judgment, the city also chose to host the state prison (designed by Wallace Dow, of course) instead of the state agricultural college. The northern heights of the city could have been occupied by a major Division I university but is instead a pile of cement, quartzite, iron bars, and razor wire. The city was not immune to crime, as made clear by John Dillinger's robbery of the Security National Bank in downtown Sioux Falls in 1934 (he got away with $50,000).[44] In 1936, an outlaw gang from Sioux City was on the run and broke into the Larson Hardware powder house east of Sioux Falls. The outlaws started arguing amongst themselves and ended up detonating the whole warehouse, setting off 3,000 pounds of dynamite and 310 kegs of powder, blowing out windows three miles away in downtown Sioux Falls and lighting up seismographs in California.[45] More in keeping with the culture of the Dakotas were the protests of farmers during the days of depression and dust in the 1930s, some of which focused on Sioux Falls and its livestock markets, and Depression-era labor strife at Morrell's.[46] Sioux Falls also could not escape the merciless furies of nature. Blizzards buried the city, grasshoppers overran the farms that the city serviced, tornadoes cut through (even taking out brick buildings), and a flood of the Big Sioux in 1881 washed away many of downtown's bridges and buildings.[47]

Through decades of growth—and periodic misfortunes and hardships—and after weathering the Great Depression, the city began to enter a new era. The new and improved airport opened in 1939. Prior to this, the only airport was the small Soo Skyway, which operated grass strip runways from 1929 to 1943 on a leased farm south of Forty-First Street. World War II brought an Army air base to Sioux Falls which, from 1942 to 1945, trained 45,000 radio operators. More than half of the radio operator-mechanics (ROMs) in the Eighth and Fifteenth Air Forces in Europe during the

42 Jon K. Lauck, "'You Can't Mix Wheat and Potatoes in the Same Bin': Anti-Catholicism in Early Dakota," *South Dakota History* vol. 38, no. 1 (Spring 2008), 1–46.

43 Marshall Damgaard, *The South Dakota State Capital: The First Century* (Pierre: South Dakota State Historical Society Press, 2008).

44 Ardyce Samp, *The Dillinger Robbery of the Security National Bank & Trust Company of Sioux Falls* (Sioux Falls, SD: Rushmore House Publishing, 1992).

45 Dorene Weinstein, "Power House Blast Was a Robbery Gone Awry," *Argus Leader*, May 31, 2014.

46 John E. Miller, "Restrained, Respectable Radicals: The South Dakota Farm Holiday," *Agricultural History* vol. 59, no. 3 (July 1985), 429–47; Lynwood E. Oyos, "Labor's House Divided: The Morrell Strike of 1935–1937," *South Dakota History* vol. 18, nos. 1–2 (Winter–Spring 1988), 67–88.

47 H. A. Ustrud, "Little of Everything," in Iver I. Oien, H. A. Hustrud, M. G. Opsahl, and J. O. Asen, eds., *Norwegian Pioneers History of Minnehaha County, South Dakota from 1866 to 1896* (Sioux Falls, SD: Historical Organization's Publication, 1928), 28; Parker, *History of Our County and State*, 73.

war were graduates of the Sioux Falls school. At its peak, the base added 28,000 troops with money to spend to a Depression-addled city of 40,000 people.[48] It led to many civic improvements, including a new sewage plant and other civil engineering advancements, and also brought Sid Epstein to town. Sid's Liquors was a fixture of a lively downtown for decades to come.[49] In the 1950s, Phillips Avenue in downtown Sioux Falls housed six men's wear stores, fourteen women's wear stores, and seven shoe stores, plus a JCPenney, a Woolworth's, a Kresge's, and a Newberry's (an old five-and-dime chain).[50] Television also came to South Dakota after the war, and all of its local news programming was developed in downtown and beamed to the rest of the state. In another sign that a new era had arrived, in 1961, a new county courthouse was built in, alas, the international, or modernist, style, all smooth and functional and devoid of ornamentation.[51]

The new postwar interstate system was a crucial development for Sioux Falls. When an early interstate plan emerged in the 1930s, South Dakota had been skipped completely (like it would be later when the Amtrak rail system was announced). By 1943, however, Interstate 90 running through Sioux Falls began to appear on planning maps and, in 1947, another chunk of interstate appeared on the map linking Sioux Falls to Sioux City and Omaha.[52] Through a bit of clever political maneuvering, South Dakota Senator Francis Case expanded the limits of the new interstate highway system by a thousand miles and he aimed to use this new mileage to benefit Sioux Falls.[53] Specifically, he wanted to extend the interstate network north out of Sioux Falls to Fargo. This was not an easy task, however, because a young South Dakotan named Hubert Humphrey, who had earlier moved to Minneapolis, wanted that mileage to run through western Minnesota.[54] Case, a close ally of Senator Robert Kerr of Oklahoma, who had the most pull on the Senate Public Works Committee, prevailed, and the Sioux-to-Fargo/Grand Forks interstate link was forged.[55] LBJ's close aide Harry McPherson said Senator Case "left a monument which archaeologists a millennium from now may find to be proof of our productive genius, or madness, or both—the Interstate Highway System."[56] For the people of

48 Lynwood E. Oyos, ***Reveille for Sioux Falls: A World War II Army Air Forces Technical School Changes a South Dakota City*** (Sioux Falls, SD: Center for Western Studies, 2014).

49 Some locals replicated Chicago's famed Pump Room during the 1950s. See essay by Patrick Lalley in this volume.

50 Alan Ehrenhalt, "Saving Downtown: Face-to-Face Markets," ***Current*** vol. 419 (January 2000), 14.

51 Larson, "Minnehaha County Temples of Justice," 26.

52 See http://www.ajfroggie.com/roads/yellowbook/.

53 Loren Carlson, "The Republican Majority: Francis Higbee Case and Karl E. Mundt," in Herbert T. Hoover and Larry Zimmerman, eds., ***South Dakota Leaders: From Pierre Chouteau, Jr. to Oscar Howe*** (Vermillion, SD: University of South Dakota Press, 1989), 302; "Road Proposal Submitted by Case Submitted," ***Argus Leader***, February 11, 1955.

54 Carlson, "Republican Majority," 302.

55 "Sioux Falls-Fargo Link Is Added to Interstate System," ***Capital Journal***, October 18, 1957.

56 Harry McPherson, ***A Political Education: A Washington Memoir*** (Austin, TX: University of Texas Press, 1995), 71. Thanks to

Sioux Falls, who now sit at the crossroads of two major interstates, the judgment was clearly genius.

The city of Sioux Falls was on the way to a robust period of growth in part because it had avoided so many of the perils that had befallen other urban areas. The city was never covered in soot and grime like a Pittsburgh or haunted by its dark, satanic mills like Manchester. Sioux Falls has never known the smog that would bedevil other American cities during the twentieth century. As some old-timers who have worked in other parts of the country and world have pointed out, there was no racketeering in Sioux Falls, no shakedowns or mafia threats, which drain away entrepreneurship, necessitating long later fights to break the control of the Cosa Nostra or to support Addiopizzo, the "goodbye to extortion" campaigns necessary in other places.[57] There was also no endemic corruption, no Boss Dennison, no Boss Daley or Tweed, no Pendergast machine. There was no overweening economic force controlling the city, no Anaconda Copper, as in Butte, or Newberry Mills, as in the old textile country of South Carolina. Since there was no dominant company in the city, it avoided the shattering losses experienced by Youngstown, Ohio, which lost its steel mill, or Lancaster, Ohio, which lost a glass manufacturer. Sioux Falls did not endure the pain of deindustrialization—Akron losing its rubber plants—as did other midwestern cities, now scarred by industrial ruins, nor did it experience crippling labor battles, like the Caterpillar fight in Decatur or the P9 strike in Austin. Sioux Falls also avoided the racial strife of other cities. It saw no lynchings, no Tulsa-like race riots, no racial violence that defined life in other postwar cities. In 1950 and 1951, there were twelve racial bombings in Dallas; in Miami, there were dozens of cross burnings from 1945 to 1951; in Philadelphia during the first six months of 1955, there were 213 documented racial incidents; Detroit saw over 200 episodes of racial conflict between 1945 and 1960.[58] Sioux Falls was never a place of slums and sprawling urban squalor, not an embittered concrete jungle, not Nelson Algren's Chicago of drug dealers, pimps, gangs, and underworld hits and terror.

Louis Wirth, a German-born Jew raised and educated in Omaha who matriculated at the University of Chicago, became the main expert on the rise of American cities and their problems.[59] In his famous work, Wirth

---

Owen Shay for sharing his work on this story. Shay, "South Dakota, Super-Highways, and Senator Francis Case" (Honors Thesis, South Dakota State University, May 7, 2014).

57 Antonino Vaccaro and Pico Di Trapani, ***Addiopizzo: Levering Consumers Responsible Purchase to Fight Mafia*** (New York: McGraw Hill, 2016).

58 Raymond A. Mohl, "Race and Housing in the Postwar City: An Explosive History," ***Journal of the Illinois State Historical Society*** vol. 94, no. 1 (Spring 2001), 17–19.

59 Zane L. Miller, "Pluralism, Chicago School Style: Louis Wirth, the Ghetto, the City, and 'Integration,'" ***Journal of Urban***

pointed to the loss of nature and the openness of rural life, the intensity of noise and smoke, and the crowded living conditions oddly combined with an erosion of community that gave shape to what Wirth called the "superficiality, the anonymity, and the transitory character of urban-social relations," where thrill-seeking is encouraged as a "means of escape from drudgery, monotony, and routine."[60] In Sioux Falls, most people know one another if they want to—the alienation and anonymity widely seen as a drag on urban life is a foreign concept. The city's many parks and local lakes kept nature ever-present. One local ornithologist started recording the local birds during the 1910s, and she found a wide variety, including various grebes, gulls, terns, ducks, geese, herons, cranes, bitterns, sandpipers, plovers, larks, crows, blackbirds, sparrows, warblers, owls, hawks, and eagles.[61] Beyond local parks, people in Sioux Falls could escape to a wide-open prairie within minutes. People were never trapped in a noisy urban core, cut off from the wild, trapped in a denuded, concrete jungle. Often members of a rural diaspora, people in Sioux Falls could easily go back to the homeplace in the country to see family and friends and go pheasant hunting and walleye fishing at a family lake cabin.

Outsiders began to notice this quality of life. One Houstonian who moved to Sioux Falls in the 1970s to run EROS Data Center quickly realized the city was a "heck of a place to raise a family," and he was known to "accuse the local populace of living in a fairytale land because they doggone do."[62] The good news spread, and by 1992, *Money* magazine announced in a cover story that Sioux Falls was the best place to live in America (Sioux City, which once overshadowed Sioux Falls, clocked in at a lowly #149).[63] *Money's* criteria focused on factors such as high school graduation rates, sunny weather (210 days a year the sun shines in Sioux Falls), low cost of living (a three-bedroom house averaged $86,000), low crime, low state and local income taxes (none, actually), low pollution, low traffic congestion, and low unemployment.[64] During the fall 1992 presidential campaign, both candidates for vice president, Dan Quayle and Al Gore, stopped in Sioux Falls and recognized the city's new status as "the No. 1 city in America" (Quayle dedicated a "Best Place" sign on the interstate).[65] A few

History vol. 18, no. 3 (May 1992), 253–54.

60 Louis Wirth, "Urbanism as a Way of Life," *American Journal of Sociology* vol. 44, no. 1 (July 1938), 12, 22.

61 Adrian Larson, "The Birds of Sioux Falls, South Dakota, and Vicinity," *Wilson Quarterly* vol. 37, no. 1 (March 1925), 18–38.

62 Marcia Brinkman, "Sioux Falls: Steady as She Grows," *Corporate Report* (April 1976), 41.

63 On Sioux City's demise, see Ralph Brown, "A Tale of Two Cities: Sioux Falls and Sioux City," *South Dakota Business Review* vol. 58, no. 2 (December 2004), 1–19.

64 Marguerite T. Smith and Debra Wishik Englander, "The Best Places to Live in America," *Money* vol. 21, no. 9 (September 1992).

65 "What's Up in America's Best Place to Live," *Money* vol. 21, no. 11 (November 1992).

years later, another national reporter came through to explain how Sioux Falls had "emerged in the 1990s as a national model for urban living."[66] He concluded that the "community has molded its identity around Leave-It-to-Beaver midwestern values, a strong pioneer work ethic, and a population that regularly attends church or synagogue."[67] A more sensible pace of life and an orderly anti-crime culture prevailed, my city planner cousin, Steve Metli, told the reporter with an Irish twinkle in his eye, an atmosphere akin to the 1950s but one open to growth.[68] Another analyst, the editor of *Governing* magazine, concluded that Sioux Falls remained a "safe, quiet, friendly outpost of upper-Midwest conservatism."[69] In recent social science parlance, it is a place with high levels of social capital.[70]

The city's leaders did not rest on their laurels. They worked to make Sioux Falls grow. The medical services sector boomed, in part because of the expanded mission of the state's medical school. Downtown was made increasingly attractive when old warehouses began to become loft apartments and Philips Avenue was extended to a revitalized Falls Park which—in a nod to the city's origins—highlighted the falls of the Big Sioux River.[71] The South Dakota business climate (ranked fourth in the nation) continued to draw in companies who wanted a new venue (neighboring Minnesota lagged far behind at forty-eight in the rankings).[72] The city became a hub for major sports events, concerts, and banking. Citibank, Wells Fargo, Metabank, and First Premier were a major presence in the city—dubbed "Wall Street on the Prairie"—and the state become the second largest home of banking assets in the country.[73] Crime remained low (the mayor said it would be even lower "if people would lock their houses and take keys out of unlocked cars").[74] Further demographic research and profiling found Sioux Falls to be a happy place and high in the categories of financial health, community, and physical health.[75] Its people were also generous and led the nation, per capita, in charitable giving (in one experiment, the Salvation Army posted donation buckets in San Francisco and Sioux Falls,

66 Todd Wilkinson, "Sioux Falls: A City of the '90s with Leave-It-to-Beaver Values," *Christian Science Monitor* vol. 89, no. 4 (November 29, 1996).

67 Wilkinson, "Sioux Falls."

68 Wilkinson, "Sioux Falls."

69 Alan Ehrenhalt, "Saving Downtown: Face-to-Face Markets," *Current* vol. 419 (January 2000), 14.

70 See Robert Putnam, *Bowling Alone: The Collapse and Revival of American Community* (New York: Simon & Schuster, 2000).

71 Jeff Martin, "Sioux Falls Builds on Its Rich Past," *USA Today*, December 26, 2008.

72 Brinkman, "Sioux Falls," 27.

73 Robert E. Wright, "Wall Street on the Prairie: Citibank, South Dakota and the Origins of Financial Deregulation," *Financial History* (Spring 2013), 24–26.

74 Brinkman, "Sioux Falls," 41. Murders per 100,000 people: Detroit, 40; Cleveland, 28; Memphis, 28; Philadelphia, 20; Sioux Falls, 2.7. See Federal Bureau of Investigation Uniform Crime Reports statistics from 2017 for the top 100 most populous cities in America that have reported data to the FBI UCR system.

75 "America's Happiest Cities," *Men's Health* vol. 35, no. 10 (December 2020).

and even though the San Francisco location had much higher traffic, at the end of the day, the Sioux Falls bucket held twice as much donated cash).[76] The story of this remarkable city, from varied angles and in differing forms, is told by way of the essays in this book, which will formally introduce the world to the strivers who made Sioux Falls.

76 Wilkinson, "Sioux Falls"; John Stossel, "Sioux Falls Beats San Francisco in Charity," *Human Events* vol. 62, no. 42 (December 11, 2006).

City of Hustle

LARRY FULLER, EVAN NOLTE, AND MIKE COOPER

Sioux Falls today would seem to be in the sweet spot for a regional midwestern city—with a metro population of more than 265,000, it's a retail, financial, agricultural, health care, transportation, and entertainment hub. The next largest cities are Denver to the west, Minneapolis-St. Paul to the east, and Omaha to the south.

Sioux Falls has received numerous national acclaims for its quality of life and strong business climate. The state has no corporate or personal income tax, either.

But the truth is that Sioux Falls has never had it easy, all the way back to its founding in the mid-1860s. Unlike its neighbors in Sioux City, Iowa, and Fargo, North Dakota, Sioux Falls didn't have a real reason for existing, much less succeeding. It was never on a navigable river, not part of a major national rail system, nor was it on any substantial trade route. Other than one meatpacking plant, there were no major industries.

The DNA of Sioux Falls is that it's a city built on hustle. From its very early days, most of the businesses were locally owned. Entrepreneurs made things like beer, flour, biscuits, brooms, candy, and cigars, and there was a thriving retail environment plus a strong agricultural market.

Emblematic of early business leaders was Richard F. Pettigrew, a lawyer, surveyor, land developer, and politician in the late 1880s who dabbled in everything from a meatpacking plant to railroads to the city's streetcar line. But his most memorable venture was the Queen Bee Mill, a massive seven-story flour mill that could process 1,200 barrels of wheat a day. The problem was that the area wasn't capable of providing that much wheat, and the adjacent Big Sioux River was not a reliable source of power. It closed after two years.

The city's biggest economic break in its earlier years was the opening of the John Morrell & Company packing plant on the city's northern edge. It was huge—and still is. Located next to the Sioux Falls Stockyards, in 1911, it was processing thousands of hogs, cattle, and sheep daily.

By 1910, with a population of 10,000, Sioux Falls was getting its footing toward uninterrupted double-digit population growth every decade, which landed it at more than 80,000 people by 1980. Sioux Falls always was considerably smaller than its sister city, Sioux City, about ninety miles south, but the gap was almost closed in 1980.

Sioux Falls entered the 1970s strong, particularly as a retail center. Like most midwestern cities, Sioux Falls tried urban renewal to save its city center. And like other cities, urban renewal programs were costly (mostly underwritten by the federal government) but largely unsuccessful.

But Sioux Falls, unlike a lot of those towns, notably Sioux City and Aberdeen, never tried to block malls outside downtown. That independent, entrepreneurial view also has been part of the city's DNA.

As a result, in 1968, the first enclosed retail shopping mall in South Dakota, the Western Mall, opened at Forty-First Street and Western Avenue. That was followed in 1975 with the Empire Mall, a regional retail center with more than a million square feet, created by the General Growth Corporation further west on Forty-First Street. This major development was joined by the Empire East expansion in 1978. Forty-First Street in Sioux Falls had become the new "Main Street of South Dakota."

Sioux Falls stumbled a bit in the second half of the 1970s and the early 1980s in both economic development and community involvement.

In the mid-1970s, a recession emerged, driven by skyrocketing oil prices and huge increases in spending by the federal government for the war in Vietnam. By 1980, the Midwest, including South Dakota, was hit by a major agricultural recession that especially affected livestock producers, farmers, ranchers, and businesses of all sizes.

There also was concern that Sioux Falls might be losing its niche as the major retail center in the region. Many South Dakota towns with a population of more than 10,000 had a small JCPenney and a Kmart. Why drive to Sioux Falls when some of the same stores were just next door?

But that old hustle emerged again as the city tried to figure out how to move ahead. It wasn't easy. The city's DNA was still there, though, and Sioux Falls eventually emerged as a regional and even national pacesetter.

One of the earlier harbingers of change was in the surprising 1974 city commission election, when a young radio personality, Rick Knobe, was elected mayor, defeating Mike Schirmer, who was supported by most of the business and professional community. Knobe won people over with his ability to listen and take suggestions for improving the city.

This headline from a 1988 issue of *Governing* magazine captures what happened: "How a Shaggy-Haired Deejay Took Over City Hall and Ended Elitist Politics." Knobe was easily reelected in 1979 to a second five-year term, this time supported by a broad range of leaders and residents.

As the turn of the decade approached, there was a malaise in parts of the community, including the business community. There wasn't much progress in attracting new business or industry. In 1978, the Sioux Falls Development Foundation was testing reactions to a business actually interested in Sioux Falls: a tire recycling plant. That never happened.

One of the problems was that there wasn't any factual basis for making decisions, including what to do about a widely held belief that people in the region didn't like Sioux Falls very much.

In 1981, the Sioux Falls Area Chamber of Commerce conducted an unprecedented regional research project with Campbell Research of Minneapolis, documenting reasons area residents visited the city. The results showed that Sioux Falls had a surprisingly strong and positive image with area residents for retail and medical services and entertainment options.

On the basis of this research, a marketing and promotional campaign, "Sioux Falls—A Good Thing Going," was developed by a task force of volunteer media, businesses, and professionals working with the chamber staff.

This campaign had a positive impact in helping solidify Sioux Falls as a great place to shop, get healthy, and be entertained. It also helped boost community confidence and pride at a challenging time. The campaign was made possible by financial support from individual businesses and in-kind media contributions totaling approximately $80,000, which was very significant for that time.

In the late 1970s, Sioux Falls had a strong retail sales economy, but the core downtown was deteriorating, especially the once-strong retail sector. There was some office building development, though, such as Wells Fargo, then Northwestern National Bank (1973), the First National Bank in Sioux Falls (1976), and Midland Life Insurance's new headquarters (1979).

Again, Sioux Falls responded with hustle by creating the Downtown Development Corporation and hiring Dick Brown as executive director in 1979. The ten companies behind the development corporation were looking for ways for the city and the private sector to collaborate in revitalizing and repositioning the downtown.

The so-called Block 11 project conceived by the Downtown Development Corporation and the city convinced the Kirby family to move their Western Surety Company to downtown, where its five-story headquarters opened in 1982 at the corner of Ninth Street and Phillips Avenue. A year earlier, IBM constructed a new office building at Eighth Street and Phillips Avenue.

But the elephant in the room—or the city—was the severe economic recession, and the big worry was that John Morrell & Company, which employed 2,800 people in a six- to eight-story building nearly seventy years old, would downsize or close. Plus, there was increasing concern among community leaders regarding the need for more economic diversification.

Then, literally out of the blue, Citicorp decided to consider Sioux Falls for a major financial services and credit card processing center following a national search. But there was a big proviso: federal law required that South Dakota's legislature had to formally invite Citi to come. That would be tough since the legislature had just ended its regular session—but would return for one day on March 12. Through the leadership and tenacity of then South Dakota Governor William J. Janklow, a legislative package was crafted and then supported by the legislature as well as by the state's banking and financial leaders.

The banks were highly competitive, especially in Sioux Falls, and their endorsement was yet another example of the South Dakota hustle. Citi did agree, however, not to compete for local business in the state.

A huge plus for South Dakota was that the recent session of the legislature had voted to drop its usury law. In New York, low usury rates set by law caused Citi to want to leave there. With extreme inflation, a bank was forced to borrow money in the high double digits, but usury laws prohibited them from charging loans more than, typically, in the 8 to 12 percent range.

These decisions had the effect of creating thousands of new jobs and increased capital investments. Citibank ultimately would employ more than 3,000 people in a three-building complex. In addition, Citibank and other financial services businesses provided additional opportunities for small businesses.

Other banks and credit card operations also brought credit card operations to Sioux Falls, but most are now gone. Citi is still in Sioux Falls. Later, Citibank and Wells Fargo located their national bank charters in South Dakota, furthering the state's identity as a financial center.

Around the same time, another leg of the service economy, health care, had an impact just as dynamic but more subtle. Sioux Falls, unlike a lot of other cities, decided to maintain a two-hospital system. Beginning in the late 1970s, both Sioux Falls hospitals grew in a competitive manner.

Also, the legislature approved adding the final two years onto its medical school and that was based in Sioux Falls. It helped solidify Sioux Falls as a provider of doctors for the region and had a major impact on the community becoming attractive to medical specialists.

A 2019 report from the US Bureau of Labor Statistics underscores the dividends those investments in health care produced: "Sioux Falls (MSA) had 14,270 jobs in health care practitioners and technical, accounting for 9.1 percent of local area employment, significantly higher than the 5.9-percent share nationally."

In the mid-1980s, the city seemed to be in the right place at the right time. Its economy was strong, including sales tax collections, up to $9.9 million in 1985 from $6.4 million in 1980, and the population was increasing by nearly 2,000 every year. Building permits, though, were $63.9 million in 1980 but only $52.3 million in 1985.

On one side, the city and the business community felt the time was right to focus on quality of life, which also can be an important factor in economic development, especially when recruiting professionals and people in the health services arena.

The city's aging performance theater, home of the South Dakota Symphony, was deteriorating. There was no public space adequate for conventions or meetings, and the Sioux Falls Arena, then more than twenty years old, was being upstaged for sports tournaments by other regional cities. The Downtown Development Corporation put together a plan for a $30 million convention and performing arts center downtown.

There was significant support from the business and professional community, but soon, strong opposition emerged from a citizens' group calling itself "Taxpayers Against the Convention Center Obligation," or TACCO. A formidable focal point for opposition was E. C. Stangland, owner of a local radio station. After an intense campaign, a special election on August 13, 1985, showed 11,825 votes for the proposal (48 percent) and 12,898 votes against (52 percent). This was a crushing defeat for the leaders of the business and professional community. Adding to that were concerns about the negative rhetoric and attitudes promoted by TACCO and its potential impact on the city's progress and economic development.

The counterpoint came two years later, oddly enough in a pitched battle over a downtown parking ramp. TACCO, reorganized as "Taxpayer Action by Concerned Citizens Organization," opposed a $12.8 million downtown parking ramp and bus transportation facility. They gathered nearly 2,000 signatures, assuming residents would vote against growth in an election.

In response, Gene McGowan, an investment adviser, helped start "Citizens for Progress." The group launched an extensive advocacy campaign on the need for the projects and their importance to all of the community. The campaign was successful in achieving overwhelming voter approval by a 58 to 42 percent margin in the election on June 16, 1987.

Clearly, much more was involved than just the projects themselves. It was an early indication that the progressive spirit and hustle of the Sioux

Falls community was alive, well, and not satisfied with the status quo.

In the mid-1980s, Sioux Falls moved ahead incrementally: the city commission was increased from three to five members, a second penny sales tax was approved specifically for upgrading streets, and a downtown development plan was adopted, setting the stage for improvements in neighborhoods near downtown.

Concern arose in 1987, though, as a strike at the John Morrell packing plant underscored the fragility of the economy. It was settled, but attention began to focus on the need for an aggressive economic development and marketing program. Sioux Falls was moving ahead, but it was not known nationally, and there was no coordinated plan for how the city could grow—and set itself apart from regional competition.

The Sioux Falls hustle kicked in again. In 1986, the Chamber invited Howard Benson, CEO of National Community Development Services (NCDS), to meet with a leadership group chaired by Lyle Schroeder, president and CEO of Sioux Valley Hospital. Benson had a strong economic development track record, including roles in starting the highly successful Forward Atlanta and Forward Metro Denver economic development initiatives.

What emerged was a case statement for an economic development and marketing program for the Sioux Falls Area Chamber of Commerce and the Sioux Falls Development Foundation, competitive community and economic development organizations now in a joint venture initiative. Included was a feasibility study based on fifty to sixty interviews with leaders conducted by Benson on the need for a new economic development initiative. He found strong support.

The feasibility study indicated that a goal of $1.9 million could be achieved to support the program's ambitious goals over four years—1987 to 1991: (1) attract 6,000 new jobs, (2) increase community payroll by $90 million and (3) increase capital investment by $105 million. Also included was a large allocation for a regional and national marketing campaign. Oversight would be provided by a Chamber-Development Foundation joint venture management committee.

The first Forward Sioux Falls campaign was announced on April 1, 1987, with Schroeder as chair. By then, the goal had been reduced to $1.4 million, but that was exceeded by $400,000.

It set the stage for an unprecedented period of sustained and increased economic growth for the Sioux Falls area that lasted more than forty years. Seven separate Forward Sioux Falls campaigns have raised more than $52 million since 1987. The mission of all Forward Sioux Falls programs, including the Forward Sioux Falls 2016–2021 program, which raised over $15 million, is to accelerate the pace and quality of economic growth and the quality of life for the Sioux Falls region.

Sioux Falls closed out the 1980s with a population just over 100,000. That pace of growth continues today. US Census data shows that between 2010 and 2019, the population of Sioux Falls increased by 19.4 percent, or nearly 30,000, to 183,793. Plus, the Sioux Falls MSA, which includes Minnehaha/Sioux Falls, Lincoln, McCook, and Turner counties, hit 265,000 in mid-2019.

A recently published book by Forward Sioux Falls offers a fitting epilogue and testimony to the benefits of community hustle. Sioux Falls received the national attention so lacking in the mid-1980s. Among others, it has ranked first for the best small place for business and careers (actually, twelve of the last twenty years), the tenth-best city for entrepreneurs, seventh among the top 100 places to live, and number one for the best city in the US for young professionals.

Dave Rozenboom, president of First Premier Bank, describes the city's success story this way: "Community leaders in Sioux Falls long ago recognized economic development is a team sport."

Hdihunni

AVERY M. JONES

Translation: *"To go and then return back to a place. To go and come back around again, as a prayer amongst a circle of Dakota people does."*

When I was young, my Unkanna, *my old man*, my grandfather, would tell me of Ehanna Woyakapi, our *history*. Our Ancestor Ma'hpiya Wica'sta, *Cloud Man*, was the Itan'can, *leader*, of I'heyata Otunwe, *Village in the Back*. I'heyata Otunwe, was located by Bde Maka Ska, *White Earth Lake*, which has been recently recognized by its true name by the settler colonial governments of the state of Mnisota, *Clear Water, Minnesota*.

Unkanna said that Ma'hpiya Wica'sta was on a winter buffalo hunt. He and his fellow hunters were somewhere north of Inyan Kabdeca Otunwe, *Shattered Stone City, Sioux Falls, South Dakota*. Tka, icamna wan hiyu, *but a blizzard approached*. Wihni Wica'sta kin, *the hunters*, dismounted and huddled with their horses. The snow piled on them. Sitting there, covered in snow for a few days, Ma'hpiya Wica'sta made a prayer to the Wa'sicu, *European*, God. He said that if he survived that he would go back home and become a Christian farmer.

Eventually dusting himself off, he went home and planted corn. I would go on to read, to the chagrin of the Indian agent, he would give away his harvest to his people instead of hoarding it for himself. His son Owanca Duta, *Scarlet All Over*, would inherit the mantle from him. Unkanna would refer to his Unkanna as Owancada, an intimate way of saying his relative's name.

Owancada took part in defending the Dakod Wico'han, *the Dakota way of life*, against the Isan Tanka, *the Big Knives*, at Birch Coulee. The Dakota War or Uprising was a culmination of theft, fraud, and injustice. Traders and Indian agents would bootleg whiskey to our youth against both our laws and theirs. The traders and agents also defrauded us and their government through credit schemes with our annuities. The final straw would be the Wa'sicu stealing and withholding our rations. Unkanna said that the trader, Andrew Myrick, laughed and told us, "Eat grass, or your own shit!" He was found dead with his mouth stuffed full of grass and cow dung.

The war would end in the largest mass execution in American history, the hanging of thirty-eight of our grandfathers, and another two who were illegally extradited from Canada a year later. Minnesota governor Alexander Ramesy would call for our genocide and exile us from our homelands. The scalps of Dakota men, women, and children were collected, and newspapers printed bounties: "$200.00 for every red-skin sent to purgatory." This was the birth of the modern-day slur of Washington's football team. The ones who couldn't flee were sent to prison camps. Owanca Duta would take the Wa'sicu name of David Weston and accept Christianity under duress to be released from prison camp to the Santee Sioux reservation in Nabdaska, *Flattened by Glaciers, Nebraska.*

Owancada would head north to Wakpa Ipak'san, *Bend in the River, Flandreau, South Dakota*. He, along with twenty-five other Dakota Tio'spaye, *extended families*, resettled upon Wakpa Ipak'san Otiwota, an *ancient Dakota campsite*. There is a place there in Wakpa Ipak'san, a stone feature on the land, shaped like a kite with a tail, indicating a game trail, placed there by my ancestors. Stone features could also be found there, indicating a certain type of grave, not "tipi-rings," a Western fantasy. Unkanna said people would come to his house and ask his Unkanna Owancada for permission to do things; they still respected him as an Itan'can.

Unkanna would tell me about our Makapaha, *burial mounds*, like the ones all along Kiwanis Avenue in Sioux Falls. About the Kun'si, *grandmother*, and her Takoja, *grandchild*, who were raped by Calvary soldiers, leading Inkpa Duta, *Red Point*, to carry out his personal war against the Isan Tanka. Dek'si, my *uncle,* told me of Inkpa Duta as well, how a town in Iowa cut his brother's head off and put it on a pike, and when he tried to be diplomatic, seeking justice from the Wa'sicu law, he was laughed at. Dek'si told me about Inyan 'Sa Ok'api, *Pipestone, Minnesota*, and what makes it wakan, *mysterious, holy*. Another Unkanna told me how our tio'spaye used to camp next to each other ehanna, *in the old days*.

Unkanna told me about Jesse James, the famed outlaw who would hide out on the Santee Reservation in Nebraska. How James and his brother married Dakota women. How John Dillinger stayed at the old St. Vincent Saloon Hotel in Flandreau. One of my favorite stories was from Kun'si. She said that Inkpa Duta burned down Sioux Falls, twice.

This land has older names, thousands of years older. I came upon a hard-to-find book called Oki'zu Wakpa, *Where the Waters Gather and the Rivers Meet: An Atlas of the Eastern Sioux* by Paul Durand. He had compiled a map of the tristate area, from our elders. Many of the entries Unkanna knew, along with my other elders. This place has names, learn about them.

I've been to Sioux Falls countless times in my life. I remember shopping at Sunshine Foods, and I still pine for Gigglebees. On the ride back home to Wakpa Ipak'san, I would look out the window as we drove the interstate, looking at different spots, landmarks, and wonder, is that where Ma'hpiya Wica'sta got caught in the blizzard?

In memory of our Dakota relatives that carried our history and stories. In memory of Dek'si Unktomi 'Sa, Red Spider, Richard "Rick" Wayne Flute Player. In memory of Kun'si Oyate Yuha Najin Win, Stands with Her People, Barbara Jean Kirk. In memory of Unkanna Chaske, First Born Son, Myron "Butch" Taylor. In memory of Taho'coka Wa'hbada Mani, Elmer "Harding" Weston, my Unkanna. His name is hard to translate into Wa'sicu. It describes him perfectly, his calm strength, his resolve, the way he carried himself everyday against this colonial experiment. Who translated Dakota POW letters and not only taught me Dakodiapi, the Dakota Language, but also how to read and write it. Who gave me the coals to restart the fire. Finally, in memory of all other great Indigenous historians whose words were poached or overlooked.

Blood Run

GEORGE W. SHURR

Humans interact with the land. The modern city of Sioux Falls is just the most recent expression of the fundamental dynamic between people and place. We often focus on dramatic, short-term, and conspicuous problems of the relationships, like the environmental impacts of new construction projects. But there's also a subtle, long-term, and nuanced connection that can be more clearly seen in older cultures. The Native American "Silent City" at Blood Run is an outstanding example of that intimate connection between people and place.

Growing up on a farm just east of Sioux Falls in the 1950s, I never heard about Blood Run. My mother taught in a nearby school district, we had relatives living in Sioux Falls, and yet I never heard about Blood Run. I was interested in archaeology and geology and went to the University of South Dakota in the 1960s, but still I never heard about Blood Run. And I wasn't the only one. The secrets of the site were somewhat protected by neglect.

When it became obvious that it was going to be difficult to make a living as an archaeologist, I became a geologist. I spent a career working in government agencies and academia in the Northern Great Plains, took early retirement, and moved back to the family farm. And then I finally heard about Blood Run. In the three decades that I was gone from the area, Blood Run had started to attract some attention.

That attention had a variety of expressions. Professional archaeologists conducted excavations on the site in order to salvage cultural resources from encroaching gravel operations. Local citizens organized an attempt to establish a national park that straddled the Big Sioux River. Although that effort was unsuccessful, the site did receive the designation as a national historic landmark as a consolation prize. And the states of South Dakota and Iowa began to acquire land that provided some protection for the site.

Then in 2013, Good Earth State Park at Blood Run was dedicated on the South Dakota side of the Big Sioux River, and several years later, a complementary master plan was carried out on the east side. Although any implementation of the recommendations for development on the Iowa side has stalled, Good Earth State Park provides an excellent introduction to the story that Blood Run has to tell.

The park is located on the bluffs of the Big Sioux River, a few miles east of Sioux Falls. If you walk around outside on the east side of the visitor center, you'll see a series of signs that take you back through the human history of this special place. In the past 150 years or so, suburban construction, intensive agriculture, highway and railroad development, gravel excavation, and bedrock quarrying have all been the hallmarks of Euro-American culture. About 200 years before that, Dakota people controlled the natural resources and transportation routes in the area.

And about 500 years ago, there was a Native American cultural group known as the Oneota that left an extensive archaeological record of a major population center. It's this "Silent City" at Blood Run that's described in the displays inside the park's visitor center. Some of our understanding of life in this Native American city comes from the Omaha, Ponca, Ioway, and Oto tribes that are the modern descendants of the Oneota. But some of the perspectives also come from scientists who have studied the physical aspects of that occupation. Dr. Dale R. Henning is one of the main archaeologists whose work is featured in the displays and who is one of the narrators in the film shown in the visitor center.

Dale Henning's professional work has centered predominately in the Midwest and has covered more than six decades. His early career was devoted mainly to teaching and careful data collection in field archaeological investigations. Later, he was more involved with administrative duties, and he developed insightful regional interpretations and syntheses of work on Oneota sites. He is currently still actively writing and thinking about Blood Run archaeology.

Although I was familiar with Dale's work from his extensive publications on Blood Run, I first got to know him several years ago when he identified some artifacts from our family farm. Recently, I had a conversation with him that followed up on an interview conducted by a professional archaeologist and sponsored by Iowa's Office of the State Archaeologist. Henning first worked on Blood Run in the 1960s after Mildred Wedel, who was an early expert on Oneota archaeology, told him about it. He co-supervised the major excavations in the 1980s and coedited a technical monogram describing that work in 2004. Ten years later, he coauthored a book intended for nonarchaeologists. It was described by the Iowa state archaeologist as "an engaging and highly readable contribution that is also a sophisticated compilation of important research knowledge."

There's been an ongoing debate about the origins of the Oneota culture. Some archaeologists believe that it's the result of influences that expanded northward from the medieval metropolitan center located at Cahokia, near present-day St. Louis. However, that interpretation may be oversimplified. Oneota sites in the Mississippi and Missouri watersheds are highly diverse, and there's a lack of substantial evidence for specific Cahokian influences. These facts strongly suggest that local cultures were even more important than the "missionary" efforts that extended upriver from Cahokia. One scholar has called Cahokia a "rurban" center that combines attributes of both rural and urban settings. Although the ties to Cahokia may be tenuous, the Silent City at Blood Run would certainly have fallen into that category.

The settlement at Blood Run was the latest and largest of the Oneota village sites. It's estimated that between 6,000 and 10,000 people lived there, which would be in the same range as Boston in 1700 or Sioux Falls in 1900. The complex of homes, fields, and ceremonial locations spread out for more than three miles along both sides of the Big Sioux River. Although it was occupied from about 1500 to 1700, it was particularly busy during the latter part of that period. Like modern-day Sioux Falls, this population center was heavily involved in agriculture and was an important hub of an extensive trading network. The trade goods included items crafted from nearby pipestone quarries, and eventually, Euro-American glass beads and metallic trinkets were included. There is no archaeological evidence for guns on the Blood Run site.

The people at Blood Run lived in round and oblong houses probably covered by hides and woven mats. They ate vegetables such as corn and squash that were raised in floodplain gardens, a variety of wild plants, and substantial bison meat. These foods were stored in cache pits dug into the ground in and around the dwellings. Their homes were also close to and mixed in with mounds that were apparently used for both burials and for other ceremonies. Blood Run is unique among Oneota sites because at one time, it had hundreds of mounds integrated within their village units. Most Oneota sites have only a few, if any, mounds.

The mounds are one of the more baffling aspects of Blood Run, but there are other enigmatic, unanswered questions. In fact, when asked about why he has continued to work on the site and remain interested in it for all of these years, Henning replied, "It's the mystery."

Dale Henning's work on Blood Run has provided a springboard for a variety of further studies. Those of us who have come later have benefited greatly from his legacy of careful observations in field excavations and in laboratory settings, as well as his insightful interpretations. Although there's not been much in the way of on-site investigations in recent years, there continues to be interest and activity in a variety of disciplines. Without the stimulus of money derived from contracted studies, people who have some connection to academia carry most of the ongoing effort forward.

As a geologist who once taught at a state university in Minnesota, I've worked on two specific aspects of Blood Run and reported on them in professional meetings. The first is the rate of erosion on the mounds that have survived. Those rates can be estimated by comparing mound heights measured in the late 1800s with those made in the late 1900s. Although there are technical limitations to this approach, the results are clear. The mounds are eroding at about the same rate as published rates of erosion associated with agricultural activity. This explains why mounds that were originally two feet tall about one hundred years ago have totally disappeared. And it suggests that the remaining large mounds should be more actively protected. They are at risk.

The second line of investigation involves comparing geological and archaeological features. Orientations of fractures in bedrock and linear stream segments match with the trends of mound patterns and artifact distribution. Both types of data point to the southeast and to the northeast. This defines a quartered circle that is an important motif in Native American traditions. And it suggests that the Native Americans made careful observations of patterns in nature and copied them.

Dr. Colin M. Betts teaches archaeology at a liberal arts college in Iowa. He has published several papers about Oneota mounds in professional journals, and some of that work has a direct bearing on Blood Run. He argues that mound building at the site represented a revitalization movement responding to cultural upheavals associated with Euro-American contact. This revitalization movement would have been similar to the later Ghost Dance ceremonies because it was meant to provide some semblance of stability in complicated new cultural interactions. Further, he has suggested that mound ceremonialism was also an important aspect of trade relationships during this time of rapidly evolving changes.

Dr. Joshua Jeffers teaches history at a state university in California and has written an essay on Blood Run for a forthcoming book about the Big Sioux River. One of his main conclusions is that the Oneota trade network that extended out from Blood Run was appropriated and altered by Euro-American influences. The Native American network that previously dealt with fabricated pipestone and ceremonies and peace morphed into one that emphasized fur trade and guns and violence. The spiraling "arms race" and instability that resulted likely led to the ultimate abandonment of the Silent City at Blood Run. Consequently, when Euro-American traders finally did make it into the area, there was no one living in the once-thriving community that had been connected by peace and trading to the land itself.

Blood Run is a special place with multiple layers of significance. Like the Native Americans who have lived in the area for thousands of years, it will endure. Both the people and the place have had a persistent presence. In contrast, it remains to be seen if the current Euro-American culture is as sustainable.

In the spring of 2021, my family and I were in Good Earth State Park when the first concert of the season was held in the amphitheater. It was a drum group from the Omaha tribe of eastern Nebraska. That was probably the first time in several hundred years that those songs had sounded out over the bluffs along the Big Sioux River. Those songs, this place, and the Native American people will all endure.

The Pomp Room

PATRICK LALLEY

Cigarette smoke and sticky floors. Grand performance and tragedy. A place where the bathroom sink was chest-level and the corners rarely saw light.

There's a parking ramp on the piece of land where the Pomp Room used to stand. But for a time—briefer than the myth would suggest—a cobbled-together bar at the corner of Eighth Street and Dakota Avenue hosted music magic.

If not magical, at least memorable.

The Pomp Room was more than a busted-up old bar. It was the zenith of a subcultural evolution in Sioux Falls that started in the 1980s in garages and basements and ended on New Year's Eve, 1998.

Duane and Jeannie Ertz bought the Pomp Room on April 1, 1971. By then it had gone through several iterations since first opening as the "Pump Room" in 1958, a few blocks away on South Main Avenue. However, the Pump Room was already a much more famous club in Chicago. A letter from the lawyers in the Windy City was enough to convince owners Chris and Mae Miller to change the name. The simple solution was to replace the "U" with an "O" on the sign, and the Pomp Room was born. It was a novel enough approach that it warranted a photo and story in the *Argus Leader*. In 1963, it moved a few blocks from Main to Dakota Avenue. When the Ertzes originally bought the Pomp Room, it was a country music bar. Then there was something of a dance phase. A few years later, the genre switched to rock-n-roll. At first, it was just one small piece of a five-building complex.

There was a bookstore and a radiator shop, among others. Gradually, rock-n-roll pushed out the other businesses. The Ertzes tore out the radiator shop to make room for a drive-up liquor store on the north side. They added on to the back of the former bookstore as well, creating a collection of levels and nooks rather than the open floor plan one might expect for live music. But that worked—the grit of the club fit downtown Sioux Falls in the 1970s, which was not a destination for the well-to-do. A wave of urban renewal in the previous decade demolished many of the old buildings and created the ill-timed "downtown mall," which closed Phillips Avenue in an effort to bring more pedestrian traffic to the area. It failed, and businesses moved south to the shopping centers on the Forty-First Street corridor. The bars stayed, creating an entertainment district that included dance clubs—disco and erotic—gritty country joints, and more than a few low-level watering holes. Frontier, Arrow, Silver Moon, Rainbow, Sportsman's. These were not the swanky cocktail clubs that populate downtown today.

This was the marketplace the Pomp Room occupied, which was something the Ertz family did not apologize for. They were West River ranchers who weren't afraid of the hard edge in search of profit. By the mid-1980s, downtown was changing again, particularly along Phillips Avenue from Ninth to Fourteenth Streets. It was slow at first. The area, nearly abandoned by commerce, was sensing a bigger national wave of city-core rehabilitation focused on specialty retail and entertainment.

In the bar business, a seismic shift was about to hit. The campaign to reduce drunk driving led to the phased increase in the legal drinking age from eighteen to twenty-one, which was completed in 1988. Then the South Dakota legislature approved expanding the state lottery to video terminals the following year. The combination of the two shrunk the pool of potential customers and changed the nightlife dynamic. The number of traditional bars serving spirits was—and is—capped by state law based on a community's population. Video lottery outlets needed only a beer or wine license, which doesn't have the defined cap. Lottery operators couldn't open fast enough. Live music as an entertainment option faded in the glare of the video screen. The old dives began closing one by one, replaced by newer buildings and more desirable tenants.

The Pomp Room carried on, catering to a crowd unburdened by convention or expectation. For many years, the bar opened at midnight on Christmas—technically December 26—to give those who needed it a place to get away. When the clocks turned back in the fall, it stayed open an extra hour until what would have been 3:00 a.m. Why not?

The Ertzs didn't create a music scene. They didn't foster the demand for live performance by the artists who crafted it. That was a product of forces larger than one bar in downtown Sioux Falls. It was a critical mass of like-minded young people looking for something, somebody, with which to connect. Along the way there were countless concerts staged in unlikely places just because the space was available. Ska punks and power poppers, who later would become international superstars, such as Green Day, the Offspring, and Neurosis, showed up in vans to play for all ages in the basement of the Nordic Hall because other bands told them there was a guy—then-teenager Terry Taylor—putting on shows in Sioux Falls. Young adults followed the trail of pre-internet handbills to find local music at the Crow Bar, Charlie's, and Phil's Pub. But to make the leap from teenage dreams to a social scene would require something greater. A triumvirate of forces came together in the late 1980s when a wave of aspirational bands and artists made original music. There was publicity starting with fanzines and then *Tempest Magazine*, a newsprint tabloid featuring arts, entertainment, and commentary in 1989.

That combination revealed to the managers of a few smaller venues—searching for a way to stand out in a video lottery landscape—an audience worth catering to. That's how the MadHatter Pub, on the main floor of the then-vacant Carpenter Building on Phillips Avenue, began booking local bands playing original music such as Flag with Hank, Janitor Bob and the Armchair Cowboys, and Children. The MadHatter begat the LimeLite, and the crowds grew when local promoter John Steever began bringing more regional and national touring acts to the club. By the time the *Argus Leader* launched a weekly entertainment tabloid in early 1993, all the pieces were in place. For a couple years, the Pomp Room and the LimeLite rode the Generation X wave of live music. But the bar game isn't for the weak, and Gen X is not the Baby Boom. Gene and Audrey Jones owned the LimeLite, and they sold the building on North Phillips Avenue to the City of Sioux Falls in 1994. Today, that building is the Anne Zabel Actor's Studio, connected to the Orpheum Theater. That left only the Pomp Room as a larger venue for local and regional bands.

It wasn't an easy path to glory.

The Pomp Room's reputation was that of a tough joint. Rugged and road-weary Harley-Davidsons often lined Dakota Avenue in front of the bar. That reputation reached its low point in October 1990 when a Pomp Room bouncer was stabbed and killed outside the club. Ward Ertz took over management of the club for his family. Eventually, he booked touring acts that could attract enough fans to fill the bar, and he picked up local bands that had been playing a couple blocks away at the LimeLite.

In late 1993, the vibe at the Pomp Room was shifting. And if a marker of that shift is available, it's perhaps Sunday, November 28, when Janitor Bob and the Armchair Cowboys first took the stage. Why this date? Janitor

Bob was a guitar-driven power pop band. While they could grind it up with the best of them, there was a hippy sensibility with roots in one of their earliest tunes, "The Happy Song." Their crowd was tie-dye, patchouli, and clove cigarettes. And it was usually a big one. The band was based in Sioux Falls and toured regionally. They were popular on college campuses and even had some radio airplay. Violet, a band with a similarly loyal following, led by iconic Sioux Falls songwriter Rich Show, also shifted to the Pomp when the LimeLite closed. That opened the door for other acts of different genres, including the all-ages events that had been booted from the Nordic Hall. For the next five years—until the Pomp Room closed for good on New Year's Eve 1998—Sioux Falls enjoyed a variety of local, regional, and national live music in a setting that today seems all but impossible.

It was a good run.

In addition to the local and regional bands—including the hard rock stalwarts with roots in an earlier time, such as Crash Alley and Wakefield—the schedule included an impressive list of notables. It's chronicled in the Pomp Room's ads in the archives of *Tempest Magazine*.

Particularly in 1997 and 1998, you'll find names such as Cheap Trick, Steve Earle, Quiet Riot, Great White, Matt "Guitar" Murphy, Indigenous, the Bad Examples, Less than Jake, and the Jayhawks. Imagine counterculture stalwarts Danzig, Marilyn Manson, and Korn—on the same night. Fargo blues guitar phenom Kid Johnny Lang—when he was still a kid. The legendary bassist Mike Watt—cofounder of the Minutemen and Firehose. The most famous appearance, however, was in 1993, and it wasn't publicized.

That's when Aerosmith showed up.

With Steven Tyler and Joe Perry, their millions of records, they were the pantheon of American rock-n-roll and had played the Sioux Falls Arena on a Monday night. Then, in a made-for-music-television moment, they popped into the Pomp and ripped through a few tunes in a stunning moment that's captured in an MTV Rockumentary. There's Kurt Loder—famed MTV newsman—doing a stand-up on Dakota Avenue with the Pomp Room's signature logo glowing in the background. Cut to the stage as the band delivers "Momma Kin" and "Walk this Way" with all the gusto they'd brought to the stage of the arena a few hours earlier.

"I would say we were in our element," front man Steven Tyler says during the rockumentary. "It's like, people were right up in my face. That's kind of like where we came from. It's like spawning, getting back to where you once came from. That was it for us." Few people knew the plans for weeks ahead of that night, primarily Ward Ertz, MTV, and the band's management, but not many.

Still, the bar was packed, which wasn't unusual after a major concert like Aerosmith. You never knew what might happen. Members of the German megastar band, the Scorpions, took the stage one night. Metallica stopped in when they were in town. These things happened at the Pomp Room.

British singer Lloyd Cole once wrote, "Nothing very good or very bad will ever last for very long." He was rephrasing Douglas Coupland, of course, who wrote, "Nothing very very good and nothing very very bad lasts very very long," in the novel that labeled post-Baby Boomers as "Generation X." The same was true of the Pomp Room. It seems fitting that the last generation to enjoy it was Generation X, that dip on the wavelength of demographics, a trough of population, buffeted by the old guard before and the swelling of the next wave after.

The city was changing, and we were changing with it.

For a while, the hope and despair, the sweat and the tears, and all those memorable moments in the Pomp Room were the culmination of something. And maybe it was the very, very best we could ask for.

The Breweries

AUSTIN LAMMERS

On October 29, 1987, a wrecking ball shot through the west face of Foremost Dairy on Second and Main in downtown Sioux Falls, showering faded bricks onto the sidewalk two stories below. For nearly a century, the bricks had comprised a high-standing Romanesque structure with round-arched windows and a battlement, described by locals as a "castle." Before housing a dairy factory for fifty years, the building had been home to Sioux Falls Brewing Company, at one time the second-largest brewery in the US.

A few weeks prior to the demolition, on October 10, a band of teenagers had lit a fire on the second floor. It took five hours, firefighters from three stations, and two aerial fire trucks to subdue the flames. Luckily, the building's lone occupant, Clyde Twiggs, a hot dog vendor who guarded the interior at night in exchange for free rent, had been in Boston on a religious retreat. That had been the extent of his luck. "I don't know what to do," he told the *Argus Leader* after learning of the blaze. "I have no place to live." Soon after, the building's owner hired a structural engineer to assess whether or not the historical building could be preserved. The damage was too much, and by November 1, its remains sat in a jagged heap. "It was not unlike having a friend die," Erna Ziegenbalg, who worked in the offices of the dairy company for three decades, wrote in the *Argus Leader*. "The new scenery at Second and Main will always elicit pain in my heart."

In 2004, the city ordered the demolition of the brewery's icehouse, which had been built on the other side of North Main Street in 1874. Carol Mashek, who was then president of the Minnehaha Historical Society, called it "the last building of the city's first industry" and fought for its preservation. The owner declared it a lost cause. Weeks later, its broken stones were hauled away by truck. The demolition left a void at the corner of Second and Main. Sioux Falls, a city built on commerce, had lost what had once housed one of its most formative industries—one that, for a time, propelled the young city into the company of midwestern metropolises such as Minneapolis, St. Louis, and Milwaukee. The birthplace of its craft beer industry had vanished, its memory reduced to grainy photos and yellowed newsprint.

In 1873, over 4,000 breweries existed in the US, and South Dakota's lone two could be found a few blocks from one another, near the edge of the Missouri River, in downtown Yankton. That year, John Foerster, of Yankton's John Foerster Brewing, looked to expand eighty miles northwest in the bustling city of Sioux Falls and hired London businessman George A. Knott to construct and manage a brewery on North Main Street. Using stones from a nearby abandoned hotel, Knott and his crew erected the state's third brewery (and icehouse) a year later. They brewed the first barrel of Sioux Falls beer in 1875.

George A. Knott & Company (renamed Sioux Falls Brewing Company in 1883), grew slowly over the next decade, until 1886, when First National Bank of Sioux Falls—which owned a third of the brewery's stock—went into receivership and was forced to make changes in the securities it held. To stay afloat, the bank sold the brewery's stock to Moritz Levinger, a Bavarian brewmaster who, shortly before, had become president of the company. The mortgage on the property, however, was sold to Porter P. Peck, who planned to foreclose the brewery. (Peck, who owned the state's first two-seated carriage, would serve as mayor of Sioux Falls from 1890 to 1894.) Levinger sued, sparking a two-year legal battle that twice reached the territorial Supreme Court before the parties involved agreed to settle in Levinger's favor in 1888. A year later, stockholders accused Levinger of fraud. He won that case as well.

Meanwhile, the new Illinois Central Railroad turned Sioux Falls into a boomtown, and despite the financial dysfunction, the brewery kept pace with the city's growth. In 1885, while under Knott's management, the brewery produced 250 barrels. Two years later, it employed sixty people and brewed 15,000 barrels, touting five different brands that the employees, unionized and well-paid, got to sample twice in the morning and twice in the afternoon, during their breaks: Blue Label, Gold Label, Ambrosia, Bohemian, and Muenchener. Sioux Falls Brewing Company operated day and night to keep up with demand from bars in bordering states and used the newly invented refrigerated railroad car to serve as the Dakotas' distributive epicenter. Ten years before the turn of the century, sixteen breweries operated across the Midwest; Sioux Falls Brewing Company was growing into one of the largest. Levinger and his treasurer, Moses Kaufmann, set sights on the brewery's expansion. But the newly established state of South Dakota had other plans.

Since 1865, the Dakota legislature had deemed beer an "intoxicating liquor," a statute that had largely been ignored until Christian women's groups and temperance societies developed campaigns declaring alcohol a catalyst for the "ruin of good families." In 1890, the "dry" state of South Dakota charged the brewery as a liquor nuisance and ordered its immediate shutdown. Levinger went back to court and lost in 1892, but he appealed to the South Dakota Supreme Court, which reversed the ruling two years later, claiming the state hadn't proven that the beer being manufactured was "intoxicating." In 1896, South Dakotans voted to repeal its statewide prohibition act, letting South Dakota taps flow freely.

Clear of tribunal restraints and thriving on regional demand, Levinger and Kaufmann refocused on development. In 1902, they constructed a malting works across the street and oversaw operations at Sioux Falls Bottling Works, where St. Louis's Anheuser-Busch and St. Paul's Hamm Brewing Company shipped their beer for distribution across the Dakotas. "The warehouses and offices of these brewing companies together with the property on which they are located comprise no small portion of the wealth and business of the community," reported a column from a 1908 issue of the *Argus Leader*. But the pair's greatest advancement, a $200,000, state-of-the-art brewery at 801 North Main Street, opened in 1904. Cut from rose quartz that was mined a few miles away, the massive Rhineland-style structure resembled a castle, featuring five connected buildings with round-arched windows surrounding a courtyard, capped with a smokestack visible from anywhere downtown. The brew crew exceeded 100 workers. Production jumped to over 75,000 barrels a year. Outside Milwaukee, Sioux Falls Brewing & Malting Company became the largest brewery in the United States.

The glory was short-lived. Levinger died in 1907, Kaufmann in 1911. South Dakota reinstituted a statewide prohibition in 1917, limiting beer sales to out of state, and the passing of the Eighteenth Amendment revoked that small privilege two years later. Rumor has it the brewery secretly supplied Sioux Falls speakeasies until the building was sold to the Crescent Creamery Company in 1920. After a forty-five-year run, the most profitable industry in Sioux Falls had evaporated, its monumental skeleton refitted to churn buttermilk.

The same year that five adolescents reduced Levinger's quartz castle to debris, Dan Zaayer walked down the block of his Sioux Falls neighborhood to the house of Dean Stalheim, his neighbor and drinking buddy, and told him of a trend he'd learned about on the coasts. "Want to buy a home-brew kit?" The two spent $100 and brewed their first batch of beer. It tasted all right, so they brewed another and then another. Eventually, they began winning awards at home-brewing competitions and visiting local brew pubs along the way. They soon fancied the idea of starting a home-brew store in Sioux Falls, hoping to join their West River counterparts in the effort to bring craft beer to the Midwest. "Screw it, let's open up a brewery,'" they decided. On Feb. 23, 1995, the new Sioux Falls Brewing Company opened its doors at 431 North Phillips Avenue, touting a ten-barrel brewing system alongside an American-bistro style kitchen. They debuted Phillips Avenue Pale Ale, Buffalo Stout, and Ringneck Red Ale, which would later medal at the Great American Beer Festival. After a seventy-five-year drought, craft brewing had returned to Sioux Falls.

But Sioux Falls had some catching up to do. Introducing craft brews to conditioned domestic beer drinkers presented its own challenge. Common complaints included:

"It's too hazy."

"It's too hoppy."

"I want something that tastes like Bud Light or Coors Light."

Eventually, years of education (and a hazy wheat beer) began to shift the way Sioux Falls thought about new brews, but even with vast acclaim, the brewery had arrived before the city revived the downtown scene. Craft beer was gaining popularity but not enough to offset high rent and spendy restaurant expenses, which spelled the brewery's closure in 2003. Sioux Falls Brewing Company had again disbanded, but Zaayer and Stalheim had planted a seed in the heart of Sioux Falls, one ready to be cultivated by the next ambitious brewer.

Enter Jerry Hauck. In the mid-2000s, after years of building and selling organic free-form furniture in a little brick building on East Eighth Street, Hauck's sales began to slip. Hauck had owned a bar in Aberdeen in the seventies before moving to Portland in the eighties, where he witnessed the beginnings of the craft beer revolution. "As a frequenter of local drinking establishments, I became disillusioned with the scarcity of good beer," he said in 2003. To keep his downtown Sioux Falls building, he knew he had to find a new use for it. So Hauck made calls to regional distributors and small breweries, looking to bring unfamiliar beers to Sioux Falls. He found enough to fill twelve tap lines, and in 2007, Monk's House of Ale Repute opened its doors. Five years later, Monk's introduced an in-house brewery,

Gandy Dancer Beer Works, Sioux Falls's first brewery in almost a decade. "When we first opened, people didn't think we'd last three months," Hauck told the *Argus Leader* in 2017. "We went against the odds, but I was pretty familiar with the craft beer industry and knew it was coming to Sioux Falls at some point." For eight years, Monk's existed as the lone spot to find unique and local beer, keeping Sioux Falls ripe for the next wave of craft brewers. They finally arrived in 2015, spearheaded by a trio of breweries looking to complete Zaayer, Stalheim, and Hauck's mission.

First, Derek Fernholz, a software engineer, and Blake Thompson, a graduate of the UC Davis Master Brewers program, combined their expertise and last names to found Fernson Brewing Company—currently the largest brewery in South Dakota—and in 2015, they opened their first taproom with Ringneck Red on tap, a nod to Zaayer and Stalheim. Next, three home-brewers with a knack for carpentry opened WoodGrain Brewing Company downtown on Phillips Avenue in late 2015. Another trio opened Remedy Brewing Company, home of the notorious Queen Bee Honey Cream Ale, in 2017. A year later, the three breweries united with other South Dakota craft brewers to overhaul a Prohibition-era law that forced breweries to sell solely through a distributor and capped each brewery's production at 5,000 barrels a year. The floodgates opened.

Black Hills-based Miner Brewing Company and Prairie Berry Winery came to town in 2018. The following year saw the openings of Severance, Obscure, Covert Artisan Ales, Minnesota-based Lupulin Brewing Company, and Fernson Downtown, followed by Look's Beer Company, an extension of the legendary Look's Market, in 2020. City limits didn't contain the boom: small breweries have opened in satellite towns Hartford and Valley Springs as well. "It's a very communal, tight-knit scene," Thompson says. "People are hopping from taproom to taproom, and to do that, you need to have a critical mass of taprooms. They are technically competitors, but the reality is, in our business structure, it's super friendly."

Therein lies the strength of the scene. While other industries might see competition as a threat, brewers in Sioux Falls view incoming brewing companies as a sign of the industry's health in the community—to the point where they trade supplies like baseball cards. If brewers at Fernson run out of a bag of oats or hops, they'll call Remedy or WoodGrain to see if they have a little extra this week and vice versa. Parallel to the collaboration between brewery and brewery is the collaboration between brewery and community. Partnering with businesses has spawned a new attention to craft beer among the denizens of Sioux Falls. Some examples:

Fernson's "Zoo Brew" with Great Plains Zoo; WoodGrain's "605 Super Shandy" for the 605 Skedaddle Half Marathon; and Look's "I Really Get Into It," a Hazy IPA for the State Theater release of the beer's namesake, a documentary about the architects of Sioux Falls's punk scene. "If they can find ways to cross promote and cultivate deeper relationships within the business community, I see that there's room for more growth in the craft beer scene," said Brienne Maner, executive director at the Zeal Center for Entrepreneurship. "They understand that they're stronger together."

Today, the site at 801 North Main Street is home to a weedy lot of trailers and decrepit cars outlined by a chain link, neighbored by an old repair shop and an abandoned antique store. No monument reminds passersby of the towering castle brewhouse that once stood there; no plaque describes how it escorted a young city into a century of growth.

But from the road, at the peak of an incline that rolls drivers downtown, one can look out and get a sense of what the brewers of Sioux Falls Brewing Company saw from the top of the tower a century ago when the quartz castle overlooked the heart of Sioux Falls. Though the origin of Sioux Falls beer no longer stands, its legacy lives on in the streets below, through the creativity of the city's new brewmasters, the quality of their beer, and the closeness of the community that unites to consume it. Though they'd likely gawk at the thought of a Hazy IPA, it would give Knott, Levinger, and the pioneers of the Sioux Falls beer great pleasure to know the brewery scene in their city still thrives today.

Joyland Park

CAROLYN JOHNSON

When examining the history of an area, certain things tend to come to the forefront. These are often the superlatives: the oldest buildings, the first politicians, the most successful industries. However, every place has more stories lurking beyond the pages of the history books. These stories tend to stay hidden, tucked away in people's memories or in boxes in attics, waiting to see daylight when someone new discovers them. Joyland Park is one of those stories.

For longtime Sioux Falls residents, Joyland Park is nothing new. Even for the younger or newer residents, it is not exactly a secret, as it has been featured in articles in the local paper and online. But a children's amusement park is exactly the kind of story that doesn't appear in formal histories of the city. And formal histories of the city were what I, as a Sioux Falls transplant, had been focusing on as I tried to learn about my new home. That is, until one warm September Saturday when the story of Joyland Park revealed itself to me.

In my work at a local history museum, I helped catalog artifacts and record information in our database so that future researchers would know what was in our collection. When I came to work and saw a box of recently donated artifacts to catalog, I never knew what I would find inside. Sometimes there were letters and carefully labeled portraits that could build a family tree generations deep. Other times the box would contain hundreds of pictures of houses, with only the house numbers to tell the story. Usually, I would skim through the contents to see what I had, maybe googling a name or place for some background information, but this time, I decided to dive in, cataloging one item at a time.

First, I pulled out a picture of a 1950s parade float, featuring a miniature locomotive surrounded by political signs. Hmm, could this be a collection of photos from a politician or campaign manager? Next, the black-and-white scene of a small amusement park. Interesting, how will these two pictures tie together? Then a close-up of that diminutive steam engine, this time on a track, pulling train cars full of smiling children. Neat, I've never seen that at a modern amusement park! Then a holiday card showing parents and two young boys sitting in the train, above a message proclaiming, "This Christmas train is coming your way." As the pictures of joyous children on the train and other rides kept coming, it became clear that this box would tell the story of the amusement park.

While I sat at a computer, cataloging photo after photo, Joyland Park unfolded before me. The pictures set the scene, and scrawled notes on envelopes and the back of the pictures wrote the story. Gene E. "Casey" Scribner bought a miniature steam train, first setting it up in his backyard in Wichita, Kansas, in 1947. He then brought the train and an automobile ride throughout the Midwest. While most of the pictures show youngsters filling the tiny train, the thrills were not limited to children—there were also several kids at heart shown in the pictures. One beaming couple and their wedding party squeezed into the train, as did the musician Tommy Dorsey when he played in Mitchell, South Dakota, in 1947.

Around Sioux Falls, Scribner set up the train at temporary locations before buying land and opening Joyland Park at the southeast corner of Duluth Avenue and Thirty-Third Street. This was 1951, when the land was in the separate community of South Sioux Falls, although a few years later, South Sioux Falls would consolidate with Sioux Falls. With this permanent location, Scribner could add more rides, so a Ferris wheel, boat ride, merry-go-round, and tractor ride joined the pint-sized train and automobiles over the years. However, the tractor ride was apparently "a mechanical headache," prompting Scribner to sell it in 1956. What was not a headache was the tunnel over part of the train tracks. This served as a storage place for the train and "added thrill for riders." Those handwritten descriptions provided so much more than just names, locations, and dates—they lent a personal touch to everything.

Soon, I came across other items in the box, more pieces that added details to the story of Joyland Park. There were advertisements for the train, one of which noted that a ton of coal could run the train for eight hours a day for a month. Another ad promoted just how "popular and safe" the coaches were. A hand-drawn map showed a potential layout for the train tracks. I could picture Casey, pencil in hand, playing with the layout, putting a straightaway here and a hairpin turn there, creating a riveting route for the train riders.

Of course, Joyland Park was nothing without its workers, and they too appeared in my box (it had begun to feel like "my box," and I looked forward to revisiting it with each work shift). There were pictures of Harold and Don Renner, the father and son who lived across the street and filled in for Casey when needed. Casey's own family—his wife Sylvia and sons Kent and Bruce—helped out as well. Many more workers were documented, by name but not face, in wage books that were also donated to the museum.

The end of the park was not recorded in the pictures, but newspaper articles fill in the missing pieces. Twelve years after opening Joyland Park, Casey and Sylvia were getting older; Casey was serving in the state legislature (ah, this explains the parade float in the very first picture I saw), and their sons had joined the military, so Casey sold the park's equipment to Burdette and Orpha Melloon. October 13, 1963, was the final day of Joyland Park, and Casey reported that it was the park's busiest day in two years.

Although Joyland Park was closed, its spirit lived on. The Melloons moved the rides and operated Lollipop Park for about ten years, no doubt creating memories for a new wave of Sioux Falls children. Even though he sold most of the rides and closed Joyland Park, Casey was not ready to hang up his conductor's hat for good, so he kept one steam train. Just as he started his adventure by bringing the train to different locations, he continued to take this train to other towns, operating Casey's Steam Railroad until 1968. Many pictures in the box were dated May 1968. Perhaps with the end in sight, Casey was especially careful to save and photograph pictures of some of these final destinations for the train.

As for me, I finished cataloging the box of Joyland Park photos and then moved on to other projects. There were new collections to catalog, new stories to learn. The Joyland Park artifacts moved into our collections storage space, waiting for the time when somebody needed those items for research or reminiscing.

It was not long before the Joyland Park collection surfaced again, as it would be featured in a new museum exhibit about South Sioux Falls. While it was my coworkers' job to research, design, and install the exhibit, it was my job to staff the front desk, sitting right around the corner from Casey Scribner's conductor outfit and the description and photos of his park. Now, instead of working on my own with a box of photos, I was talking to people who had visited the park as children and seeing others learn about Joyland Park for the first time.

As visitors reminisced about Joyland Park, suddenly the story was so much more than the items left behind. Suddenly, the smiling, laughing children from the photos were standing in front of me. They were certainly taller—and their hair presumably grayer—than in those black-and-white pictures, but here, decades removed from their childhood, they were bringing this little bit of the past right into the present. In many cases, they were sharing their memories with their children or grandkids, bringing the story of the park to a new generation.

Of course, many visitors were not seeing the exhibit with someone who had once been to Joyland Park. While these people didn't have a personal connection, they could all relate to the childlike wonder and joy in the pictures. Although it may not have been as historically significant as some of the other things in the exhibit, Joyland Park's story drew people in. The story was largely hidden for decades, but everyone appreciated this little piece of Sioux Falls history once they knew about it.

Today, the exhibit is gone, and the Joyland Park items are once again in storage. But now, other artifacts and their stories fill that exhibit space, bringing more hidden stories to light.

The Big Sioux River

CHEYENNE MARCO

Stand on the shores of a river. Watch its contents tumble by. You'll see more than water: ducks, leaves, candy wrappers. After a moment or two, you'll notice the reflections—of the tangled trees, a passing cloud, or a sentry boulder. But the reflections run deeper than outlines on a glassy surface. They permeate the depths and color the course. A river reflects the communities who claim its shores. Cloudy water and empty soda cans mirror a people's values as clearly as water mirrors the sky.

Though I have only been an official resident of the state for a handful of years, I've always felt somewhat South Dakotan. Growing up in extreme southwest Minnesota, snow days and tornado warnings came courtesy of KELO. My parents did their grocery shopping at the Sioux Falls Randalls and—after that closed—the Walmart on Louise. Birthdays and holidays were celebrated at the Ramkota water park. Celebratory meals were eaten at Coyote Canyon. Each school year was punctuated by a field trip to the Washington Pavilion. We always felt drawn to Sioux Falls; it was like there was something in the water.

When we look back on our lives and start to create a story, it's easy to see patterns. As I excavate these memories from my childhood, it seems somewhat inevitable that I would end up in the Mount Rushmore State, pulled here by restaurants and fond remembrances. But there are a number of reasons I landed in South Dakota—not the least of which was the University of South Dakota. USD offered the two things I wanted most from a school: (1) an advanced degree in writing and (2) a campus close to home.

Upon receiving my acceptance into the USD English Department's master's program, I moved to Vermillion and began living the unenviable life of a grad student. Though the hours were long and the work difficult, the department consisted of some of the kindest and brightest scholars I have had the privileging of working with, including Dr. Paul Formisano. As the director of writing, Dr. Formisano served as a papa bear to all the wide-eyed grad students who were only just realizing what they'd gotten themselves into. It was in this capacity that I first encountered Paul, and we discovered an intersection in our scholarly interests: regionalism and environmental attitudes. Paul's research revolved around aridity and water politics in the Mountain West while my interest was agriculture and its complicated relationship with environmental stewardship.

Paul thought of me when a want ad landed in his inbox. A Sioux Falls nonprofit wanted someone who could help them with their mission of improving water quality in eastern South Dakota. Paul forwarded the job ad to me, and I applied to work for Friends of the Big Sioux River.

Friends of the Big Sioux River (FBSR) began as a coffee group, composed of river enthusiasts. The group talked of canoe trips and scenic walks. As they shared stories, they reflected on the condition of the Big Sioux. They mourned the doleful browns and the dangerous levels of E. coli. Wouldn't it be great to canoe down sparkling waters at home? Wouldn't it be great if there wasn't always something in the water?

Their discussions started to center on this dream. A clean river. A safe river. A swimmable river. They researched river-positive practices and swapped stories about the power of prairie grasses and low-impact development. Over the years, their discussions led to the solidification of the belief that others shared their ambitions, and talk turned to action. The group filed 501(c)3 paperwork and officially began their work as an environmental nonprofit, spreading the word of the economic, aesthetic, and environmental benefits of a clean river.

To be perfectly honest, when I applied for the job, I knew little about the Big Sioux. What I lacked in content knowledge I more than made up for in research skills, and as I patiently waited to hear back from FBSR, I took to the internet. I learned that the Big Sioux flowed 419 miles south from Roberts County, South Dakota, to the Missouri River in Sioux City, Iowa. The river coursed through the middle of a subtle plateau called the Coteau des Prairies. Both the Big Sioux and the Coteau were developed as a result of repeated glaciation. As the Laurentide ice sheet advanced on prehistoric South Dakota, hard shale split the ice into two lobes. The ice eroded the lands on either side of the shale, leaving a sliver of slightly elevated land in extreme eastern South Dakota and southwest Minnesota. The retreating ice carved out the James River Valley to the west and the Minnesota River Valley to the east, leaving the Big Sioux and Cottonwood Rivers to drain the plateau.

Something about this region has always attracted people; it's like there's something in the water. According to the Siouxland Heritage Museum, the dramatic sweep of the river drew its first human inhabitants 10,000 years ago. Little is known about these first inhabitants. Between 500 and 800 AD, a second group of nomadic Indigenous peoples moved into the area; however, like those who came before them, their occupation of the territory seems to have been short-lived. Eventually, the Oneota, attracted by the region's fertile soil, settled in the region and established an agrarian society. Native peoples continued to settle along the river. In the eighteenth century, the Lakota were driven into the region by their enemies who had obtained guns and horses from European settlers. The Lakota used the Big Sioux and the falls as an important reference point. They called the area above the falls "Watpaipakshan," meaning "where the Sioux River bends," and the region below the falls "Tchan-Kusundata," meaning the "thickly wooded river."

As Europeans pushed westward, the falls became a location for trade between French and Lakota fur trappers, kicking off a long history of the falls being used as a focal point for commerce. The territory changed hands between the French and Spanish before finally being acquired by the United States as part of the Louisiana Purchase. On their voyage to the Pacific, Lewis and Clark observed the confluence of the Big Sioux and Missouri Rivers. Their interpreter, Mr. Durion, noted that the Big Sioux was navigable up to a falls. There, the water tumbled down a cliff of red rock that the Native people considered so sacrosanct that they had developed "a sort of law of nations, by which the banks of the creek are sacred, and even tribes at war [met] without hostility." Several decades later, Joseph Nicollet, exploring for the US government, came across the Big Sioux and reported it to be a "stream of clear, swift-running water meandering across an immense prairie." A few years after that, Captain James Allen led a military expedition up to the falls. Initially unimpressed with the Big Sioux, he changed his tune upon seeing the falls; he remarked that the party "came to a great picturesque fall. . . . These falls present a remarkable feature of the river and country."

Through the mid-nineteenth century, European settlers flocked to the falls of the Big Sioux. There was certainly something in the water: agricultural promise and other economic opportunity. After initial settlers abandoned the area in 1862 following conflict with Native Americans, the US military established Fort Dakota near the falls in 1865. In 1877, residents incorporated to form the village of Sioux Falls, and in 1883, Sioux Falls officially became a city.

The new residents of the Big Sioux River region did not hold the same reverence for the area as the Native people before them, and the landscape was suddenly subjected to a massive overhaul. Settlers took to their plows and established farms. As for the falls, while they were certainly beautiful, the settlers were more interested in the economic potential of the river. Quarriers removed rocks from the river, and a hydroelectric plant installed a dam. Settlers also began to use the river for waste disposal, dumping sewage, garbage, and animal carcasses in the water. Capitalizing on the notion of the Big Sioux as a place for waste, a coal plant established a landfill on the river. Though the land was soon converted and sold to the Milwaukee Railroad Company, enough environmental damage had been inflicted that the effects would linger into the twenty-first century.

Beyond using the river to ferry refuse out of the community, entrepreneurs obsessed over ways to exploit the falls of the Big Sioux. Richard F. Pettigrew, a lawyer and land developer, believed he could use the falls as a source of hydropower. Pettigrew set out to construct a mill after he saw the large amounts of grain that were harvested from the region's fertile soils. After securing funding from investors, Pettigrew began work on the Queen Bee Flour Mill in 1879, and construction was completed in 1881. The mill could process 1,200 barrels of wheat per day when working at full capacity, and the site was served by five rail lines. Unfortunately for Pettigrew, harnessing the power of the falls turned out to be better in theory than in practice. A drought, which led to inadequate river flow and grain shortages, put strain on the new business, and after just two years, the mill closed. In the early twentieth century, several attempts were made to revamp and repurpose the Queen Bee, but each attempt was met with limited success. The building caught fire in 1956, and the property was eventually donated to the City of Sioux Falls.

In 1883, the same year the Queen Bee declared bankruptcy, a friend of Pettigrew's, James H. Drake, established Drake Polishing Works just above the falls. Drake Polishing used the falls to power polishing equipment in their work with stone monuments and petrified wood. The polishing works experience marked more success than the mill. Drake's works were exhibited around the country, including at the 1904 World's Fair in St. Louis. However, over the next several decades, the company decreased its productions and finally called it quits in the 1940s.

The economic development of the river continued into the twentieth century. In 1908, the shores of the Big Sioux also became home to Sioux Falls Light and Power. The dam on the old Queen Bee Mill site was raised, and a river spur was blocked off to push more water through the river's main channel. The increased pressure provided enough hydroelectric power for three 500-kilowatt generators. The plant wasn't decommissioned until 1972.

Perhaps the most influential economic development for not only the Big Sioux but also the city of Sioux Falls came in 1909. John Morrell & Company, a meatpacking plant, expanded operations in the United States. John Morrell had established a facility in Chicago but closed it down to move operations to Iowa. The company desired to push further west and saw Sioux Falls, with its easy railroad access, as a prime new location. They leased their first building in 1909. However, in 1911, finding Sioux Falls to be particularly suited to their needs, plant officials opted to build a more permanent and modern processing facility located near the railroad—and subsequently, near the river. John Morrell would prove to be an impressive adversary to the health of the Big Sioux River. Throughout the twentieth and twenty-first centuries, the plant would continue the community's early practice of dumping the undesirable into the river, including slaughterhouse waste and high levels of ammonia.

To say commercial development devastated the Big Sioux would qualify as a grotesque understatement. The river rock bore scars left by quarriers. Natural flow routes had been cut off by dams. By 1908, an entire river channel was filled with garbage. Sioux Falls residents began bemoaning the deterioration of the river as early as 1878. According to the Siouxland Heritage Museum, the writer of a newspaper article published in the *Dakota Pantagraph* on May 9, 1878, proclaimed that business interests had so marred the falls that they were "smeared and no longer a major attraction." An undated Minnehaha County Historical booklet claims the site surrounding the falls "has passed oblivion, a victim of commercialized aggrandizement." In 1951, an opinion piece submitted to the *Argus Leader* accused the Sioux Falls community of undervaluing the beauty of the falls. Unfortunately, these voices were ignored, and the condition of the river continued to deteriorate. The notion of the Big Sioux as a dump only solidified. Pitts, Inc., a scrap metal recycler, purchased the land from the bankrupted Milwaukee Railroad Company, and a junkyard sprung up along its shores. Among the overgrowth of weeds and sprawl of leaking automotive parts, some of Sioux Falls's homeless sought shelter, pitching tents along the Big Sioux and using the river as a bathroom.

With a history such as this, I wasn't surprised that plugging "Big Sioux River" into a news search yielded results that focused on pollution and poor water quality. I found a dozen articles, ranging in publication from as early as 1996 to as recently as 2011, on fines levied against John Morrell for EPA violations. I discovered a 2008 EPA press release announcing Menards would settle a lawsuit after destroying a Big Sioux tributary. And I was surprised to find a page on the city's website dedicated to water quality monitoring. I sifted through a few more articles on flooding, fishing, and cleanup projects—nothing that particularly stood out.

However, in the midst of my research, I came across an article that caught my attention. I found it in the *Sioux City Journal*, though it appeared originally in the *Argus*. The article, written by Cody Winchester, was simply titled "SD's Big Sioux among Dirtiest Rivers in Nation." After a few lines contextualizing the river and its plight, I was shocked by Winchester's assertion that the Big Sioux was listed as the thirteenth-dirtiest river in the nation. I started to run through a mental list of waterways—the Missouri, the Mississippi, the Hudson, the Columbia, the Cuyahoga. There had to be thousands of rivers in the US. I remembered stories of some catching fire and some spawning mutant fish. Of all this water, the Big Sioux, that humble little country river, rivaled them in filth? I was beyond shocked and unsettled.

There was definitely something bad in the water.

My outrage over the Big Sioux's conditions was by no means new. Before me and even before Friends of the Big Sioux River, community members expressed a desire to address the environmental abuses inflicted on the river.

In the 1960s, Hazel O'Connor, a champion for preserving the history of Sioux Falls, adopted the Big Sioux River as one of her causes. She began advocating for the river from her position as a leader of the city federation of Women's Clubs. In 1961, after nearly a decade of talk about a possible park, the city agreed to dedicate $5,000 to improving the area around the falls. The issue gained momentum, and O'Connor, as well as other members, chartered the River Improvement Society (RISE) in 1969. RISE sought to clean up the Big Sioux River for the purpose of recreational development and worked with local volunteers to pull everything, from water heaters to car tires, out of the river. The founders of RISE also envisioned a massive greenway that would provide a peaceful spot for tourists and residents to enjoy the splendor of the falls. The group attracted all kinds of river enthusiasts, including local businessman Roy Nyberg, who excitedly promoted RISE's plans for a river greenway. Nyberg felt so strongly about the project that he led a group to Texas to show off a greenway in San Antonio that he felt exemplified the potential of RISE's proposition.

Members of RISE began to pressure city officials for change. In 1974, the organization found the new mayor, Rick Knobe, to be sympathetic to their cause. A native of Chicago, Knobe came from a place where stretches of tress grew alongside rivers and there were rules telling developers not to touch them, and he wanted to bring that philosophy to Sioux Falls. Knobe appointed Steve Metli as city planner, and the two dedicated themselves to improving the conditions along the river. Within Metli's first year, the city approved the Big Sioux River Greenway Plan, which made provisions for parks, trails, flood control, picnicking, archery, nature study, camping, motorized recreation, horseback riding, winter recreation, water activities, and historic sites.

In addition to the greenway project, Knobe targeted major river polluters using new federal policy established by the 1972 revisions to the Clean Water Act (CWA) to begin working with major polluters, including John Morrell and the city of Sioux Falls. The CWA pressured John Morrell to correct its bad behavior, and in conjunction with the city, the meatpacking plant developed their own wastewater treatment facility and filed plans and permits in line with CWA regulations. Likewise, the city redesigned its sewer system, creating separate treatment systems for stormwater and raw sewage.

Slowly but surely, Sioux Falls residents began to observe change on the shores of the Big Sioux River. In 1980, an opinion piece published in the *Argus Leader* celebrated the local efforts to improve the river. Knobe claimed that by 1986, people could begin to get close to the water. In 1987, the city adopted a second Greenway Plan, which expanded the scope of the original project. In 1994, a Sioux Falls Parks and Recreation newsletter announced a multiphase redevelopment of Falls Park. The first phase would include the installation of new roads, parking lots, sidewalks, and lights.

Today, the Sioux Falls Greenway boasts a paved bike trail, parks, and historic markers. The crown jewel, Falls Park, has become one of Sioux Falls's largest attractions. Tourists can snap photos of the iconic falls, look down on the course of the river from the observation tower, or peruse the ruins of the Queen Bee Mill. The Greenway stitches together the natural beauty of the river and the urban amenities of downtown Sioux Falls.

Still, though the car batteries and scrap metal disappeared and the tangle of weeds was tamed, the plight of the river remained. The water still ran cloudy, still foamed at the falls, still stank on hot days. After all, even after all these restoration efforts, the Big Sioux was the thirteenth-dirtiest river in the nation. There was clearly still something in the water.

After a series of interviews, I managed to talk myself into a job with Friends of the Big Sioux River. Though they admitted they'd been searching for someone with a background in science, they could see the value of a writer, and they brought me on to compile research and develop outreach materials. My job would be to give a voice to the Big Sioux River and to those who advocated for it.

Without yet knowing too much about the organization, I guessed that FBSR was a twenty-first-century extension of RISE—concerned citizens looking to hold Smithfield (formerly John Morrell & Company) and other bad urban actors accountable for EPA violations.

"That's certainly part of it," FBSR Chair Dana Loseke told me when I first met him, "but not even close to the whole story."

At our first meeting, Dana came prepared with overstuffed folders and the down-to-business attitude I expected from a former general manager of a major food products company. A Nebraska native and longtime Sioux Falls resident, he exuded the open friendliness mixed with serious stoicism that characterizes many from the Great Plains. He cared about his community and made no secret of his keen intelligence. His demeanor was kind and commanding in a way that indicated to me that—if all the Big Sioux needed was some midwestern grit and a good dose of elbow grease—he'd roll up his sleeves, take care of it today, and find something more difficult to do tomorrow. Unfortunately, the situation was a bit more complicated than that. It would require education, politics, and—perhaps worst of all—patience.

"Sure," Dana said, "Smithfield posed a perennial threat to the Big Sioux's water quality."

Following the brief bout of proactivity in the seventies, the meatpacking plant had regressed to a "see something, say nothing" environmental policy, which incurred some federal wrath in the nineties. The plant still exceeded

EPA allowances and disregarded the community's desire to reclaim the river. While the best thing Smithfield could do for the river is pack up and follow in the footsteps of Drake Polishing Works and Pitts Salvage, the Chinese-owned giant makes too much money to go anywhere. Not to mention that South Dakota's lax environmental laws and enforcement guarantee no better home for an operation so ready and willing to (as my father would so colorfully put it) shit in its own nest. Smithfield was a problem, but a quantifiable one that could be litigated into compliance if need be.

Apparently, the real threat to the river boiled down to a concept I briefly recalled from my sophomore environmental science class: nonpoint source pollution (NPS). According to the EPA, NPS, more commonly known as runoff, is pollution that "comes from many diffuse sources. NPS pollution is caused by rainfall or snowmelt moving over and through the ground. As the runoff moves, it picks up and carries away natural and human-made pollutants, finally depositing them into lakes, rivers, wetlands, coast waters and ground waters." Many states have reported NPS at the leading cause of water quality issues.

According to Dana, the biggest threat to the Big Sioux was not mustache-twirling CEOs backing dump trucks full of sludge into the water. Rather, the threat came from the hundreds of thousands of people in the Big Sioux River watershed going about their daily lives—driving cars, walking dogs, watering lawns. These actions are so small that most of us don't even think about them.

Take, for instance, our lawns. Few things serve as such an obvious signifier of American life as a lush green lawn of Kentucky bluegrass, freshly mowed and bereft of weeds. But in the Northern Plains, attaining and preserving that kind of lawn requires dedication and a lot of fighting with Mother Nature. In its natural state, the Plains are given to tall, deep-rooted prairie grasses, like Bluestem or Green Needlegrass. These plants are designed to deal with the whims of the region's climate, including sporadic drought. Kentucky bluegrass, on the other hand, is far more delicate, requiring just the right balance of water and nutrients. Homeowners install sprinklers and apply fertilizer, herbicides, and pesticides to create more conducive growing conditions. And when they succeed and the grass grows as desired, it means mowing—and plenty of it. This is a ritual plenty of us dedicate ourselves to every spring and summer. However, every time it rains, the chemicals put into and onto those lawns make their way to the river. All the chemicals on all the lawns rush into the Big Sioux in a big toxic wave.

But it's not just the lawn chemicals. It's the leaked fluids from cars, uncollected dog poop, sidewalk salt, and loose soil. It's plastic bags and cigarette butts that find their way to storm drains. These are the somethings in the water. When the annual average of twenty-seven inches of rain and thirty-eight inches of snow fall on Sioux Falls, the precipitation picks up hitchhikers and makes its way straight to the river.

As Dana explained the concept of nonpoint source pollution, I remembered yet another topic from my environmental science class: the Gulf of Mexico Dead Zone. At the mouth of the Mississippi River there's a 6,000- to 7,000-square-mile hypoxic zone resulting from intense eutrophication. Nutrient rich runoff from the American breadbasket triggers large-scale algae blooms that remove oxygen from the water. As a result, aquatic life suffocates and leaves a large stretch of "dead" water.

In essence, what Dana was describing to me was the smaller mechanisms behind this larger problem. When looking at actions in isolation, one person, one lawn, or one farm was a drop in the bucket, but when you compounded those actions, creating one community, one city, and one state, the drops became a flood. One person had not poisoned the Gulf of Mexico, but one nation had. One person was not responsible for the condition of the Big Sioux River, but one community was.

My crash course in river ecology continued. Since NPS comes from a variety of sources, determined by the actions and habits of a watershed's inhabitants, each community creates its own unique toxic concoction and resultant complications. For instance, on the US West Coast, runoff tainted with cat feces has caused problems for California sea otter populations. In northern states, where residents struggle with icy roads and sidewalks, salty runoff poses a threat to lake and river health. For the Big Sioux River, several NPS contaminants contribute to the water's murky, unhealthy condition with the three biggest problems being TSS, E. coli, and nitrates.

TSS, shorthand for total suspended solids, is what most of us think of when we think of water pollution: the stuff that makes water look dirty. TSS refers to the "dry weight" material mixed with water that could be filtered out—things like sediment or litter. This material can be organic or inorganic, including grass clippings, leaves, sticks, topsoil, plastics, and cigarette butts. Essentially, TSS consists of all the visible particulates interspersed with the water. Like NPS, TSS can result from a number of practices, from dropping a gum wrapper to running a backhoe. Much of TSS results from soil disruption, the kind that occurs as a result of irresponsible farming or land development practices. To keep the Big Sioux in line with its designated use (DU) of supporting warmwater semipermanent fish life, the state of South Dakota has established that TSS levels should be below 158mg/L on a daily basis and average below 90mg/L over thirty days. Higher levels of TSS can interfere with aquatic life's ability to breathe, breed, and feed. TSS tends to be higher in the spring and early summer with the snowmelt and frequent precipitation picking up debris as it flows through the city. According to data provided by the city of Sioux Falls, TSS levels remain relatively consistent as the river cuts through Sioux Falls, but water quality testing in Canton's Newton Hills, just south of Sioux Falls, reveals significantly higher levels than those observed just north of Sioux Falls at the I-90 location.

E. coli, unlike TSS, is an invisible contaminant but a critically important one because it reveals an unsettling truth about the water: there's poop in it. E. coli occurs naturally in the intestines of warm-blooded animals, and small amounts are excreted during defecation. E. coli contamination results from raw sewage, pet waste, and manure leaching into the river. For its designated use of immersion recreation, the state has established a maximum daily level of 235 colony forming units (CFUs) per 100mL with an average below 126 colonies per 100mL over thirty days. E. coli levels frequently exceed the established standard. Demonstrating that the E. coli contamination is undeniably the result of NPS, water quality tests performed after rainfall events reveal incredibly high colony counts with results registering upwards of 14,000 CFUs per 100mL!

Finally, nitrates straddle the border between visible and invisible contaminants. Nitrates can end up in the river as the result of improper or incomplete wastewater treatment. However, as an NPS contaminant, nitrate pollution primarily derives from chemical fertilizer runoff. Homeowners, striving for their perfect lawn, often apply nitrate fertilizers to feed the grass. If applied before a rainstorm, or if fertilizer winds up on an impermeable surface (like a sidewalk or driveway), this plant food can end up in the river. Plant material, such as lawn clippings, that absorb nitrates can also contribute to the problem. If lawn clippings are left on an impermeable surface or deposited in a storm drain, they can carry nitrates to the river as well. Once deposited in the river, nitrates do what they do best: fuel plant growth. However, instead of lush green grass, the result is a lush green river. Algae thrives in waters with excess nitrates. When the conditions are just right, nitrates—a previously invisible contaminant—can fuel hard to ignore blue-green river rot. Many waterbodies across the Northern Plains, from Lake Erie to Wall Lake, from the Mississippi River to the Big Sioux, suffer from nutrient loading, contributing to large scale algae blooms and aquatic dead zones. In South Dakota, nitrate pollution is a relatively new concern; however, it's one that is becoming increasingly concerning as studies reveal links between various health conditions to the presence of nitrates in local water, including Blue Baby Syndrome and various cancers. The state of South Dakota has established a 50mg/L threshold for nitrates, though experts agree that 10mg/L is closer to an acceptable standard. In Sioux Falls, nitrate levels have yet to break the 10mg/L criteria. However, over the years, numbers have been on the rise, and numbers steadily increase as the river flows through the city.

Following all the bad news, Dana followed up with plenty of good news. He handed me a folder full of research on Low Impact Development (LID). LID focused on ways of incorporating a landscape's natural hydrology into urban community designs. Strategies included reducing impermeable surfaces, protecting topsoil, preserving wetlands, planting riparian buffer strips, rethinking lawn care, and maintaining storm drains. In some cases, like simply securing topsoil or rethinking lawn care, the pollution could be stopped all together. In other instances, where the pollution or landscape alteration is unavoidable, the strategy is to slow water down, allowing pollutants to settle out before hitting the river.

I left that first meeting with plenty of material. With the obvious heft of my previously empty messenger bag, the folders spilling out of my arms, and the preloaded thumb drive and CD that made all the printed information seem inconsequential, one thing became clear. As dire as the situation was, as dirty as the river may be, as high as the Big Sioux was on the polluted river's list, there were as many solutions as there were problems. There were things to be done—if anyone wanted to do them, if anyone wanted them done. In the end, something else—something good—could be put in the water, but it was going to be a lot of time and hard work to get it there.

For the next five years, I learned more about the Big Sioux River than can be committed to a single essay. I wrote dozens of newsletters and articles, composed PSAs, designed a website, compiled water quality data, researched urban and agricultural NPS, and produced brochures. On my desktop lives a folder of all the writing—just the writing—and some of the research I did for FBSR. The properties menu tells me the folder is a paltry 4.07 gigabytes in size.

During my time with the organization, I watched the state struggle with a riparian buffer bill that would incentivize conservation along the river's edge. I read the 2016 *Argus Leader* article that announced the School of Mines' discovery of dangerous Shiga toxin producing E. coli in 95 percent of samples drawn from the Big Sioux—yielding results comparable to undeveloped countries where people die in widespread outbreaks. I read the 2017 follow-up article that revealed 34 to 50 percent of water samples contained E. coli strains that caused diarrhea, 72 percent contained strains that caused intestinal lesions, and 11 to 22 percent contained genes that could trigger more serious health problems. I watched with bated breath as the Des Moines Water Works tried and ultimately failed to reclaim its own NPS-polluted rivers, making clear—much clearer than any water in the region—the uphill battle FSBR would be facing in its fight for clean water.

More than reading through news articles and sorting through numbers on water quality reports, I began to watch. I became more aware of my environment. As I drove from Sioux Falls to Lennox in a rainstorm, I noticed the way water carved through uncovered soil in a field. As I patiently waited through the spring thaw, I noticed the dirt-stained snow in the ditches. As I enjoyed a walk on a warm winter day, I noticed the salt crystals crackling under my feet. At the park, I noticed dog walkers who ignored their pets' poop. During trips to the park, I noticed the shifting shades of the water's chocolatey hue.

Above all, I noticed a culture of disconnect. We've become disconnected from our environment. South Dakota is famous for its wide-open spaces, and the generosity of landscape has given us a false sense of security. We've confused a plentiful land with an inexhaustible one, mistakenly believing that there will always be a new, pristine environment to replace the one we've destroyed. We haven't considered what will be lost if we don't change our course; we haven't considered what we're already missing. Had I never worked for Friends of the Big Sioux River, I wouldn't have considered it.

I would have never thought about how nice it would be to go for a quick dip in the river, never worried about the otters that call its shores home, never imagined a falls without foam. I would've continued to take it for granted—like so many Sioux Falls residents do every day. We've forgotten that this place—our home—sustains us, and it's our responsibility to sustain it in return—to protect it from exploitation and to protect those things that make it unique.

But it's not just our environment; we've also become disconnected from one another. Though South Dakota feels like America's biggest small town, we've grown. Especially in Sioux Falls, we're a little bit bigger than we used to be, and we need to understand the dynamics of a larger urban environment. One dropped cigarette butt, one unraked yard, one unswept sidewalk doesn't amount to much, but together, those actions compound and contaminate. The choices I make on my front yard may not seem like such a big thing, but when added to my neighbors' and my neighbors' neighbors' and my neighbors' neighbors' neighbors', it becomes a different story.

On the bright side, the consequences of compounding actions don't have to be negative. If enough people band together to make river-positive choices, goals can be accomplished, and victories can be achieved. As Sioux Falls continues to experience unprecedented growth, the city has an opportunity to grow sustainably with forward-thinking developers implementing LID strategies. This, paired with residents who are willing to make changes in their own backyards, can make a huge difference. These seemingly small choices can add up fast and return the Big Sioux to its former glory—to what it was before the pets and lawns, before the junkyard and flour mill, before the garbage and sewage. If we work together, we can see the river that drew so many people to Dakota territory, the one that Joseph Nicollet describes as a "stream of clear, swift-running water."

To do so, we cannot let ourselves become complacent or let ourselves remain disconnected. We have to recognize we all put something in the water.

Between Sixth and Eighth Street in downtown Sioux Falls, a monumental stainless-steel sculpture called the "Arc of Dreams" spans the Big Sioux River. Two arms reach toward each other from opposing sides of the river, leaving a fifteen-foot gap in the middle that represents "the leap of faith dreamers take to see their dreams come true." According to the sculpture's website, this sculpture "is a tribute to the dreamers of the past, present and an inspiration to the dreamers of the future."

The river is not unlike the sculpture that adorns its shores. A symbol of what the community stands for. A testament to the past, present, and future. An emblem of hope. In the coming decades, the residents of Sioux Falls will have a choice to make about the kind of river it wants, about what it will put into the Big Sioux: pollutants or potential. And that choice will be a clear reflection of the kind of people who live next to that river with the breathtaking falls. Either way, there will be something in the water.

Zandbroz and Phillips Avenue

JEFF DANZ

A couple of years ago, Zandbroz Variety celebrated our thirtieth anniversary. Going through the archives for press clippings and photos for our window display reminded me just how much downtown has changed in that time. A brief history of Sioux Falls would take us from the first winter, when a small band of settlers huddled together for safety and warmth, in the appropriately named Fort Sod, to the state-of-the-art dog park recently built on its site. Yes, a lot happened in between.

For most of its history, downtown Sioux Falls saw steady growth as the business and entertainment center for the regional marketplace. This all worked pretty well until the city expanded and a shopping mall was introduced. One by one, the department stores and national brands like JCPenney, Montgomery Ward, and Woolworth's either moved to the mall or closed. A national program called "Urban Renewal" was seen as a sound approach to save downtowns. Sioux Falls embraced it and, like many others, lost a lot of history and replaced it with architecture that will inspire future urban renewal.

The next school of thought to save downtowns was the pedestrian mall. Sioux Falls gave that a try when the 200 block of Phillips Avenue was closed to cars and buses. While it had some small green spaces, it was still mostly concrete and not very inviting. Conventional wisdom said that the pedestrian mall would be the final nail in the coffin of downtown. Contrary to that observation, there were a number of stores like Scotts Limited, Dee's Leather Shoppe, Prairie Star, Kitchen Cordial, and Chopping Block Antiques, all of which were owned and operated by women, most of whom continued to be in business for many years. People often tell me that Zandbroz started the rebirth of retail downtown, but we just joined a group of feisty entrepreneurs. The downtown we all enjoy today started with those women and their shops. They knew the future of downtown retail was to find your niche and be special.

In 1988, my brother Greg and I started looking for a building for our business. There were many to choose from; empty storefronts were like missing teeth in downtown's smile. A lot of it was owned by Louis Hurwitz, a founding partner of what is now Davenport Evans Law. Mr. Hurwitz, in his late seventies, was an old-school gentleman who knew how to wear a three-piece suit. We took him out to lunch and made our pitch to which he patiently listened and followed with, "Here's what we're going to do boys." He gave us a contract for deed at a reasonable price because he knew no bank would give us a mortgage. (There had been a recent crash in commercial real estate.) Mr. Hurwitz thought our retail concept made no sense: "You're going to be a variety store and you aren't going to carry pantyhose, film, or batteries?" He spent his winters in Florida and, for us, one sign of spring was his visit upon returning. I think the first five years it was just to see if we were still there. He liked to tell us he sold Minerva's building to its founders and was so proud of their success. I think he would be completely amazed at the vibrancy of downtown Sioux Falls today, and I'd like to think that he would brag a little about giving Zandbroz their start.

When we started, I thought the rebirth of downtown was just around the corner—I was wrong. It would take many years. But our timing was good because there was a growing movement in the community, and City Hall was taking action. A business investment district was established and the Main Street program was adopted to promote and advocate for downtown. Main Street later evolved into Downtown Sioux Falls (DTSF). There were lots of meetings and brainstorming sessions. I remember we had a presentation from Sherry Kafka Wagner, an urban planner who had been instrumental in creating the San Antonio River Walk. Sioux Falls, like many communities, was built around a river and the falls that are its namesake. It might seem strange, but thirty years ago, you wouldn't venture there alone, and the idea that we could make a visitor attraction from the falls was met with a great skepticism. Nevertheless, the "Phillips to the Falls" initiative was launched, and work continued through the administrations of the next three mayors.

When my brother and I were working to restore the building in 1988, we would open Zandbroz when historic preservation was not a guiding concern of the city. We had to fight to keep its architectural metal crown and tin ceiling. That began to change quickly as others began restoration projects and the community began to embrace and encourage it. The city's Façade Easement Program has been the key to dozens of historic restorations.

Downtown has been fortunate to have brave souls undertake these restoration projects, like the Shriver Building and Eighth & Railroad.

Then there are people like David Dyke, who restored the derelict Carpenter Hotel Building, and Dave Dandar, who has restored a number of buildings downtown including the Boyce Greely. Jeff Hazard and the Houman brothers have been longtime developers who have also left their mark.

While the city and civic leaders have been crucial for progress, the passion of countless dreamers who started businesses, and the people who supported them, have made downtown thrive. Some of these folks would volunteer for events, bring friends and visitors on a tour, as well as shop and eat. Most of us shopkeeps and chefs have been lucky to have their support, especially in the early years—they are the rare patron.

Just before we opened in the spring of 1989, I went to introduce myself to the neighboring businesses. I went into the first shop across the street, telling the proprietor that we were going to be open in the evening and on Sunday afternoons. When I invited her to join us, she looked at me and said, "Young man, if I wanted someone to tell me what to do, I would be at the god damned mall!" It made me laugh, but her point was made. We all do our own thing, but we have learned to work together when needed. We are competitors, we are also neighbors, and we're friends. We've shared success and failure, tragedy and triumph—melodramatic but true.

In Zandbroz Variety's three-plus decades, a lot of things have come and gone in downtown. Some retired, some moved, many failed. Some failed because they weren't great ideas (think combination discotheque, clothing store, bar and grill) and there were those ahead of their times (remember the Brew Pub Restaurant twenty-five years ago)? There were also, of course, those that discovered working for themselves wasn't what they thought it would be.

We are still here, thanks to a combination of modest expectations, stubbornness, and the support of our wonderful customers. Sometimes people ask me why I don't sell my building and retire. I tell them I'm just starting to have fun because downtown has become a destination not just for our visitors but also for Sioux Falls. Young people are staying or coming back as well as opening new businesses. But more than that, this is my neighborhood. I live here, work here, and being the old man on the block, I need to keep an eye on it.

Building a Cathedral

HANNAH REDDER

St. Joseph's Cathedral, which looms on that hill above Main Street, began the way most churches do: with fire. In 1881, a wooden iteration of the current massive structure, located a block or two away, succumbed to a blaze on the prairie, which was nearly impossible to avoid with so much prairie to burn. The church, then St. Michael's, was rebuilt—this time using brick.

Meanwhile, French architect Emmanuel Masqueray was building cathedrals across the Midwest in places like St. Louis and St. Paul, which caught the eye of Bishop O'Gorman. In 1915, construction began on Masqueray's newest cathedral, and though he wouldn't live to see it completed, it was finished in May 1919. Today, its twin spires guide planes into the city, home now to 120,000 Catholics.

When I set out to write about St. Joseph's, I set out to write about this. About beginnings. Of Sioux Falls, one scholar said its citizens essentially manifested its early success, their "language of anticipation" around a *theoretical* railway system attracting very real businesses and workers. That's useful, I thought—hopeful. We could use a bit of that. But now, as in the darkest days of 2020, I find it impossible to think about the start of anything—to conceive that anything can grow beyond the fire that licks at its ankles.

Equally hard is writing about religion in a state like ours—of building a church on stolen ground. The driving out, the othering of native people is evident in South Dakota more than in most other places, the seizure and redistribution of sacred land still raw after centuries of removal. In the cathedral's foyer, a statue of Kateri Tekakwitha, a Mohawk woman canonized in 2012, sits beneath a recessed window. As a girl, she was mostly blinded from a smallpox outbreak that killed her family. Tekakwitha means "she who bumps into things."

I'm not so much interested in building, then, as in rebuilding. In what can be done with what we have. Luckily for me, churches have plenty of that, too.

In July, I take a tour of the cathedral for the first time. My parents, still devoted Catholics (myself only nominally at this point), come with me. We meet our guide in the cool dark of the foyer, cross floors of imported Italian marble, past Kateri, and into the nave. We gawk, heads straight back, while she turns on the lights.

Over the course of the tour, I'm most interested to find that many of the cathedral's most arresting features aren't even original. Most of the paintwork is new; this greets you first, the brilliant golden angels in the rafters. The altar is new as of the 1940s, replacing the much smaller one recycled from the brick version of the church decades before, and the stained-glass windows, French now, replaced frosted ones in 1947.

As we make our way toward the altar, the timing of those renovations strikes me. While quite a bit of French stained glass was being imported to the US at that time, much of it came from churches bombed out in a war that had just taken 400,000 American lives. South Dakota alone gave nearly a third of its own population up to serve, with women, children, and "city workers" left behind to keep farms running.

Even so, part of the 1940s renovations were these: huge circular windows in the north and south transepts, dedicated to Joseph and Mary, respectively, that feature vocations appropriate for that saint's gender. The guide is quick to remind us that the vocations for women were those considered appropriate in 1947: mother (of course), teacher, nurse, and nun. The male vocations, she says somewhat wryly, remain appropriate today. I can't help but laugh.

We linger a long time in the transepts. Far below the stained glass, the stations of the cross begin and end. These, too, were renovated in the forties, the sculptures painted and set back into the wall so as not to blend in, and they are mesmerizing to me in their detail, their precision. Our guide points out the sky, for example—the hazy blue of morning in the first panel, and by the last, a gloomy twilight streaked with setting sun. The artist took great care to show the long stretch of Jesus' misery, and it's really quite effective. Beside me, Mom sniffs softly.

I, too, am moved, but less by the panels themselves than with the effort of their making. The continuity of the sky pleases me the way a callback in a novel might: the artist cares enough to remember and so takes care of us. Then again, I think, how could someone living in a barely postwar America ever forget the concept of miserable, stretching time? How so much anguish can be packed into one or two or three revolutions around the sun, which moved at a pace both the same as and completely unlike any other revolutions before them?

How time can warp this way is certainly not something I'll ever forget. Of the past two years, I have maybe a handful of memories: Thanksgiving by myself, Christmas alone, my birthdays in quarantine. They're my own stations, everything in between lost to that specific brand of time—a dull ecru, like plaster.

But then, that bright rebirth. We know a bit about that, too. The news in the *Argus* those years after the war (at least the news pertaining to St. Joseph's) was not about the renovations to the altar and stained glass. The news was about *weddings*. Pages and pages of them packed to the margins, so many delayed in the years before. Many of them were at the cathedral, beautiful as it is, and it's in these tediously, deliciously detailed announcements that we can see what a church really means to its parishioners in a time such as that:

> the Christmas setting of green in the sanctuary studded with Royal Blue lights, the altar in its rich red and all the white cathedral candles, reflected the colors of her wedding party. She was in white velvet, her maid of honor in American Beauty red and her many attendants all wore royal blue. It was a setting that harmonized perfectly in color tones. And the new blue stained glass windows added another delightful color touch to the entire cathedral.

This from 1948. A Christmas wedding washed in blue. No mention of the images on the glass—the popes, the martyrs with the instruments of their deaths—but of the light coming through the pieces.

As someone who identifies now only as "culturally Catholic," this nearly century-old scene helps me explain, mostly to myself, what such a concept can mean. Because there are certain things I no longer do: confess my sins, seek advice from priests. But I will say a rosary at a beloved grandparent's funeral, which I did twice this past year, and hope they hear it wherever they are. I will, on a Christmas spent alone, pull up the livestream of Mass at my parents' church and look for their pew, and though it's empty, I will feel at home.

After the end of World War II, the decade was almost out before people really started to notice what had been built for them. In 1949, the Catholic Women's Literary Society met in the nave so a monseigneur could explain the new additions, using opera glasses to peer into the rafters. I wonder how many of those women served in the war themselves or, if they'd stayed, had dropped out of school to run a farm or serve on jury duty or perform any number of things considered men's work. I like to think they exchanged looks and nudged each other in the ribs when they saw the windows.

Neither my parents nor I had ever been to the cathedral before that day in July. But during the pandemic, when they were still dragging dining room chairs into the living room to watch Mass, sometimes they'd tune in "just to mix it up." Devoted Catholic though she is, my mom is also a lover of beautiful things, and she was there for the moments the camera's eye drifted into the ceiling; she was there for the angels.

She tells the guide this when we first arrive, and the woman chuckles. She says dozens of people emailed in last year, asking for the camera to focus on this or that thing they'd never noticed when going to Mass in person. "I guess you don't really look up," she says. For the three of us, mouths practically unhinged, this seems insane.

There's a Mark Twain quote I've seen circulating recently: "History doesn't repeat itself, but it often rhymes." It's a sentiment the purpose of which I'm unsure. To comfort? To warn? There's a bit of both in the air these days as the sky darkens on this, our second pandemic year. But there's something peaceful, at least to me, in the sameness of these scenes: the Catholic Women's Literary Society, opera glasses in hand, safe and secure and finally wedding-ed out, winking down the aisle at the idea that only a man can be a soldier, and the parishioners of St. Joseph's, nose to their TVs, hungry, in their isolation, for what's been there all along.

It's fitting, I think, that so many churches burn in their infancy. Perhaps as retribution, but perhaps as a reminder, as well, of that most basic Christian tenant that from death comes life; from destruction, a chance to rebuild. To gut what's rotten and replace it with angels—what an act of hope that is.

John Morrell

MICHAEL J. MULLIN

This paper is dedicated to Ralph Dally and Sarah Telahun Birhe's mother, both of whom spent years working at the John Morrell (Smithfield) plant in Sioux Falls, South Dakota.

Until April, 2020, it is doubtful that most Sioux Falls residents gave much thought to one of its iconic employers: Smithfield Foods. This is somewhat surprising given the fact that Smithfield is Sioux Falls's third-largest employer.[1] However, unlike the two largest employers, Sanford and Avera Health Systems, Smithfield has long since lost its place as the "gateway to the middle class."[2] As was the case throughout the meatpacking industry, wages had stagnated since the early 1980s.[3] One result of this income decline was that Smithfield's employees were now more likely to be immigrants and refugees;[4] this stands in stark contrast to the historic employment pattern of the plant where American-born and regionally recruited employees made up more than 95 percent of the workforce. That is why, when Smithfield Foods experienced an outbreak of COVID-19 among its workers, the Sioux Falls community's collective response centered on "those people."[5]

That many Sioux Falls residents felt a distance between themselves and the meatpackers indicates how different Sioux Falls is today from its twentieth-century roots, where working at John Morrell & Company meant economic security and social mobility. The story of meatpacking

1 See Sioux Falls Development Foundation Listing at http://www.siouxfallsdevelopment.com/majorEmployers.cfm, last accessed December 22, 2020.

2 James and Deborah Fallows. ***Our Towns: A 100,000 Mile Journey into the Heart of America*** (New York: Pantheon Books, 2018), pp. 23–24.

3 Some of this wage loss was the result of companies like John Morrell breaking the labor unions that represented workers. See Michael J. Broadway, "From City to Countryside: Recent Changes in the Structure and Location of the Meat- and Fish-Processing Industries," pp. 17–41, especially pp. 22, 25, in Donald D. Stull, Michael J. Broadway, and David Griffith, editors. ***Any Way You Cut It: Meat Processing and Small-Town America*** (Lawrence, KS.: University of Kansas Press, 1995).

4 Today it is estimated that 65 percent of Smithfield workers are people of color; this trend of hiring immigrants and refugees is not unique to Smithfield in Sioux Falls. The trend began in the 1980s in the midst of labor strife throughout the meatpacking industry. See, for example, Lourdes Gouveia and Donald D. Stull, "Dances with Cows: Beefpacking's Impact on Garden City, Kansas, and Lexington, Nebraska," pp. 85–108, Mark A. Grey's, "Pork, Poultry, and Newcomers in Storm Lake, Iowa," pp. 109–128, or David Griffith's "***Hay Trabajo***: Poultry Processing, Rural Industrialization, and the Latinization of Low-Wage Labor," pp. 129–152, all in Donald D. Stull, et. al., editors. ***Any Way You Cut It: Meat Processing and Small-Town America.***

5 For how the outbreak of COVID-19 affected the immigrant workforce, see Jaweed Kaleem, "As state took its stand, refugees took the brunt," *LA Times*, December 24, 2020, Section A, page 1.

in Sioux Falls, then, is the story of city's growth and evolution. By the late 1980s, meatpacking employed fewer than 3.5 percent of the Sioux Falls workforce;[6] it has shrunk since then, but, for most of the twentieth century, John Morrell & Company was the largest employer in Sioux Falls, and the second-largest in the state. At one time, nearly 20 percent of the city's labor force worked at John Morrell & Company.[7] Despite the growing awareness that Sioux Falls has moved beyond "meatpacking," it is difficult to imagine Sioux Falls without a meatpacking plant.

John Morrell & Company owned the meatpacking plant in Sioux Falls for most of the twentieth century. Smithfield Foods purchased the plant in 1995. In 2013, Smithfield sold the plant to Shuanghui International Holdings, Ltd.[8] Whoever the owner is, the meatpacking plant remains an important, if often overlooked, economic cornerstone of the Sioux Falls economy. John Morrell, and the Sioux Falls Stockyards located directly across the street from the packing plant, drove Sioux Falls's emergence as the region's economic linchpin.

Before examining some important moments in John Morrell's Sioux Falls history, it is important for the reader to understand the subtle ways John Morrell & Company influenced Sioux Falls. The presence of the plant along the Big Sioux River, and what is now Rice Street, influenced the placement of the city's wastewater treatment plant;[9] it dictated which roads were paved first. The first paved highway in Minnehaha County, for example, ran from Canton to Dell Rapids and directly east of the Morrell plant. South Dakota farmers were some of the most dependent on trucks (rather than trains) for delivering their animals to market. Later, the two interstate highways that provide access to Sioux Falls served the same purpose. In town, nearly 700 automobiles brought 1,950 workers to the plant daily by the early 1930s.[10] Paved roads became the order of the day. As time went on, Morrell workers shaped some of the distinct neighborhoods of Sioux Falls.[11] While its workers lived in Sioux Falls, Morrell required the

6 Steve Erpenbach, "Morrell: Dispute may close plant," *The Argus Leader*, November 13, 1988, p. 2a.

7 The figure 20 percent might be low, but it is derived from Arthur G. Horton's economic analysis of Sioux Falls on the eve of World War II. He reported 1,950 employees at the packing plant and a city population of 30,028. Of that total population, just over a third of them were nineteen years old or younger. See Arthur G. Horton, *An Economic and Social Survey of Sioux Falls* (Sioux Falls: Sioux Falls Chamber of Commerce, 1938).

8 For Smithfield's purchase of Morrell's plant, see https://www.cruchbase.com/acquisition/smithfield-aquires-joh-morrell-co-c2bca1db, accessed August 28, 2020. For Shuanghui's purchase, see Michael Felberbaum, "Owner of John Morrell Food Group Sold to Chinese Company," *Dayton Daily News*, business section, May 29, 2013. Accessed at https://daytondailynews.com/business/owner-john-morrell-food-group-sold-chinese-firm.wzhHMDI6fG0ogMSev4xsN/, August 28, 2020.

9 By 1941, Morrell's used approximately one million gallons of water per day, and it needed to be treated before being released back into the Big Sioux River. See Lynwood E. Oyos. *Reveille for Sioux Falls: A World War II Army Air Forces Technical School Changes a South Dakota City* (Sioux Falls: Center for Western Studies, 2014), p. 11.

10 Horton, *An Economic and Social Survey of Sioux Falls, SD 1938–39*, p. 130.

11 Tom Dempster (with an historic overview by Gary Olson), *North of Twelfth Street: The Changing Face of Sioux Falls Neighbor-*

input of the countryside for its existence, and so with the assistance of the Sioux Falls Stockyards, farmers brought their cattle, hogs, and even sheep to town nearly every day of the year.

Agricultural producers who came to Sioux Falls could drop their animals off at the Sioux Falls Stockyards in the morning, have breakfast at the Stockyards Café, see their animals sold later in the morning, and then shop along Phillips Avenue in the afternoon. By the time the producer left town later in the day, many of the livestock they had delivered had traveled across the street and already been butchered. As for the Phillips Avenue merchants, they had more receipts in the till because of the producer's presence. It was in this manner that Sioux Falls became the focal point, or regional capital, of the surrounding countryside.[12]

John Morrell & Company was not the first meatpacker in Sioux Falls. The first efforts at meatpacking began in 1883, but the city condemned the plant as a nuisance due to the odors produced. Two other efforts, one in 1885 and another in 1890, attempted to establish Sioux Falls as a meatpacking center. These efforts also failed. By 1900, "meat packing in Sioux Falls" remained "confined largely to the operations of local butchers."[13] In 1905, however, E. R. Green of Sioux Falls opened the Green Packing Plant. It operated sporadically, and it was this facility that John Morrell & Company president, Thomas D. Foster, leased when he decided to expand Morrell's footprint beyond Ottumwa, Iowa, in 1909.[14] John Morrell & Company had arrived in Sioux Falls.[15]

John Morrell & Company's appearance in Sioux Falls coincided with a change in agricultural production in the surrounding areas. At the time of statehood, wheat was king. But by the turn of the twentieth century, corn had begun to make inroads. Indeed, the number of acres farmers devoted to corn more than doubled between 1910 and 1930.[16] Unlike wheat, corn could be fed to ranch animals, and this helped stimulate cattle production in southeastern South Dakota.[17] Moreover, the region was beginning to raise more hogs, and that is the animal most often processed at the Sioux Falls plant. By 1929, the plant was processing over one million hogs a

---

hoods (Pierre: South Dakota Historical Society, 2012), p. xxxiii.

12 James Richard Smith. *Some Changing Features of a Regional Capital: Sioux Falls, South Dakota, 1920–1970*, Phd dissertation (Lincoln, NE: University of Nebraska, 1971) p. 2., 38, 46, 53–56.

13 Ray A. Beck, "The Meat-Packing Industry: With Special Reference to its Development in South Dakota," M.A. Thesis (Vermillion, SD: University of South Dakota, 1938), p. 41.

14 *1909–1949* (Sioux Falls, John Morrell & Company, 1949), p. 3.

15 Beck, "The Meat-Packing Industry: With Special Reference to South Dakota," pp. 31–42.

16 Beck, "The Meat-Packing Industry: With Special Reference to South Dakota," p. 23, table 3.

17 James Richard Smith. *Some Changing Features of a Regional Capital: Sioux Falls, South Dakota, 1920–1970*, PhD dissertation (Lincoln, NE: University of Nebraska, 1971), p. 29.

year, drawing animals from Iowa, Minnesota, Nebraska, North Dakota, South Dakota, and occasionally Montana.[18] The presence of the Sioux Falls Stockyards ensured an adequate number of animals for the plant's operations, and what differentiated the Sioux Falls plant from other meatpacking enterprises, other than a reliance on trucks to deliver animals, was the fact that the Morrell plant processed hogs, cattle, and sheep. Most meatpacking plants processed a single type of animal.[19]

Morrell was the first company in South Dakota to offer paid vacation to its employees. Any worker who had worked for a year and met specific criteria was eligible.[20] In 1925, 245 Sioux Falls plant employees took advantage of their one week at full pay opportunity.[21] This was just one-way Morrell & Company changed the workers' experience in Sioux Falls. People wanted to work at this "progressive" company. Eventually, John Morrell & Company would also offer a pension plan, but that would come later and after a major strike in 1935.

Morrell's growth buoyed Sioux Falls. Within two years of opening, Morrell had a regional impact of $25 million per year. Having begun with the ability to process 200 to 500 head daily, expansion allowed the company to process ever greater numbers. By 1920, the Sioux Falls Stockyards sold Morrell & Company 265,333 animals yearly. By 1938, the company was processing 24,581,400 animals.[22] These numbers meant a significant number of "visitors" entered the city every day. These visitors did more than just deliver animals to the market; they shopped too.[23] By 1938, Sioux Falls's businesses reported their reach into the countryside as varying between forty and one hundred miles.[24] Today that reach extends even farther.

Unlike meatpacking plants elsewhere, Morrell drew its workers from the surrounding countryside. Until the 1980s, Morrell's did not depend on immigrant labor, and unlike Omaha, Nebraska, and Fort Worth, Texas, Morrell's never recruited African Americans to break a labor strike. This fact helps explain why Sioux Falls was one of the whitest cities in the United States for much of the twentieth century.[25] As the largest employer in town,

18 Arthur G. Horton. *An Economic and Social Survey of Sioux Falls, South Dakota 1938–39* (Sioux Falls: Sioux Falls Chamber of Commerce, 1939), p. 124.

19 Steve Erpenbach, "Morrell: Disputes may close plant," *The Argus Leader*, November 13, 1988, p. 2a.

20 The criteria included not missing any workdays except for some excusable cause. See footnote 21 for citation.

21 "Vacations for 1925," in *the Morrell Magazine*, II:6 (Decemer,1925), p. 5.

22 Arthur G. Horton, ed. *An Economic and Social Survey of Sioux Falls, SD 1938–1939*, (Sioux Falls: Sioux Falls Chamber of Commerce and City of Sioux Falls). p. 33. The breakdown in animal numbers was 15,042,000 hogs, 7,915,000 cattle, 58,700 calves, and 1,565,700 sheep.

23 Tom Dempster (with historical overview by Gary D. Olson). *North of Twelfth Street: The Changing Face of Sioux Falls Neighborhoods* (Pierre, SD: South Dakota Historical Society Press, 2012), p. xxiv.

24 Horton, *An Economic and Social Survey of Sioux Falls, South Dakota 1938–39*, pp. 124, 127.

25 Sioux Falls was 99.6 percent white in 1937, and 98.4 percent white in 1976. See Horton, *An Economic and Social Survey*

Morrell drew its workers from the children of South Dakota's original settlers—overwhelmingly Northern European in origin. For the few who were not citizens, Morrell celebrated their decisions to become Americans.[26]

Most of these workers were males, but there were also some women working at the plant. Initially, the only women employed at the Sioux Falls plant worked in the administrative offices, not on the line. This was not unique to Sioux Falls, but World War II changed this. By 1945, at least one woman worked in 68 percent of the departments at the Sioux Falls plant.[27] Shortly after the war, women were reassigned to some specific plant areas, and their presence within the Morrell workforce began a decades-long decline.[28] Today, meatpackers continue to funnel women into specific areas of the meatpacking enterprise, and these areas tend to limit promotion and pay increases.[29] Whether male or female, workers for most of the twentieth century were drawn from within the region.

One of those drawn to a job at John Morrell & Company was Ralph Dally. Originally from northern Minnesota, Dally arrived in Sioux Falls shortly after World War II. His timing was fortuitous. The labor unrest that created Local 304A was over.[30] Working at John Morrell's now offered an opportunity to become middle class. Workers had steady hours and good pay. The job allowed workers to send their children to college.[31] For nearly a century, working the line at John Morrell's meant the next generation of family members would have options unavailable to earlier generations. Ralph Dally spent nearly forty years working at John Morrell & Company. He sent his son Nate to Concordia College in Moorhead, Minnesota. Nate's brother and sisters also had the opportunity to attend university. None of them chose meatpacking as a career, but Nate and his siblings did work summers there during their college days to offset their college expenses. Today, Nate Dally wears a suit and tie to work every day; he works with the Sioux Falls Area Community Foundation in donor relations. Nate's career is what many Morrell employees hoped for their children.

Unfortunately, working in the meatpacking plant is no longer seen

---

of Sioux Falls, South Dakota 1938–1939, p. 72 and *Horizons: Sioux Falls in the 70s* (Sioux Falls: Sioux Falls Development Foundation, 1976), p. 14.

26 "Three More Americans," in *The Morrell Magazine* II:8 (February, 1926), p. 4

27 *Morrell Magazine* 22 (July, 1945), pp. 12–16.

28 Marvel Vander Kooi, "'It was like Family': A History of Women Working in the post-World War II Sioux Falls Morrell Plant," unpublished paper (Sioux Falls, 1998), p. 3–5.

29 Deborah Fink. *Cutting into the Meatpacking Line: Workers and Change in the Rural Midwest* (Chapel Hill: University of North Carolina Press, 1998), p. 82.

30 For a discussion of the union's founding and its fight against John Morrell in 1935 see Lynwood E. Oyos, "Labor's House Divided: The Morrell Strike of 1935–37," *South Dakota History* 18:1&2 (Spring/Summer, 1983), pp. 67–88.

31 See, for example, Gail Eiesland, "The Morrell Strike: 1935–1937," student paper, 1981, p. 1. in the Lynwood Oyos Collection, Center for Western Studies, John Morrell Strike, 1935–37: Student Papers, 1979–81, 30363, LO 1/1.

as a stepping-stone into the middle class. The late 1980s and early 1990s saw profound changes in meatpacking and wages; by 2013, "meatpacking workers' real wages were 40 percent less than they had been forty years earlier."[32] Declining wages created a different type of workplace and a different type of worker. These declining wages have a ripple effect for the community of Sioux Falls. The Sioux Falls School District finds more and more of its students qualifying for free and/or reduced lunches.[33] Employment in meatpacking might offer an alternative to poverty, but it does not provide an opportunity to join the middle class.

The reason Ralph Dally was able to provide for his family was that he worked at John Morrell between the two most important labor strikes in Sioux Falls's history. These two strikes define John Morrell & Company's relationship with the city, and these strikes shaped the direction of Sioux Falls (and perhaps South Dakota as a whole). The first strike occurred in 1935 and lasted until 1937. The second strike took place in 1987. The first work stoppage eventually produced one of the strongest labor unions in South Dakota; the second strike eventually broke the union, and some might say unions in general, within South Dakota.

The 1930s were a period of change in management-labor relations; unlike earlier periods, management found that workers had newfound rights as a result of New Deal legislation. Perhaps the most important of these rights was the right to unionize. The Morrell plant had seen earlier efforts to unionize, but they had come to naught. As one writer noted, the company simply ignored these efforts, and the union effort fizzled.[34] Now, in the midst of the Great Depression, workers tried again. In March 1935, Local 304 initiated a new strike. The company informed employees that 108 additional men and women would be laid off. These layoffs followed on the heels of an earlier round of redundancies totaling 107.[35] All told, the layoffs represented more than 10 percent of the meatpacking plant's workforce.

The 1935 strike produced the first sit-down strike in American labor history. The Sioux Falls workers took their on-site "break" five months before the Akron Tire Strike and nearly a year before the more famous

---

32 Wilson J. Warren, *Meat Makes People Powerful: A Global History of the Modern Era* (Iowa City: University of Iowa Press, 2018), p. 143.

33 Sioux Falls has seven schools that have more than 70 percent of their students receiving reduced or free lunches; it has another nine schools with at least a third of the student body qualifying for reduced or free lunches. See https://www.sdstate.edu/remast/2019-free-and-reduced-lunch-percentage-south-dakota-public-schools; last accessed May 23, 2021.

34 Matthew Oyos, "Blood, Sweat, and Tears: The Story of the Morrell Strike of 1935," unpublished paper, 1980, p. 1; in the Lynwood Oyos Collection, Center for Western Studies, John Morrell Strike, 1935–37: Student Papers, 1979-81, 30363, LO 1/1.

35 Lynwood E. Oyos, "Labor's House Divided: The Morrell Strike of 1935–1937," *South Dakota History*, 16:1 & 2 (Spring/Summer, 1988), pp. 72–73.

Ford Motor Company sit-down strike of 1936,[36] and just like the "Battle of the Running Bulls" in Flint, Michigan, Sioux Falls had its own "Bloody Friday" on July 19, 1935.[37] What separated the two sit-down events was that the Sioux Falls workers were not trying to prevent any "scabs" from taking their jobs. Instead, the Sioux Falls workers chose the sit-down strike model because they thought they would only be on "strike" for "twenty or thirty minutes at most."[38] Indeed, one of the things that precipitated the strike was a union proposal to reduce hours at the plant from thirty-two to twenty-hours for the workers. The idea was to prevent additional layoffs in the midst of the Great Depression. Morrell management wanted to hire and fire at will.

The most important legacy of the 1935–1937 strike was the recognition of Local 304A to bargain on behalf of the meatpacking workers at Morrell. In the years that followed, pension and health plans became an accepted part of the worker-employer relationship. As one participant noted:

> There's no doubt that the strike was worth it. They were very tough times but definitely worth the effort. I realize it each month when my pension check comes in the mail or each time they take care of my hospitalization or prescription needs. These are things that never could have been realized before the events of 1935.[39]

However, there is something else that makes the strike important. It marks the final defeat for inhouse "associations," or what was called "welfare capitalism," in the 1920s.[40] Welfare capitalism had envisioned management and employee working together to solve the problems facing a given industry. But, here, in Sioux Falls, the idea that management had "accepted an obligation for the well-being of its employees" had been shown to be a lie.[41] The strike had initially been about workers requesting

36 See https://www.encyclopedia.com/history/united-states-and-canada/us-history/sit-down-strikes for the Akron strike, listed as the first sit down strike in American history, and https://www.history.com/this-day-in-history/sit-down-strike-begins-in-flint for the Flint, Michigan strike; both accessed January 6, 2021.

37 Oyos, "Labor's House Divided," pp. 78–80.

38 This quote comes from a June 16, 1988, interview between Janet O'Donnell and Sam Twedwell. The interview is part of O'Donnell's unpublished paper on John Morrell & Company and its workers; see Janet O'Donnell, "A Mid-30s Labor Problem in Sioux Falls," p. 8. in the Lynwood Oyos Collection, Center for Western Studies, John Morrell Strike, 1935–37: Student Papers, 1979–81, 30363, LO 1/1.

39 Brian J. Bauer, "The Morrell's Strike of 1935," p. 6; in the Lynwood Oyos Collection, Center for Western Studies, John Morrell Strike, 1935–37: Student Papers, 1979–81, 30363, LO 1/1. Bauer interviewed Joe Johnson, who was one of the twenty-nine workers blacklisted by John Morrell & Company after the initial strike of July 1935. Eventually, Johnson was hired back by the company.

40 For a discussion of "welfare capitalism" and its role in American labor history, see David Brody, "The Rise and Decline of Welfare Capitalism" pp. 48–81; in David Brody, ***Workers in Industrial America: Essays on the Twentieth-Century Struggle*** (New York: Oxford University Press, 1980).

41 Brody, ***Workers in Industrial America***, p. 61.

fewer hours to save other people's jobs. Management had rejected this idea. In this sense, then, the John Morrell & Company of Sioux Falls has an important place in the labor history of the United States.

The post-World War II years saw labor peace, and John Morrell's Sioux Falls plant dominated city employment. A steady supply of men and women spent their careers at John Morrell. As late as 1976, Morrell employed more than twice as many workers as the next business.[42]

If the strike of 1935 created the twentieth-century American union, the labor contracts of 1983 and 1985 marked how fundamentally changed meatpacking had become at the end of the twentieth century. The emergence of Iowa Beef Processors (IBP) as a major meatpacker created new dynamics within meatpacking. IBP not only worked to mechanize as much of the process as it could, but it also refused to abide by the long-established "master contract" which had guided management-labor relations across the industry.[43] IBP's actions forced old-time packers such as John Morrell & Company or Geo. A. Hormel & Company to become more efficient—meaning management sped up the production line. To become more economically viable, the old meatpackers had to reduce wages, and that process began in Sioux Falls in 1983.

The 1983 contract cut hourly wages by $2.44 an hour; workers went from making over $10 an hour to a base rate of $8.75. At the time, the minimum wage for an American worker was $3.35 an hour. Morrell's management claimed the cut was necessary because meat processing had become "unskilled" labor. Following IBP's lead, Morrell had simplified each worker's task, allowing it to speed up the line and reduce its alliance on skilled butchers.[44] Now, Morrell told union leaders that their competition was not high-end meat producers, but IBP and ConAgra. The wage contraction of 1983 set the stage for the labor problems of 1985, and they began even before contract negotiations did. In May 1985, 250 beef-production workers went on strike; this represented roughly one-tenth of the company's total employee count in 1985 for Sioux Falls.

The strike was precipitated by a production line speed up. Not only did this increase the likelihood of someone missing a prescribed cut, but it also had the potential to create work hazards such as a pressure hose breaking.[45]

42 *Horizons Sioux Falls in the 70s* (Sioux Falls: Sioux Falls Development Foundation, 1976) p. 40. Morrell employed 2,789 people while Sioux Valley Hospital had 1,150 workers.

43 By mechanizing as much as the production process as possible, IBP was able to claim that its workers were not "skilled" workers but unskilled laborers. See Deborah Finks, *Cutting into the Meatpacking Line: Workers and Change in the Rural Midwest* (Chapel Hill: The University of North Carolina Press, 1998), pp. 42, 93.

44 Fink, *Cutting into the Meatpacking Line: Workers and Change in the Rural Midwest*, p. 93.

45 This is what happened at the Monfort plant in Greeley, Colorado, when management sped up the line there in 1979. See

The speed-up led one man to miss a cut. He was promptly suspended by the company. His coworkers felt that was unfair, and they walked out. A federal judge ordered the workers back to work, but five men lost their jobs over the incident.[46] Labor unrest continued that year as the labor contract under which workers operated was due to expire on September 1, 1985, and early negotiations had not proven fruitful.

The union opened with a demand that the $2.00+ per-hour wage cut of 1983 be restored. On the day before the contract expired, company officials countered with another proposed wage cut.[47] For the next six weeks, nearly 2,400 workers striked at John Morrell's Sioux Falls plant. This produced a variety of responses, with many in the community complaining that Morrell workers, even with the wage cut, made more than most Sioux Falls workers. When the strike ended in November 1985, both sides had given up something.[48] What was different, though, was that management and union workers were clearly at odds about the future of meatpacking work. Both sides were angry, and this anger set the stage for Morrell's decision in 1987 to destroy the union financially.

The final blow for Morrell workers came in 1987, when the company sued the union for an "illegal" strike. Sioux Falls workers refused to cross a picket line set up by Morrell workers from the company's Sioux City, Iowa, plant. The negotiated contract specifically forbade Sioux Falls workers from striking, while union representatives argued a "sympathy" strike was not outlawed by the contract. The Sioux City episode occurred behind an earlier sympathy strike on behalf of Morrell workers striking at Arkansas City, Kansas.[49] Morrell took the union to court over the matter. Although an arbitrator originally ruled in favor of the union, Morrell & Company appealed and won in federal court.[50] The verdict: punitive damages of $24.8 million.[51] The verdict amounted to nearly half of the total assets of the 1.4-million-member union.[52] This doomed the union. The lawsuit bled into contract negotiations between the company and its Sioux Falls workforce. After eight different efforts to

---

Carol Andreas, *Meatpackers and Beef Barons: Company Town in a Global Economy* (Boulder: University Press of Colorado, 1994), p. 65.

46 Jane Olsen, "250 walk off jobs at Morrell's" *The Argus Leader*, May 17, 1985, p. 1a.

47 Anne Willette, "Union to Austin strikers, stay away" *The Argus Leader*, September 18, 1985, 1a.

48 Jane Olson, "Morrell, union reach tentative agreement," *The Argus Leader*, Nov. 19, 1985, p. 1a.

49 Brenda Wade, "Morrell, union end standoff," *The Argus Leader*, August 5, 1986, p. 1-2a.

50 There were actually two court cases, the first, in March 1987, decided that Morrell workers had staged a series of illegal strikes. The second case determined the "damages" John Morrell & Company were entitled to. See Steve Erpenbach, "Jury decides in Morrell's favor," *The Argus Leader*, March 11, 1988, p. 1a, and Steve Erpenbach, Morrell wins $24 million suit," *The Argus Leader*, November 11, 1988, p. 1a

51 "John Morrell Wins Lawsuit Against Striking Union," *The Dessert News*, November 12, 1988. Article at https://www.deseret.com/1988/11/12/18783791/john-morrell-wins-suit-against-striking-union; last accessed 11-May-2021.

52 Steve Erpenbach, "Morrell wins $24 million suit," *The Argus Leader*, November 11, 1988, p. 1a.

find common ground, the company declared an impasse in negotiations and unilaterally imposed an 18 percent pay cut; though union workers voted overwhelmingly to reject the contract, no strike was called. Instead, union leaders simply noted that the company had "destroyed 50 years of bargaining."[53] The union was in no position to strike; now, longtime workers began to leave the plant in droves.

Breaking the union created a new dynamic at John Morrell & Company. No longer were workers American born; instead, the new workers that Morrell drew were recently resettled refugees, themselves a new development in Sioux Falls's history. Sponsors of the new arrivals often settled the refugees in the neighborhoods surrounding the meatpacking plant, which were neighborhoods previously occupied by earlier American-born plant workers. Those former workers had either retired (some of whom left Sioux Falls for the communities they had grown up in, as was the case with Ralph Dally) or gone to work elsewhere. In the process, one neighborhood was abandoned for another.

Beginning in the late 1980s, Lutheran Social Services began supporting Sudanese refugee resettlement in Sioux Falls. Their sponsorship occurred just as labor tensions between the meatpacking union and John Morrell & Company reached their nastiest level. The wildcat strike in support of workers in Sioux City, Iowa, precipitated a legal showdown that left the meatpacking union bankrupt. In the aftermath of the work stoppage, longtime workers found themselves working alongside new workers who did not look like the traditional Morrell worker and often spoke English with an accent. Whether it was Dinka, Bari, Nuer, Zande, or Spanish, the dialects spoken at John Morrell & Company marked another transition for the city of Sioux Falls. Sioux Falls's population was diversifying. Whereas Sioux Falls was 98.4 percent white as late as 1976,[54] that figure has dropped to just over 80 percent in the most recent census. If you look at the demographics of the Sioux Falls School District, people of color now comprise 39.8 percent of the student body.[55]

While longtime residents might comment on the growing diversity of Sioux Falls, the transition from "white" to "people of color" as employees fit into the national trend within meatpacking during the 1990s. New meatpacking employees were not only people of color but were also

53 "2,000 Morrell Workers Get Pay Cuts Under New Pact," *LA Times*, February 21, 1989, article at: https://www.latimes.com/archives/la-xpm-1989-02-21-fi-236-story.html; accessed May 11, 2021.

54 See ***Horizons: Sioux Falls in the 70s*** (Sioux Falls: Sioux Falls Development Foundation, 1976), p. 14.

55 Figures for today come from Census Bureau at https://censusreporter.org/profiles/16000US4659020-sioux-falls-sd/#race; figures for the Sioux Falls School District appear in a presentation entitled "2020 District Demographics Report, slide five, see http://www.sf.k12.sd.us/images/docs/school_board/school_board_reports/2020/13B-2020DistrictDemographicsRpt.pdf; both last accessed on May 17, 2021.

nonunionized. This transition coincided with declining wages paid to meatpacking workers.[56] Fortunately for Sioux Falls, other industries had arrived in Sioux Falls during the 1980s (think credit cards). Longtime residents in Sioux Falls now looked to white-collar positions at Citibank, Wells Fargo, and other enterprises for careers. The result: John Morrell became the domain of resettled refugees and Latinx workers who had heard of job opportunities in Sioux Falls and at nearby meat processors, such as the JBS Meatpacking plant in Worthington, Minnesota, about fifty minutes east of Sioux Falls.

The transition occurring at John Morrell & Company during the 1990s went largely unnoticed by locals. The reason for this was the arrival of a new economic enterprise: credit cards. Sioux Falls was transitioning from a blue-collar economy to a white-collar community. The change was led by women, who comprised nearly 70 percent of Citibank Sioux Falls's payroll at the time of the Morrell strike.[57] Working-age residents now had options other than John Morrell for employment and a career. John Morrell's role as the dominant employer of Sioux Falls was winding down but not before its legacy for Sioux Falls and South Dakota was secure. Still, meatpacking's impact on the evolution of Sioux Falls was not over.

Declining wages, a new workforce model, and other opportunities allowed longtime residents to consign meatpacking to Sioux Falls's past. They did this despite John Morrell & Company being the city's largest employer as late as 1992. Still, other industrial occupations emerged to push meatpacking down the pecking order of largest employers. Credit card payments, education, and then health care all jumped above Morrell in terms of employing Sioux Falls residents. As Smithfield entered the twenty-first century, the future of Sioux Falls looked beyond the local agricultural sector for its economic future. Morrell remains an entry point for some of Sioux Falls's newest residents to establish themselves in an ever-changing city.

56 This phenomenon was not unique to Sioux Falls. See Peter Rachleff, ***Hard-Pressed in the Heartland: The Hormel Strike and the Future of the Labor Movement*** (Boston: South End Press, 1993), p. 46. Smithfield advertises a starting wage of $16.50 per hour, with a fifty-cent pay raise after ninety days.

57 Corrine Olson, "Smokestacks to greenbacks: Sioux Falls becoming a finance hub," ***Argus Leader***, August 27, 1988. Article was cut out from newspaper and is found in the ***Citibank Folder***, Museum Research Center, Siouxland Heritage Museums.

Fear and Loathing: McGovern '72

DANIEL MAX GERLING

Who knew that the 1960s died at the Holiday Inn in Sioux Falls, South Dakota, on the evening of November 7, 1972? For those alive at the time and tuned into politics, this particular death—Senator George McGovern's monumental loss to Richard Nixon in the 1972 US presidential election—wasn't a great surprise. This unfortunate detail was my only point of reference for Sioux Falls before moving here in the summer of 2010. And it eventually led me, an avid book collector, on a mad hunt to find what has become the jewel of my collection.

I learned about McGovern, Sioux Falls, and the circus of an election from reading Hunter S. Thompson's *Fear and Loathing on the Campaign Trail '72* in my formative years on the Illinois prairie in the 1990s. Thompson's account of the election was to me, a young fan of New Journalism for its rejection of the artifice of objectivity in journalism, Hunter S. Thompson—aka Dr. Gonzo, aka Raoul Duke—at his zenith. After struggling to keep a job writing for a bowling magazine in Puerto Rico early in his career, and after years of reporting from South America, Colorado, and California, Thompson caught a break when he wrote a story for the *Nation* on the Hells Angels biker gang in 1965. The article garnered enough curiosity that he spent the next year riding with the Angels for a book-length manuscript for Random House. The Angels were always suspicious of Thompson for being an outsider taking notes on them and asking too many questions. By the end of their time riding together, they stomped him to a bloody pulp when he criticized one of the gang for beating his own wife. But in the meantime, they seemed to enjoy Thompson for his propensity to flirt with "the edge," the line between life and death, sanity and insanity, truth and fiction. He was a hard drinker, a gun lover, and he entertained the bikers with his connection to people and drugs that were on the other side of the counterculture—namely, the Haight-Ashbury hippies of San Francisco, Jefferson Airplane, Ken Kesey, Allen Ginsberg, and Neal Cassady.

As a young and dynamic writer with deep connections to the various parts of the counterculture, Thompson was an ideal author for magazines such as *Harper's*, *Scanlan's Monthly*, and *Rolling Stone*. His voice jabbed and pounded with the energy of a machine gun. And with the bellicosity of an angry psychopath, he berated the people and institutions he felt were ruining America in one way or another. He routinely assailed the politicians responsible for the war in Vietnam as well as the wealthy, the overzealous police, racists, and J. Edgar Hoover. Even hippies and fellow writers that he felt to be subpar were on the receiving end of his verbal brutality. (He once wrote a letter to Anthony Burgess, calling him a "lazy cocksucker" and "cheapjack scum" for delaying a think piece he promised to *Rolling Stone*.) The real antichrist for Thompson took the form of Richard Nixon, whom he routinely called a "lying dog" and a "werewolf." In a eulogy of sorts for Nixon decades later, titled "He Was a Crook," Thompson wrote, "Some of my best friends have hated Nixon all their lives. My mother hates Nixon, my son hates Nixon, I hate Nixon, and this hatred has brought us together. Nixon laughed when I told him this. 'Don't worry,' he said, 'I, too, am a family man, and we feel the same way about you.'"

And while Thompson cast a skeptical eye on the Horatio Alger version of the American dream, he did believe in the dream of the sixties—that of civil rights and racial equality, of the end of foreign intervention, of a government that left people alone to enjoy indulgence in drugs and sex with whomever one pleased. He was plugged into the music of the era, gushing in letters and published work about Bob Dylan, the Dead, the Stones, and Buffalo Springfield. By 1968, when he witnessed the Chicago police beating peaceful protesters and journalists at the DNC convention, he began to doubt that the dream of the sixties would succeed. And by 1971, when he published his most famous book, *Fear and Loathing in Las Vegas*, he had already begun mourning the end of the cultural sixties. In perhaps the most famous passage of the book, Thompson writes:

> You could strike sparks anywhere. There was a fantastic universal sense that whatever we were doing was right, that we were winning. . . . And that, I think, was the handle—that sense of inevitable victory over the forces of Old and Evil. Not in any mean or military sense; we didn't need that. Our energy would simply prevail. There was no point in fighting—on our side or theirs. We had all the momentum; we were riding the crest of a high and beautiful wave. . . . So now, less than five years later, you can go up on a steep hill in Las Vegas and look West, and with the right kind of eyes you can almost see the high-water mark—that place where the wave finally broke and rolled back.

And with passages like this, I too grew nostalgic for this decade I never experienced in the first place.

Thompson was my first lens into the culture of the US in the 1960s. As a teenager, Thompson brought this strange and wild decade to life for me in a way that no history book could. Thompson was smart, hilarious, and free. He was inside this whirlwind of music and violence and drugs, and somehow, he was able to write lucid narratives that made sense of it all. I followed all of his leads, reading *The Ginger Man* and *The Great Gatsby* because he admired them so much. I listened to Dylan and the Stones. And because my mother wouldn't let me get a motorcycle at sixteen, I got a 50cc Honda Spree in hopes that I could experience "the edge" as well. Topping out at thirty miles an hour downhill on the scooter, I did not in fact experience "the edge," but I continued chasing down even more leads that would help me understand his time and place, reading about Muhammed Ali, Ernest Hemingway, and Kesey. Thompson had already begun his pivot to politics, aware that real change was effected by those in power, and I developed a fascination with that sphere as well.

In 1970, at the onset of his shift toward politics, Thompson ran for sheriff of his adopted home in Aspen, Colorado. Competing against a staunchly conservative ex-military man, Thompson shaved his own head so he could refer to the crew-cut incumbent as "my long-haired opponent." His platform involved renaming Aspen "Fat City" to discourage tourism, disarming the law enforcement, and targeting dishonest drug dealers, as "it will be the general philosophy of the Sheriff's office that no drug worth taking should be sold for money." He lost, narrowly, but between this race and his sour experience in Chicago in 1968, he felt the only way to leave Vietnam, make real gains toward racial equality, and build a kinder culture was through elections.

So Hunter Thompson spent a year, from December of 1971 through December of 1972, covering the presidential campaign for *Rolling Stone*. He wrote without the pretense of objectivity and usually injected himself into the stories. Thompson disliked the primary candidates of Humphrey and Ed Muskie ("a vicious 200-pound water rat"), and he even reported that there was a rumor Muskie was addicted to a root called ibogaine, given to him by a mysterious Brazilian doctor: "given the known effects of ibogaine . . . Muskie's brain was almost paralyzed by hallucinations. . . . [H]e looked out at the crowd and saw gila monsters instead of people." It's true that this rumor did circulate, but it's also true that Thompson started it. Despite the book including some elements of fiction, McGovern's campaign manager,

Frank Mankiewicz, famously called Thompson's book "the least factual, most accurate account" of the race. McGovern himself called it the best book that emerged from the campaign.

Quite early in the primaries, Thompson found a savior in George McGovern, the Mitchell, South Dakota, native who had been sharpened by a PhD in history and a strong social gospel ethic. He was honest to a fault and didn't play the election game he was supposed to play. He told Floridians that he would likely cancel the space shuttle program that would bring thousands of jobs. He told nervous white people that he supported busing because it's "among the prices we are paying for a century of segregation in our housing patterns." Thompson wrote that McGovern was the only candidate who "lines out the painful truth," and his reward was to be "mocked, vilified, ignored, and abandoned as a hopeless loser by even his good old buddies."

And Thompson adored him for it. Unabashedly.

For as much as Thompson himself relied on creating the character of Hunter Thompson to promote his own brand, his cynicism was offset by McGovern's sincerity and authenticity. Among democratic operatives, this forthrightness was called "the McGovern problem." But his sincerity garnered enough enthusiasm for McGovern to win the primary to face off with Nixon. Still, the incumbent spun McGovern's sincerity into a weakness by painting him as a radical who would force white kids to be bused to dangerous Black neighborhoods. His plan to cut $30 billion from the defense budget, appoint women to the Supreme Court, and offer everyone a decent job building up run-down neighborhoods was common sense for McGovern. He saw the plan as something deeply American; he saw it as an "intelligent modern application of the Puritan work ethic. It's saying that we shouldn't waste labor, we shouldn't waste human life." His "Come Home, America" speech was like the tail end of a jeremiad that promised a way out and a way back to America's roots:

> Come home, America, from Saigon, where we are wasting young blood in support of a political regime that does not even have the respect of its own citizens. . . . From the evils of racism to the dignity of brotherhood, come home, America. . . . From the hunger of little children, from the loneliness of the aging poor, from the

> despair of the homeless. . . . Come home, America, to that sense of community that opened the country and gave us nationhood. For what we need most of all is the assurance that each one of us is part of a nation where we care about each other.

Addressing racism, Vietnam, hunger, homelessness, joblessness, and creating hope—this was a message poured straight from well of the 1960s. But the Eagleton affair (the revelation that McGovern's running mate had gotten electroshock therapy to treat depression), the dwindling US casualties in Vietnam, Nixon's Southern strategy, and Nixon's ability to paint McGovern as a commie all doomed him.

McGovern flew back to Sioux Falls on November 6 so that he could make the hour-long drive to Mitchell the next day—Election Day—to vote. McGovern was confident he would win at least eight to ten states, including Illinois, New York, and California, to run up the electoral count. Upon his arrival at the Sioux Falls airport, a collection of his friends and supporters gathered to welcome him home. According to Thompson, the local Jaycees erected a sign reading "Welcome Home, George." Thompson noted that the mood of the gathering was sullen. One notable figure at the airport for the welcome was Dan Garry, the chief of staff for South Dakota Governor Dick Kneip. I sat down with Garry in the bar at the downtown Holiday Inn and asked him about the mood when McGovern's plane landed. He said it felt more like a wake than anything else. The journalists on the "Zoo Plane" following McGovern around looked beat, the McGovern staff were tired and worn down, and McGovern himself gave a short speech noting the "love and devotion" in the air. But by all accounts, the oxygen was being sucked away from McGovern.

The next day, after McGovern voted in Mitchell and made the rounds talking to high school students and visiting his beloved Dakota Wesleyan University, the caravan headed back to the Holiday Inn on Eighth and Phillips for the election night festivities. Thousands of Sioux Fallsians descended on the Holiday Inn for what one news anchor called "the biggest thing to happen to the city." Hundreds pushed their way inside where the local and national media were set up to report on early results, but McGovern went straight to his suite on the eighth floor. The smart set, including Garry and the journalists on the Zoo Plane, knew McGovern would lose, but few predicted just how bad it would be. Thompson was a chronic gambler, and even he bet with his heart instead of his mind, predicting that Nixon's win would be within 5.5 points instead of the

23.3 point spread that resulted. Thompson spent much of the evening in the top-floor lounge of the Holiday Inn with prominent journalists Bob Greene and Ron Rosenbaum: "we just talked about how strange it was to be sitting in Sioux Falls at the top of the Holiday Inn . . . wondering what songs were on the jukebox. . . . It was like going to visit a couple on the verge of a really nasty divorce scene, where you know it, and you're invited over for dinner, but no one mentions it." Despite the early throngs around the Holiday Inn, the crowds thinned as the night wore on, and no one caused any disturbances. The Sioux Falls police spokesman said, "It was an extremely quiet night downtown. We've had nothing happen, and we really don't expect much to happen."

The lead local story in the *Argus Leader* the next morning read, "McGovern, Sioux Falls will recover." Thompson, however, was cut deeply by the results. Twenty-five years later, on a panel discussing the election, he said, "You're talking about Sioux Falls, South Dakota, right? That remains one of the truly heinous nights of my life . . . it's like one of those scars that heals but has nerve endings in it." And his writing grew even more cynical as the seventies went on. Thompson and McGovern remained friends long after the election ended. They first reconnected in December to discuss what went wrong, and the tone of their discussion was more akin to pals discussing why their football team lost. Thompson asked McGovern if he thought the sixties ended in 1972, but McGovern was unwilling to let the end of a remarkable decade rest on his electoral failure. Still, McGovern was deeply appreciative of Thompson's support and loyalty, and he even wrote a eulogy for Thompson after the author's suicide in 2005: "Hunter was disheartened after the campaign, and it fell to me on several occasions to try to persuade him not to give up on what he called "this f—— up country." And McGovern seemed to love the book Thompson wrote that exposed many ugly truths about campaign journalism, campaigns in general, and the crookedness of Nixon that would come into full light within the following years.

This unusual and iconic friendship told me so much—not only about politics and journalism—but also about the strange alliances one can find in the rich cultural history of this country. Here we have a fast-talking, atheistic, and scabrous alcoholic writer enamored by a well-intentioned and mild-mannered son of a Methodist preacher from deep within the Northern Plains. And their mutual admiration was, to me, an escape from the pessimism one will inevitably experience following American politics. So that's why I—a new transplant to Sioux Falls—badly wanted to find

McGovern's copy of *Fear and Loathing on the Campaign Trail '72* at the senator's estate sale in 2013. I'm not a memorabilia or autograph kind of person, but books are another story. And both McGovern and Thompson were heroes to me at certain points in my life. Furthermore, I had just completed my PhD in American studies, a nine-year endeavor that was in large part inspired by the path this book set me on.

It was a crisp and icy January morning in Sioux Falls when I arrived at McGovern's estate sale, which was set in his daughter's modest duplex on the west side of town. I expected thousands to be lined up around the block, but by 7:00 a.m., there were fewer than 100 people. I recognized a few prominent locals, and there was a muted giddiness in the cold air as we crowded into the garage in groups of forty or so while the line advanced. Some I spoke with had traveled across the country for this, but in Sioux Falls, it was just another Saturday. One man hoped to buy McGovern's car. Another asked me to take a picture of him with an armful of lamps, a crystal bowl, and a photo of McGovern with Bill Clinton as proof that these items had indeed belonged to McGovern. But most emitted the energy of folks waiting for a midwestern rummage sale to open up. I headed straight through the maze of items and scanned every bookshelf I passed. And then I found it. $4. Whoever priced these books didn't realize its significance in the history of politics and journalism, and I was okay with that. I was also impressed with the number of works that a presidential candidate couldn't get away with showcasing on a bookshelf these days—*Writings and Speeches of Eugene Debs*, Castro's *History Will Absolve Me*, Herbert Matthews, and progressive history by Walter LaFeber and others highlighting the toxicity of McCarthyism. As Obama was reelected shortly after McGovern's death and inaugurated earlier in the week, I thought back to McGovern's "Come Home, America" speech and its insistence that community, the resolve to cure hunger and homelessness and to invest in America's cities, and the notion that we should care for each other were not communist conspiracies but rather deeply engrained in our history dating back to the Puritans. Obama wasn't about to repeat the perceived mistakes of McGovern by opening himself up to McCarthyist charges. And for that, he served eight years as president. We know that some political losses turn into delayed victories, such as Ronald Reagan's speech at the 1964 RNC, when Goldwater was clobbered but Reaganism was born. Was McGovern's redemption to be found in Obama's success? Or in the election of another deeply honest democrat, Jimmy Carter? I don't know.

Now, I live a few houses down from the museum home of South Dakota's first senator, R. F. Pettigrew, who started out conservative but drifted toward anti-imperialism and became a vociferous critic of the shortcomings of capitalism. In fact, he almost ended up in prison for the same charge that sent Eugene Debs away. I also live four blocks away from the downtown Holiday Inn, and I walk my dog past it nearly every day. Occasionally, I think back to that night in Sioux Falls about fifty years ago, when the wind was knocked out of the town and the sixties died a quiet, somber, and unremarkable death.

Some Sioux Fallsians at the Holiday Inn that night were suspicious of McGovern for getting too big for his britches by seeking the highest office in the land. Some were surely excited to be near the national press, as they rarely stop by these parts. Some like Thompson felt tragedy in the overwhelming rejection of "one of the few men who've run for President of the United States in this century who really understands what a fantastic monument to all the best instincts of the human race this country might have been." While history can often seem ethereal—something that happened once out there some time ago—that book I bought is a palpable recognition of the exact time and place an enormous and collective sense of hope was lost.

But Sioux Falls doesn't like to get too upset about things. Economic bubbles and crashes hardly register here. Its modesty is its trademark. Our local music festival is called "That Sounds Decent," and sometimes it gets canceled for weather. No big deal, we'll try again next year. As the newspaper headline assured its readers the morning of November 8, before they could even experience the gravity of the loss, "Sioux Falls will recover."

Theodore Roosevelt in Sioux Falls

DUANE JUNDT

As letters go it's a doozy: thirty-six typewritten pages composed for the United States Secretary of State John Hay by his boss, President Theodore Roosevelt. But given the scope of the letter's subject, Roosevelt's "Great Western Tour," a 14,000-mile trip covering twenty-five states in April, May, and June of 1903, the missive's length may not seem quite so remarkable. Even a letter of this length could not catalog all of the "nearly 150 towns and cities" visited by TR, and while major cities like Kansas City, Denver, and Albuquerque merit mentioning, Roosevelt spends far more time detailing his visits to lesser-known locales like Butte, Montana, Cheyenne, Wyoming, Medora, North Dakota, and Sioux Falls, South Dakota.[1]

Why would Roosevelt devote a lengthy paragraph to his time in Sioux Falls while giving his stops in Milwaukee, St. Paul, and Minneapolis a mere two sentences? The answer lies in TR's belief that when he arrived in Sioux Falls, he "began to get into the real West, the Far West, the country where I had worked and played for many years, and with whose people I felt a bond of sympathy."[2] For this most western of presidents, entering South Dakota meant entering "Dakota," where from 1883 to 1887, he managed two ranches and worked cattle alongside his cowboys in the valley of the Little Missouri River in western North Dakota.[3] Arriving in Sioux Falls on a Sunday (April 5, 1903) also gave Roosevelt the chance to rest, putting aside the whistle-stop appearances, endless hand-shaking, and speech-making that would mark the tour. Even though he had been riding the rails for only five days, Roosevelt, in a letter to his son Kermit (written on Cataract Hotel stationery), wrote that, "It has been a <u>very</u> tiring trip."[4] While he welcomed the opportunity to rest, TR relished the chance to play in the West once again in the company of one of South Dakota's most notable denizens.

---

1 Edmund Morris, *Theodore Rex* (New York: Random House, 2001), 214.

2 Theodore Roosevelt to John Hay, 9 August 1903 in Louis Auchincloss, ed., *Theodore Roosevelt: Letters and Speeches* (New York: The Library of America, 2004), 278.

3 Roosevelt did not completely liquidate his ranch holdings until 1898, but the disastrous winter of 1886–1887 effectively ended his career in cattle raising. See Clay S. Jenkinson, *Theodore Roosevelt in the Dakota Badlands: An Historical Guide* (Dickinson, ND: Dickinson State University, 2006).

4 Letter from Theodore Roosevelt to Kermit Roosevelt. 5 April 1903. Theodore Roosevelt Collection. MS Am 1541 (54). Harvard College Library. Theodore Roosevelt Digital Library. Dickinson State University.

Theodore Roosevelt first met Seth Bullock in 1892 while Roosevelt was undertaking an inspection tour of Indian reservations in his capacity as a United States civil service commissioner. Following Roosevelt's lead, Bullock volunteered for cavalry duty in the Spanish-American War, and though he saw no combat, his service endeared him to TR. Bullock appeared alongside Roosevelt when he campaigned in South Dakota as McKinley's running mate in 1900, and he was a familiar figure at the White House following Roosevelt's elevation to the presidency. Just as TR equated South Dakota with the West, he saw in Bullock, the former sheriff of Deadwood and one of the owners of the S&B Ranch, the perfect embodiment of the westerner. Though Manhattan born and Harvard educated, Roosevelt, by his own admission, saw himself "as much a westerner as an easterner,"[5] and to TR, Bullock "and Bill Sewall [one of Roosevelt's ranch hands] represent the type of men with whom I really believe I have more in common than with almost any others."[6]

For these two ranchers, the best form of play at hand was horseback riding. After a morning church service and a dinner, around 4:00 p.m., the president and his posse—his doctor, Surgeon General of the Navy Presley M. Rixey, Judge Oliver Pendar of Sioux Falls, and Bullock—stole away from the Cataract in a bid to leave the press and public behind and secured rides at the stable of E. W. Coughran. They rode south before crossing the Big Sioux River, heading to East Sioux Falls, then heading north and west back across the river, covering about twenty miles.[7] Roosevelt, in a nod to his western setting, said the ride "reminded him of the days when he was a genuine cow boy on the prairies of North Dakota."[8] The Sunday Sioux Falls ride would initiate a series of such outings during the tour, which would include rides at Yellowstone and Yosemite National Parks, the Grand Canyon, and a sixty-mile gallop from Laramie to Cheyenne, Wyoming.

Roosevelt more than met his Sabbath obligations in Sioux Falls by attending two church services on Palm Sunday. In his letter to Hay, TR offered this note about Senator Alfred B. Kittredge (who acted as the president's host while in Sioux Falls): "Not being himself a church-going man he had naturally fallen helpless when faced with the church problem, and I found he had committed me to a morning and an evening service."[9] The early service at the German Emanuel Evangelical Lutheran Church

5 James F. Vivian, *The Romance of My Life: Theodore Roosevelt's Speeches in Dakota* (Fargo, ND: Prairie House, Inc., 1989), 10.

6 Letter from Theodore Roosevelt to Theodore Roosevelt, Jr. 24 February 1903. Theodore Roosevelt Papers: Series 2: Letterpress Copybooks, 1897–1916; Vol. 38, 1903, Jan. 5–Mar. 9. Manuscript/Mixed Material. Library of Congress.

7 For details on the ride, see *Sioux Falls Daily Press*, 7 April 1903, pp. 1, 4 and *Daily Argus Leader*, 6 April 1903, p. 5.

8 *Daily Argus Leader*, 6 April 1903, p. 5.

9 TR to John Hay, 9 August 1903 in Auchincloss, *Letters and Speeches*, 278.

was conducted entirely in German, including the singing at TR's request of one of his favorite hymns, "*Ein feste Burg ist unser Gott*" ("A Mighty Fortress is Our God").[10] "At its conclusion the president stepped forward and shook hands with the ministers. 'I understood and enjoyed every word of it,' he said and then proceeded to give a brief outline of the sermon in German to show that he understood and remembered the discourse."[11]

After his horseback ride and supper, Roosevelt went to the Livingston Memorial Reformed Church for the evening service. One wonders what went through TR's mind when Rev. Henry Schipper remarked in his sermon that, "The statesman has schemes in abundance for the good of his country and for his own glory, but fell disease or the hand of the assassin lays him low and his schemes are never carried out."[12] TR admitted to Hay that "contrary to my expectations," he enjoyed both services.[13] Bishop William Hobart Hare of South Dakota's Episcopal church, after learning that he could not host the president at his cathedral, settled for walking arm in arm with TR to the Cataract's dining room and giving the blessing at the afternoon dinner.[14] In what may have been a delicate act of denominational diplomacy, the following morning's procession of dignitaries saw Thomas O'Gorman, the Roman Catholic bishop of the Sioux Falls diocese, seated in the fifth carriage while Hare occupied a seat in the sixth.[15] Both prelates no doubt relished a chance to bend the president's ear, especially about the administration's policy toward their respective Native American schools.[16]

The following morning, Monday, April 6, the president and his party braved a raw and blustery daybreak and made their way to the city's auditorium, where Roosevelt was set to address a large gathering of schoolchildren. TR opened his brief remarks, like he would innumerable times across the Great Plains, by praising the production of his favorite crop: "But a good deal better than the best product of the farm or of the mine is the product of the home."[17] As Roosevelt biographer Edmund Morris so pithily put it, "His robust views on childbearing were bolstered by spaces so wide and soil so deeply fertile."[18] The remainder of his remarks resembled

10 Letter from Theodore Roosevelt to Thomas E. Stewart. 16 March 1903. Theodore Roosevelt Papers. Library of Congress Manuscript Division. Theodore Roosevelt Digital Library. Dickinson State University.

11 *Sioux Falls Daily Press*, 7 April 1903, p. 1.

12 Ibid., p. 4.

13 TR to John Hay, 9 August 1903 in Auchincloss, *Letters and Speeches*, 278.

14 *Daily Argus Leader*, 6 April 1903, p. 5.

15 *Sioux Falls Daily Press*, 7 April 1903, p. 4.

16 On the Protestant-Catholic competition and lobbying of the administration over funding of schools for Native American children and Bishop Hare's role, see William T. Hagan, *Theodore Roosevelt & Six Friends of the Indian* (Norman, OK: University of Oklahoma Press, 1997).

17 Address of President Roosevelt to the school children at Sioux Falls, S. D. 6 April 1903. Theodore Roosevelt Papers. Library of Congress Manuscript Division. Theodore Roosevelt Digital Library. Dickinson State University.

18 Morris, 224.

the McGuffey Readers and Horatio Alger dime novels of the time: work hard, play fair, be nice to the weak, character counts. Not surprisingly, the preacher of the strenuous life emphasized the life lessons that could be gained on the football field.[19]

After exhorting the latest generation of South Dakotans, Roosevelt's retinue returned to the Cataract Hotel, where the president mounted a speaker's platform in front of the hotel's Ninth Street entrance. The return to the hotel also meant a return to the campaign trail, though that fact remained largely unexamined by the press and president. According to long-standing custom, as a sitting president, Roosevelt could not actively campaign on his own behalf in 1904.[20] Having canceled a trip west, including a stop in Sioux Falls, in the fall of 1902 because of a serious leg injury and the pressing needs of a national coal miners strike, "the trip in 1903 seemed so essential" to the accidental president's election prospects.[21] Because of his much photographed toothy grin and frequent exclamations of "Bully!" and "Dee-lighted!" one would think that "the cheers and the crowds were fuel for his exuberance,"[22] but a reading of Roosevelt's correspondence from the tour, from beginning to end, reveal a man "jaded, and nerve-weary and bored" by the daily speeches and the glad-handing and company of local politicians.[23]

One of those politicians, Senator Kittredge, did his best to not add to the president's boredom, introducing him to the crowd as "Our President."[24] Roosevelt, in a long coat and top hat, struggled to make himself heard over brisk winds as he read from his text, "The Wage-Worker and the Tiller of the Soil."[25] Given that the venue for the speech was South Dakota, TR smartly addressed the tillers of the soil first. Presidential historian Doris Kearns Goodwin notes that the policy speeches prepared for the trip were "neither 'particularly original' nor profound," and Roosevelt's Sioux Falls address fits that description, consisting mostly of a laundry list of the administration's bureaucratic and legislative achievements (irrigation for the arid West under the Newlands Act, encouraging the planting of trees, mediation of the anthracite coal strike, improvements in railroad safety).[26]

19 On Roosevelt and football and the popularity of the college game at the turn of the twentieth century, see John J. Miller, *The Big Scrum: How Teddy Roosevelt Saved Football* (New York: Harper-Collins, 2011).

20 Henry F. Pringle, *Theodore Roosevelt: A Biography*, rev. ed. (San Diego, CA: Harcourt Brace Jovanovich, Publishers, 1984), 243.

21 Ibid.

22 Ibid.

23 Letter from Theodore Roosevelt to Henry Cabot Lodge. 23 May 1903. Lodge-Roosevelt Correspondence. MS. N-1584. Massachusetts Historical Society. Theodore Roosevelt Digital Library. Dickinson State University.

24 *Daily Argus Leader*, 6 April 1903, p. 5. The *Sioux Falls Daily Press* claims that Kittredge used the lengthy "Gentlemen, the president." *Sioux Falls Daily Press*, 7 April 1903, p. 4.

25 *Sioux Falls Daily Press*, 7 April 1903, p. 4.

26 Doris Kearns Goodwin, *The Bully Pulpit: Theodore Roosevelt, William Howard Taft, and the Golden Age of Journalism* (New York: Simon & Schuster, 2013), 350.

While they may not have been inspired by TR's address, the citizens of Sioux Falls could take pride in the fact that their modest city of 10,000 had been deemed worthy of hosting one of the tour's major policy speeches.[27]

Senator Kittredge, who shared with TR the inheritance of his office, having been appointed to his post upon the death of Senator James H. Kyle in 1901, and who was always at Roosevelt's side during his time in Sioux Falls, no doubt benefited from basking in the president's glow as he secured a full-term appointment from the South Dakota legislature in 1903. Secretary of Agriculture James Wilson spoke to TR's cowboy sensibilities when he wrote the president in July that "Senator Kittredge grows on acquaintance, is firmly fixed in the saddle and is above the short grass average."[28] Seth Bullock, who had joined the tour in Sioux Falls to participate in the Sunday afternoon horse ride, would serve as the cowboy court jester of Roosevelt's entourage through much of the trip, entertaining TR and his East Coast advisers with western tales both true and tall. The Friendship Tower above Deadwood, commissioned by Bullock shortly after TR's death and soon before his own, memorializes not just a man but a friendship between two ranchers who stood in awe of each other.

Roosevelt would make his third and final trip to Sioux Falls in September 1910 (having also visited the city in 1900 as President McKinley's running mate) as he began to lay the groundwork and test the waters for his 1912 presidential campaign. South Dakota, unlike its northern neighbor, would thank the Rough Rider for his persistence in pursuing its affections by rewarding him the state's electoral votes in his final campaign.

---

27 Morris, 217.

28 Letter from James Wilson to Theodore Roosevelt. 9 July 1903. Theodore Roosevelt Papers. Library of Congress Manuscript Division. Theodore Roosevelt Digital Library. Dickinson State University.

Jewish Sioux Falls

MARA W. COHEN IOANNIDES

It was not until the arrival of the railroad that the Jewish community of Sioux Falls began. This is a common theme throughout the American Midwest. Because most Jews, both immigrant and native born, were merchants, they tended to settle in areas that had economic potential. There were few Jews in the territory during this period anyway; in 1877, the Jewish population of the region was only about ten.[1] In 1878, the railroad arrived, and this led to a dramatic influx of population, so much so that in 1890, the town became the largest in the newly founded state.[2] Professor Gary D. Olson calls Sioux Falls a typical midwestern boom town after the arrival of the railroad,[3] and this also translates into the typical experience of the Jewish population.

As in the rest of the Midwest, the first Jews to arrive were German or of German heritage. These German Jews immigrated for the same reason that their Christian counterparts had: to flee the recession and violence of civil wars, plus the additional privations put upon them in the German states of limited housing and the constraint in some states limiting marriage to only the oldest son. The idea of moving to a country that did not have a state religion or restrictions on travel and business was enticing, and so the Jews sent their second and third sons, and daughters to marry them. The men would come first and establish themselves and then bring over their families. Sometimes they would bring sisters, nieces, or daughters specifically to marry their Jewish business partners.

In 1882, Jacob Blum, a German immigrant, arrived in Sioux Falls. He had been a wool and hide dealer in another part of the county and so opened the same business in town.[4] That same year, Alexander Stern, also a German immigrant, left Yankton where he'd been for four years, and moved to Sioux Falls. What we see are merchants realizing the growth potential of this railway town. It is not surprising that two years later, Alexander married Augusta Blum, daughter of Jacob.[5] With almost no

---

1 "Statistics of Jews," *The American Jewish Year Book 5675*, Herman Bernstein, ed., JPS, 1914, p. 352.

2 Kermit L. Staggers, "Sioux Falls, South Dakota," *Encyclopedia of the Great Plains*, 2011, plainshumanities.unl.edu/encyclopedia/doc/egp.ct.048.

3 Gary D. Olson, "A Dakota Boomtown Sioux Falls, 1877–1880," *Great Plains Quarterly*, 2004, vol. 24, p. 17.

4 Dana R. Bailey, *History of Minnehaha County, South Dakota*, Brown & Saenger, 1899, p. 454.

5 Baily, p. 707.

other Jews in the area, a match between these two was almost guaranteed. In 1884, Morriz Levinger arrived from Oskaloosa, Iowa, with his friend Moses Kaufman and opened a brewery.[6] By 1887, Blum and Kaufman were in business together. Along with buying wool and hides, they also bought rags and rubber to resell out East to be reused.[7]

In 1888, Solomon Kuh arrived with his family and opened a broom factory just before statehood was announced.[8] With statehood, the town continued to grow. Solomon also invested heavily in real estate.[9] He eventually gave the factory to his sons, Julius and Louis, who by 1907 had the largest broom factory in the country.[10]

Joseph Abraham Agrant, who became known as John, began his life in America in the Cremieux Colony, but in 1894, John and his wife, Clara Lebovitz, moved from Sioux City to Sioux Falls. They had two daughters; the first was born in 1894. John's jewelry business began by buying diamond rings from divorcees, and he became the best watchmaker in the city, though he never charged what he was worth. Both John and Clara were well known for their charity. John would send poor people he encountered to his house, where Clara would feed them. John brought numerous Judaica with him from Russia, including a small Torah, and the family hosted High Holy Day services in their home before a synagogue was built.[11]

In 1896, Charles Fantle Jr. opened the Cash Dry Goods and Carpet Emporium. His father, Charles Sr., owned stores in Ann Arbor, Michigan, St. Paul, Minnesota, and Hudson, Wisconsin. His brothers, William and Moses, ran Fantle Brothers in Yankton. Clearly, Sioux Falls had grown to be a major hub for the Fantle family to consider it as a place for expansion. By 1899, Charles Jr. owned three consecutive storefronts, which shows that the family was correct in their guess. Then, his brother Samuel moved to Sioux Falls to help with the business, and the name changed to Fantle Brothers Department Store. They expanded in 1910.[12] Zaidee Plechner, a sister of Mrs. Charles Fantle, married Louis Kuh in 1898.[13] Julius Kuh married his first cousin, Clara Greenstein, in 1901. Clara worked at Fantle's store.[14]

---

6 Bailey, p. 601.

7 "Rags and Rubber," ***Argus Leader***, 22 April 1887, p. 6.

8 Baily, p. 599.

9 "Deceased was one of the most tireless of Sioux Falls' Business Men Boomers," ***Argus Leader***, 11 May 1908, p. 3.

10 "S. F. Broom Works, ***Argus Leader***, 25 Nov. 1907, p. 32.

11 Jennette L. Agrant, Interview, South Dakota Oral History Project, 11 Sept. 1976. Transcript.

12 "Fantles store took service seriously," ***Argus Leader***, 27 Dec. 2014, https://www.argusleader.com/story/life/2014/12/27/looking-back-fantles-store-took-service-seriously/20938903/.

13 Wedding announcement, ***Argus Leader***, 19 April 1898, p. 4.

14 "Wed in Sioux City," ***Argus Leader***, 5 Apr. 1901, p. 5.

The second wave of Jews, the Eastern Europeans, changed both American and American Jewish demographics. Between 1880 and 1910, over 1.5 million Jews from Eastern Europe immigrated to the United States.[15] It is estimated that in 1880, there were about 400,000 Jews in the country, and by 1910, over 2,000,000. South Dakota's Jewish population grew from 250 to 300 between 1901 (the first year there was an estimate) and 1907[16] and then exploded to 1,262 in 1918.[17] Culturally, they were different from their German co-religionists. The German Jews were part of a reformation of Judaism because they had been part of a Jewish Emancipation, so their services took place mostly in German, rather than in the traditional Hebrew the Eastern European Jews were used to. They had also adopted modern dress and hairstyles and stopped keeping the Jewish food laws (*kashrut*) that the majority of the Eastern European Jews adhered to. For the most part, Eastern Europeans were not securely educated, nor did they come with any money—something that gave the German Jews an advantage over German Christians. Thus, there were inter-Jewish conflicts that were not as obvious in Sioux Falls, but elsewhere. However, these differences are important to understand how the two communities created their homes of worship.

The Eastern European immigrants who arrived in Sioux Falls were very much like Morris Ackerman, who left Lithuania and settled in Mankato, Minnesota, before arriving in Sioux Falls in 1906. First, he ran a garage, then a dry goods store, and finally found success with Ackerman Furniture. He and his wife, Lillian Fineberg, had four daughters.[18]

There were also people like Nathan Koplow, who left Russia in 1911 and eventually arrived in South Dakota to join his brothers Meyer and Louis, who were already in the state. He homesteaded outside of Landeau, and when it was difficult to find work, he spent almost three summers on this land; the winters were too harsh. After the First World War, he sold his homestead.[19]

Israel Seide, as a young married man, arrived in Sioux Falls in 1914 alone. He left his wife and daughter in Poland. During World War I, he opened a scrap business, became a naturalized citizen, and enlisted. In 1920, he returned to Poland to bring Fannie and Clara to Sioux Falls.[20] Their

15 Joseph Jacobs, "Jewish Population of the United States Memoir of the Bureau of Jewish Statistics of the American Jewish Committee." *Jewish American Year Book*, vol. 16 (1914–1915), pp. 341, 346.

16 "Jewish Statistics," *American Jewish Year Book 5671*, Herbert Friedenwald, ed., Jewish Puyblication Society of America, 1910, p. 277–278; "Statistical Summary by States," *Jewish American Year Book* 5662, Cyrus Adler, ed., Jewish Publication Society of America, 1901, p. 149.

17 "Statistics of Jews," *Jewish American Year Book 5680*, Harry Schneiderman ed. Jewish Publication Society, 1919, p. 605.

18 "Morris L. Ackerman, Veteran S.F. Businessman, Dies at 69," *Argus Leader*, 3 Aug. 1950, p. 18.

19 Nathan Koplow, Interview by Fred Hosen, South Dakota History Project 10 July 1974. Transcript.

20 "Israel Seide," *FindaGrave*, n.d., www.findagrave.com/memorial/158533069/israel-Seid#view-photo=135968507.

American-born son, Morris, became a physician in Hartford, Connecticut.[21]

Despite the small Jewish population in the state, by 1900, there was a B'nai B'rith Lodge in the region that also included members from Illinois, Iowa, Minnesota, Michigan, Nebraska, and Wisconsin.[22] B'nai B'rith (Children of the Covenant) had only been founded in 1843 as a group to provide funerary costs and stipends for children whose fathers belonged. It grew into an organization that provided charity for orphans and disaster relief around the world.[23] The South Dakota lodge continued well in the twenty-first century.[24]

The Jews socialized with everyone. They were not exclusive to their co-religionists. In 1899, Alexander Stern was elected to the board of the German Harmonia Lodge No. 56 of the International Order of Odd Fellows.[25] This was not uncommon. Germans were less interested in their fellows' religion than that they were also German, so they included German Jews in almost every social group they organized.

However, socializing and doing charity work with non-Jews could not take the place of a religious community. The first arrivals, the German Jews, incorporated a cemetery, Mt. Zion Cemetery, in 1903.[26] It is on the 2300 Block on East Twelfth Street. Since prayer services could take place anywhere but a burial had to take place on Jewish ground, this was not an uncommon order of creation for Jewish communities in the Midwest.

The Orthodox, Eastern European, Jews had organized and started planning to build a synagogue. During the 1910 High Holy Days, a subscription was begun. The local press noted: "There are about forty eligibles [sic] for membership to the Jewish church in this city at the present time."[27] It is unclear if this was a count of all Jews or all Orthodox Jews in the city at the time. Although it seems this counted the Reform Jews, because in 1916, Sons of Israel was incorporated and it included both communities.[28]

This Reform Jewish community broke from Sons of Israel and formed Mt. Zion Temple in 1919 and immediately aligned themselves with the Union of American Hebrew Congregation.[29] The first full-time rabbi,

21 "Morris Jacob Seide," *FindaGrave*, n.d., www.findagrave.com/memorial/158557661/morris-jacob-seide.

22 "Directory of National Organizations," *The American Jewish Year Book 5661*, Cyrus Adler, ed., JPS, 1900, p. 106.

23 "About B'nai B'rith," B'nai B'rith, 2021, https://www.bnaibrith.org/about-us.html.

24 "A Finding Aid to the B'nai B'rith International Archies, 1843–2015, undated," MC 900, American Jewish Archives, n.d., http://collections.americanjewisharchives.org/ms/ms0900/ms0900.html.

25 "German I.O.O. F.," *Argus Leader*, 7 Dec. 1899, p. 5.

26 "About Our Temple," *Mt. Zion Congregation*, n.d., www.mtzionsf.com/about.php.

27 "The Jewish New Year," *Argus Leader*, 5 Oct. 1910, p. 5.

28 *75th Anniversary and Reunion Mount Zion Congregation Sioux Falls, South Dakota*, 3–5 June 1994. Program.

29 "About Our Temple."

Salvador J. Schwab, was hired in August 1920 to serve the congregation of thirty-five families. He only stayed for two years.[30] In 1924, Mt. Zion Temple purchased the First Lutheran Church building, built in 1894, and has remained there ever since.[31] The original renovations, like the replacement of the stained-glass windows, were finished after the first service was held in the building in January 1924.[32]

The 1920s was a time for action in the Jewish community. Along with the congregations, a B'nai B'rith chapter was formed in 1920 with over twenty members. It was the only chapter in the state, although in 1921, because there were members from outside Sioux Falls, there was discussion of creating more chapters. During their first year, they donated money for both local and European Jewish relief.[33]

In 1934, Sons of Israel dedicated their new building.[34] This was the only building in the state specifically designed as a synagogue.[35] This decade, despite hard times elsewhere, brought stability to the Jews of Sioux Falls. Phillips Avenue was filled with Jewish-owned stores. The congregation hired a rabbi and flourished as well.[36] A social hall was added to the building in 1951,[37] and in 1958, a school annex was provided by the Pitts family to aid the growing religious school.[38]

There was a Hadassah chapter in Sioux Falls, founded in 1937,[39] that provided aid to the Jews and Palestinians in the Holy Land during and after World War II.[40] By the turn of the twentieth century, the chapter folded into Hadassah of the Upper Midwest.[41] Additionally, the Women's League of Sons of Israel raised money during the war for the Red Cross.[42]

While the Mt. Zion congregation flourished in the 1970s, Sons of Israel folded in 1973.[43] This is not unusual in the Midwest, as Orthodox congregations found it difficult to keep members because the children often left the town where they grew up and left the Orthodox Movement because they found the Reform Movement provided easier access into American

30 *75th Anniversary*, p. 4–5.

31 "About Our Temple."

32 "Service Jan. 25 in synagogue," *Argus Leader*, 15 Jan. 1924, p. 14.

33 "Jewish Lodge, B'nai B'rith, is Growing Here," *Argus Leader*, 29 April 1921, p. 9.

34 "New Synagogue to be Dedicated Today," *Argus Leader*, 12 Aug. 1934, p. 3.

35 Freda Hosen, "South Dakota Jews Inherit Interesting Story," *Argus Leader*, 15 July 1976, p. 40.

36 *75th Anniversary*, p. 6.

37 *75th Anniversary*, p. 7.

38 *75th Anniversary*, p. 8.

39 "About Us," *Mt. Zion Congregation*, n.d., http://www.mtzionsf.com/about.php.

40 "Hadassah Members Aid in Supplying Palestinian Needs," *Argus Leader*, 8 Oct. 1944, p. 10.

41 "Who We Are," Hadassah, 2021, "Hadassah, Sioux Falls chapter records," *Upper Midwest Jewish Archives, umja0097*, University of Minnesota, https://archives.lib.umn.edu/repositories/15/resources/7316.

42 "City Briefs," *Argus Leader*, 4 Feb. 1944, p. 4.

43 "About Us."

society.[44] Its precious Deadwood Torah, which had spent years touring the South Dakota countryside, was presented to Mt. Zion for safekeeping,[45] and the building was sold to St. Paul's Evangelical Lutheran Church.[46]

The Jews of Sioux Falls felt that most of the anti-Semitism they suffered was due to ignorance, not really hate.[47] That is not to say that people did not experience name-calling and other such anti-Semitic incidents.[48]

Between 1977 and 2001, Sioux Falls boasted a population of 195 Jews.[49] By 2007, the Jewish population in the state had dropped to an estimated 295,[50] and the only welfare organization listed in the *Jewish American Year Book* for the city was the Jewish Welfare Fund.[51] In 2020, Mt. Zion congregation had only about fifty families of various Jewish denominations and has not had a full-time rabbi since 1978. Instead, they use student rabbis studying at Hebrew Union College in Cincinnati, Ohio.[52]

Chabad, a Jewish movement founded in the mid-1800s that stresses conservative interpretation of Jewish law and practice, sent Rabbi Mendel Alperowitz in 2017 to open a community center in Sioux Falls. While there had been Chasidic rabbis visiting the state in the late 1900s, this was the first permanent position in the state. The mission of the Chasidic community is "to bolster and revitalize Judaism in every part of the world."[53]

The Jewish community of Sioux Falls is typical among Jewish communities in the United States. It developed because of the expansion of the railroads in the country and shrank because of intermarriage and economic opportunities elsewhere in both the state and the country. However, that it remains vibrant, though small, into the twenty-first century, suggests that it can withstand change and provide the needed religious and social practices necessary for its members to maintain their Judaism.

44 Sidney Goldstein, "American Jewry, 1970: A demographic Profile," ***American Jewish Year Book 1971***, Morris Fine and Milton Himmelfarb, eds, American Jewish Committee, 1971, p. 57.

45 ***75th Anniversary***, p. 9–10; "About Us," ***Mt. Zion Congregation***, n.d., http://www.mtzionsf.com/about.php.

46 Hosen, p. 70.

47 Rose Rimmerman, Interview by F[red] Hosen, South Dakota Oral History Project, 27 Sept. 1976. Transcript, p. 15.

48 Jennette L. Agrant, Interview by F[red] Hosen, South Dakota Oral History Project, 11 Sept. 1976.

49 "Jewish Population in the United States, 2007," ***Jewish American Year Book 2007***, David Singer and Lawrence Grossman, eds., American Jewish Committee, p. 192.

50 "Jewish Population in the United States, 2008," ***Jewish American Year Book 2008***, David Singer and Lawrence Grossman, eds., American Jewish Committee, p. 178,

51 "Jewish Federations, Welfare Funds, Community Councils," ***Jewish American Year Book 2008***, David Singer and Lawrence Grossman, eds., American Jewish Committee, p. 679.

52 "About Us."

53 Menachem Posner, "Chabad Opens Center in 50th State: South Dakota," ***Chabad News***, 27 Nov. 2016, https://www.chabad.org/news/article_cdo/aid/3500266/jewish/Chabad-Opens-Center-in-50th-State-South-Dakota.htm.

Statues and Sculptures

VIRGINIA OLSON

Ecclesiastical stained-glass windows grace Gloria Dei. Ceramic mosaics decorate the corridors of the Sioux Falls Regional Airport. Sixteen expansive murals painted in the early 1900s adorn the walls of the Old Court House Museum. The Great Plains Zoo and Delbridge Museum of Natural History displays an amazing mounted collection of over 150 legally hunted animals. A stone arch made of petrified wood and created in 1926 serves as the entrance of Woodlawn Cemetery.

Public art is right in front of our eyes. Best of all, it's free.

Though each piece of the city's public art is special in its own right, you will come to appreciate particular ones, even after reading their backstories.

Landlocked City Wants Its Battleship

Though dynamic as it is today, the city's public art scene sputtered and lurched along for many years. The USS South Dakota Battleship Memorial was Sioux Falls's first major public art project. Because the original idea was so grandiose, the project took seven years to complete. It got underway in 1962.

The *USS South Dakota* was the most decorated battleship of World War II. Built in Camden, New Jersey, it was launched June 7, 1941. The battleship fought in every major naval battle in the Pacific from 1942 to 1945 and was the most decorated of World War II. When it was announced that the mighty ship was going to be recycled for scrap in 1962, a Sioux Falls citizens' group enlisted the support of the late Congressman Ben Reifel to save it and work to have it brought to South Dakota. They specifically asked Reifel for help in finding a way to navigate the 37,970-long-ton ship, towing it from a Philadelphia naval shipyard through various waterways to the Mississippi River, then to the Missouri River to Sioux City where it would travel the Sioux River. Reifel letter responded that though this was a noble idea, it would not work and went on to suggest that Iowa or Nebraska would be better suited to house the behemoth vessel.

With impossible sailing logistics, the citizen's group gave up on the original idea. Instead, they laid out a second plan that was minimalist in nature—a four-foot high concrete outline of the 680-foot battleship on the grounds of Sherman Park.

Though retrieving the full ship was impossible, the citizens' group, along with the Sioux Falls Chamber of Commerce, did manage to salvage the ship's mast, anchor, radar screen, nine sixteen-inch gun barrel muzzle ends, a ninety-four-ton gun barrel muzzle, and an eighteen-ton bronze propeller. Because of their massive size and weight, special transportation arrangements were necessary to move the salvaged parts. Once in Sioux Falls, extra large cranes were required to put them in place. The memorial was finally completed and dedicated in August 1969. The well-known landmark serves as a tribute to the crew of the *USS South Dakota* and also to World War II.

Two Michelangelos

In 1971, the public art scene suddenly became both intriguing and controversial when Thomas Fawick, a former resident and famous inventor, gifted two grand sculptures—Michelangelo's statues of David and Moses—to Sioux Falls and Augustana University. Moses was to be placed near the Augustana Commons, which wasn't a problem. The eighteen-foot statue of David, on the other hand, was placed in Fawick Park, facing the Tenth Street viaduct. Some found it distasteful, and there were public outcries to remove the statue all together. A minister's letter to the *Argus Leader* objected to David's nakedness, calling it, "not art, but sin." The city responded, turning the statue away from the viaduct. *USA Today* picked up the story and poked fun at the city's decision of modesty with editorial cartoons that covered up David.

The news-making didn't end there when a scandal arose around the commissioned artist, Felix W. de Weldon. De Weldon had created hundreds of public art pieces across the US. His most famous was the Iwo Jima sculpture. When the statues were dedicated in 1973 and 1974, de Weldon spoke in detail about the problems he had in getting permission from the Italian government to make casts from the original statues. But de Weldon made the whole thing up. It seems making casts of the original sculptures had been outlawed in Italy since the 1800s. There was no "special permission"; de Weldon had used his own plastic casts of Moses and David and had never gone to Italy at all. People across the country were shocked at the artist's audacity, and Sioux Falls again looked foolish.

The SculptureWalk and Arc of Dreams

After the "scandals" of David and de Weldon seemed to fade away, the Sioux Falls art scene went dormant. It wasn't until 2004 when SculptureWalk debuted. The concept was simple—display local and regional sculptures on the sidewalks of downtown. Sculptures would be chosen from entries in SculptureWalk's national contest. It was public art in its truest sense. The first year SculptureWalk kicked off with thirty-four unique sculptures.

It didn't take long for the community to develop a comfort level with this new brand of art. It was a fresh take and out of the ordinary. Unlike art in a museum, there was no feeling of intimidation, no judgment, and no prior art knowledge was required. The ScupltureWalk was a leisurely outdoor activity. Individuals could stop and admire a sculpture or simply walk by. It was all about art for art's sake. Most of all, the SculptureWalk was fun.

Since its beginning, 857 world-class sculptures from thirty-two states and ten countries have been exhibited downtown and viewed by more than 300,000 people annually.

SculptureWalk "upped its game" when the metaphorical Arc of Dreams was dedicated in 2019. It was public art on a grand scale. Dale Lamphere, South Dakota's premier artist of large sculptures, created the Arc. The massive stainless-steel sculpture, which spans the Big Sioux River between Sixth and Eighth Streets, is as long as a football field and rises nearly seven stories. At the center of the Arc is a fifteen-foot gap representing the leap of faith dreamers must take to achieve their dreams. Though it sits impassively during the day, at night the Arc lights up. Owned by ScupltureWalk, the Arc was funded by 720 donations, which raised $3 million.

Jim Clark was SculptureWalk's founder, and for him, art in Sioux Falls has come a long, long way. "I had big dreams and goals for SculptureWalk," he says. "We have worked extremely hard to get this far, but we are never satisfied with the status quo. Our efforts to achieve excellence will never end."

Eleven Sioux Falls Statues Cataloged by the South Dakota State Historical Society

In 2020, the South Dakota State Historical Society surveyed the statues of the state. To make their list, statues needed to depict a person or personage and couldn't be in a cemetery or on private land. Following the guidelines of the three P's—public, person, and permanent—the historical society came up with a list of 172 entries. Their list is still ongoing. Though most of the statues cataloged across the state are patriotic in nature, most of Sioux Falls's statues don't fall into that category:

Statue of David
Statue of Moses
Ole the Viking
The Muse of Music
St. Francis of Assisi
Edwin A Sherman
Going Home
Joe Foss
Rich Greeno
Richard Pettigrew
Helen McKennan

Why Sioux Falls and Sioux City are Different

MARY HARTNETT

Sioux Falls is for hipsters. The gateway city is called the hipster capital of South Dakota, with its downtown artisanal breweries, coffee bars, restaurants, boutiques, gift shops, art galleries, and live music (Milne). In 2020, COVID-19 devastated cities and towns across the country, but not Sioux Falls. At the end of 2020, Mayor Paul Tenhaken said that smart budgeting and millions of dollars in pandemic relief would be put toward a new $30 million initiative called "Sioux Falls for All" (Conlon).

According to the mayor's office, over 20,000 people have moved to the city since 2015. Those moves have put the population just over 190,000, and it is a population that is still changing and growing more diverse. The Latino, Black, and Asian communities have nearly doubled, according to 2020 census data and the *Argus Leader* (Mitchell).

However, Sioux City had been less fortunate long before the pandemic. The city has a population of approximately 80,000 people. In fact, at a rate of 4.1 percent in 2020, Sioux City had the highest rate of out-migration of any metropolitan area in the state ("Sioux City Has Largest Net Population Outflow"). This outflow was hardly a surprise, as the community has been witnessing a dwindling population since the 1970s. Downtown Sioux City once hosted department stores, restaurants, nightclubs, professional offices, and movie theaters. However, most doctors, dentists, retail shops, lawyers, and bankers have been leaving the city for the more favorable tax climate up the road in the Dakota Dunes, South Dakota, since the early 1980s. At the time, the two cities were quite similar.

However, while Sioux City focused on local industry and blue-collar jobs, Sioux Falls looked ahead and upward. In 2004, University of South Dakota Professor Ralph Brown studied the economic growth of Sioux Falls (Brown 2004). In the 1980s, Sioux Falls brought in Citibank credit card call centers, which made the city one of the country's most extensive banking and credit centers. The arrival of Sanford Health's hospitals and health centers added many more jobs and investments in Sioux Falls (Brown). And in 2021, the creation of a large Amazon distribution facility will put Sioux Falls in a privileged place amidst economic calamity.

Sioux City has lagged behind Sioux Falls, which is not what its founders predicted. As the population of Iowa grew exponentially in the 1850s, settlers continued to move west. The future looked bright for Sioux City, which was seen as a boomtown on which "great dreams and visions" were dependent (Silag, "Sioux City"). The city's first white settler was French trapper Theophile Bruguier. In 1849, Bruguier settled near the mouth of the Big Sioux River, three miles from Sioux City, in a cabin he was still occupying in July 1870 ("The Founding of Sioux City"). Bruguier lived peacefully among the Native Americans and solidified his relationship with the tribe by marrying the daughter of Chief War Eagle. But Bruguier did not create the city. In 1854, John Cook and Joe Jackson of Council Bluffs organized the Sioux City Township Company (Silag, "Sioux City"). Cook had offered state lawmakers many shares of the townsite's company stock in return for help in "establishing Sioux City as the political and economic center of northwest Iowa" (Silag, "Sioux City" 588).

Sioux Falls and Sioux City had a lot in common. Both were riverfront frontier cities, with Sioux Falls on the Big Sioux and Sioux City on the Missouri, and both were initially settled in the mid-1850s. A group of promoters laid claim to the area in and around what is now Sioux Falls in the mid-1850s. However, violent encounters with local tribes caused settlers to leave the area or stop coming entirely (Ohdenbach 1970; Olson 2004). Sioux City gained momentum, and a federal land office opened in 1855. Land speculation was rampant, and buildings rose on overpriced land. Missouri River towns like Sioux City, and Omaha down the road, were significant points of departure for westward travelers (Silag, "Sioux City"). Riverboat, dock, and steamboat workers lived in hotels and boarding houses along the levee (Silag, "Sioux City"). There were also bankers, landowners, business owners, builders, and people who wanted to settle down with their families and make a new life.

A national financial panic in September 1857 coincided with the founding of Sioux City (Rustin, 1894; Silag, "Sioux City" 599). In addition, the constant speculation by investors had caused a real estate bubble. When that bubble burst, most of the city's banks closed, and all land sales stopped for a time (Silag, "Sioux City"). In addition, despite earlier promises, the railroad did not reach Sioux City until after the Civil War, and many people left Sioux City in the 1880s and 1890s. Those that stayed were families and businesspeople who were looking to prosper and make a new start.

Fueled by the Homestead Act of 1862, the Dakota Boom opened the Dakota Territory to settlers, who each rushed to lay claim to 160 acres of farmland. Olson notes that at the land office in Sioux Falls in the spring of 1878, the pace of business increased significantly. On April 2, 1878, the *Sioux Falls Pantagraph* reported that "crowds of home seekers" could be seen at the US Land Office in Sioux Falls (Olson). On March 29, the *Sioux City Journal* reported 175 homestead entries, eighty-eight timber culture entries, sixty-two homestead declarations, and more, totaling over 58,000 acres as compared to the week of March 24 (*Sioux City Journal,* March 29, 1878). The land office continued to do brisk business in May, with 50 percent more customers (Olson).

The railroad arrived in July of 1878, and by 1880, Sioux Falls had over 2,000 inhabitants, according to the federal census and local newspaper reports (Olson). Olson argues that after the "Dakota Boom," Sioux Falls has had a relatively stable growth pattern, making it more fortunate than many other small midwestern cities (Olson). Sioux Falls had a different way of doing things, and through the years, it pretty much escaped the cyclic rise and fall of most small cities. Sioux Falls could have built and maintained a state university, but it decided instead to locate the state penitentiary in their city, securing steady jobs. Colleges, churches, businesses, and organizations slowly grew in Sioux Falls and prospered.

In contrast, Sioux City grew in fits and starts and was hurt by the kind of events that plague small cities, such as the loss of key businesses and the lack of connections to national and international markets. Mahoney (2004) says that the small cities of the Midwest sprouted and grew from the 1840s to the 1880s. As small cities began to grow across the Northeast and Midwest, there was often little or no accompanying vision or ideology. Many boosters overinvested in local improvements and railroads and were ruined by the financial reversals caused by the panic of 1857.

But Sioux City also had reputational issues. From its early years, it was heralded as a place where the good times rolled, along with all that the good times entailed such as saloons, prostitution, gambling, and violence. Hewitt points out that Sioux City was known in popular culture and the press for its vice and violence. He gives an example of how Sioux City cropped up in the John Wayne film *Angel and the Badman.* Wayne said that if the bad guys had known his gun was not loaded, they would have unloaded their guns in a standoff. His character in the film, named Quirt Evans, says, "It would have been like Saturday night in Sioux City" if things had gone the other way (Hewitt 123). Almost fifty years since the film's release and the frontier town's worst violence, Sioux City's bad reputation remained intact.

The notorious murder of Rev. George Canning Haddock has haunted Sioux City since the 1880s. Haddock preached on the evils of alcohol and vice in a city where both were rife. Much of Iowa was dry because of Clark's Law, which was passed in 1882 and closed saloons across the state, except for those in Sioux City. It had 7,500 residents and seventy-five saloons, or one saloon for every 100 residents. But saloons, gambling, and prostitution funded the city by paying fines of $25 to $100 a week (Hewitt 1991; Max 1998). This atmosphere sustained a lot of violence in the riverboat city (Max 1998). After about a year of constant campaigning against the saloons, Haddock was gunned down in front of the notorious Columbia House on August 3, 1886. His murder was a scandal that the media milked for all it was worth. Local and national channels extensively covered both trials of the alleged killer John Arensdorf, who was then found not guilty (Max 1998). A memorial to Haddock now resides in downtown Sioux City.

Haddock's murder, and the accompanying publicity, lit a fire under city officials, and they finally began to clamp down on saloons and prostitution. Liquor and brothels were conveniently relocated across the Missouri River to Stanton, which is now South Sioux City (Hewitt 1991). However, in the 1920s, Prohibition resulted in bootleggers running up and down the Missouri. Sioux City was called "Little Chicago," both for its large stockyards and supposed gangster connections. The Chicago House hotel was known as a retreat for gangsters. However, rumors that Al Capone had visited Sioux City have never been substantiated (Margarici 2018).

Sioux Falls has also had its "seamier" early days. In 1878, the city had a dozen saloons and two houses of prostitution. In 1878, there were no murders and only a handful of criminal cases (Olson 2004). But Sioux Falls was the divorce capital of the country for a short period during the late 1800s. Women fled to South Dakota because obtaining a divorce was against the law in most states (Crossen 2007; Schaffer 1990). From 1887 to 1906, when the divorce law was in effect, more than 7,000 divorces were granted in South Dakota and more than a thousand of those divorces were granted in Minnehaha County, where Sioux Falls is the county seat. Yankton and Sioux Falls competed for the title of "divorce capital" of the country, but Sioux Falls won the battle with the help of a sympathetic judge (Schaffer 210).

Economically, Sioux Falls and Sioux City had different trajectories. Even during good economic times, small cities' growth was stunted by one-dimensional industrial bases. Prosperity arrived later and ended sooner (Mahoney 2004). Small cities were also very vulnerable to volatile cycles of growth and decline. Sioux City was the home of the famous eighty-acre Sioux City Stockyards. However, the yards finally shut down for good in 2002, leaving a Home Depot in its place (Dreezin 14 November). A few years later, the homegrown Gateway Computer factory closed up shop and moved overseas, taking hundreds of local jobs ("Gateway to End"). Sioux City still draws small-scale meat-packers, and its efforts to draw more white-collar jobs have ended in disappointment.

Sioux Falls took a different route and became the home of the South Dakota State Penitentiary. A century later, in the 1980s, the city made a deal with Citibank, making it the credit card capital of the Midwest. A rapid increase in population and housing soon followed. The company's operations included more than six million Mastercard and Visa accounts from all fifty states, and Citibank was accused of paying South Dakota to repeal its usury laws or the cap on what lenders in the state could lawfully charge to borrowers (Wright 2013). Nonetheless, the Citibank investment has left its mark on Sioux Falls and opened the doors to greater prosperity.

Sioux Falls also has Avera and Sanford Health facilities, which have become economic engines for all of southeast South Dakota, with Sanford Health now one of the largest health care systems in the United States. The city's downtown area has also been called its "crown jewel" because of the city leadership's ability to change with the times (Huber). The *Argus Leader* traces the many changes the downtown area has seen from the 1970s to the 2020s, from empty storefronts to a vibrant mix of local and national stores, restaurants, and bars, as well as residential properties. The city also connected the scenic Falls Park to the rest of downtown, making it a major attraction, with rippling water flowing over ancient rocks in the middle of the neighborhood (Huber).

But Sioux City's economy is improving, just not at the rate of Sioux Falls's. Housing is being built, jobs are coming to town (mostly meatpacking), and efforts are being made to lure more business to several downtown hotels that the city has approved. Redevelopment is also afloat, with Ho-Chunk buying up the historic Fourth Street. Ho-Chunk is the economic development corporation of the Winnebago Tribe of Nebraska. Ho-Chunk President and Chief Executive Officer Lance Morgan said at the announcement of the deal that Ho-Chunk has "bet big on Sioux City" (Docker).

In some ways, Sioux City has a good reputation. Take, for instance, the response to the crash of Flight 232 in 1994. The plane's hydraulic system had failed, and the pilots had to land in a cornfield near the Sioux City Airport. First responders raced to save more than 180 passengers. Sioux City emergency workers became a model for ideal disaster response and volunteer spirit. Moreover, the beauty of the Loess Hills, proximity to the Iowa Great Lakes, abundant natural beauty, and scandalous local history all add to the allure of Sioux City. It is also home to generations of families, like my own. The legacy of the work of Sioux City settlers made the area a fine place for families and businesses, and the city still is today.

Sioux City and Sioux Falls are what we make of them, what we, as citizens, are willing to do to make those cities safer, more diverse, and more prosperous for all. Diversity is hip and better housing is hip, just as new brewpubs, coffeehouses, and art galleries are hip. They draw the hip, the unhip, and those who want to live in an evolving and family-friendly city.

Sources

Brown, R. "A Tale of Two Cities: Sioux Falls and Sioux City." *South Dakota Business Review.*

Conlon, S. "Mayor Paul Tenhaken's Vision for 2021 Means Creating A 'Sioux Falls for All.'" *Argus Leader,* 30 Dec. 2020.

Docker, M. "Progress: Ho-Chunk Capital Buys Properties on Sioux City's Historic 4th Street." *Sioux City Journal,* 21 Mar. 2021.

"Gateway to End Sioux City Production." *Rapid City Journal*, 12 May 2004.

Hewitt, W. "Wicked Traffic in Girls: Prostitutes and Reform in Sioux City." *The Annals of Iowa.*

Hunter, W. & Stewart, R. "The Population of Iowa: Its Composition and Changes." Ames, 1930.

Max, M. "The Prohibition Rule: Murder in Sioux City." *NET.edu.* Originally published in *Wild West Magazine*, 1998.

Mahoney, T. "The Small City in the Midwest." *Indiana Magazine of History.*

Margarici, M. "Back in the Day, This Quiet Iowa Town was a Mafia Mecca." *Only in Your State.*

Milne, B. "Downtown Sioux Falls Named 'Hipster Capital' of South Dakota," *Argus Leader*, 17 October.

Mitchell, T. "Census 2020 Data Shows Sioux Falls' Population is Growing—And Becoming More Diverse." *Argus Leader*, 12 Aug. 2021.

Ohdenbach, B. *A History of First Lutheran Church, Sioux Falls, South Dakota.* 1970. University of Nebraska at Omaha, Master's thesis.

Olson, G. "A Dakota Boomtown: Sioux Falls, 1877–1880." *Great Plains Quarterly.*
"The Founding of Sioux City," *Sioux City Journal,* 30 July 1870.
Schaffer, C. "Money Versus Morality: The Divorce Industry of Sioux Falls." *South Dakota History.*
Silag, W. "Sioux City: An Iowa Boom Town." *Annals of Iowa.*
———. "Citizens and Strangers: Geographic Mobility in the Sioux City Region, 1860–1900." *Great Plains Journal.*
"Sioux City Has the Largest Net Migration Outflow Among Iowa Cities," www.thecentersquare.org, 2 June 2020.
Wright, Robert. "Wall Street on the Prairie: Citibank, South Dakota and the Origins of Financial Deregulation." *Financial History.*

The New Sioux Falls

CHRISTOPHER VONDRACEK

The woman smoking a cigarette outside the courthouse in Elk Point, South Dakota, stood two blocks down from an outboard motorboat stacked on concrete blocks near the abandoned service station and told me exactly what she thought about the trial inside, now ending its second week.

"They ruined a lot of jobs," she said, inhaling her cigarette.

I sheepishly nodded, kicking my scuffed dress shoes against the concrete pavers. *Welcome to the meat trial of the century.*

Weeks earlier, during my interview for this job in Sioux Falls, the western bureau chief of a legal news service—flown in from San Francisco—kept repeating his fascination with the meat trial down the Big Sioux.

"We'll definitely want that covered," he said. "It's got Dianne Sawyer. Something called pink slime. And like, $5 *billion* in potential damages. Unreal."

Later, I'd learn this wasn't exactly accurate. Technically, BPI (formerly Iowa Beef Products and now, Empirical Foods) asked for only $1.7 billion from ABC for tarnishing their good name.[1] And the phrase "pink slime" was not the industry term—that was *lean finely textured beef* product (LFTB)—constituting the goop, the scoria, the meat-like substance they sold and that had *been* invoked (as "pink slime") over a dozen times by ABC News's Sawyer over three nights of broadcasts in March 2012.

Predictably, pandemonium followed. Parents called school cafeterias, asking for boycotts. Chagrined executives at McDonald's, Burger King, and Wendy's pulled LFTB from their meat mix. Even grocery stores, which mixed LFTB into lean beef, spec'd-out the stuff.

And, hey, it wasn't necessarily killing people or even making folks sick. It was scraps of usable beef attached to carcasses after all the rest was removed on assembly lines, what Upton Sinclair might've called, "all the cow but the moo." The product had even already gone through the public scrutiny ringer, notably from the *New York Times*, which squared up LFTB in their sights for a Pulitzer-winning piece on food safety.

Most importantly, the "pink slime" moniker, conjuring up a car-eating blob from some 1950s horror film, was coined not by Nielsen-

1 Though $1.7 could be "trebled" up to over $5 billion under South Dakota's agricultural defamation law.

seeking Manhattan producers but actually by scientists two hours east at laboratories in Ames, Iowa, with the US Department of Agriculture back in the late 1990s. They had tested LFTB to determine just what in the world this mystery meat was and wrote down, "this stuff is like pink slime."

Nevertheless, Sawyer and ABC were a more satisfying target. Especially for a madder-than-hops meat company, as the periwinkle meat paste was their baby, invented by Eldon Roth, and fed their company's bottom line. Soon they throttled facilities, laid off workers, and in an America with rapidly depreciating *bonhomie* between Mayberry and Madison Avenue, Sawyer—along with her correspondent, Jim Avila—became the face of corporate, coastal elitist vegetarianism, for breaking a rule, that even I, as a lifelong rural Minnesotan who'd grown up the son of public school teachers *in town*, knew to be sacrosanct out in the country.

You can't diss someone's meat.

My own mother once scolded me as a child when—in front of my Uncle Steve, a cattle rancher from central Nebraska—I'd repeated what I'd heard on a radio broadcast.

"Isn't red meat bad for you?" I asked.

Mom escorted me so fast to the back porch.

"Never say that again in front of Steve."

And I was chilled into silence, not because what I said was wrong but because it was rude. But in my defense, it was a question increasingly hard not to ask.

When I'd moved from St. Paul to Sioux Falls a year earlier, in 2016, I found the wafting meat smells from Smithfield Meats, a slaughterhouse near our brownstone apartment downtown, frequently souring not just the air but also my jogs along the river. There were days I could barely breathe in, instead turning off the path to lumber up a hill near the cathedral to fill up my airways again. When I asked around town, though, I always got the same response.

"Smells like money," said Mike Haskett, owner and chef of a bistro on Phillips Avenue, slapping his white apron over his chest.

Years later, in DC, a woman who worked as a lobbyist but who had proudly grown up in Sioux Falls, leaned in as we talked about her hometown's pungent cloud.

"Smells like money," she whispered, before breaking into a laugh.

And these were the liberals.

It's why BPI had fought to get the trial into Elk Point, and why ABC had fought for removal to the federal court in Sioux Falls. The latter, of course, had lost that fight, and now, nearly five years onward, here we were. And I thought it opportune for me, a new reporter. This was a generational story, one that might land me on *All Things Considered* reporting on emotional divisions in Trump's America. But after talking to the clerk, ready to dig in the journalistic tenterhooks, I heard a crashing sound—*crunnnnch*—and looked up.

Across the street, a reporter who worked for the *Argus Leader* in Sioux Falls was parking his red sportscar.

"Hey, man," I said, walking over. "Gonna be a big day today, huh?"

He inspected his bumper.

"Dude, we barely showed up ourselves," he said, standing up. "The editors didn't know if they could justify sending someone every single day. So we're alternating days with the *Sioux City Journal.*"

I turned to face my courthouse, my stomach tightening in a knot.

"But this is, you know, the meat trial of the century?"

He shrugged. "There's just hardly any interest back in Sioux Falls."

Behind us, a gal with sketchbooks walked in, followed by that clerk, stomping on her cigarette butt. Dispirited, I clutched my notebook and trudged toward this tiny courthouse in the middle of nowhere, home to this gigantic lawsuit about meat, which no one really cared about anyway and was about to get underway.

Let's give Sioux Falls an alibi or two for their disinterest. First off, this was a *beef* trial. Morrell slaughters *pigs*. Second, even if this epicurean distinction feels too fine a point, Elk Point is an hour's drive south from the Queen City, and with whole floors of the *Argus Leader* Building downtown sitting empty, local news was king.

But the citywide apathy toward the biggest event going on in the wider state circumscribing Sioux Falls could be explained by what my boss, Bernie Hunhoff, at *South Dakota Magazine* told me when I interned there in 2007: "Sioux Falls just never felt like the heart of the state. It's never captured my imagination."

Folks in Sioux Falls mostly like to figure themselves distinctly *away from* the prairie—the agricultural economy, the dusty feed silos, the pink slime, the farm boys from Humboldt hooping and hollering with Natty Ice in the tailgate and flying a Confederate flag. It's a city that wants to be leisurely and clean and free of soil stains and pig smells.

This doesn't mean that Sioux Falls isn't *here*, largely, because of the money earned from soil stains and pig smells. There's a river walk with bluestem grasses. There's some reclaimed barn-wood décor at a café or two on Phillips Avenue where they might serve bison. But over the last couple of decades, maybe since its founding, there's been a concerted effort to draw some aesthetic distance with its country past. In 2006, the city partially collapsed its iconic feed tower, and in 2009, they closed the stockyards. By 2016, an old diner called Bob's Chicken, frequented by the slaughterhouse workers, even shuttered, with talk of a new locale out by the byway.

And when I moved to Sioux Falls, my now-wife Carrie and I would walk downtown and see the names of banks, the health care companies glittering in the night sky. These were the words Sioux Falls wanted to use to sing its song—not the names of seed companies or tractor manufacturers or storied, AM radio agronomists. That was another city. Maybe Elk Point.

My first day in the courtroom, I gaped at what I saw. At the foot of the stairs, two bailiffs stood guard outside the courtroom, and inside, roughly twenty, maybe thirty, maybe 100 attorneys in black and blue suits sat. In the back row, marked "media," roughly half a dozen, and sometimes far fewer, reporters found their seats.

"Please rise for . . ."

In walked the judge with the bangs. Judge Cheryl Gehring bounded in like Pat Summit following a victory going to shake hands with the opposing team's coach. Journalists from the East Coast who'd rented Sioux City hotels for the opening day had not been disappointed a week earlier when, quashing a flurry of motions from both sides, Judge Gehring passed on advice to the attorneys that had been told to her by an old South Dakota attorney. "Litigators are wine drinkers," Gehring said, in a Dakota drawl. "Trial attorneys drink whiskey."

But by the time I arrived in Elk Point, the John Ford-qualities of the trial's debut had subsided. Instead, attorneys delved into the legal nitty-gritty: *Did Avila want to tell both sides of the story? Did other reports on LFTB exist? How many shipments were cancelled by Hy-Vee?*

A retired lawyer sat next to me. He'd moved back from Minneapolis to his hometown of Elk Point and had opted to spend a cheap vacation coming down to the courthouse each day.

"Not much else going on in town," he shrugged.

We watched the jury that afternoon, all twelve plus an alternate or two, who looked like the people you'd find pushing a cart through the grocery aisle at the Walmart with a box of frozen ham steaks, which is to say exactly who BPI had in mind when they organized the case here instead of up in the federal courthouse in Sioux Falls.

"Some of these folks probably haven't seen a vegetarian," the retired attorney told me.

That Friday afternoon, Rich Jochum, a bald company official, recounted his attempts to work with the film crew for Jamie Oliver's show. Jochum said BPI opened up their plant in South Sioux City to ABC, but that the network used a photograph published earlier in the *Washington Post.*

"How did you feel when you saw Oliver's show?" asked BPI attorney Dan Webb.

"Outraged," replied Jochum.

"Was anything accurate?" Webb pressed.

"Only that we separate beef from fat," Jochum said. "Otherwise, nothing."

Then Webb played a segment from *Jamie Oliver's Food Revolution*. The whole courtroom watched as the telegenic culinary host threw a slab of red meat into a Maytag drying machine, whirling centrifugally the beef product at warp speed, showcasing the separation process of meat from, well, not-meat. The *au gratin* jurors held up hands to their mouths as if witnessing a father accidentally back over his son.

In fairness, a meat trial of the century wasn't good branding for a big town looking to be a city. I recall the day in 2017 that the *Argus Leader* said the community's population—using estimates of US Census data—topped 170,000 residents.

"Totally inaccurate," railed my mentor, Jack Marsh, a former editor of the paper, on Facebook. "Look at the most recent Census Report."

Nevertheless, the number boosted cosmopolitan attitudes. A year earlier, the town added a much-ballyhooed reverse parking along Dakota Street just north of downtown, after an urban-planning enthusiast had won a small battle at a city council meeting. And a greengrocer for city dwellers landed downtown, too, causing Sioux Fallsians I'd gone to college with who'd moved away to say things on social media, like, "Wow. Maybe I *will* move back!"

In lieu of mass transit or gritty street scenes[2] or skyscrapers, people really wanted things to work. And there were flashes of that farm and country and even *western* life in the twenty-first-century city. One night at the Top Hat Bar, a dive with a long mirror running along the tables and Hanks One and Three on the jukebox, a man in a flannel shirt, a friend of Carrie's who'd come out in college, told us he'd just inherited the family farm. There were the hipster kids hanging out by the record store down the block from the courthouse, émigré from the punk club in the Nordic Hall basement in the early 1990s. And there was the night we ended up at Jennifer White's art gallery, Post-Pilgrim, below a record shop on East Tenth Street, where she showed us her paintings, a row of elongated Native men in suits and twin feathers, or her Indigenous women standing against Warhol-esque colors. This felt like the consciousness of a city suitable for the twenty-first century.

But by other measuring sticks, things faded. The city soon painted over the reverse parking strips, citing safety. And about a year after the opening of the grocer, I walked in one night to see the shelves had succumb to wilted lettuce and squishy peaches. Wandering around while the owners balefully watched me from their forlorn smocks, reeking of cigarette smoke, I tried to not give offense by rummaging past empty shelves and purchasing a $7 box of cereal and non-expired milk, the local meat completely off the shelves. By January, the place was another sophisticated, generic cocktail bar.

In between my travels down to Elk Point, however, I fortunately picked up another gig that summer, teaching summer school at Washington High. The courses were to be a remedial English curriculum. And my supervisor, a grandmotherly white woman who cut almost blithely past cultural lines that a younger teacher wanting tenure might loathe to cross, gave me an introduction.

"We've got mostly kids whose parents work at Morrell's," she said. "The worst are the Congolese girls. They have real attitude."

One student—Grace—I remembered from my stint as a substitute teacher because I'd kicked her out of class at George McGovern Middle, the school for mostly immigrants and, curiously, "alternative" learners, when she kept interrupting our assigned movie. "Routine flyer," the principal

2 We lived in a brownstone, maybe one of the few in town, and out our back window, we could see streaming senior photographer after senior photographer.

told me when I signed out at day's end. But when Grace showed up that first day at Washington, stuck with her age group in the fourteen- and fifteen-year-old class (or "beginner"), I noticed the problem.

She was way better than her grade level allowed.

"Everyone just figured I was the same as my cousin," said Grace, "Cuz we're the same age."

So I put Grace to work, asking her to help other students. But when I stuck her with a sweet, tiny boy, Kahlil, from Somalia, he walked up to me in his khaki pants and sandals to lob his grievance.

"I don't want to be helped, professor," he said. "Not from *her*."

Faced with an impossible situation, I eventually allowed Grace to read by herself in the hallway—poring through chapter books her peers might not visit for months.

This was the life of kids from all over the world who'd ended up in this place called South Dakota. Their parents found work at the slaughterhouse, part of the growth happening that few in the city were aware of. Another student, who was sixteen and had just arrived from China, didn't know a single word in English. We sat next to each other on a picnic bench under a shade tree on a break one morning, communicating to each other through Google Translate on his cellphone. He wrote furiously into the phone and then handed it over to me. "I am a chef," he wrote. "I have already graduated from high school. I do not know why I'm here."

After a moment's pause, briefly iced by the thought of his overwhelming circumstances, I told him, "This will be good review, then. You will help the others learn."

He sat in back for another week and then never returned.

But the rest of us shouldered forth. We read *Winn-Dixie,* spending inordinate attention on Southern Gothic literature references, and then plowed through a dystopian novel about children living in an underground city. And when we finished that, while other teachers emphasized worksheets, grammar, games with dice and flash cards, I wanted them instead to pile up words. So I'd build off our reading with PowerPoints.

"Prairie."

"Forest."

"Desert."

They'd write the words down. Use them with their conversation partner. And then we'd add more words. Once, we landed on a picture of a dust cloud, some wide, tornadic ghost hollowing out the frame of the picture on a dust-swept horizon.

"What is this?" I asked. "Anybody?"

A boy called Hope, from Sudan, a mischievous if ultimately just energetic boy in the back, began laughing.

"I know what that is. My mother told me."

"What's that?" I asked him, holding my chalk piece, quizzically.

"That's the devil," said the boy, his laughing continuing. "I know what that is. That's the *devil.*"

All the kids began laughing, as did I, as I looked back up at that menacing cloud, wondering if he weren't more right than wrong. And then Grace peeked in, clutching her chapter book, seemingly growing taller already this year, and quietly slipping back in the doorway, her multicolor beads dangling.

On my second day in court, ABC's defense attorneys sparred with Olivera Abel, CEO of Jensen Meats in San Diego, a frozen hamburger patty maker who'd removed LFTB from its "spec sheet" in the aftermath of the Dianne Sawyer broadcasts and subsequent public outrage about the meat's color.

"Was it pink?"

The attorney repeated his question with the vigor of Tom Cruise in *A Few Good Men* interrogating Jack Nicholson.

"Why can't you call it pink?!"

When BPI's attorneys followed up on newsman Avila's claim that pink slime was "only good for dog food and cosmetics," Chad Martin of Tyson Foods sat on the stand, insisting Avila's claim was false because they turned LFTB into hot dogs.

"Is hot dogs something a human would eat?" asked BPI's attorney, a man, presumably, who'd gone to law school for this moment.

"Yes," said Martin.

"Thank you for your time."

The attorney sighed heavily as we broke for lunch.

The reporter told me he had what he needed for the day. "It's just all prelude," he said, "till they can appeal the ruling." The radio people said the claimants' strategy was legally technical. But maybe in my ignorance, joining the fight at the very end, I thought the questions had reminded me of my classroom questions to the English-language-learning students: What do you call *beef?* What is beef and what is cow? How come in Spanish, they call "chicken" "*pollo*" when you want to eat it, but "*gallina*" otherwise?

For lunch, I drove out to a roadside diner I knew from college, but about fifteen feet from the door, a woman in dark sunglasses and a pencil skirt put up her hand.

"It's closed," she said.

She meant it was closed *for me.* Mysteriously, I watched people from the defense team enter the diner behind her. Later, the retired attorney told me the BPI attorneys had bought up another closed restaurant or bar across town for a midday debriefing headquarters.

So I went across the street to Casey's and got an apple, a bottle of water, and some cheese.

"A store full of temptations and this is what you buy?" the cashier laughed. "It's the most healthy selection I've seen today."

If a teacher displays a picture of a city and asks me, "What is this?" I would say a marketplace. A gathering space. Greens on the street, with saxophone's wail and someone selling CBD and lemon tarts or the noise of airplanes passing overhead, or fervent discussions about politics while someone inspects cherries, her child petting a stranger's dog. If nothing else, a city is a variety of foods, impossibly arranged in an urban expanse far from a field.

But I don't know if I would answer "Sioux Falls."

In the fall of 2016, a short article published by the *Argus Leader* cited a 2009 study from the Centers for Disease Control and Prevention that found Sioux Falls was last among 180 metropolitan areas for eating vegetables and fruits.

Since moving to Sioux Falls, I couldn't help but notice not only the health care facilities—particularly heart hospitals—that ringed the community's perimeter, presumably from the lack of things (walking and vegetables) you find in a city, but I also noticed the lack of conversation on the streets, save for obnoxious billboards boasting about atheism or carbon pollution. Politics, in other words, felt impolite. So maybe Sioux Falls didn't care about this trial because they didn't see anything *wrong* with what was happening: a journalist getting punished for largely just telling the truth, albeit rudely, about a product made and sold here in America. Those reporters had been nosy.

On a Thursday of the fourth week of the trial, I sat in a screening of the film *Guardians of the Galaxy*, which we'd given the students as a celebration for the last day of summer school, when I got a call from the attorney.

I'd been looking forward to the second month of the trial when, I imagined, the defense would start up with stirring orations in favor of the free press. But none of that happened.

"Just thought you should know," my confidential informant said. "They're going to settle. The judge just announced it."

"Just like that?" I asked.

"Just like that."

I felt a chill to my bones. Hanging up, I went back to finish the movie, where on the screen, a Harrison Ford stand-in piloted his war-weary spacecraft through an asteroid belt, cursing out his monster-like sidekick, and the room was filled with laughter, as our students, the new Sioux Falls, laughed and laughed at this movie that, through the genius of Hollywood producers, could be enjoyed in any language.

When I was a kid, I knew Sioux Falls as a place where my grandmother and her older sister, Marie, still into their eighties, would drive up to from Beresford to find the salad bar at Minerva's on Phillips. They'd get dressed up, put on lipstick, walk leisurely to and from the building in heels, and before leaving town, they'd drop down to the falls to peek at the purple granite, to hear the water, and then they'd smell the stockyards, squeeze up their windows, and drive home.

I don't know what they would've thought of the trial. The structure of the "pink slime" deal, of course, would never, officially, be announced. Nor the rationale. Both sides claimed some sort of victory. Months later, Eldon's wife spoke at a Sioux City Chamber of Commerce meeting and said the check contained "lots of zeroes." A *subsequent* fiscal year-end filing from Disney, ABC's parent company, reported a special litigation fee of over $177 million.

Eldon said he'd hire some workers back. The company reformed under a new name. LFTB showed up again on menus. But I still can't shake what I heard on my second day in court: that Avila said a burger made 100 percent of LFTB was "chewy." It couldn't be eaten. It just looked close enough.

By the end of December, Carrie and I would move away, waving to friends and family in a Penske truck. But over the final months we had in town, I vowed to start walking more, along the river, or through the downtown at night. By October, with the snow falling past the old nineteenth-century storefronts, I would look up at the courthouse, and then I'd peel around the corner past the cramped fine dining establishment owned by a failed Democratic candidate for US Senate, where when diners finished up, they wrapped themselves in big, black coats before scampering across the street to the theater or the symphony. A little farther down, I could also see the second-story dance studio, where on a wintry night, you might catch a tawny silhouette above the street of young ballerinas, doing pliés to a sixteen-count. And then down a few more blocks to the west, I'd reach the Vietnamese restaurant where, ordering a bowl of pho, you might sit in the window finding a quiet, neon place, where the owner brought out a sheet cake one night to surprise Carrie on her birthday.

Something, I understood, was still here, or emerging, huddled not out by the mall or the new university center or the minor league diamond but here along the river, with its old steel mill and punk club housed in the Nordic Hall's basement or over at the ice-skating rink in McKennan Park, still buried into the soil or wrapped in the hot stench from over near the river's bend, curling like a cat's tail around the Wonka-esque brick slaughterhouse.

That December, on an unseasonable Saturday afternoon, just weeks before we moved, Carrie and I would be walking in Falls Park when I ran into Grace with her family. She'd been living with her cousin's family when I taught her. I asked her how her reading was going ("good"), how her classmates were ("they're fine"), and then what she thought of her new hometown, now almost a year in.

"I like Sioux Falls," she said, shrugging her shoulders. "It's a good place."

I said goodbye and walked across the bridge, over the half-frozen gurgling rapids, and when I looked back, I saw Grace with her father, in a tall, fine suit, slowly walking along the autumn river, with the glint of tall buildings behind him.

KELO

BETH JENSEN

KELOLAND Television, the first station to sign on in South Dakota, filled the screen with a black-and-white test pattern in the spring of 1953. It started taking shape the summer before, when Joe L. Floyd and partners Eddie Ruben and Larry Bentson purchased Midcontinent Company, the operator of KELO radio. And on May 19, 1953, the station signed on from its first location, the second floor of the Hollywood Theater Building at Eighth Street and Phillips Avenue. Joe L. Floyd's son, Joe H. Floyd, was a senior in high school and worked on the first newscast.

"We'd been rehearsing for about a week. So, for me, it was just another rehearsal. But it started off with the opening, with both my father and Evans Nord, talking about how this was going to be their first real broadcast. And I said, 'Wow, that's the first one!' Up until then, everybody was watching test patterns," Floyd said. The newscasts weren't live. They were recorded at 3:30 in the afternoon, and it was Floyd's job to take the raw, six o'clock film strip to Harold's Photography for processing. Then he would take the film back to the KELO studio for the commercials to be spliced in.

"Then I would take that master reel and drive it out to Schindler, where the transmitter was, and they would put it on a film chain and that was the six o'clock news," Floyd said. The delay would occasionally create issues. "Occasionally, the weatherman would be forecasting partly cloudy, and by the time the show ran, it would be raining like hell."

The station introduced live programming in the fall of 1954, giving viewers access to sporting events and network shows. The arrival of live studio cameras in January of 1955 allowed the station to broadcast live news, weather, and sports. Many of the commercials were also live. Even in the early days, Floyd knew his father was creating something special.

"My father is an old vaudeville guy. He was a stage manager at the Orpheum Theater in the Twin Cities. And he saw television just like a stage play. That's why programming was such an important deal to him," Floyd said. "In later times, I remember him talking to the staff about how important our television news was because we covered so much of the state. And how closely we would have to follow and should follow the news guidelines from CBS, which he called Cronkite guidelines."

That meant delivering content without opinion.

"He would watch the newscast and he insisted that we never gave any kind of a smile or a smirk after a story. Just straight all news."

In March of 1955, KELO made history again by launching what would become the longest continuously running children's show in the world. *Captain 11* signed on, with host Dave Dedrick, who patterned his character after a show of the same name in Minneapolis. The station designed the set, using pinball machine parts, and gave Dedrick a distinct royal blue suit. The program aired daily and attracted crowds of children and their parents to the KELO studios.

"He was my hero from the get-go, when we first got television in '53," said former KELO anchor Doug Lund, who watched *Captain 11* as a child. "He was so special, and he just understood the kids so well."

"As far as the viewers were concerned, Dave Dedrick *was* KELO," former KELO anchor Steve Hemmingsen said. "Dedrick was just a showman. He had it in his gut."

In 1959, KELO Television had outgrown its original studio and moved to its current location at Thirteenth Street and Phillips Avenue. Dedrick also worked as the station's weather forecaster and he, along with Hemmingsen, Lund, and Jim Burt, made up the station's successful anchor team. Hemmingsen arrived in 1969 after an early radio career at the "Polka Station of the Nation" in New Ulm, Minnesota. "I came in one night and did my audition," Hemmingsen remembered. "I was always a very good sight reader, reading two or three lines ahead." Joe L. Floyd noticed that talent and cut the audition short.

"That's enough, that's enough, you're a hell of a sight reader."

But Hemmingsen didn't want to be an anchor, he wanted to report.

"The stipulation was that I was to be a reporter. So, he didn't bother telling anyone I was a hell of a sight reader," Hemmingsen said.

That agreement lasted until they needed a last-minute anchor on the midday broadcast and Hemmingsen was tapped in.

"In those days, if someone left, they looked at the bench and said, 'Who's next?'" Hemmingsen said. "If you could read, they didn't worry if you were beautiful or handsome. KELO was lucky. We always had pretty good bench strength."

Doug Lund joined the team in 1974.

"People took a shine to us, and we were the only show in town for a long, long time," he said. "The concept of Joe Floyd and the whole group of people that were there was just to be good and to be honest and fair and get the best equipment you could possibly get." In addition to having great instincts about news, Joe L. Floyd was also a gifted promotor. He once launched an advertising campaign aimed at getting the attention of national advertising agencies with his photo and the tag line: "I'm Joe Floyd. I consider myself a helluva salesman."

In August of 1961, he launched his most ambitious and successful campaign, the KELOLAND Gold Rush. The promotion drew more than 100,000 people to a field near Manchester, South Dakota. Hundreds of contestants received gold shovels to dig for prizes like $10,000 and a new car. Celebrities like Lawrence Welk and Clint Eastwood were on-site and added to the excitement. Floyd's gift for promotion also extended to the branding of the station as KELOLAND, to represent its regional reach. While most stations covered one city or part of a state, KELOLAND reached viewers in South Dakota, Minnesota, and Iowa, and later expanded to communities in North Dakota, Nebraska, Montana, and Wyoming. While in 2021, the Sioux Falls designated market area ranks as the 113th largest in the country, the geographic coverage area is one of the largest.

"People used to laugh at the statement 'KELOLAND,' but they all recognized it," Hemmingsen said.

The reach is also thanks to the decision to sign on KDLO in Aberdeen (Florence) in 1955, KPLO in Pierre (Reliance) in 1957, and KCLO in Rapid City as a full-power satellite station in 1988. But when Joe L. Floyd pushed to expand to Rapid City, initially, the decision was not an easy one.

"When we built the station out there, we had to build in a one-hour delay. The programming was on a one-hour continuous tape system that was difficult to run. And it continued that day, I was in the Twin Cities by that time, when the Gulf War started, and I called my partner and said you can't cover a war on a one-hour delay. So, we shut down the tape system and went live," Floyd said.

The regional reach only expanded the popularity of its anchor team.

"Joe Floyd just knew what people wanted. He could look at an idea in a minute and say, 'Yeah, that will work.' In a strange way, that was good management," Hemmingsen said. "There was a real good nexus that put this thing together. Joe Floyd put together a damn good team."

That team of anchors was all men until Julie Francavilla was promoted to anchor the evening news in 1989. "I was the first female anchor on the 10:00 p.m. news at KELO, so that was a truly extraordinary opportunity I was given," Francavilla said.

When she left to become a reporter in Seattle in 1991, twenty-five-year-old Angela Kennecke was promoted from the morning show.

"It's like the Mount Rushmore of KELOLAND. There were these old guys that were my father's age that had all of this gravitas and following. They were like gods," Kennecke said. "You have to remember there were only like three channels. People didn't have everything they have today with the internet and all of the channels and all of the options and streaming services. They had three channels, and everybody watched KELO, nobody watched the other ones. So, these guys were huge. The big news. And they were big in a lot of ways."

With experience came appreciation.

"I have to say, it wasn't easy working that job as a very young, blonde, naive woman. But it was an education. I learned fast. And I became a better writer and a better reporter because of those guys, for sure," Kennecke said. She credits Hemmingsen and Lund with creating a powerful foundation. "The kind of old-fashioned newsmen that they were really brought up the level of news for this station, and it's a legacy we've tried to carry on."

Legacy is a term that is frequently mentioned by those both in front of and behind the scenes, like assignment editor Dexter Gronseth, who started working in the master control area of the station right out of high school. After spending more than four decades at the station, he feels a great responsibility to build on what the early employees established.

"I think you have a lot of people who understand the legacy and who will work hard to keep the legacy going. The big four certainly put us at a higher level, and I think we've just taken the game a little bit higher than that," Gronseth said.

He got his start on the assignment desk while Hemmingsen was both evening anchor and managing editor, which also gave Hemmingsen content approval.

"Working alongside Steve Hemmingsen, I learned more about TV news than I ever thought I would," Gronseth said. "To this day, I make decisions based on Hemmingsen's philosophy."

The job gives those in the newsroom a front row seat to Sioux Falls history.

"I drive up and down these streets every day. And I'm reminded of story after story that I've covered at this location and that location," anchor Don Jorgensen said.

In May of 1996, the station changed ownership for the first time. Midcontinent Communications sold the station to Young Broadcasting. This was also the year that *Captain 11* signed off and Dave Dedrick retired. In 1997, KELO made a strategic investment in its weather coverage by building the first and only live Doppler radar in the coverage area. Initially branded the Live Doppler 2000, the network included two radars, located in Beresford and Huron. A third radar was later added in Wall in 2001.

"It was a bold move to spend a lot of money to try and improve the technology for us and our viewers," said meteorologist Jay Trobec, who joined the station as a reporter but earned his meteorological seals when he moved to weather. "I think it's shown over time that it paid off."

The same year, KELO made the important strategic decision to launch a website, and on December 3, 1997, KELOLAND.com went live. Through all of the changes, the station has maintained a powerful role in helping the community by hosting events like a telethon for the Spencer Tornado victims.

"I think actually what I'll remember most is the uniqueness of this community and how people really rally around whatever is happening in our world here," Kennecke says. "I would say I really remember the Spencer Tornado and raising a million dollars for people. And people just coming in the front doors of KELO and kids just opening their piggy banks and standing there and taking that money."

Each year since 1998, KELO has donated resources and thousands of dollars of airtime to produce public service announcements for more than 130 organizations in more than twenty communities as part of its National Emmy Award-winning community service campaign, Tradition of Caring. "We have a responsibility as a station to use our platform to help the communities we serve," says KELOLAND Media Group vice president and general manager Mari Ossenfort. "The station has a long tradition of using the power of KELO to give back."

KELO also continued its tradition of investing in technology by launching HDTV programming in 2003 and making the full HD conversion in 2011. It changed ownership again in 2013 when Young Broadcasting merged with Media General. In 2017, Media General merged with Nexstar Media Group and KELO became part of what would be America's largest local television and media company. The ownership changed, but the commitment to local viewers continued. First with the launch of lifestyle program on *KELOLAND Living* in 2018 and a $1 million remodel and launch of a new set in February of 2020. "Our priorities have always been local news, weather, and sports," Ossenfort said. "And investments in technology allow us to find the best ways to deliver that content to our viewers." And through it all, KELO has won every newscast time period since it signed on the air. KELO's commitment to its legacy has continued too.

"I don't think we take it for granted. I think we work hard, and we instill an attitude with our workers that we expect to be successful," Jorgensen said. "My biggest motivation is the fear of failure." Jorgensen, who was promoted to evening anchor, after Hemmingsen's retirement in 2000, still remembers Hemmingsen's parting words: "When he left, he said don't screw it up."

Sources
All quotes are from interviews conducted personally by Beth Jensen; recordings are housed at KELO studios.

Theatre

BOB WENDLAND

First, a brief history. Sioux Falls has always been a big little city that quietly supports art of multiple disciplines while fostering an environment that encourages entrepreneurial endeavors and building a sturdy platform for big money businesses.

Since the early 1920s, when Phillips Avenue was home to multiple vaudeville touring house theatre spaces, theatre and entertainment have lingered on the fringe and modestly blossomed with the support of small groups of community members. Homegrown theatre ebbed and flowed throughout the following decades and helped build the stage for the robust theatre community that Sioux Falls is home to today. Until about fifteen years ago, theatre lived in the shadows, but a little ember started to glow in the late 1990s that began a blaze that sparked the five theatre companies that Sioux Falls knows today.

In the summer of 1997, Bare Bodkins Shakespeare Theatre Company changed the game with the first independent theatre company devoted to one playwright. They picked a good writer to build a brand and a reputation on. In partnership with the Sioux Falls Parks and Recreation Department, Bare Bodkins was able to offer free performances of an abridged Shakespeare play every summer. Bare Bodkins took it one step further. Not only did they offer a very specific form of theatre, but they also decided to do it professionally. They paid their artists for their time and talent in a way that had not previously been established in the Sioux Falls local theatre scene. Additionally, they cast a small group of actors to play all the parts in the show. Many actors played anywhere from three to eight characters in one production. And as if that wasn't boundary-pushing enough, they took a simplistic approach, citing that, just as Shakespeare did in his day, the actors use minimal costume pieces and props to tell the story. They used limited pieces and relied heavily on natural surroundings. Launching a vital chapter in the Sioux Falls theatre scene, Bare Bodkins was the source of a monumental wave of creative momentum.

Five years later, a small group of theatre enthusiasts started meeting to discuss reviving a community theatre. With input from the city of Sioux Falls, the Sioux Empire Arts Council, the business community, educators, neighbors, and artists, the Sioux Empire Community Theatre was born. It has seen many different leadership teams and employed multiple production directors in its nearly two decades. Producing shows from niche, virtually unheard-of, small-cast plays to big, blockbuster musicals. With thousands of volunteers on and off stage in those years, this community theatre has fostered connections between creatives that have launched several other theatre projects and motivated several fully fledged companies.

A city the size of Sioux Falls, with the creative horsepower that exists in the corners of this community, requires a community theatre, and Sioux Empire Community Theatre has always held up that mantle: giving a platform to theatre hobbyists and trained professionals, creating opportunities for folks in the area to build community with like-minded individuals and providing entertainment for a broad swath of Sioux Fallsians.

The year 2016 was notable. Two theatre companies formed by two groups of recent theatre graduates emerged. First, in the spring of 2016, Monstrous Little Theatre Company introduced a wild, fresh concept to the theatre scene: they performed in the back room of a bar. This was followed by theatre in a church basement and then a grocery store, a recording studio, and a used bookstore. They made a big splash with their aim to bring new and provocative plays to the community in unconventional theatre spaces. The company continues to produce an average of three plays a year, bouncing around from one unique venue to another and telling envelope-pushing stories through a fresh lens with honesty and integrity.

Continuing the "Year of New Theatre Companies," a musical-theatre-focused company made a big debut in the Fall of 2016. Four friends, who met during a production of *Mary Poppins* at the Sioux Empire Community Theatre, dreamed up what would later become the Good Night Theatre Collective. They noticed a missing piece in the live entertainment game in Sioux Falls and introduced the community to cabaret-style musical theatre at the Icon Lounge. With a quirky theme and four outstanding vocalists, each month brought a new set list of songs and helped craft the company's self-coined approach to cabaret theatre: "two parts live concert, one part theatre." The success of this new style of storytelling opened doors for the company to produce a world premiere of an original musical written by local artists that quickly became an expected staple of each subsequent season. In their third season, they began producing fully staged, nonoriginal musicals as well. The company currently offers a season of eight shows from September to July: four themed cabarets and four musicals—two nonoriginal musicals, one locally written original musical, and a family-focused musical.

A few years later, in the fall of 2019, a group of "women of a certain age" came together after meeting during a production of *Calendar Girls* at the Sioux Empire Community Theatre. They decided to start a theatre company that told the stories and experiences of middle-aged women by actors fitting that demographic. The group performed Nora and Delia Ephron's *Love, Loss, and What I Wore* in several different venues throughout Sioux Falls to launch their new company and, just a few weeks later, they found themselves in the same unprecedented situation as the other theatre companies: the COVID-19 global pandemic.

Prior to the pandemic, the community was overflowing with talented theatre artists collaborating and creating, building impressive momentum around a movement toward a level of quality in the theatre arts that Sioux Falls hadn't previously seen. All of a sudden, theatre at its core, as an arts medium which required strangers to come together in large groups to enjoy the stories told, became an unwise idea. So while many theatres and live entertainment venues across the country, and the globe, closed their doors and waited out the pandemic with varied optimism, the scrappy theatre companies of Sioux Falls decided to put their talents to work and get creative. The Good Night Theatre Collective pivoted immediately to online cabarets. Asking their performers to record themselves singing their parts of the songs in their own homes, they spliced together isolated video footage in order to keep their audiences entertained, even while stuck in their own homes. The Sioux Empire Community Theatre followed suit with a series of radio plays later that summer. Producing some classics and some locally written works with a small crew of actors, they posted their new entertainment outlet onto social media and gave people an opportunity to listen in and support them with donations.

A new theatre and dance fusion company burst through the doors shortly afterward. Headlights Theatre was a group of dancers who decided to start doing outdoor shows in parking lots. With masked performers and audience members staying inside their vehicles to watch the show due to the pandemic, this new performance troupe was creating something new and unique. Their "Park and Art Series" invited local bands and the theatre scene's own Good Night Theatre to partner with them by providing live music to accompany their choreography and movement.

The Good Night Theatre Collective took their newfound video editing skills and put together two virtual variety shows, the first in July of 2020 with a "Christmas in July" theme and the second in February 2021 with a "Valentine's Day" theme. These variety shows had original and public domain music as well as several original stories and *Saturday Night Live*-style sketches. In the fall, the Good Night Theatre Collective decided to partner with other local arts entertainment groups (Monstrous Little Theatre, Broad Cast, and Sioux Falls Chamber Collective) to bring a Garden Party Series to the Washington Pavilion's Paladino Hohm Sculpture Garden. These brief, thirty-minute shows happened outdoors with a masked audience. The format of the short-form entertainment was live music and storytelling stitched together with a very small group of performers and offered to the public for free.

The owners and artists of the Good Night Theatre Collective were beginning to get a name for themselves and their tenacity toward finding safe ways to provide entertainment to their fans. They produced virtual and outdoor shows, built unique collaborations, and even sold magnets with the proceeds being split among the five theatre companies in Sioux Falls. These efforts did not go unnoticed. They won the "Hey Sioux Falls Award" for Best Pivot of the Year and received the Sioux Falls Arts Council's "Innovative Project Award."

As vaccine numbers began to rise, and performers and artists around the world began sharing their innovative ways of continuing to create, every one of these theatre companies found ways to create again.

As I write this, the pandemic is far from over, and all of these companies are still facing uncertainty about what the future has in store. One thing is certain, though, the theatre community in Sioux Falls is resilient. It's chock-full of creatives who never back away from a challenge and who come together to overcome obstacles.

Though this essay features five of the most prominent theatre companies in Sioux Falls, many other organizations have made their presence known in the entertainment sector over the past several years. LiRa Dance Theatre is a professional dance troupe that performs one feature dance show each year. Improv Falls and Basement Dwellers Improv perform improvisational theatre. Augustana University and the University of Sioux Falls both have thriving theatre departments. The Dakota Academy of Performing Arts at the Washington Pavilion has been educating the youth of Sioux Falls and the surrounding area in the theatre arts for over twenty years.

Sioux Falls has always been a big little city. Lately, that little city has been building a big little theatre community with more stories to come.

Seney Island

JONATHAN ELLIS

On a cold, windy Saturday on October 30, 2004, Sioux Falls Mayor Dave Munson held a ribbon cutting commemorating the opening of "Phillips to the Falls." The ceremony marked the final achievement that generations of city residents had strived for: a park and direct access from downtown to the scenic falls of the Big Sioux River. Munson, who had personally negotiated with BNSF Railway CEO Matthew Rose about moving its operations from the area so that Phillips Avenue could be extended, acknowledged the collective effort that it had taken to get to this moment.

"We're all here today as part of a historic moment," he said. "It's going to be something that we'll reflect on. We'll forget about the wind and being cold here today and will reflect on the fact that we saw the beginning of a transformation of this part of the downtown area of Sioux Falls."

Not far from where Munson spoke near Fifth Street and Phillips Avenue was a piece of land that had once been the city's oasis—an island on the west side of the Big Sioux River.

Known originally as Brookings Island (after Wilmot Brookings, whose Western Town Company had claimed 320 acres of land along the falls and Big Sioux River in 1856), the island later became known as Seney Island after a wealthy New York banker, George Seney. He invested in the Queen Bee Mill, buying land along the falls, including the island that would bear his name.

A channel of water that jutted northwest from the main channel of the Big Sioux before reconnecting with the river at the falls formed what was a ten-acre, wooded island with a grassy spot at its center. As settlers built Sioux Falls in the late 1800s, Seney Island became the city's retreat. It hosted picnics, band concerts, speeches, and all types of events, allowing pioneers a relaxing, scenic spot to luxuriate. Charles A. Smith, author of *Comprehensive History of Minnehaha County* (1949), described it as the "Town Hall of its time." He further added, "It was surrounded in springtime by the turbulent waters that started their rapid descent over the rocky ledges to the lower river bed some 200 feet below. Here, in profusion, budded the flora indigenous to the western streams and undulating prairies—great trees, ferns and tall rose bushes that towered above the grassy spot in its center."

It was, of course, a natural park for the budding new city. In the spring of 1887, Methodist leaders in the state proposed a plan to jointly acquire the island with the city and transform it into a summer resort that would serve as a park. The *Argus Leader* mightily approved and was already cross that the city's business community had failed to act on a proposal from the same Methodist reverends two years earlier, who had proposed establishing a Methodist college in Sioux Falls. Because of lackluster support in the city's business community, the college was established in Mitchell. A park at Seney Island, the paper concluded, would be a boon for Sioux Falls.

"Surely the city stands to do whatever is generous and fair to secure this institution. It is not putting it too strongly to say that if this summer resort is established here, it will be equal to having another railroad built into this city."

But the asking price, $10,000—$1,000 an acre—proved to be too high. The *Argus Leader* was still optimistic that a deal could be reached. In May 1887, George Seney visited the city, and later that year, two representatives of the city—Judge Brookings and the Rev. Hartsough—visited Seney in New York about acquiring the island, but no deal could be made. Although Seney Island boosters couldn't consummate a deal, the island continued to be used by the community. The 1894 Independence Day celebration was typical: a parade weaved through the city streets, ending at the island, where there was singing, including "The Star-Spangled Banner," the reading of the Declaration of Independence and other oratory, band music, and athletic contests. In 1906, the island's new owner, E. W. Coughran, the president of the Sioux Falls Light and Power Company, had a new offer for the city: In exchange for exempting from tax twenty-eight acres of river land that had belonged to the Queen Bee, as well as the revenue generated from the "privileges" at the park from concerts, dances, and other social events, which amounted to between $500 and $800 a year, the city could use Seney Island as a park.

After much debate, the city's aldermen voted to accept part of the offer—the tax rebate. At a subsequent meeting, they learned the rebate they thought they'd voted for was only half a year's taxes. After that, they walked away from the deal. The next year proved to be the beginning of the end for Seney Island. The 1907 legislature reformed the state's water laws, and the Sioux Falls Light and Power Company moved quickly to harness the power of the Falls into a source of electricity. Work began that fall to build a dam above the island and retaining walls that funneled the river's water into a

600-foot-long penstock that channeled the river water into a powerhouse with three turbines capable of generating electricity.

The retaining wall on the western side of the Big Sioux effectively sealed off the channel that had made Seney Island an island. Its loss was offset by a large jump into modernity, however, with electricity now available to power streetcars and factories. The October 24, 1908, edition of the *Commercial West*, a grain and finance industry newspaper, heralded the new electrical power in Sioux Falls:

> At last the falls of the Big Sioux River at this city have been brought under control; at last the waters are flowing through a huge penstock with turbines at the lower end, and electricity equaling several thousand horsepower is being developed; and at last the hopes and dreams of the old settlers of Sioux Falls are realized, after thirty-five years or more of waiting. For there are citizens here today who have waited many years for someone with capital, energy, inclination and the confidence to come along and properly develop this great water power, mostly going to waste.

As the *Argus Leader* proclaimed, "Power for a Half Hundred Factories." The decision to harness the river for water sealed Seney Island's fate. The effort to gain control of the island, or what was now called the island, didn't end. In 1909, Coughran went to the city's equalization board to complain about the taxes on Seney Island, which had been assessed at $200 an acre, claiming the island was not worth that sum. Commissioner Edwin Sherman challenged Coughran to sign the deed for Seney Island and he would pay $200 an acre. Coughran walked out of the meeting. A year later, Coughran's real estate company, the Equitable Realty Company, granted a perpetual easement to the Milwaukee Railroad Company for land in the area. The railroad company gained control over portions of land around what had been the island and began filling in the channel that had separated Seney Island from the mainland. While social events continued to take place, Seney Island began to take on a new character. A June 1, 1914, *Argus Leader* headline summed up that new character: "Police Chase Vags off Seney Island: Department Starts Cleanup on the Notorious Loafing Place of Rough Element." Still, the nostalgia of Seney Island wasn't lost. In 1921, the Young Men's Booster Club supported a proposal to clean it up and create an outdoor swimming area above the falls. The idea was endorsed by several prominent residents, as well as the

Federated Club of Women. While nothing came of these endorsements, the *Argus Leader* editorial board agreed: "When we get a breathing spell, the city must add Seney Island to its holdings and develop that as a fully policed and very beautiful breathing spot for the northern part of the city." But less than two years later, the city's paper of record changed tack, and there was one reason. The Milwaukee Railroad Company had asked the city to vacate several blocks of streets and alleys on North Phillips Avenue and Second Street to expand its operations, and that was favored by the city's business community. It would mean the end of Seney Island.

The Milwaukee's proposal evoked a backlash among those who wanted to save Seney Island, and after the city council voted to vacate the roadways to the Milwaukee, the pro-Seney Island people sought to refer the issue to a public vote. The *Argus Leader* published numerous testimonies about how bad Seney Island had degenerated. The channel that had once separated the island had become a town dump, and the only people who went to the island now were criminals and prostitutes. George L. Hoffman, a nearly forty-year resident, wrote a long letter reminiscing about the island's glories. Besides city residents enjoying the island's natural wonders, farm families from outside the city would visit: "Shade trees on the farm, at that early date were rare indeed and so it was always a great treat to come to town and spend a few hours on the island and, for the time being, forget about the shadeless shanty and sun-browned prairies."

Hoffman then described a recent visit, writing that what he saw, coupled with his memories of the place, was enough to make a strong man weep. The shade trees were gone and what Hoffman found was a dump: "Every disgusting and disease breeding thing can be found there, strewn three and four feet deep over nearly the entire island and extending south to within less than a block to one of our most prized institutions, the Manchester Biscuit Co. Carcasses of dead dogs and parts of other dead animals, decayed fruit by the wagon load and every kind of refuse and rubbish that the human mind can possibly conceive." As opponents of the Milwaukee proposal collected signatures to refer it to a vote, the *Argus Leader* greeted them with a snarky editorial:

> After several weeks of agitation and comment on the Milwaukee terminal proposition, a "mass" meeting was held in the auditorium and 55 citizens voted against the proposal. This would not appear on the surface to be a great outpouring of indignant citizens bent on saving the scenic beauties of Seney Island—the historic home

> of the hobo and the tin can. And isn't it astonishing how beautiful that wonderful resort has become—all of a sudden.

When the Seney Island proponents filed enough signatures to force a vote, the Milwaukee supporters filed a lawsuit, alleging that two of the referendum sponsors who had collected signatures were invalid because one was a convicted felon and the other not a US citizen. The issue was finally resolved in 1926 at the South Dakota Supreme Court, which ruled that a vote on the referendum would go forward.

That vote, on April 20, 1926, resulted in a victory for the Milwaukee Railroad Company. A majority of voters agreed to vacate the city blocks to the railroad company, and Seney Island disappeared. Soon, it went from being a cherished nature preserve to a malevolent entity. People complained about burning rubber gas emanating from the former island, as well as crime and prostitution.

Even the name got bastardized. The majority of references to the island in the 1930s started adding an extra *e* to the name, Seeney, including the Depression-era book on South Dakota from the Works Progress Administration, *The WPA Guide to South Dakota.*

But as the decades passed, the *Argus Leader* looked back on the glories of the island before modernity arrived, without acknowledging its own perfidy. In a 1955 reflection, Lucia Watson, a settler who arrived in 1878, remembered the island as a favorite gathering place for all public events. Jesse Harrington, another early settler, recalled that for many years, a cannon was mounted facing north and that it was fired every Fourth of July. The island also included a "large bowery dance hall."

At some point in the collective memory, Seney Island became a public park that had been turned over to industry rather than having always been privately owned. In 1961, Earl McCart campaigned for the city commission on a platform of bringing back Seney Island and the falls as a city park. He reflected on his boyhood, remembering how glorious the area had been. In 1972, McCart tried to make good on his campaign promise: he supported a resolution from the city's Parks and Recreation board to condemn land owned by the Sioux Steel Company, one of the many industrial firms that was located near the falls at the turn of the century, and the Milwaukee Railroad Company. The goal of the resolution was to restore a city park that had never truly existed. But Ted Woods, a lawyer for Sioux Steel, explained to the commission that the city had never owned the land that had once been Seney Island. The city backed down. Shortly after winning election as the first "strong mayor" of Sioux Falls in 1994, Gary Hanson's administration put together a plan to wipe away everything in Falls Park and rebuild the park, including Seney Island. But as restoration began, they started finding hulks of burned-out railcars, garbage, and polluted soils. The Environmental Protection Agency told the city to cap the area.

"We were told, 'Don't dig, because you're going to find more items you're going to have to deal with,'" he said. So the city capped much of the land that had been the most popular retreat in the city's early decades with clay to seal in more than a century's worth of pollution and debris.

"I would have loved to have had Seney Island," Hanson said.

Culinary Sioux Falls

CHRIS MADSEN

"Tell me what you eat, and I will tell you who you are."
—Jean Anthelme Brillat-Savarin

Food, in one form or another, has historically been big business in Sioux Falls. It wouldn't be much of a stretch to say food put Sioux Falls on the map. As home to Smithfield Foods, formerly John Morrell & Company, Sioux Falls puts a lot of hams on holiday tables. Other industries, notably financial services and health care, have played a substantial role in keeping Sioux Falls on the map and enlarging the city's footprint and influence. Yet food remains as relevant as ever because this town loves to eat.

The menu, however, tells a story about the community.

It is not much of a stretch to say Sioux Falls, like most small cities in the area, was not a particularly diverse community in terms of race or economics. That's not a criticism; it's a statement of fact. You just need to look no further than what was on the menu. Dining out, as opposed to grabbing fast food, usually meant a sit-down restaurant where the adults smoked at the table. The food—probably burgers, fried chicken, a hot roast beef sandwich, or a BLT—was served on heavy plates. Huge salads of iceberg lettuce served in stainless-steel mixing bowls with hard boiled eggs and sliced cold cuts and cheese, all drenched in Thousand Island dressing was considered "diet" food. You got a drink, not a liter-sized cup and unfettered access to the soda dispenser. Dessert choices lived in a rotating glass cabinet near the host stand, where there were also Andes Mints or York Peppermint Patties available for a nickel, if you could panhandle one from a parent.

The food landscape was also dotted with some "ethnic" places to eat. Pizza was considered "Italian," and chances are, enjoying one was a sit-down affair. "Chinese" meant egg drop soup, fried wontons, General Tso's chicken (or any stir-fried thing involving little ears of corn in a gloppy sauce), and fortune cookies. "Mexican" meant Taco John's, Taco Bell, or Chi Chi's. If you were really lucky, you could find a smorgasbord (aka a buffet) and overindulge in any or all of the above.

A fancy night out probably involved a relish tray on the table, a trip through a salad bar, a hunk of beef, a big baked potato with sour cream and butter served in little pats, and a blended boozy ice cream drink for dessert. Fortunately, in those sorts of joints, the Andes Mints were gratis.

None of the food most of us knew as kids was bad. It was what it was. But Sioux Falls was on the brink of big changes because lurking just over the horizon were tremendous opportunities in the financial services and health care industries that would soon turn a big town into a medium metropolitan community. The food scene and how the community approached eating out was about to change.

Two things signified these changes. The first was the opening of Champps Americana at the Western Mall. By the late 1980s, long before becoming home to a few popular big box stores, the Western Mall was the retail equivalent of the Island of Misfit Toys compared to the Empire Mall down the street. Then, seemingly out of nowhere (well, actually the Twin Cities), along comes this kind of sports bar/restaurant/open-kitchen concept. Bartenders served ice cold beer in huge twenty-two-ounce glasses across a polished hardwood bar. Champps offered diners an exhaustive array of pasta, burgers, sandwiches, appetizers (including spicy wings), and all the other things we see everywhere today. The portions were nothing short of gargantuan. Even the serving plates and utensils were upsized. We all got a little upsized too, but that's another story. The place was usually packed, and we would happily wait in line.

The coming of Theo's at Thirty-Third and Spring was the second seminal event. Located in a former seafood restaurant, Theo's had a couple things going for it. Like Champps, the bar area hopped. The who's who of Sioux Falls bellied up for happy hour at Theo's. And the food, under Chef Dominique Fontenelle, was quite a bit, well, *foodier* than what people were used to seeing on their plates. Theo's had the standard filet mignon on the menu. What stands out, however, are memories of pasta dyed black with squid ink. That sort of thing tends to make an impression, and Theo's most certainly made its mark on the local scene.

Dining out in Sioux Falls became more than a convenience; it became a full-fledged form of entertainment. And just as people would stand in line to make last call at Nite City, they'd stand in line to get a 5,000-calorie bowl of fettucine alfredo. Champps and Theo's are now only memories, but their legacies and impact live on.

Today, more than anything, the Sioux Falls diner hungers for what's next. The grand openings of new eateries, including certain fast-food franchises are met with nearly the same enthusiasm as a major concert announcement, and about as many attendees. When the city's first Popeye's franchise opened on East Tenth Street (on the exact same spot as the former Pizza Inn), traffic backed up for blocks as devotees mobbed the drive-through. Fortunately, for commuters on West Forty-First Street, the long-deprived fans of Chick-Fil-A can now line up their vehicles in the Empire parking lot as they await their turn for chicken strips or a sandwich.

A craving for franchise food is a definite hallmark of today's Sioux Falls food scene. It is relatively fast and easy to travel around the region to places like Omaha, Kansas City, and Minneapolis-St. Paul for short trips. It's in places like that where many Sioux Falls locals get exposed to the likes of Cheesecake Factory, Chipotle, Chick-Fil-A, Jersey Mike's, and P. F. Chang's. One bite of these forbidden fruits and diners will trade their immortal souls for a foil-wrapped burrito and free guacamole. And when some of these franchise joints eventually make it here, they get mobbed for weeks straight, and then fold right into the larger food landscape. This cycle repeats itself often and is seemingly only limited by the availability of liquor licenses. (A word to the wise eyeing the Sioux Falls market, however: good service and good product are baseline requirements. Fail in either category, and diners will go elsewhere.)

Sioux Falls also has a penchant for casual bar-and-grill-type places that all seem to offer chicken wings, burgers, wraps, pasta, salads, and flatbread pizza. In other words, the legacy of Champps lives on. Our appetite for this now ubiquitous menu is apparently insatiable.

Fortunately, Sioux Falls has an appetite for more adventure than chicken strips. Some midwesterners like to celebrate their cultural roots by gathering in the basement of Lutheran churches in the dead of winter to eat cod that has been dried and reconstituted, in a process involving lye, until the protein structures are denatured to the point where a fishy, thick, Vaseline-like substance remains. No thanks. Keep the lutefisk. Pass the aquavit, please! Some of these folks swore they wouldn't be caught dead eating raw fish, but that changed in a hurry. Sioux Falls now supports about a half dozen restaurants offering sushi. Local grocery stores sell it too. And, indeed, thanks to the miracles of modern logistics, a diner can visit a place like Sushi Masa and enjoy fish as fresh and skillfully prepared as one might expect in San Francisco, or even Osaka.

As the world has become a smaller but no less troubled place, Sioux Falls is now home to many immigrants seeking a safer, if not better, way of life. The community is far more diverse than it was in 1990. In 2020, Sioux Falls School District students spoke ninety different languages. Nevertheless, as a wise parish priest once observed, "Everyone has to eat!" And nothing gives people of different backgrounds and cultures the opportunity to learn from each other like sharing a meal.

Even in the 1980s, any foods from south of Texas was dubbed "Mexican." Fortunately, the use of such ill-fitting and improper labels is on the decline. Chi Chi's closed and most of us recognize Taco John's as a regional favorite, but it's about as Mexican as Cheyenne, Wyoming. Instead, we can visit places like Inca, Puerto Vallarta, Azteca, Giliberto's, and Jacky's for dishes much more faithful to the authentic flavors of Latin America. If you want to know if you're at such a place, you won't need to brush up on Spanish. Just look for big pickups in the parking lot bringing hungry work crews to lunch. Look around. Have what they're having.

We are also seeing the same diversification when it comes to Asian cuisine. Notably, there are a growing number of places where you can enjoy the pleasures and nuanced flavors of other cuisines of southeast Asia. Several restaurants specialize in Vietnamese cuisine. The aptly named Phnom Penh on North Minnesota Avenue offers Cambodian dishes. Yummy House and Lao Szechuan have huge menus that offer Chinese dishes that go far beyond stir-fried chicken and vegetables in a brown sauce. Thai is finally starting to find an eager audience in the area.

Of course, Asia is far more than southeast Asia. The vast continent includes India and Nepal, which offer heady curries and other dishes with seemingly unending depths of flavor. Diners will also find various offerings of "Mediterranean," which around here is code for flavors of the Middle East. Syria and Lebanon both border the Mediterranean. All of these flavors are stunningly bright and are often vegetarian or vegan. If you don't believe a meatless meal can light up your palate like a pinball machine, go visit Sanaa Abourezk at Sanaa's Gourmet. Or try the eggplant bouranee at Khorasan Kabob House. It will change your life, or at least your feelings toward eggplant.

Sioux Falls has also become home to a number of Africans from countries such as Sudan, Eritrea, and Ethiopia. In the coming years, expect more African cuisine. If you want to enjoy the flavors and fun now, visit places like Lalibela to tear off a chunk of spongy injera to dip into a huge communal platter of savory stewed meats and vegetables. Wash it down with ice cold Meta beer. It may take time to get used to using injera instead of a fork, but the flavors and love in the food will speak to you.

And, of course, where people want to eat, cooks will appear, and we have been lucky enough to attract some great culinary talent. Chefs are learning that Sioux Falls has a great appetite for all sorts of things, and we are ready to blur some lines and enjoy great flavors. Indeed, we've been fortunate enough to attract world-class culinary talent. Remember that edible *objet d'art* you enjoyed at a little place in Paris? You might find the same thing, or a pastry just as delicious and beautiful, at CJ Patisserie downtown. Or visit Queen City Bakery for a quiche and try not to leave with a whole cake. If your Instagram page needs a food-porn infusion, check out the highly stylized dishes at Harvester Kitchen.

And, of course, old favorites like Minerva's, Gregg's Substation, Rosie's Café, and others are all around if you want a heaping side of nostalgia with your meal.

To paraphrase Brillat-Savarin, if a city is what it eats, the Sioux Falls menu looks good. Sometimes, the town can seem a little set in its ways, but we're always hungry for what's next.

Pettigrew

TOM DEMPSTER

Perhaps it's time to forgive Senator Richard Frank Pettigrew. He might even ask for it.

His statue seems to lord over the Levitt at Falls Park West, almost as if it owns the park and everything around it. Truth is, Pettigrew once pretty much did.

He first came to Sioux Falls seven years after the evacuation order by Governor William Jayne that emptied the Dakota Territory village. Judge Amidon's son had been found riddled with over a dozen arrows, and the judge himself was shot dead on the hilltop overlooking Sioux Falls. The Dakota Indian War of 1862 would leave its blood in the marrow of South Dakota history, marked by the mutilated bodies of Minnesota settlers and the hanging of thirty-nine Santee Sioux in Mankato, Minnesota—the largest mass execution in the history of the United States. The Wounded Knee massacre was to come twenty years after Pettigrew first set foot in Sioux Falls.

Bill Hoskins, director of the Siouxland Heritage Museum, told the story of Pettigrew on SDPB's *In the Moment*. Another pioneer, Nye Phillips, roomed with Pettigrew in the barracks of Fort Dakota. Nye Phillips, said Hoskins, did all the cooking and would wash the frying pan out with his trousers. Finally, as the weather turned colder and the grease-laden trousers stiffened, Phillips just left them standing by themselves under a tree. Phillips (though not the Phillips of Phillips Avenue) was to become the register of deeds, a village trustee, a city alderman, and the Minnehaha County sheriff.

Pettigrew came to Dakota Territory with the eye and temperament of a surveyor, one whose feet and instruments surveyed not only the minutes and seconds of latitude and longitude but also the soon to explode values of land in a village that was to become a city. This was especially true if Sioux Falls acquired a railroad, and with Pettigrew's initiative, it finally did in 1878.

Pettigrew's real estate legacy is everywhere. Augustana University rests partially on land donated by Pettigrew. Flandreau was founded by Pettigrew and his brother. Go to Granite, Iowa, just minutes away from Blood Run, and again, Pettigrew is there. But the tract of land that is most of Pettigrew legend is the 160 acres he bought in what was to become the Knob Hill of Sioux Falls, the historic district, the Cathedral Heights.

Real estate titles, abstracts, deeds, and mortgages are all intricate documents—documents that attest to ownership and encumbrances on land as they pass from one owner to another. And different types of landowners sometimes have different requirements in order to establish a title that is clear of any cloud or encumbrances. Pettigrew became increasingly worried that he, in fact, did not have a clear title to his 160-acre plot overlooking downtown Sioux Falls. Another claimed the land due to this sense of muddled ownership. A simple document would clear the matter. Pettigrew just needed to get a signature from a previous owner or heir and file it at the Register of Deeds Office in Sioux Falls. Once filed, the title would be clear. A race ensued. Pettigrew, in haste, traveled to Minneapolis and secured the necessary signature, as did the other man. Both were on the train headed to Sioux Falls, both with the document that, once filed, would give him clear title to the land. Pettigrew's solution? He knew the conductor, who had purchased land in the tract. Pettigrew boarded the locomotive, the conductor unhooked the passenger car in Valley Springs, and off to the register of deeds traveled Pettigrew in the locomotive, leaving the passenger car stranded behind. Pettigrew won the race and filed the document. Stories of this conquest were carried nationwide with Pettigrew "as a western cowboy, wearing a buckskin coat, a broad-rimmed hat and two revolvers and a belt full of cartridges, pulling the pin uncoupling the locomotive" (Fanebust 97).

One can only smile here, and marvel at Pettigrew's panache.

Wayne Fanebust, in *Echoes of November*, a biography of Pettigrew, tells the story of Pettigrew's travels to the Black Hills. In one especially rich trip, Pettigrew and his fellow travelers got to Deadwood in their nine passenger, six-horse stagecoach only after Pettigrew had shot an antelope. Once they were in Deadwood, he hosted an antelope feed. Later in the trip, Pettigrew hiked down Harney Peak and shot a deer. He quartered the deer, carried it down the mountain on his back, and sensed that he was being followed by a mountain lion. He dropped the deer in the hopes the mountain lion would feed on the deer rather than him. He returned the next day to find only the bones of the deer remaining. Later, back in Deadwood, he stood with Seth Bullock on Main Street. A gunfight was happening down the street. A prospector came along and, despite Bullock's warnings, said, "I've got a right to go down that street and I'm going to go." The miner exercised his right and immediately suffered a shot to the head. Today, the epitaph on his grave reads, "He had a right to go down that street."

Following the shooting, Bullock and Pettigrew sidled into a bar and a "young man" by the name of Calamity Jane bought them drinks. Staying at the Welch Hotel, Pettigrew was disturbed by a fight in the hallway and discovered one of the men to be Major Marcus Reno, a survivor of Little Big Horn. But no matter—the hotel was on fire and Pettigrew escaped by kicking out the window in his room. He climbed up the hill to the house of his political friend, Judge G. C. Moody—both of whom would become US Senators. Moody's house is one of the few structures in Deadwood to survive the fire of 1879. The next morning, Pettigrew found a still-standing saloon and saw George Hearst drunk and celebrating the recent purchase of a gold mine.

On still another trip, this one as part of Pettigrew's campaign for Dakota Territory delegate to Congress, his stagecoach was held up by a gunman close to Buffalo Gap. The passengers were ordered out, recounts biographer Fanebust. Believing he recognized the thief, and with a gun pointed at him, Pettigrew whispered in his ear, "Kemsley, what am I to tell your mother?" Here, too, Pettigrew is a man of substance, of courage, of good humor, a man of the prairie, a pioneer, a man who could kill and dress a deer, a man who can take life as it comes.

Darwin Wolf's statue of Pettigrew has him facing southwest, as if looking at his real estate holdings throughout Sioux Falls: Knob Hill, his office building on Phillips. But turn the statue around and Richard Frank Pettigrew would be looking at the ruins of the Queen Bee Mill. He brought railroads to Sioux Falls and attracted investors and gilded capital. He was an entrepreneur, a one-man economic development machine. Most of his plans didn't succeed, and during the hard times, during banking panics and the recessions of the late 1800s, Pettigrew's investments, his speculations, turned to ruin—as did the Queen Bee Mill.

At the age of twenty-seven, Pettigrew was elected to the Dakota Territory legislature. He was then elected as Dakota Territory representative to Congress and finally, along with his Deadwood friend Judge Moody, to the US Senate. A "people's candidate" to his friends, he was "a gambler and whiskey gurgler" to his enemies. He was dubbed "the Pickeral Statesman" because if you have ever caught and tried to land a northern pike, you'd understand Senator Richard Frank Pettigrew. A northern pike, a predator fish, hits a fishing lure hard, and once caught, it twists and dives with astonishing ferocity, its jaw lined with rows of over 300 to 500 razor-sharp teeth. Pettigrew had come to Sioux Falls and was instrumental in who and what the city was to become; he had come to Dakota and was instrumental in who and what the territory and state was to become.

Senator Pettigrew—shrewd, smart, and aggressive—could also be imprudent and intemperate. But that doesn't mean he wasn't right. Years before John Meynard Keynes, he knew viscerally the importance of an expanding money supply for an expanding country. He knew the chokehold of railroad trusts, he believed in the direct election of the US Senate, and he believed in the initiative and referendum. He spoke against the Spanish-American War, spoke against the annexation of Hawaii, and spoke against the gold standard. In his second term in the US Senate, he walked out of the Republican convention, effectively leaving the Republican party. And when it came time for his reelection, the Republican Party left him. The South Dakota legislature, in an era when US Senators were elected by state legislators, turned him aside. Pettigrew, likely in agony, had no choice but to stand his ground and suffer the consequences.

Twenty-two years after Pettigrew left the US Senate, he wrote *Imperial Washington*. In it, presidents are imbeciles, Senators are dishonest bribe-takers, and the US Supreme Court has no power to review acts of Congress. In his chapter entitled "Capitalism," Pettigrew writes, "The leisure class, having nothing better to do, play at ducks and drakes with international affairs, plunges the country into economic and military conflicts, heaps up great debts, and wastes its own and the country's resources while the workers do the mass-fighting, pay the taxes, and suffer from starvation and disease." Wayne Fanebust talks about Pettigrew interpreting the Russian Revolution as being the most meaningful human event of his time. Fanebust states that Pettigrew wrote to both Lenin and Leon Trotsky, requesting copies of their books in Russian. He called Lenin "the greatest man who ever lived."

Political lives are inherently tragic because they bear the grief between what is and what should be, between what we dream or pray ourselves to be and the hardness of what we really are. Perhaps that's the meaning of the distance between the three-ton prayer rock and the eighty-inch round concretion marking the entrance of the Pettigrew Home and Museum. Perhaps too that is the meaning of the framed Declaration of Independence hanging next to Pettigrew's federal indictment of the Espionage Act of 1917. Pettigrew was charged with "attempting to obstruct the selective draft and making anti-war utterances." He was arrested and the next day posted $5,000 in bail (*New York Times*, Nov 15, 1917).

Pettigrew's will dictated that the two must forever hang together in his museum, the distance between our dreams of ourselves and our reality. One can almost feel, as reported in the *New York Times* of April 15, 1918, the crowd that "daubed the offices of Richard Frank Pettigrew with yellow paint." Pettigrew's bust and portrait inhabit the front living room of his home and museum. His presence in the room is tangible. So too is Pettigrew's legacy as a pioneer, an entrepreneur, South Dakota's first US Senator, a man of immense energy, passion, courage, and controversy.

Falls Park

MARTY MCGOEY

> I love Dakota more and more—
> Her prairies vast, her mines of ore—
> I love her mountains and her glades,
> But most her beautiful cascades.
>
> —poem published in *American Miller*, 1880

All water has a voice. Whether it is moving or still, water calls to us. Many communities are built because of water at the confluence of rivers, on gulfs or bays, or where rivers meet larger bodies, be they oceans or lakes. The functional purpose for building on water is for the faster and easier transportation of goods, but I think water also beckons to us. We are drawn toward it, maybe out of respect for the past and the ancestors who crossed over it, maybe because we are biologically mostly water, or maybe because we are thirsty and water brings life? Perhaps it's due to religious connections with baptism, Noah's ark, and Moses's infant journey down the Nile? It could also be the smell of fresh or saltwater or the play of light on the surface that we can stare at for hours, fishing or just meditating.

Located in the north central part of Sioux Falls, the falls of the Big Sioux, and the city's namesake, offer so many sensory delights of light variations, smells, and sounds. On a pleasant day, people congregate at Falls Park as though it were a kind of church or gathering place. Visiting the park is an obligation for travelers and longtime residents, as it is a place of natural and human history. Calm days with perfect weather can be rare, but when they happen on weekends, you can bet that the park will be filled with people staring at the water, fishing in the Big Sioux, walking dogs, picnicking, and browsing the posted signs that reveal the history of the falls and the city.

The falls were formed thousands of years ago by a melting glacier that poured over bedrock quartzite. Archeological evidence suggests that prior to European exploration, the area around the falls was used as a camp by nomadic hunters who constructed burial mounds nearby. Later came the Oneota, ancestors of the Mandan, a more permanent and agricultural society than the nomads. The Lakota arrived in the area in the eighteenth century to find the mounds and camps as ancient ruins.

Stories of the falls were one of the major draws to the area, long before the rocks in the area were quarried or when the sidewalks of the park were paved. The history of the falls is inextricably tied to the city named for them. A description of the falls by French scientist and explorer Joseph Nicollet—who called them "beautiful and picturesque"—was one of the first draws for town settlers and developers. Local Native tribes called the river "Te-han-Kas-an-data," which translates to "thickly wooded river." It's hard to imagine thick woods on the Big Sioux, even though photographic records prove otherwise. Many other historic photos of the area only miles away from the falls show rolling plains broken only by sparse trees and new buildings built by early residents. Before my research, I'd always imagined the falls as surrounded by tall prairie grass, with the original discoverers drawn to them by the noise of rushing water, hidden somewhere, until they stumbled upon the Big Sioux, not thickly wooded with oaks but scored deep into the sand and soil, like the Platte or parts of the Missouri.

Shortly after the discovery by white explorers, the cascading waters of the Big Sioux became a sought-after piece of property. In 1856, the falls were claimed by the Western Town Company along with 320 acres of land suitable for the development of a small city on the plains. Disappointed that they were too late to lay claim to the falls themselves, the Dakota Land Company founded an adjacent plot of land and called it Sioux Falls City.

Like so many places in the city, the falls were a major focus of one of the city's most influential founders. R. F. Pettigrew saw the promise that real estate in the city held, and with the falls, he saw an opportunity for growth and progress, ideas which led to the building of one of the most prominent structures at the falls: the Queen Bee Mill.

Inspired by the success of other mill towns, especially Minneapolis to the northeast, Pettigrew envisioned similar success for his mill. Construction started in August 1879 with funding by George Seney. The eighty-one-acre site was purchased for $38,000, nearly $1 million in current value. Construction took two years and cost nearly $500,000, or $13 million today. The dimensions of the mill were eighty by one hundred feet, and it was seven stories high. It was said, at the time, to be the tallest structure west of the Mississippi and east of the Rockies. Standing at the base of what are now the ruins of the mill, one can only imagine what it must have been like to work there in the years that it ran. Its workers must have felt swallowed up by the gargantuan structure, and I imagine they would have felt either a strong sense of pride in working in an industrial setting, while not far away, their neighbors and relatives lived in sod houses and farmed open fields. Or maybe the workers felt a kind of doom hanging over them, perhaps a certainty that this industrial complex would be the first of many and would one day be dwarfed by larger mills and endeavors. They worked at the forefront of the industrial West, enhanced and supported by the iron horse and the railyards. The industrial West held the promise of extraction of resources from the land, of ownership, of millions to be spent and millions more to be earned. Over a hundred years later, the CenturyLink Tower in downtown Sioux Falls was built, and, at eleven stories, it is currently the tallest in the city and the state. Nonetheless, one can imagine the site of the Queen Bee Mill as a lone sentinel or a Tower of Babel to industrial progress. At its full capacity, the mill could produce up to 1,200 barrels (235,200 pounds) of wheat per day. In contrast, the Pillsbury A. Mill, built two years later in Minneapolis, was designed to produce 5,000 barrels per day, and it later increased to a potential of 17,500 barrels per day. Compared to Pillsbury, Queen Bee was insignificant, and it never became the powerhouse that Pettigrew had envisioned. The rapids below the falls proved to be too weak to power the mill, and a lack of wheat to grind further complicated things. In 1883, the mill closed and stood as an abandoned tribute to progress for twenty-eight years until it was reopened by the United Flour Milling Company in 1911. The company converted the mill to electric power in 1916, though it again closed that year due to more efficient flour-production methods. Again, the mill fell to the wayside as the industrial world passed it by. Thirteen years later, the mill was opened as a warehouse until it was destroyed by a fire started by a lightning strike in 1956. Seven years later, the ruins and the grounds were donated to the city of Sioux Falls.

As a feature of Falls Park, the ruins serve as a kind of centerpiece in pink quartzite. The ruins are gated but opened every so often in good weather for live music, events, and productions by Bare Bodkins Theatre Company, which performs Shakespeare plays. The builders and mill workers of the Queen Bee Mill could never have expected the outcome of their labor to become a Shakespearean stage. Bare Bodkins has been around since 1997, and so, in only a few years, the mill will have been known longer as a stage, then a warehouse, and then as a mill. Its ruins are portions of the exterior walls, still forming a complete rectangle, though the floorboards have been replaced by grass. The arches and the unevenness of the tops of the walls give it an atmosphere of antiquity, as though they were remnants of a less-documented past built by a king or Caesar himself, which only makes sense that Bare Bodkins would choose this setting as a backdrop for their productions. Like the water, people are also drawn to ruins, the older and more ruined the better so as to give them a chance to fill in and imagine things on their own. The ruins are similar to the much larger ruins at the Pillsbury A. Mill in Minneapolis, which have also been turned into a venue and museum, though I think the Queen Bee ruins are more aesthetically pleasing, as their pink bricks blend so well with the rest of the park and the general aesthetic of downtown and the city's historic buildings, linked together by the same materials. The ruins seem strangely natural here, an extension of the ground, the industry long since swept away by the passage of time.

Though the Queen Bee Mill is probably the most noteworthy building in Falls Park, there were other business ventures as well. In 1883, the Drake Polishing Works was established by James H. Drake, a friend of Pettigrew. The Polishing Works was most notable for polishing petrified wood obtained from Arizona. The company gained notoriety for having several works in the St. Louis World's Fair of 1904. Some of this polished petrified wood can even be seen in the entrance to Woodlawn Cemetery in Sioux Falls. Drake Polishing Works lasted until the 1940s, when it ceased production. The current visitor center in Falls Park now stands in its place.

Drake also built the smaller Cascade Mill at the falls in 1883, which was fitted with an electrical generator in 1887—a precursor to the larger Sioux Falls Light and Power Building, which was built in 1908—which powered the city's electric streetcars and streetlights. The Cascade Mill is gone, but the pink quartzite of the Sioux Falls Light and Power building is still intact and now houses the charming Falls Overlook Café, a prominent feature of the park.

The construction of so much industry was not without cost. Seney Island was one of these casualties. The former island was a popular place for picnickers and was filled with trees. Seney Island could very well have been the site where Joseph Nicollet viewed and described the falls, which helped lead to the city's development. This "birthplace" of the city became a dumping ground for trash (encouraged by the railyard) until an entire channel was filled in and the island became part of the shoreline. Afterward, the rail companies built tracks on the new shore. While the Minnehaha County Historical Society tried to save the island with an appeal to the mayor, he scoffed and said, "It would be a hangout for bums."

Ironically, Falls Park would later become entirely a hangout spot for outcasts. While the city owned the land, the park fell into disuse and became overgrown in the late 1960s when it acquired the name "Hobo

Road." It's hard to stand at the foot of the falls now and imagine them overgrown and surging with pollution, but that was the reality until the mid-1990s when the restoration of the park began on the orders of Mayor Gary Hanson. The sidewalks and visitor center were constructed in 1999, and the park was mostly transformed into its current appearance. Now there are current talks of a makeover, and not unlike the historical competitions by developers, companies are once again competing for designs and bids, though this time to win the contract for the makeover.

Anyone who has spent time in Sioux Falls has an anecdote they remember with fondness, whether it be graduation photos, marriage proposals, or family drives through the park when it glows with Christmas lights. My favorite memory of the park will always be crossing the bridge with my wife on a cold day in January. When the temperature turns subarctic, the park is almost always empty, and that day, we were alone. I always carry a hat and gloves with me tucked away in my winter coat, but my wife had neither. I offered both, but she said no, so I cupped my gloved hands over her ears and we moved slowly over the bridge—our little bridge—looking at our little frozen trickle on the Big Sioux, at least for this moment, until the air started to sting our lungs and we made it back to the car. The entire visit lasted ten minutes, and she asked me later in the car why I'd even bothered. I gave her my canned midwestern answer that it was "something to do" but that I've also always loved watching the falls.

The Big Sioux and the river of time have made Falls Park a place of constant change. From their carving by the glaciers in prehistory, to the mound-building hunters, the agricultural Oneota, the Lakota, the European explorers, the developers, the industrialists, the displaced, and now the tourists and citizens seeking respite on a pleasant day, the falls can be seen as the cascading heart of the community, its blood being both the waters of the Big Sioux and the visitors here. Its presence in Sioux Falls cannot be denied as it is the city's namesake, and the pink quartzite here can be found throughout the city in buildings on Phillips Avenue, in the Old Courthouse Museum, and in the prison walls, which were quarried by the prisoners themselves. The river is no longer thickly wooded, but it is thickly peopled, and a pleasant day in this heart of the city will never fail to lure visitors.

Sources

Bragstad, Reuben. *Sioux Falls in Retrospect.* Privately printed, 1967.

"Falls Park: A KELOLAND.com Original." KELOLAND.com, 2021.

Milton, John. *South Dakota: A Bicentennial History*. W.W. Norton, 1977.

A New South Dakota History, Second Edition. Harry F. Thompson, editor. The Center for Western Studies, 2009.

Rambow, Dave. *The Falls of the Big Sioux River*. Siouxland Heritage Museums, 1999.

Smith, Charles A. *Minnehaha County History*. Educator Supply Company, 1949.

South Dakota's Main Street

JOHN KENNEDY CLAUSSEN SR.

Some people are fortunate to have been raised in an intriguing setting. It may be near an ocean, on the prairie with waving grains, or perhaps in the mountains. For me, it was just a few blocks from County Highway 148, which over time became Forty-First Street and the new heart of Sioux Falls as shopping downtown waned.

It's an area Jesse James, Charles Lindbergh, and John Dillinger all once graced. Perhaps these men were signs of things to come with this street's importance. Jesse James and his band held up a stagecoach on the Yankton Trail where it traversed what is now Jefferson Park—just a few hundred feet north of Forty-First. In August 1927, Lindbergh landed his plane at the Soo Skyways Airport on the south side of Forty-First—between what are Western and Kiwanis Avenues today. Seven years later, John Dillinger crossed Forty-First after he and his gang robbed a Sioux Falls bank of $46,000 and headed south in a green Packard.

All of this history I learned later in life, while as a child I thought about the Natives and buffalo that once traversed my home's yard. What I really didn't understand was the growth I was witnessing as a child just south of my home on Elmwood Avenue—that was just two blocks north of Forty-First—would shape my life as well as the city I grew up in.

One of my first true memories of Forty-First Street would have been in the summer of 1966, when heavy rain flooded that street's ditches. Yes, Forty-First once had ditches. I remember a hoard of people walking down to the county road to see the standing water, and we even watched a boy canoe the future Forty-First along the ditches. I also witnessed the last harvest along Forty-First as a farmer gathered his last bounty. My mother informed me that it would be the last gathering of crops because a new shopping center called the Western Mall would soon be built there—the Park Ridge of its time. In just a few years, the canoe, rain, and crops would give way to traffic due to the Western Mall and complementing places like one of the very first Here's Johnny restaurants (founded by Johnny Carson), an A&W with its iconic dome, a Bonanza Steakhouse, an Earl May's Garden Center, new car dealerships, the Western Mall Theaters, a Shakey's Pizza where you could watch them flip the dough, and one of the first 7-Elevens in town with an adjoining Coney Island hot dog shop. Big elm trees and a chicken coup on Forty-First were replaced by Village Inn Pizza, which became my first job in high school. There was a malt shop, too, whose name eludes me, but I remember walking the ditches to that shop with my older sister who had a friend that worked there.

There were gas stations like Standard Oil, Phillips 66, DX, and Husky. The first tacos came to Sioux Falls in 1971 with the arrival of Taco John's on Forty-First. The Western Mall had an actual firetruck on display at Lavergne's Junior Shoes. Church's Chicken made a brief appearance, although most don't remember it, where Sheldon Avenue and Plaza Forty-One are now. Montgomery Ward in the Western Mall became a mecca for me as a nine-year-old checking out the latest mini-bikes on sale. Incidentally, the old MW door handles can still be found on what is now Graham Tires. One of the twin apartment complexes, one with a Monopoly-piece quality, still stands on Forty-First near Jefferson Avenue. Streets north of Forty-First were still gravel in the late 1960s but with curbs and gutters already installed. I guess they were signs of things to come. As a kid, I also remember buying my first forty-five record at MusicLand in the Western Mall. I believe it was "In the Ghetto" by Elvis. Of course, there was the candy shop, Hubbard's Kupboard, in the mall, too, where I bought not only strings of red licorice but also football and baseball cards of such greats as Namath, Unitas, Crew, and Killebrew. The Del Farm grocery store was where a sixteen-ounce glass bottle Pepsi was either fourteen or sixteen cents (depending upon which clerk rang you up). The liquor store next to the candy shop had a public bottle opener where a kid like me could get their pop opened. I remember summer nights, lying in bed without air-conditioning and listening to the Dan Dugan trucks shift through their gears as they left their station—where Costco is now—as they headed out for I-29. In 1972, Tempo, the Walmart of its day with a Target "red" marketing scheme, had a major fire, which caused them to have a half-off fire sale during the Christmas season. The 7-Eleven during blizzards became the nerve center of survival for cars that could make it there and lines of snowmobiles too.

As Forty-First Street expanded westward beyond the Oxbow area, I remember watching earth movers on a hot and windy June day in 1974. They were gouging out the land for the new Sioux Empire Mall, which would soon dwarf the Western Mall. I also recall a tragic accident in the summer of 1978 between a fire truck and a dump truck during a downpour—it symbolized the hurried pace of growth at all costs. In my lifetime, two new bridges have been built over the Sioux River, and I've seen O'Gorman High School rise on the corner of Forty-First and Kiwanis. In fact, I've watched

Forty-First Street become the busiest street in the entire state. In time, the Empire Mall would become more popular than Mt. Rushmore in terms of visitors. I worked in the Empire Mall, and I remember managers saying that one would have to be "brain dead" not to have a growth in sales due to Forty-First Street and the malls people came to visit from a five state region. But I've also seen—in both May of 1993 and August 2015—the mighty street of my youth narrowed to just a single lane due to torrential rains.

Further west of the Empire Mall was the Penny Addition on the west side of I-29, where an abandoned gas station and restaurant once stood for many years. Let us also not forget the growth of perpendicular streets on Forty-First with names like Louise, Carolyn, Shirley, Madelyn, Terry, and Marion. They are said to have been named for the developer's old girlfriends, but who can know? As growth continued in the 1980s, southwestern Sioux Falls began to experience power outages from time to time. The western part of Forty-First was called Western Heights and later became home to Roosevelt High School and continual growth at the intersection of Tea and Ellis Road.

As Forty-First Street matured, new challenges and changes came to this street. One of the oldest commercial buildings still stands just south of it, on Louise Avenue. Through the years it has been a veterinary clinic, a health clinic for woman, and it is now a sub sandwich shop. In September of 2019, a tornado roared down Forty-First Street and caused substantial damage to the Western Mall region. Protests and even riots at the Empire Mall erupted in the summer of 2020. Ironically, the protesters who walked down Forty-First were unknowingly passing the former sites of such politically incorrect restaurants like Smitty's Pancake House and Sambo's—both places are now long gone. So Forty-First Street has a history of progress and social change as well.

Many of the avenues in my childhood neighborhood were plotted by Senator Richard Pettigrew, and I've heard it explained that because Jefferson, Lincoln, and Garfield were his favorite presidents, that's how the streets got their names. Kiwanis was once called Harvard Street, and Elmwood was once known as New York Avenue. Thus, it was a perfect world for a kid like me, who was named after JFK, to grow up in. In some ways, my innocence was lost on a tragic night in the early 1970s when a horse got lost—yes, there used to be horses and a corral on Forty-First Street—and I remember hearing the echo of a gunshot fired by a police officer. He had to take the animal out of its final agony. Just shortly before this, it was running wild through my neighborhood while I was riding my blue Schwinn Stingray bike. And thus, that terrible echoing ushered in the realities of a new world for me.

Today, Forty-First Street is a path to success for the city. But that old county road of my youth, which is now a busy avenue of progress and growth for a modern Sioux Falls, is still there if you look for it.

City of Hospitals

MARGARET PRESTON

During the late nineteenth century, as emigrants ventured further west, doctors came with them who wanted to set up their own medical practice.[1] What these doctors found was a place where one's reputation and survival could rise or fall on being quick-witted and resourceful.[2] Many of these doctors spent their time trying to convince residents of the benefits of various sanitary practices, including proper waste disposal and the importance of clean water. As immigrants settled on the prairies, doctors would first use horse and buggy and then cars to make house calls; however, as technology improved, doctors would increasingly send their most challenging cases to hospitals. While hospitals were once seen as places for those who could not afford a house call, with improved medical technology, enhanced understanding of sterilization, and increasing knowledge of germ theory and vaccination, the hospital became the center for health care.[3]

In the late nineteenth century, a group of Sioux Falls businessmen, clergy, and doctors met to discuss the creation of a hospital for the city. In the summer of 1894, and with subscriptions from locals of over $3,000, a hospital opened in a house located near Terrace Park. The *Argus Leader* described that all the subscribers and stockholders were Scandinavian but that the hospital would welcome all patients. While South Dakota had only become a state in 1889, Fort Dakota (now downtown Sioux Falls) had been established in 1865, and the *Argus Leader* noted that there had been a "crying need for years for such an institution as this in Sioux Falls." However, the building quickly became too small, and the hospital soon relocated to the larger Cameron House which sat at Tenth and Dakota Avenues.[4]

---

1 See Ken Burns, *Mayo Clinic: Faith, Hope, Science* (2018), https://www.pbs.org/kenburns/the-mayo-clinic/.

2 Volney Steele, *Bleed, Blister and Purge: A History of Medicine on the American Frontier* (Montana: Mountain Press Publishing Co., 2005), 167–9.

3 See Peter Temin, "An Economic History of American Hospitals," in *Health Care in America*, H. E. French III ed. (California: Pacific Research Institute for Public Policy, 1988) 80–81.

4 "Sioux Falls Hospital" *Argus Leader*, August 30, 1894, 5. In addition to the doctors, the hospital's new staff also included two trained nurses from the Lutheran Deaconess Order. In 1899, the Sioux Falls Training School for Nurses was established but would, within twenty years, become integrated into the hospital. See Narcy Recker, *An Institution of Organized Kindness* (Sioux Falls, Sioux Valley Hospital, 1996), 2–5; Gary D. Olson and Erik L. Olson, *Sioux Falls, South Dakota: A Pictorial History* (Virginia: Donning Company, 2003), 77.

The hospital continued to grow, and plans to build a new structure were hatched; in 1900, the hospital's directors purchased land near Nineteenth Street and Minnesota Avenue. Construction began immediately, and that year, Sioux Falls Lutheran Hospital, South Dakota's first community hospital, opened. While the hospital was not formally supported by the Lutheran Church, the name chosen was "to acknowledge the church affiliation of the original organizers, the deaconesses who provided early nursing service and the majority of shareholders."[5] The completed structure could house twenty patients and contained a room that could act both as a surgical or delivery room. However, by 1906, Sioux Falls Lutheran Hospital was still too small for the growing city, and a local woman provided the funding for another hospital.

When Helen McKennan peered out of the window of her Sioux Falls mansion, she viewed the eighty acres that surrounded her home, scenery that Edwin A. Sherman, executor of McKennan's will, described as "unsurpassed."[6] The *Argus Leader's* article was headlined "A Good Woman Gone," and it described her funeral held on October 2, 1906, where Reverend Frank Fox, pastor of First Congregational Church, presided. Fox next described how McKennan wished to leave all that she had to others. First, she desired to offer to Sioux Falls "a place where tired mothers could come with their babies and rest," and thus she left twenty acres for the park. While today McKennan Park still offers shade to all visitors, in the twentieth century, the park was home to the city's first public baseball diamond, pool, and zoo.[7] Ultimately, once distributed, fully half of Helen McKennan's estate, valued at nearly $50,000, went in various ways toward the "betterment" of Sioux Falls, including toward establishing an institution that would provide medical care to the city's neediest citizens.[8]

Over the next few years, there began a search for an organization to establish the hospital. Finally, Roman Catholic Bishop Thomas O'Gorman wrote to Mother Joseph Butler, leader of Aberdeen's Sisters of the

---

5 Recker, *An Institution of Organized Kindness*, 6.

6 "Mrs. M'Kennan Died this P.M." *Argus Leader,* September 29, 1906. Edwin A. Sherman, 1844–1916, fought to ensure that McKennan's will was respected. See Margaret Preston, *A Journey of Faith a Destination of Excellence: Avera McKennan Hospital's First Century of Caring* (Sioux Falls: Avera McKennan Hospital, 2010).

7 A few years after McKennan's death, Sherman followed McKennan's example and donated fifty-three acres, which is today known as Sherman Park. In 1956, the *Argus Leader* announced that Helen McKennan was the "Mother of the City's Parks" because her gift of a park to the city was her idea . . . not Sherman's." See Olson *Sioux Falls, South Dakota*, pp. 9–11, 13, 30–31, 79; Harry F. Thompson, ed., *The New South Dakota History* (Sioux Falls: Pine Hill Press, 2005), pp. 166–7 and 172; Richardson, "McKennan Park Historic District," n.d.; "Dedication of Sherman Park to Sioux Falls" *Argus Leader,* September 4, 1911, and "Mrs. McKennan Was 'Mother' of City Parks" *Argus Leader* June 15, 1956.

8 Mrs. George E. Cox, *First Congregational Church: A Congregation of the United Church of Christ Centennial 1872–1972* (n.p.,1971), located in Caille room, Sioux Falls Main Library. "Hospital for Sioux Falls" *Argus Leader,* October 2, 1906, 1–2. Helen's brother, Artemus, was the recipient of some of her estate.

Presentation of the Blessed Virgin Mary, who, despite the fact that the order was already running hospitals in Aberdeen, Mitchell, and Miles City, Montana, consented for the presentation order to open a fourth hospital in Sioux Falls. The hospital slowly became a reality, and by early 1911, there was great anticipation as the building took shape upon the city's landscape.

The newspaper was able to supply a picture of how the inner workings of the hospital reflected the increasing trend throughout the country to improve the safety and sanitary nature of municipal services. The *Argus Leader* noted that "the building will also be absolutely fireproof and as sanitary as modern ingenuity will make it."[9] The modern amenities included electricity throughout, telephone service, an elevator, a silent signal, and a dumb waiter. All of this would provide Sioux Falls, as the paper noted, with an institution that "will compare with [those in] even larger cities." McKennan Hospital's dedication was set for Sunday, December 17, 1911, and in his opening remarks, Bishop O'Gorman made clear that the hospital would be a place where patients of all faiths and the ministers of those faiths would be welcomed.[10]

Despite another hospital, the need for medical care in Sioux Falls continued to increase, and in response, in 1925, Sioux Falls Lutheran added a three-story addition, which raised the hospital's capacity by another thirty beds. The following year, Sioux Falls Lutheran, which was renamed Sioux Valley Hospital, purchased land near Eighteenth and Grange Avenues and completed its first building in 1930.[11] And yet the demand continued; in response, other facilities opened.

Included among these new facilities was the Moe Hospital. Dr. Anton J. Moe of Minnesota built a small but sophisticated structure on Fourteenth and Main Street that offered a variety of services including surgical, obstetrical, and dental care: "The structure was highly advanced for its time."[12] In 1915, two additional clinics opened in the city. The first, was established by Dr. Goldie E. Zimmerman, the city's first pediatrician and first female doctor.[13] The second was the Donohoe Clinic founded by Drs. S. A. Donahoe and Geoffrey Cottam; it was was originally located on the ninth floor of the National Bank Building in downtown Sioux Falls. After

---

9 "Sioux Falls Magnificent New Hospital Under Construction," *Argus Leader,* January 28, 1911.

10 "The M'Kennan Hospital Impressively Dedicated," *Argus Leader,* December 18, 1911, 3

11 Recker, *An Institution of Organized Kindness*, 7–8 and 14–17 and "Sioux Valley Hospital Now Being Operated in Full Force" *Argus Leader,* July, 30, 1930.

12 Recker, *An Institution of Organized Kindness,* 8, and Harrington, *A Woman's Will . . . A Sister's Way: The McKennan Hospital Story* (Sioux Falls, 1961), 90. The Moe Hospital "flourished" until Dr. Moe died in 1939. For a few years after, Dr. Moe's son, Edgar Alan Moe, ran the facility as a nursing home.

13 Recker, *An Institution of Organized Kindness,* 9.

expansion and relocation, the clinic was renamed Central Plains Clinic, and over the years, the CPC partnered at times with both McKennan and Sioux Valley Hospitals.[14] Dr. John McGreevy established McGreevy Clinic in Sioux Falls when he relocated his practice from Mitchell in 1946. McGreevy's brother, Ed, soon joined the practice, and they rented space in the building that housed the Moe Hospital. In the 1960s, the two men decided to build near McKennan Hospital, which led to a strong working relationship with the hospital.[15]

Two additional facilities also served the particular needs of the region. The first was the Royal C. Johnson's Veteran's Memorial Hospital established at the end of World War II and named for South Dakota native Royal C. Johnson, who helped create the Veterans Administration. The hospital opened on July 24, 1949, and it included beds for 283 patients. In addition to South Dakotans, the hospital also served veterans from Minnesota and Iowa. The second was the "Crippled Children's Hospital and School" that opened in 1952 and was able to accommodate nearly 100. Prior to this time, the facility had been functioning for two decades as part of Sioux Valley Hospital, but the polio epidemic of this era inspired supporters to campaign to have a separate facility built. The hospital expanded over the years and is known today as Lifescape.[16]

In the early twentieth century, all of the medical facilities of Sioux Falls were tested as the nation struggled through World War I and the flu pandemic that swept the globe at the end of Great War. What became known as the "Spanish Flu" continues to challenge scientists, though recent research suggests that, in addition to the influenza virus, a second "bacterial infection led to most of the deaths during the 1918–1919 pandemic."[17]As the highly contagious flu outbreak began to spread, by the spring of 1918, the United States was quarantining its military bases while cities began to shut all public gathering spaces.

The flu's progress can be seen through the *Argus Leader*. On September 18, 1918, it featured a reassuring article that suggested that despite cases of influenza arriving on a ship into New York, the city's annual death rate

14 "Central Plains Clinic LTD," *Eyes on You Magazine* (1992) and Dr. Loren Amundson, "Historical Marker Text" April, 2006. The historical marker dedicated to the Donahoe clinic sits at Ninth Street and First Avenue in Sioux Falls, and it states that the clinic was established in 1949. In 1976, CPC, now with close to seventy physicians on staff, bought seventeen acres of land on Kiwanis Avenue and moved into a new facility.

15 Kathleen A. McGreevy, "A History of Avera Health," unpublished paper (September 2001), 10. McGreevy Clinic became part of Avera Health in 2006.

16 Olson, *Sioux Falls, South Dakota,* 121 and 146; "Patient Comfort Must be Guarded" *Argus Leader*, September 20, 1950; Harrington, *A Woman's Will*, 91, and https://www.lifescapesd.org/about.

17 David M. Morens, Jeffery K. Taubenberger, and Anthony S. Fauci, "Predominant Role of Bacterial Pneumonia as a Cause of Death in Pandemic Influenza: Implications for the Pandemic Influenza Preparedness" *Journal of Infectious Diseases* 198 (1 October 2008), 1–2.

for the flu was half what it was the prior year.[18] However, on September 25, the news quickly changed as the *Argus Leader* stated that the "Spanish Grip is Spreading Rapidly [in the] East" with calls by federal and state officials for more effective measures to fight the flu. On September 26, the paper described how influenza had spread to army camps, and that the government was now mobilizing medical and nursing units for those areas of the country where the epidemic had "gained considerable headway." There were demands to cancel the draft as influenza swept through all but thirteen Army camps and was "apparently beyond control in many eastern communities" as the death rate rose from 2.3 to 4.4 percent in a week. On October 3, the *Argus Leader* related that the flu was "rapidly spreading among the civilian population." In addition, the article featured the fact that cities had closed their schools, churches, and "places of public assemblage" indefinitely.[19]

The Red Cross mobilized forces to combat the contagion and would enroll nurses "and will freely use its accumulated hospital supplies to fight the epidemic." Next, on October 12, the *Argus Leader* stated that local authorities had issued "sweeping orders effective at noon today, closing practically everything in Minnehaha County, except the public schools. Churches, all public meetings, theaters, movies and every place where crowds assemble in or outdoors are barred until further orders." As for children, it seems that authorities felt that they could be more "readily handled" if they remained in school.[20] As the flu spread throughout the country, there was increasing pressure on public services because workers, including teachers, firefighters, and police, also became sick. Naturally, the demand for doctors and nurses increased as the US Public Health Services sought to educate the public on how the disease spread.[21]

As scholars reflect upon the 1918 flu, they describe that it appears to have arrived in waves, the first in the spring of 1918 being less deadly than those that followed. Persons who were sick with the earlier bout, researchers suspect, may have been protected against the ravages of the later influenza. As a result, the late-1918 strain was particularly virulent to those aged twenty to forty and less so for the very young and elderly. The worldwide death toll for the Spanish Flu is estimated to be as high as 50

18 "No Danger of Epidemic of Spanish Grip" *Argus Leader*, September 18, 1918, 1.

19 "Spanish Grip is Spreading Rapidly East," *Argus Leader*, September 25, 1918, 1; "Stamping out Spanish Grip War Measure" *Argus Leader*, September 26, 1918, 1; "Cancel Draft Calls Because of Epidemics" *Argus Leader*, September 27, 1918, 1.

20 "Grip in Army Better; Spreads with Civilians," *Argus Leader*, October 3, 1918, 1; "Sioux City Schools Closed," *Argus Leader*, October 8, 1918, 1; "Close all Public Places But Schools," *Argus Leader*, October 12, 1918, 1.

21 Rhonda Keen-Payne, "We Must Have Nurses: Spanish Influenza in American 1918–1919," *Nursing History Review* 8 (2000), 143, 149–151, 154.

million; in the United States it appears that a quarter of the population became sick, with some 675,000 dying as a result—this is more Americans than US soldiers who died in combat in World War I, World War II, Korea, and Vietnam combined.[22]

The flu certainly played a role in South Dakota, and the *Argus Leader* described that in 1918 alone, influenza killed 1,847 in South Dakota, "whereas in the year 1917 only 54 people succumbed to the malady."[23] Throughout the state as well as Sioux Falls, flu cases challenged the resources of all hospitals.[24] As one McKennan nurse recollected, patients came to the hospital "already black-looking from the high temperature, and many were in the last stage of pneumonia. I worked three weeks all day except for three hours off. Fifteen of the student nurses were ill, none died, but some lost their hair. I helped the undertaker carry out the bodies, there were so many."[25] The flu challenged Sioux Valley Hospital, where "corridors, offices and even the parlor were used to house the patients," and many of the hospital nurses were also serving the Red Cross during the pandemic.[26] The epidemic, which forced hospitals to place patient beds in hallways, made clear what the city already knew: Sioux Falls's hospitals needed to expand.[27] Yet new construction was a costly investment as the price tag of medical care crept higher nationwide.

The increasing expense was, of course, the result of advancements in technology, research-improved pharmaceuticals, and the benefit of experience. Medical personnel gained significant knowledge on the battlefield. The First World War and those that followed provided medicine with a greater understanding of trauma and emergency care. The Great War provided greater understanding of how to care for trauma patients better. During World War II, improvements, particularly in pharmaceuticals, brought important advancements. The most significant may have been Alexander Fleming's 1928 discovery of penicillin; and while it was not

22 Gina Kolata, *Flu: The Story of the Great Influenza Pandemic of 1918 and the Virus that Caused It* (New York: Farrar Straus and Giroux, 1999), ix–x, 80, and G. R. "Experiences during the Influenza Epidemic" *The American Journal of Nursing* Vol. 19, No. 3 (Dec., 1918), 203–205.

23 "Flu Worst Enemy of State During 1918; Takes Toll of 1,847" *Argus Leader,* May 8, 1919, 10. In truth, the number was probably higher as Pierre's Vital Statistics Bureau had broken out the 544 who died of pneumonia.

24 McKennan, between September of 1918 and March of 1919, listed 173 with the virus, though that number was likely higher as those with pneumonia, not included in the count, had probably contracted the flu. Harrington, *A Woman's Will,* 23, and Robert F. Karoleritz, *With Faith, Hope and Tenacity: The First One Hundred Years of the Catholic Diocese of Sioux Falls: 1889–1989* (Mission Hill, SD: Dakota Homestead Publishers, 1989), 173; Harrington does not state the number of pneumonia cases at McKennan.

25 Anonymous Typed Manuscript (1911–1918), McKennan Hospital Scrapbook # 3, Presentation Archives.

26 Recker, *An Institution of Organized Kindness,* 10; 12.

27 McKennan, for example, added a new wing in 1919. In November, the *Argus Leader* would reveal that McKennan's $160,000 extension was rapidly heading for completion and it hoped to open on April 1, 1919, "Addition to M'Kennan Hospital, to be Built this Summer, Will Make it One of Finest in West" *Argus Leader,* June 18, 1918, p. 7.

available for mass production until 1943, widespread use of penicillin enabled injured soldiers to be evacuated from the battlefield without fear of infection. Such improvements made their way into hospitals, and soon, medical personnel were advocating the use of pharmaceuticals and increasing their focus on the importance of scientific research as it related to medical advancements. By the mid-twentieth century, hospitals had replaced the home as central to the provision of health care. For example, in 1873, there were 178 hospitals in the United States, but there were 4,357 by 1909; then between 1909 and 1946, hospital numbers increased by 44 percent. Nevertheless, the demand for more beds continued.[28]

Throughout the twentieth century, the steadily growing population in Sioux Falls and the region increased the need for medical care. All health care facilities were buffeted by the changes to health insurance, regulations regarding specialty care, and the new expectation that hospitals and clinics market the care they could provide to the wider public. Television, newspapers, and even billboards appeared, describing the services that were offered in Sioux Falls. The hospitals' histories took the same twists and turns that much of US health care experienced throughout the twentieth century and into the twenty-first. In 2006, T. Denny Sanford donated $400 million to Sioux Valley Hospital, and Sioux Valley changed its name to Sanford Hospital. In addition, Sanford donated $20 million to the University of South Dakota's medical school, and its name became the Sanford School of Medicine. For McKennan Hospital, the impact was also upon the changes experienced by the religious order of nuns who administered it.

The Presentation Sisters administered McKennan Hospital and had long collaborated with the Benedictine Sisters of Yankton, South Dakota. The Benedictines established Sacred Heart Hospital in Yankton in 1897. Their collaboration strengthened over the twentieth century and by century's end, that relationship became permanent, and the two orders formally joined together under the new name Avera Health, which was announced in the *Argus Leader* on March 12, 1998.[29]

Since the turn of the century, both nonprofit hospitals—each now having thrived for over 100 years—continue to provide care for Sioux Falls and the larger surrounding region. Both hospitals have expanded the range and complexity of services and are essential to the medical care needed by the communities that surround them. Whether it be in oncology, heart

28 Paul A. Brinker and Burley Walker, "The Hill-Burton Act: 1948–1954," *The Review of Economics and Statistics* Vol. 44, 2 (May, 1962), C208–212.

29 Joyce Terveen, "Presentation to be renamed Avera Health," *Argus Leader*, March 12, 1998.

health, or orthopedic care, both hospitals continue to challenge each other. Longtime former CEO of Avera McKennan, Fred Slunecka, reflected on how the challenge for both nonprofits to be financially sustainable continues to the present and how hospitals continue to seek to balance the need to be fiscally responsible while continuing to offer quality of care.[30]

30 Kathleen McGreevy, Russell McKnight, and Margaret Preston, "Interview with Fred Slunecka," November 30, 2009.

City of Banks

DOUGLAS J. HAJEK

How would a state like South Dakota come to lead the nation in banking assets? Or for that matter, how would Sioux Falls end up being the designated main office of two of the four largest financial institutions in the United States? Citibank's decision to move its credit card business to South Dakota in 1980 is a story about a remarkable moment in South Dakota history—one that continues to impact our state and its people in many ways.

It is difficult to comprehend how utterly astonishing it was that Citibank—a bank that would soon become the world's largest issuer of credit cards—would move its credit card operation to Sioux Falls in 1980. It was so surprising that some people seem to think it was all part of a carefully designed plot. But even if it had been possible to design, such a plan would have been well beyond the edges of credibility and too audacious to be taken seriously.

Others say it was just a fluke, and to a large extent, they would be correct. Indeed, it would not have happened at all had it not been for the confluence of highly unusual circumstances. Still, it is at its heart a story of vision, leadership, and action that allowed our state to make the most of a historic opportunity.

It is a common perception that it all happened because South Dakota repealed its usury law (which limits the amount of interest that can be charged on a loan) to lure Citibank here—a perception created by reports like this from the *New York Times* on August 16, 1981:

> The story began in the winter of 1980, when Citibank, frustrated [with New York's usury law] looked afield for a friendlier state. At Citibank's urging, South Dakota promptly stepped forward, eliminating its usury ceiling and winning the bank's credit card operations.

Since this myth is by now so well established, it is useful to examine the facts. From the facts, a different conclusion emerges: Citibank had nothing to do with the change in South Dakota's usury law.

Background

In 1972, I started a career in banking. Those were the days of pots n' pans deposit premiums, and bankers spent little time worrying about how much interest to pay on deposits because under Regulation Q, the Federal Reserve dictated the maximum rate of interest banks could pay depositors, and nearly every bank paid it. For most of the 1970s, the maximum rate for bank savings accounts hung around 4 percent, and for accounts at savings institutions, a quarter of a percent more.

By 1979, high inflation had been entrenched for nearly a decade, and there had been several high-profile efforts to uproot it. In August 1971, President Nixon used his authority to impose wage-price controls. He was afraid that if he didn't do something, the Federal Reserve would impose tight money control that could lead to a recession in 1972, the year he would be up for reelection. The controls worked for a while, and Nixon was reelected in his race against South Dakota Senator George McGovern. When the controls came off in April 1974, prices quickly shot up even faster than before.

Nixon resigned in August 1974, and Vice President Gerald Ford succeeded to the presidency. After Ford had been president for two months, in October he announced his "Whip Inflation Now" campaign to much fanfare. We enthusiastically wore WIN campaign pins around the bank (for about a week). The WIN campaign included measures to control costs—more food production, less energy consumption, and a requirement that all legislation be evaluated for its inflation impact. Later, President Jimmy Carter used an authority, which had never been invoked before, in signing an executive order directing the Federal Reserve to impose consumer credit controls. To show how little respect economic forces have for good intentions, none of these efforts were of lasting impact, and most did more harm than good.

None of these measures worked. Yet in their failure, they set the stage for a drama in which, quite by chance, South Dakota found itself cast in a leading role. Here's how it happened.

The Volcker Solution

Things changed in August 1979 when President Carter decided to make Paul Volcker chairman of the Federal Reserve. Until then, the Federal Reserve's traditional approach in carrying out monetary policy was to manipulate interest rates, particularly the fed funds rate. With inflation stubbornly clinging to double digits, Volcker made a radical break from the past. He wanted to control the money supply more directly by focusing on nonborrowed bank reserves, leaving the fed funds rate to float. When he was ready to make his move, Volcker, on short notice, called a secret meeting of the Reserve Board to adopt the new procedure on Saturday, October 6, in what became known as Volcker's "Saturday Night Special."

Interest rates went to unbelievably high levels. By December, the fed funds rate and the prime rate had jumped to over 20 percent. Nationwide, mortgage rates were in the range of 15 percent. To illustrate in dollar terms what this meant, consider that in 2020, the median list price of a home sold in Sioux Falls is $230,000. If you paid 10 percent down and financed the rest over thirty years, at the 2020 mortgage rate of about 3 percent, the monthly principal and interest payment would be $872. At 15 percent, the payments on the same home would be three times as much at $2,617. The home construction business was in a deep coma.

In this environment, Regulation Q, rather than protecting banks by limiting what they could pay, was rapidly draining them of their deposits as their customers found other places to get better returns on their money. The easing of Reg Q's limits, beginning in 1980, stemmed the tide of deposit withdrawals but also led to much higher money costs for banks, and soon, banks were paying out more in interest on deposits than they were earning on loans. Where usury limits applied, every new loan was a money loser for the bank; borrowing became very difficult, especially for farmers and small businesses.

South Dakota Changes Its Usury Law

These were the conditions when the legislative committee of the South Dakota Bankers Association met in November 1979 to discuss its priorities for the 1980 legislative session. My bosses at Western Bank—T. M. and T. J. Reardon—invited me to attend the meeting. With money costs soaring, the usury limit was on everyone's mind and was first on the agenda. But bankers were conflicted—they didn't want to appear greedy by asking for another increase in the usury limit because they had just gotten the legislature to go along with an increase from 10 percent to 12 percent in the 1979 session.

T. M. Reardon listened patiently while the other bankers talked. After a half hour, seeing that the discussion was going nowhere, he moved that the association propose a permanent solution—one that would exempt "regulated lenders" from the state's usury limits. The motion was seconded without delay by a gentleman sitting directly across the table from us—T. M.'s brother-in-law, Chuck Burke, a distinguished Pierre banker and a member of the South Dakota Banking Commission. With little discussion and no dissent, the committee passed the motion. I was not aware until twenty years later, when T. M. gave me a copy of his memoirs, that he had arranged all this with Mr. Burke ahead of time. Mr. Reardon was worried that if he had not done so, his proposal might have died for lack of a second. His plan worked—with little discussion and no dissent, the committee passed the motion.

After the meeting, Milt Schwartz, the association's executive director at the time, went up to Tom Adam, the association's longtime legal counsel, and said, "Tom, what in the hell just happened?" Milt was just as surprised as everyone else and now faced the sobering prospect that he and Mr. Adam would be tasked with selling this concept to the legislature.

The bankers recruited Rep. Don Clements from the town of Armour to serve as the prime sponsor, and the usury exemption bill (HB 1046) was introduced on January 8, 1980, the first legislative day. At the Joint House and Senate Committee on Commerce hearing on January 18, 1980—when public testimony was taken before it went to the House floor—four bankers, two lobbyists, and the chief investment officer of the South Dakota Investment Council all testified in favor of the bill. Not a single person testified as an opponent. It passed the House on Jan. 22 (59–8). Then, on February 6, the twenty-second day of the thirty-day session, it passed the Senate 30–0. Having passed both houses, the bill now needed the governor's signature to become law.

The Marquette Bank Decision

While this was happening, New York's usury limit was causing huge losses in Citibank's credit card operation. Walter Wriston, its legendary chairman, was desperate to find a solution. Citibank had already lost a billion dollars in the credit card business, and the future looked even worse. But Wriston could not convince New York Governor Hugh Carey to support easing the state's usury restriction. Governor Carey, a friend of Wriston's, was sympathetic. He just saw no chance to get the New York legislature to agree to any easing of the state's usury law.

A United States Supreme Court decision the previous year gave Citibank options. Marquette Bank, the Minneapolis bank owned by Carl

Pohlad, was a successful credit card issuer, but it was losing business to First National Bank of Omaha. With Minnesota's usury limit of 12 percent, Marquette charged an annual fee. Nebraska's limit was 18 percent, which made it feasible for the Omaha bank to offer a card without an annual fee. When First National Bank of Omaha started offering an 18 percent "no annual fee" card to residents of Minnesota, Marquette Bank sued.

By the time the case made it to the United States Supreme Court, First National Bank of Omaha was represented by Robert Bork, who had served as the US solicitor general until 1977. During oral argument before the Supreme Court, it was evident Justice Thurgood Marshall was not impressed with Marquette Bank's case. It seemed to him that Marquette mostly had a marketing problem that it was trying to solve by upending the structure of the national banking system. To make his point painfully clear, Justice Marshall presented Marquette's lawyer with this rather blunt observation: "I really feel Marquette Bank would have done better to take their case to an advertising agency."

The Court ruled in favor of Bork's client, First National Bank of Omaha. The Court held, in a unanimous decision, that under the National Bank Act, the laws of the card issuer's state of domicile determined the maximum rate, not the laws of the state where the cardholder lived.

The Big Hurdle: The Douglas Amendment

There probably weren't two people in South Dakota who gave a hoot about the Marquette Bank case at the time, but it turned out to be one of the most important Supreme Court decisions in our state's history.

Citibank, on the other hand, did care. Because of the Marquette Bank decision, it knew if it operated from a state with a more favorable usury law, it could export that usury law throughout the United States. But the Douglas Amendment to the Bank Holding Company Act of 1956 prohibited Citicorp from coming into a state without an invitation from that state's legislature. In other words, the Marquette Bank decision and favorable usury laws in another state would do Citibank no good without an invitation from that state to open a bank there. More importantly, Citibank faced this sobering reality: no state legislature had ever approved such an invitation.

Yet, as it was losing $300,000 per day, it became clear in January 1980 that Citibank could expect no relief from New York and would have to move. Now it faced two questions. First, was there a state with more favorable usury laws? Second, if so, would it be possible, on relatively short notice, to get an invitation from one of these states?

As to the first question, it was well known at headquarters that California had no limit on its consumer loan rates, but with that state being the home of Bank of America, Citibank's leaders saw no hope of getting an invitation there. So Citibank's legal department examined the laws of all the states to see if there were other options. Being unaware that South Dakota was in the process of passing its usury exemption, Citibank's lawyers determined, on the basis of their existing statutes, that five states deserved a further look: Rhode Island, Nevada, Hawaii, Missouri, and South Dakota.

As to getting an invitation, Rhode Island and Nevada were crossed off because their legislatures were not in session. Hawaii was eliminated because even if that state would invite Citibank, operating the credit card business from there would have been a logistical nightmare. That left Missouri and South Dakota. Both states had the additional advantage of being centrally located, an important consideration at a time when virtually all statements were sent by mail, since Citibank's cardholders were spread all over the United States.

Charles E. Long, senior vice president of card operations, was Citibank's point man. Charlie preferred Missouri because he had been a TWA executive there for nine years and had many contacts in business and government. He had none in South Dakota, so Citibank scrambled internally to find someone who could help them contact Governor Janklow. Now in the second week of February, it had grown to an urgent matter because there were only a few days left in South Dakota's thirty-day legislative session.

Citibank Meets South Dakota

How, in 1980, would a New York bank get connected with the governor of a place so foreign to them as South Dakota? Well, a lawyer at Citibank (an Aberdeen native and Harvard Law graduate) came up with the name of Michael Crew, a Harvard Law alum, and called him. According to Harry Christianson (Governor Janklow's legal counsel), it was Mike, practicing in Vermillion at the time, who made the first call to the governor's office. The assistant who took Mike's call wanted him to talk to Janklow's chief of staff, Ron Williamson. Ron was away from his office, so Mike left a message with the assistant.

When Ron didn't return his call by the next morning, Mike Crew asked his sister, Margaret (then a lawyer with the South Dakota attorney general), to pay a personal visit to give Ron more details. Margaret walked down a flight of stairs to his office and told him of the urgency of the matter: Citibank wanted to talk to the governor and it could mean jobs. A meeting was promptly arranged. Margaret observed that "in their experience, quite understandably, it probably wouldn't have occurred to a New Yorker that if you want to talk to the governor of South Dakota, you could just call him." South Dakotans would have no reason to doubt this, because according to longtime aide Jim Soyer, "Janklow's home number was in the Pierre phone book, and he routinely took evening calls there."

On February 14, Charlie Long cut short a business trip to Panama and came to Pierre to meet with Janklow in the governor's mansion. Charlie had never been to South Dakota and knew nothing about the state. I figure that made him and our governor about even because until that week, Janklow knew next to nothing about Citibank.

The governor assumed Charlie was there because of the recently passed usury legislation. But Charlie said that was not the purpose of his visit. He said Citibank had no mechanism to track state legislation as it was happening so he didn't even know about South Dakota's usury bill. Now Janklow was puzzled. Why was it so urgent for them to talk? Charlie explained that Citibank needed to move to a new state but because of the Douglas Amendment, it could not come without an invitation from the legislature. He was there to see if South Dakota would invite Citibank.

Janklow now had to figure out what to do. Dealing with the bankruptcy of the railroad that transported much of the state's agricultural products, an agriculture sector struggling from impact of a grain embargo, and other challenges, the governor was as eager to diversify the state's economy and find new jobs as Citibank was desperate to find a solution to its problem. But this was unlike anything with which the governor had ever dealt. He had to determine what kind of a commitment to extract from Citibank, and he worried that he would ask for too little. More urgently, he had to figure out how, with only two legislative days left, he could get the legislature to do something no state legislature had ever done—that is, to invite an out-of-state bank holding company to establish a bank in their state.

Convincing South Dakota's Bankers

Governor Janklow called on Jeremiah Murphy, a lawyer and prominent lobbyist from Sioux Falls. Jeremiah told the governor that with such a short time left in the session, that unless the governor had the support of the South Dakota bankers, there would be no chance of getting the legislature to approve an invitation to Citibank. The governor had to somehow convince the independent bankers and the regional banks that supporting the invitation was in their interest. The twenty-ninth legislative day passed, and there was a twenty-five-day break before the final day. During this interim, the governor and Jeremiah prepared the groundwork with legislators and bankers.

Charlie went back to Missouri, which was the state he favored. Charlie said he wanted to go to Kansas City because "it had computer rooms, programmers, [a] good communication system, good labor pool, and so on. Sioux Falls was an unknown." After spending a few days there talking to the governor's staff, the mayors of Kansas City and St. Louis, the leaders of Missouri's legislature, and the bankers association, Charlie could see that Missouri would be a challenge. With over 700 banks in Missouri at the time, and downright hostility among some of them, it would be extremely difficult to convince them that they should not oppose an invitation, much less actively support one.

Back in South Dakota, Murphy told Janklow he should meet first with the Sioux Falls bankers to get their reaction. On the morning of Friday, February 29, Janklow called Murphy to ask him to set up an afternoon meeting. Jeremiah thought the downtown Holiday Inn would be a good neutral offsite place to meet, but due to the short notice, the hotel didn't have a good meeting room available, so he settled for the lounge on the top floor. At the meeting, Janklow gave the Sioux Falls bankers a summary of Citibank's plan, and he told them that Charlie Long would be in Pierre the following Monday to discuss the matter with the Banker's Association Executive Council. Janklow asked if they would come to the meeting to hear out the New Yorkers, and several agreed to do so.

Monday came, and Charlie was back in Pierre to meet with the Bankers Executive Council. The governor made it clear to Charlie that he (Janklow) couldn't get this done by himself—Charlie would have to play a big part in convincing the bankers to support an invitation. They met with the bankers in the governor's conference room. Going into that critical meeting, Janklow had a pep talk for Charlie: "You're coming out here with a Brooklyn accent. We don't like slick guys from Wall Street out here. We've all seen *The Music Man* many times, and we're not buying trombones from strangers. You've got work to do." Charlie, with Citibank's general counsel Patrick Mulhern at his side, leveled with the bankers and told them Citibank would accept whatever restrictions they decided to impose. Yet he also told them that if Missouri extended the invitation, Citibank would put the charter there but would still establish an operation in South Dakota. Charlie also added that he didn't think Missouri could get it done.

At first, several influential bankers expressed concerns that Citibank would go after their customers. For his part, Janklow emphasized all the benefits this could mean for South Dakota. He also told the bankers they could kill it if they wanted to. Charlie told the bankers Citibank would accept whatever restrictions they decided to impose.

When the Q and A session was over, three bankers—Bill Dougherty, the former lieutenant governor and one of the founders of SunBank in Sioux Falls; Harold Torness, from the Sisseton bank; and Chuck Seaman, from the Warner bank—stood up and expressed their support for the invitation. Janklow recalled:

> I'll never forget those three in a row. [Then] we went around the room. It was just like everybody coming to the rail at a revival, one after the next, signing up for Jesus. The next thing I know, they got around to the president (Glenn Waltner of Freeman), and he said, "Well, when you left the room governor, we were gonna hold a secret meeting and vote on it. But it sounds like everybody but me has voted, and you can count me in."

Moments later, the Executive Committee of the Bankers Association passed a resolution supporting a bill to invite Citibank.

Later, Charlie Long expressed how radically different the South Dakota bankers had been compared to what he encountered in Missouri. His meeting with the bankers in Missouri was very unpleasant; he felt beat up by them. In South Dakota, he saw everyone in the room together, and on the spot, he was able to address their concerns.

It was quite a statement about the progressive attitude of South Dakota's bankers that they would all be willing to set aside parochial concerns to accomplish something much bigger for the state.

The Citibank Bill

Work continued on the bill to invite Citibank. On March 12, the last legislative day (a day normally reserved solely for considering vetoed bills), the legislature suspended its rules and allowed the bill to be introduced, acted upon without the usual public hearings and without the usual second reading. And so HB 1370 was introduced, passed by the

Senate (33–1) and the House (64–2), and signed by the governor. With an emergency clause, it went into effect immediately.

Although the Session Laws of 1980 unapologetically referred to the legislation as the Citibank Bill, the authorization was not limited to Citibank. It also allowed other out-of-state holding companies to come here as long as they satisfied three requirements: first, the holding company could establish only one bank in South Dakota; second, the bank must have capital of at least $25 million; and third, the bank must operate out of a "single office . . . at a location which is not likely to attract customers from the general public."

To anyone who didn't know what was going on, this might seem like an odd invitation. But these conditions were not a problem for Citibank. They ultimately invested $250 million in capital, and it wasn't interested in competing with South Dakota banks.[1]

Next Steps for Citibank

There was still a lot of work to be done, including the regulatory approval Citibank needed to obtain. Federal Reserve approval was especially critical to South Dakota, because although Citibank had assured Janklow it would hire a minimum of 300 to 500 South Dakota workers, it left open the potential for significantly more if the Federal Reserve would approve moving the entire credit card operation to our state. Neither commitment was in writing though—it was all based on a handshake.

Complicating things was the fact that some members of Citibank's board were not thrilled with the idea that they would be moving this massive operation and many jobs to South Dakota in the midst of a national recession. They were taking a lot of heat from the public and the New York media. So Governor Janklow had to continue to give this a lot of attention, so much so that the Citibank board began to affectionately refer to him as the director emeritus.

1 Note: In 1988, Michigan National Corporation, in reliance on the statute enacted by the passage of the Citibank Bill, applied to and received approval from the Federal Reserve Board of Governors to establish a national bank in South Dakota from which to conduct Michigan National's credit card business. The Independent Community Bankers of South Dakota appealed the board's decision. The Eighth Circuit Court of Appeals observed that the statute violated the United States Constitution because the "restrictions [the statute] imposes on an out-of-state bank holding company's ability to compete in local markets are precisely the type of 'parochial' regulations the Commerce Clause prohibits." So the Court remanded the case to the Board of Governors to withhold approval until South Dakota modified its statute to bring it into conformity with federal law. The Court's decision was delivered on January 28, 1988. The legislature, which was in session at the time, repealed the offending language three weeks later (as part of HB 1314), and with an emergency clause, the repeal went into effect immediately when it was signed by Governor George Mickelson on February 20, 1988. Ironically, while the ICBA succeeded in convincing the Eighth Circuit Court that the statute created by the Citibank Bill was constitutionally flawed, the Court's proposed remedy ultimately led to the repeal of the provision that was most critical to getting bankers to support passage of the Citibank Bill in 1980.

The *New York Times* seemed shocked that Citibank would go through with this. Here's what the *Times* reported on June 29, 1980:

> It sounded like saber rattling, but Citibank really means it: It has signed a one-year lease for three floors of the . . . Western Bank building . . . in downtown Sioux Falls . . . that will serve as a temporary base of operation [and] is negotiating the purchase of 10 acres . . . where it plans to build its permanent headquarters. . . . And Richard D. McCrossen, the newly-appointed head of the operation expects to close on the purchase of a home in nearby Brandon next month.

The New York legislature's resolve weakened when Citibank announced it was leaving, and on November 24, 1980, it enacted a moratorium on its usury limit. But by then it was too late. On February 19, 1981, Citibank (South Dakota), N.A. received its charter from the comptroller of the currency and officially opened for business.

Six months later, August 16, 1981, the *New York Times* noted New York's belated but unsuccessful attempt to salvage the situation:

> Alarmed, New York followed suit [by changing its usury law]—but Citibank had promised South Dakota, and that promise it did keep. Did this herald a sweep of business to South Dakota? . . . Well, First Bank System of Minneapolis did warm up to South Dakota. . . . But no one else has.

State leaders who knew what was actually happening found parts of this report amusing because first, there were several substantial operations that had come or were in serious negotiations to come to South Dakota, and second, First Bank System had operated in South Dakota since 1929.

Richard McCrossen

The day the Citibank bill passed, Charlie Long called Richard McCrossen (Citibank South Dakota's first president) and blurted out, "Dick, you're going to love South Dakota," then abruptly hung up. I've wondered if that was a prediction or an order.

McCrossen got Citibank off to a great start as he led the organization's move here and built the operation into the most profitable part of Citibank's business. He was a strong, disciplined leader, and he left no doubt among his troops that he had high expectations of them, which, I might add, they were very reluctant to disappoint.

Dick McCrossen was determined to make Citibank work for South Dakota as well as South Dakota did for Citibank. It was evident from the community involvement of the entire Citibank South Dakota executive team that this was a commitment they all shared, and it became a permanent part of the corporate culture of the Sioux Falls bank.

Walter Wriston, Citibank's chairman, and John Reed, his successor, could not have been more pleased with how well things were turning out in South Dakota. Large New York companies bad-mouthed Sioux Falls and warned Wriston that South Dakotans would be undependable workers, but Citibank found the opposite to be true. One executive observed that "South Dakotans worked harder than New Yorkers," which allowed the Sioux Falls bank to perform the same work with fewer employees. Wriston was also impressed that a letter could make it from Long Island to Sioux Falls a half-day faster than a letter from Long Island to Manhattan.

More Big Things

Subsequent to Citibank's initial move to Sioux Falls, several other credit card banks came to South Dakota. These entrants included, among others, First City Bank, a South Dakota affiliate of a Houston-based organization, which opened in Sioux Falls, and First National Bank of Omaha, which began issuing cards through its affiliate in Yankton. An existing Sioux Falls-based institution, First PREMIER Bank, through its PREMIER Bankcard division, entered the credit card business in 1989 and today is one of the top twenty Master Card issuers in the United States.

Since then, there have been several key banking developments for South Dakota. In 2004, Wells Fargo, N.A. designated Sioux Falls as its main office. Its CEO at the time, Dick Kovacevich, had been a top executive with Citibank and was personally familiar with the quality of Citibank's South Dakota experience. In 2008, Wells Fargo acquired Wachovia Bank and consolidated the two banks in 2010, which made it a $1.2-trillion bank with its main office in Sioux Falls. Then in 2011, Citibank (South Dakota) merged with Citibank, N.A., and Citibank, N.A. designated Sioux Falls as its main office. It, too, was a $1.2-trillion bank.

When 2011 came to a close, two of the four largest financial institutions in the United States had designated Sioux Falls as the home of their main offices, making South Dakota number one among all states in banking assets, a position it held from 2011 to 2018. Today, it ranks number two, closely behind Ohio, the home of JP Morgan Chase Bank's charter.

Additional favorable legislation has led to South Dakota's growth in other segments of the financial services industry. Sioux Falls is also the home of the nation's largest prepaid card issuers, MetaBank and Bancorp Bank. South Dakota is recognized nationally as one of the best states in which to site long-term (so-called "dynasty") trusts, and consequently, the state now hosts over 100 trust companies, which hold assets from all over the world in excess of $350 billion. Banks have come here because South Dakota has had a solid reputation established over four decades, with all the components of a good environment for banks: reasonable regulation and taxes, a talented, educated, experienced, and conscientious workforce, and a strong communications, technology, and distribution infrastructure. Just as important—our policymakers have for the most part been predictable in showing their belief in the value of an industry that's benefited our state in so many ways.

The 1980 legislation and the journey of Citibank to South Dakota is an extraordinary part of the state's history. While it was never part of anyone's grand design, there can be no doubt that the 1980 legislation has had a transformational impact on South Dakota well beyond anything anyone could have imagined. It has brought billions of dollars to our state, opened the door to many promising careers, significantly expanded the technological capabilities of our state, and greatly enhanced our state's investment in research and education. It has also brought us closer to the larger world and given us a new sense of potential.

Yet this could have simply been a missed opportunity that none of us would have ever heard about if Governor Janklow—in that moment on Valentine's Day 1980, when he met with Charlie Long—had simply said, "Charlie, with only two legislative days left, there is no way I can get this done."

But luckily for Sioux Falls and South Dakota, that was not in the nature of Governor Janklow.

Sources

Bingner, Gary. *South Dakota Banking: The Lowdown of High Finance in Middle America, A History of the Citibanking Revolution, 1980–1983.* Unpublished record of events at behest of Governor Janklow. Available at the State Library in Pierre, South Dakota.

Ethan G. Sribnick, *A Legacy of Innovation*. Philadelphia: University of Pennsylvania Press, 2008.

Frontline. "The Secret History of the Credit Card." PBS. Aired, November 23, 2004.

Independent Community Bankers Association of South Dakota, Inc. v. Board of Governors of the Federal Reserve System, 838 F.2d 969 (8th Cir. 1988).

David E. Lindsey, Athanasios Orphanides, and Robert H. Rasche, "The Reform of October 1979: How It Happened and Why," *Federal Reserve Bank of St. Louis Review*, March/April 2005, Part 2, 187–236. https://doi.org/10.20955/r.87.

Marquette National Bank of Minneapolis v. First of Omaha Service Corp., 439 U.S. 299 (1978).

South Dakota Legislative Research Council, Legislative Record, 1980 and 1988 Sessions.

Zweig, Phillip L. *Walter Wriston: Citibank and the Rise and Fall of American Financial Supremacy*. New York: Crown Publishers Inc., 1995.

City of Stone

APRIL WHITE

From a distance, the quarries expanding just east of Sioux Falls in the late 1880s were a dark scar across the prairie. But up close, the exposed quartzite formed a brilliant rainbow. The rock face was streaked with cherry red, royal purple, and chocolate brown. Elsewhere, even without the benefit of polishing, the stone glowed pink, lilac, and peachblow, the warm, orange-red hue of a Dakota sunset.[1]

Early white explorers in the region had marveled at the beauty of this unusual material. The artist George Catlin, who visited the Coteau de Prairies plateau in the 1830s, painted canvases of the region's Indigenous people mining the red pipestone found between layers of quartzite; the soft stone had been prized by the tribes for centuries to make tools, ornaments, and ceremonial pipes. But it was the harder rock that entranced Catlin. "I became completely surprised and charmed; and I resolved to procure specimens of every variety," he wrote. He broke off "small bits from them with my hammer; until I had something like a hundred different varieties, containing all the tints and colours of a painter's palette."[2]

Decades later, though, the white settlers of Sioux Falls saw something very different when they looked at the outcroppings that dotted the landscape. They saw the promise of prosperity. A city could be built—both literally and economically—from the same stone that formed its namesake cataract.

The stone that would become known, for a time, as "Sioux Falls granite" or "Sioux Falls jasper" began as sediment deposited at the bottom of a long-lost sea that stretched from the Arctic Ocean to the Gulf of Mexico. As quartz crystal and silica built up, so did the heat and pressure, until about 1.7 billion years ago when the sand recrystallized as quartzite, a stone so dense it is stronger than steel.

The durability must have appealed to members of the Western Town Company of Dubuque, Iowa, who staked their claim on 320 acres on the

1 Arthur Phillips, E. W. Caldwell, and Henry Austin, "The Dakota Metropolis," *New England Magazine*, 1891.

2 George Catlin, *Letters and Notes on the Facts, Manners, Customs and Conditions of North American Indians* (Philadelphia: J.W. Bradley, 1859), 703.

western bank of the Big Sioux River in 1857. They built Sioux Falls's first hotel, the Dubuque House, from rough-hewn blocks of the abundant stone. The hotel did not last, but the stone did. Abandoned and likely burned during the Dakota War of 1862, the Dubuque House was razed when town development began again in the 1870s. The salvaged rock was repurposed to construct the city's first brewery on Main Avenue. E. A. Sherman, one of Sioux Falls's first citizens, used the stone for many of his buildings, and in 1880, architect W. L. Dow used it in his debut commission, the Dakota Territorial Penitentiary, the first of many projects he would design from quartzite over the next two decades.[3]

The earliest buildings were formed from the most easily accessible stone, wherever glacial and water erosion had exposed the rock face. The inmates themselves quarried the quartzite for their prison from the grounds of the penitentiary, and the mills growing up along the Big Sioux cut the stone directly from its banks, forever reshaping the river. But these small deposits could not meet the growing demand for stone. Quartzite, it was said in the tone of immoderate enthusiasm characteristic of the city's early days, "combine[d] beauty and strength more perfectly than any other stone in America."[4] It was marketed as "indestructible," and the supply was described as "inexhaustible."[5]

C. W. Hubbard was among those who recognized the money to be made. Originally from Vermont, Hubbard had come west in the 1870s, settling first in St. Paul and then relocating to Sioux Falls in about 1881 to oversee the construction of the Queen Bee Mill. The project was the most ambitious the Dakota Territory had ever seen: the massive seven-story mill was designed to produce 1,200 barrels of flour a day. But the waterpower from the river was insufficient to meet the demands of the mill, and it never operated at full capacity. By 1883, the company was bankrupt.[6]

Despite that failure, Hubbard still saw opportunity in the region's natural resources. The Queen Bee Mill had been constructed of Sioux Falls quartzite, and as early as 1883, Hubbard was operating a quarry of his own. Those early years in the stone business were rocky ones. Some of the city's biggest names—Seney and Drake among them—jostled for the best sites, and charges of bribery, theft, and trespass flew. When the dust finally settled in 1886, Hubbard had established himself six miles southeast of

---

3 On W. L. Dow, see Jennifer Dumke, ***W. L. Dow: The Architect Who Shaped Sioux Falls*** (Charleston: History Press, 2013).

4 "Sioux Falls Granite" quoted in "It is Jasper," ***Daily Argus Leader***, August 20, 1889.

5 For example, "Another Letter from T. M. James," ***Weekly Commonwealth*** (Topeka, Kansas), December 2, 1886; and "Sioux Falls Stone," ***Daily Argus Leader***, June 17, 1889.

6 On C. W. Hubbard and so many other things, see Wayne Fanebust, ***Where the Sioux River Bends*** (Freeman, SD: Pine Hill Press, 1984).

Sioux Falls at the Ives quarries, so named for an early settler in the area. With a contract from Kansas City for 1,200 yards of paving stone, the business expanded from two stone cutters to 100 in just a few months, and the Illinois Central extended its tracks to the quarry. In 1887, Hubbard incorporated as the Sioux Falls Granite Company.

In the late 1880s, the quartzite business seemed as indestructible as the stone itself. The Sioux Falls Granite Company and at least four other quarrying businesses nearby—the Minnehaha Granite Company, the Sioux Falls Quarry Company, Drake's Monarch Quarries, and Jasper Stone Quarry—shipped stone to Omaha, Chicago, and Detroit, along with countless cities in between. In Sioux Falls, the schools were made of quartzite (among them, All Saints, the South Dakota School for the Deaf, the Lincoln School and the Lutheran Normal School); the houses of the city's well-to-do were made of quartzite (architect W. L. Dow's house, fittingly, sat on a quartzite foundation); the shops and offices that lined Main Avenue and Ninth Street were made of quartzite; even the streets were paved with quartzite, a luxury more common in larger cities. In 1888, Hubbard's quarries produced hundreds of thousands of stones to line Phillips Avenue between Fifth and Twelfth Streets, the first finished road in the territory.

"The first man who will build of anything but jasper in Sioux Falls ought to be open to the same imprecation for disloyalty as he who would pull down the American flag, and be shot in his tracks," the *Daily Argus Leader* opined in 1889.[7]

Quartzite also built the city of East Sioux Falls. The company town was not constructed of the coveted stone it sold, but it boomed with C. W. Hubbard's successes. Known as Ives until the Illinois Central christened its wooden depot East Sioux Falls, the community grew from a single farmhouse in the mid-1880s to 400 people in 1888. Cottages and a general store, a schoolhouse, a post office, and a town hall popped up. The town also had a cricket team—many of the skilled stonecutters Hubbard recruited were English—and a baseball team. A local fishing hole attracted day-trippers from Sioux Falls, as did the saloons. East Sioux Falls was a wide-open place, allowing Sioux Falls citizens to indulge

7 "The first man who will build," *Daily Argus Leader*, September 28, 1889.

in vice while still decrying it.

By 1890, the population of East Sioux Falls stood at about 600—the number needed to petition to become a city in the new state of South Dakota. In August of that year, with approval by the county commission and a vote of the populace, East Sioux Falls was incorporated, but that wasn't the biggest news of the month. An enormous block of quartzite—fourteen feet long, three feet wide, and "without a flaw"—cut from a quarry in the new Sioux Falls suburb got more attention.[8]

But there were already signs that the market for Sioux Falls's quartzite was softening. In April of 1891, the Sioux Falls Granite Company was placed in receivership, and much of the town was unemployed as Hubbard struggled to collect debts and secure new contracts. In 1892, the company was sold, providing hope to the community, and Hubbard rebounded, temporarily, when he was awarded a contract to supply quartzite for the new post office. It would not be enough. The Panic of 1893 sent the country into a five-year depression and shuttered the Sioux Falls quartzite industry. In East Sioux Falls, the quarries filled with water.

As late as 1899, when he wrote his *History of Minnehaha County, South Dakota*, Dana R. Bailey expressed optimism for the industry that had created East Sioux Falls. "This valuable stone is still there in large quantities," he wrote of the quartzite. Of the city: "[A]lthough in a dormant state at the present time, it is not a Rip Van Winkle sleep that has overtaken this enterprising little berg."[9]

The quartzite boom never revived. By the early 1900s, concrete was the modern building material of choice. Even W. L. Dow, the architect who had shaped Sioux Falls from its famed stone, embraced the newly fashionable medium. In East Sioux Falls, the population dwindled. In 1913—after twenty-three years as a city—the government dissolved. Over the decades, the buildings crumbled, until finally, in 1991, the boomtown was razed.

But the stone unearthed during the heyday of the 1880s has proven as durable as its boosters claimed. It can still be seen throughout Sioux Falls, an unshakable foundation for the city.

8 "South Dakota," *The Dickinson Press* (North Dakota), August 16, 1890.

9 Dana R. Bailey, *History of Minnehaha County, South Dakota* (Sioux Falls: Brown & Saenger, 1899), 289.

City Governance

TOM GRECO

In a little over 140 years, Sioux Falls would change its form of government seven times, electing over 200 of its own to provide for a "healthy and prosperous community in which to live and to engage in business."[1] Such changes were not "shake-ups" resulting from major scandal, graft, or corruption. Instead, each change reflected the collective desire of its citizens for a government best able to respond to the challenges of growth and modernization, while at the same time reflecting and preserving the ideals and values that continue to shape the city. This is not to say, however, Sioux Falls's government escaped its share of heated debate, instances of questionable behavior, or public criticism.

Sioux Falls would not become a city until 1883, when it was incorporated under a special law of the territorial legislature.[2] For the six years prior, the Sioux Falls Village Board of Trustees would govern with a president and four trustees under limited powers granted by the legislature in 1877.[3] As the village grew, so did the needs and expectations of its residents. In early April 1883, a mayor and eight aldermen (two representing each of the city's four wards) would sit for the first time as the Sioux Falls City Council. The city incorporated again in 1889, but that time it would be under the general laws of the territory.[4] A total of nine mayors and ninety-eight aldermen would serve on the city council between 1883 and 1909. Among them were George Burnside, who would go on to serve an unprecedented seven terms as the mayor of Sioux Falls, and Alderman Joseph Sampson, who would earn the dubious distinction of being the only elected official of the city ever expelled by their peers.[5]

To provide for an ever-growing city, the council focused their attention on many of the things we take for granted today: utilities, public safety, health, and recreation. While there were many successes, several important issues "went unresolved for years as the City Council argued, procrastinated,

1 From the pamphlet "Charter of the City of Sioux Falls, South Dakota" (Sioux Falls, SD: Sessions-Mannix Printing, 1911), 66.

2 "An Act to Incorporate the City of Sioux Falls," Fifteenth Session of the Territorial Legislature of Dakota.

3 "An Act to Incorporate the Village of Sioux Falls," Twelfth Session of the Territorial Legislature of Dakota.

4 The question of adopting "Chapter 73 of the General Laws of the Territory of Dakota of 1877" was adopted by the voters of the City at an election held on March 19, 1889 (Sioux Falls City Council Minutes, March 20, 1889).

5 Sioux Falls City Council Minutes of June 7, 1895. Sampson deposited $767.50 into his personal account, but was never indicted by a court of law.

or reversed itself. Issues of water, electricity, and sewer service are prime examples."[6] For years, the council would rely on franchise agreements or contacts for water, lighting, gas, and public transportation. In fact, the council would still be granting private sewer permits up to 1908.[7] By 1907, citizens were looking for a government that was able to tackle these challenges.

The tide shifted dramatically when leading businessmen latched on to a nascent form of government enacted into South Dakota law in 1907—the commission form.[8] One year later, Sioux Falls adopted the new form and in mid-April 1909, the Sioux Falls City Commission officially replaced the city council with a mayor and four commissioners, all elected at large. Unlike their aldermanic predecessors, commissioners would serve full-time, and each of them would have responsibility for specific functions of city government.[9] Despite a strong start in 1908, the five-member commission would suffer from infighting that elicited public discontent and frustration so strong that two commissioners would face recall.[10] In October of 1913, the voters narrowly ushered in change again, this time to a three-commissioner form, in the hope that a smaller body would better manage the affairs of the city.[11] This particular form would remain unchanged from 1914 to 1986, warding off seven ballot measures to change it and weathering three more recall elections, only one of which resulted in the incumbent, a mayor, losing their seat. [12] In 1986, the commission reverted to five members, again by popular vote, only to last nine years. During the commissions' eighty-six years, thirteen mayors and thirty-one commissioners served throughout a period of substantial growth and prosperity, but by the 1990s, this form would outlive its appeal.

In the early 1990s, a local group comprised of "business people, laborers, teachers, and even some city employees," raised concerns about the way the city was growing and the way it delivered services.[13] Instead of relying on the "one-size-fits-all" forms of government found in state law, they would take advantage of a state constitutional provision allowing the city to structure its own form of government. "Home rule," as this

6 Gary D. Olson and Erik L. Olson, "Sioux Falls, South Dakota: A Pictorial History" (Norfolk, VA: The Donning Company, 1985) 77.

7 R.E. Bragstad, "Sioux Falls in Retrospect" (Privately published, 1967) 91.

8 Bragstad, "Sioux Falls in Retrospect," 13.

9 Bragstad, "Sioux Falls in Retrospect," 16-17.

10 "First Recall in South Dakota," ***The Mitchell Capital***, October 3, 1912 and ***Sioux Falls City Commission Meeting Minutes***, August 15, 1913.

11 Canvass of October 21, 1913 election.

12 City Election of April 19, 1921 (Mayor George Burnside Retained his seat); Election of October 21, 1930 (Burnside and Comm. Alex Reid retained their seats); Election of December 19, 1961 (Mayor Fay Wheeldon lost to Vinton L. Crusinberrry).

13 Corrine Olson, "Citizens Propose Revised City Hall," ***Argus Leader***, February 17, 1994.

is known, allows cities and counties to "choose any form of executive, legislative, or administrative structure" and provides them with the ability to "do anything *not* prohibited by the state." This stands in contrast to the established forms of government in state law, which allow local governments to do "only those things authorized by the state."[14]

The structure proposed by the group was unique to any other form previously contemplated. It provided for a city council consisting of a full-time mayor, vested with all executive and administrative powers, and eight part-time council members who possessed all legislative and policymaking powers. With powers clearly separated, the charter also includes a series of checks and balances, such as the mayor's power to veto and break tie votes or the council's power to approve the budget and appropriate funds. Among the council members, five are elected by each of the five council districts (wards), while three serve at large—the intent being to provide sufficient attention to localized concerns while not losing sight of broader city issues. Both the mayor and council members are subject to term limits. Importantly, the powers of the city would not be limitless. Under state law, neither the charter nor any local ordinances can "set standards or requirements which are lower or less stringent than those imposed by state law," and there are a series of expressed restrictions on home rule power (in addition to acts "prohibited by the state").[15]

When the charter came before a public vote in 1994, the voters narrowly adopted it, and the new city council convened for the first time on Tuesday, January 3, 1995. A little over a year later, the *Argus Leader* would comment, "It's getting difficult to recall the last really ugly turf fight in Sioux Falls city government. . . . [City government] has made a surprisingly smooth transition."[16] As the years progressed, things would not be quite as harmonious, but the new form of government would show itself more than worthy of representing and serving such a bustling city. Since 1995, the city limits grew by more than thirty square miles and 90,000 people. Major investments in road infrastructure, wastewater treatment, and water supply continue to be made; the city's planning and zoning strategy was overhauled; affordable housing, public safety, and health remain top priorities; and, very often in partnership with a range of local, state, and federal partners, the city continues to take steps to attract new industries, development, and investments in the community.

14 Tom Magedeanz, "Home Rule in South Dakota – An Update" (Pierre, SD: South Dakota Legislative Research Council, August 7, 2000) 2-3.

15 "Home Rule Charters," *South Dakota Codified Law,* Chapter 6-12.

16 Editorial Board, "Sioux Falls Serves as Good Example," *Argus Leader*, January 12, 1996.

Four mayors and thirty-five council members have served thus far under the current city charter. Owing to the part-time nature of the council members' positions, a diverse mix of candidates have sought and found a seat on the city council over the years. And mayors, with significantly more powers than their predecessors, have each managed a sophisticated enterprise of professional and appointed administrators who conduct the day-to-day affairs of the city while simultaneously preparing for the next twenty, fifty, and one hundred years. Sioux Falls's government will no doubt evolve in the future. Whether it changes in form again will be a question only its citizens can answer.

USF

STEPHEN JACKSON

If you step foot on the University of Sioux Falls (USF) campus today, you are very likely to be inundated with references to cougars. You would probably first encounter Doug Baer's imposing statue of a cougar just north of the Stewart and Cleveland Professional Development Centers. You might then head into the official university store, Cougar Central, to pick up a T-shirt or a textbook. And when you are done shopping, you might grab a cup of coffee at Cooper's Café, named after the university's mascot, Cooper the Cougar. The imagery is similarly inescapable at events and on social media. Annual homecoming events, replete with alumni reunions, family visits, and an annual 5K, are all organized as "Cougar Days." Cooper the Cougar can be found at sporting events, leading chants of "Let's go, Coo" to adoring fans. On social media, you can search for #SuFuCoo or #CooFalls.

In other words, the symbolism of the cougar is deeply interwoven into the very identity of the University of Sioux Falls. It might be surprising to find out, then, that the cougar mascot was only adopted in the late 1970s. For more than half a century before that, the institution, then called Sioux Falls College (SFC),[1] was closely associated with Native American symbolism. Students and alumni were known as the Braves. Debates over the appropriation of Native American imagery as mascots are extraordinarily controversial, so how and why did a small Baptist liberal arts college in Sioux Falls South Dakota make this transition?

The origin of the Braves symbolism can be traced to the early 1920s. English professor Lawrence Nelson started a tradition of the Purple Feather in 1921 to recognize outstanding students, and purple and white subsequently became the school colors (as they remain to this day).[2] Two years later, the annual "Tepee Day" tradition, celebrated at homecoming, began. According to the college newspaper, the *Stylus*, in 1942, the name Tepee Day was selected "because of the Red Man's significance in this locality." Every year, they would crown a Tepee Day chief and princess, who would don full headdresses and Native American attire before awarding Purple Feathers to outstanding students. The Braves nickname quickly became a staple of SFC

1 The institution changed its name from Sioux Falls College to the University of Sioux Falls in 1995.

2 Indeed, of all the traditions adopted in the 1920s, only the tradition of the Purple Feather remains. There are, of course, no actual feathers involved in the process anymore.

at athletic events and other university functions. A close association with Native American imagery became a defining feature of college life at Sioux Falls College for more than half a century. The college yearbook, for instance, was named *The Sioux Brave*, and during the Second World War, SFC students who went off to fight were nicknamed "The Fightin' Braves."

There were few signs as late as the 1950s that the Braves mascot or associated imagery caused any controversy on the Sioux Falls College campus. A 1959 student editorial criticized the mascot but only because "there is nothing characteristic of SFC about the name." It also stated that "many other institutions and organizations have Indian traditions." But things gradually began to change in the late 1960s. A series of articles in the *Stylus* entitled "A History of Despair" told students about the contemporary Native Americans experience, including the problems of racism and poverty evident in places like Pine Ridge. This may have led to President Reuben Jeschke's offhanded comment about the annual Tepee Days that "questions have been raised about the propriety of the title, but not the significance of the event." The implication of his writing indicated, however, that he did not consider this a particularly significant issue.

The situation rapidly changed in the early 1970s. After a decade of tremendous expansion in the 1960s, the time of the baby boom generation, the college experienced a financial crunch and a problem of declining enrollment. For the first time, SFC college administrators began to actively recruit minority students to campus. Almus Larsen, an administrator in charge of admissions, visited "all of the Indian high schools in South Dakota and a few Indian junior colleges" during the 1971-72 academic year. A growing but still very small number of Native students came to campus in an era of intense Native American activism. The fiftieth anniversary of Tepee Days at Sioux Falls College occurred in the same year as the American Indian Movement occupied Wounded Knee, South Dakota. In an increasingly charged atmosphere, some members of the SFC Native American community began to criticize the caricatures so frequently used at athletic events and during Tepee Days.

Pressure for change began to mount, but it was not until 1976 that any definitive action took place. This was also the year that the college adopted its first nondiscrimination policy, declaring, "Sioux Falls College admits the students of any race to all the rights, privileges, programs, and activities generally accorded or made available to students at this college," a policy which specifically included "athletic and other school-administered programs." Homecoming activities in 1976 made it "painfully apparent" that many of the practices surrounding Tepee Days were "no longer acceptable" to the SFC community. For the next year, the campus engaged in a lively debate over whether or not to continue using their traditional mascot.

President Owen Halleen made it clear that any mascot decision would not be made by administrative fiat but would instead be the product of a highly democratic process. By January of 1977, the SFC administration unveiled a plan to gather as much input as possible from various college constituencies. Several campus meetings were held to openly discuss the appropriateness of the Native American imagery on campus. Faculty, students, alumni, the student body, administration, and the SFC Women's Board all had the opportunity to vote on the best option regarding the college mascot.

As part of these discussions, the *Sioux Falls College Bulletin*, the alumni news publication, printed position papers both for and against continued use of the Braves mascot. The author defending current practice suggested that these long-standing traditions "are frequently seen as the reservoir for school spirit" and a way of cementing the institution's identity. The author argued that they were, in a sense, historical symbols with little ethnic or racial significance. The second position paper argued that choosing "a particular nation of people as a mascot is to dehumanize or depersonalize them, and value them only for some supposed magic or animal quality."

By April of 1977, the votes had been cast and analyzed, and SFC settled on a compromise solution. More than eighty percent of students voted to keep the Brave as the school's mascot, and out of all the groups, only the faculty and administration voted to abandon the traditional imagery. With these results in hand, SFC attempted to "retain the nickname 'Brave' but with no racial overtones for the sports groups and yearbooks." One might suspect that this was simply a rhetorical device to keep the traditional symbolism, but in fact it involved a series of highly significant changes, including instructions to:

> (1) avoid use of Indian caricatures and other Indian symbolism, (2) eliminate title of Tepee Days from Homecoming, (3) eliminate use of Indian headbands and costumes in homecoming activities, (4) eliminate title of "Chief" for Homecoming Chairman, (5) change Homecoming evening meal to Royalty Banquet rather than Chief's Barbeque, and (6) eliminate use of teepees in campus decoration for Homecoming.

In other words, stripping offensive depictions of Native American culture from the school's traditional symbolism involved meaningful changes to campus celebrations and practices.

Homecoming 1977 was the first true test of a new paradigm whereby Sioux Falls College would continue using the label "Braves" while doing their absolute best to avoid racial overtones in campus activities. The compromise solution proved to be a complete failure. As the *Alumni Bulletin* put it, "as long as we were still the 'Braves,' the mascot had Indian connotations that could not be denied." Students also found it "difficult to break away from the theme" and that, in the absence of chiefs or tepees, "felt they had nothing to rally around." In a dramatic reversal of their vote earlier that year, a majority of the student association voted to drop the name Braves entirely, and the student senate quickly agreed. Since the faculty had already indicated their opposition to the title Braves, the SFC board of trustees voted in November of 1977 to empower the president to search for a new mascot for the college.

President Halleen again adopted a very democratic approach, and he organized a vote by all campus constituencies to help find a new symbol for the institution. Prospective names were solicited from everyone in the SFC community, and a committee composed of students, faculty, staff, and alumni chose the top five options. The four runners up were Comets, Spartans, Bears, and Colts, but it was Cougars which won the vote. Over the next few years, the new mascot and imagery replaced the troubling Native American symbolism of the past.

The decision to change mascots at Sioux Falls College may not seem of great historical significance. But it revealed several notable features of the campus culture. The entire SFC community was willing to listen to criticisms and to engage in open dialogue on a difficult subject in a respectful manner. The decision-making process was highly inclusive, involving nearly all major college stakeholders.

Those of us in an increasingly polarized twenty-first century might be able to learn something from this episode in the history of a small liberal arts college in Sioux Falls. At the very least, we can appreciate what was, inarguably, a brave decision.

Sources

Board of Trustee minutes, Sioux Falls College.

Jeschke, Reuben. *A Decade of Growth* (Sioux Falls: University of Sioux Falls, 1968).

The Sioux Brave.

The Stylus.

The Sioux Falls College Alumni Bulletin.

Augustana

SANDRA C. LOONEY

Augustana University's outdoor sculptures invite response and initiate reflection. These works of art become part of a campus legacy students experience day to day. Each sculpture has its own story. Although some stories have been forgotten, students have their own vision of them. Students pass by the sculptures, as their schedules and planners propel them to class, laboratory hours, and campus activities. They are a seen and unseen presence, part of the physical and interior landscape. In many ways, the campus sculptures exemplify the institutional values of a liberal arts education at Augustana: faith, heritage, excellence, community, service.

When I came to Augustana as a student in 1960, few sculptures existed on the campus. The limestone *Moses* had been completed in 1954 by art professor Ogden Dalrymple and installed at the entrance to the Mikkelsen Library. During Viking Days, a giant wood-frame version of *Ole the Viking* appeared for a student all-night vigil to protect *Ole* from marauders up the street, the Sioux Falls College Cougars. Over time, more sculptures appeared, many of them designed and executed by professors and students.

The most prominent campus art in my student days was the statue of *Moses* with its inscription: "The fear of the Lord is the beginning of wisdom." Many days, I rushed past those words, words that gave study a higher purpose. I noticed the silver and gold horns on the head of *Moses* and learned they represented divine radiance. *Moses*-at-the-library sits atop the central campus hill. At the bottom of the hill, directly outside the Commons, is a companion sculpture, *The Owls: Foresight, Hindsight, and Insight*, the smallest owl. Its guiding inscription is "Seek ye wisdom and gain understanding" from Proverbs 4:5. *The Owls* is one of the collaborative sculptures on campus by two late art professors, Palmer "Poly" Eide and Ogden Dalrymple. I have a treasured picture of Poly and Mr. D. at work on the owls in 1986. In September 1992, I wrote in an article for the campus that "Eide and Dalrymple's collaboration was so true that it is difficult to say who did what. They themselves were not interested in who did what but what the finished piece would say." Gallery Coordinator John Peters says those two were a dream team and fun to watch working together because they understood each other so well.

Peters acknowledges Poly and Mr. D. as the backbone of Augustana's sculptures on campus. Among their sculptures is *God's Creatures*—the fish and creatures of the sea, the birds of the air, the bison of the earth, and man and woman carved into four limestone blocks on the east facade of Mikkelsen Library. Their collaboration also produced *The Muse of Music*, which depicts the muse with a tear of ecstasy falling down her cheek. This sculpture is located on the west side of the Fryxell Humanities Building.

In 1967, Augustana placed a permanent *Ole* sculpture in the center of campus. Here, heritage and school spirit are personified. Augustana had been seeking the permanent presence of Ole so a contest was initiated—$300 would go to the artist and $200 more if the institution agreed to install the sculpture. I remember one entry clearly. It was a wholly heroic Viking. Alan Berdahl, class of 1976 and brother to the winning artist, the late Pete Eide, says the Eide family had teased Peter, class of 1966 and son of Palmer Eide, about creating the world's largest self-portrait. The *Mirror*, Augustana's student-run newspaper, had this account in its October 13, 1967, issue: "In 1966 an idea was born and Peter Eide embodied Ole's spirit into a squatty little Viking on a much too small ship. It was not love at first sight on the part of the campus." People might be surprised to know that some critics suggested the artist should return the contest money. The *Mirror* declared 1967–1968 to be a trial year for *Ole*. But *Ole* captured the campus. Squatty-Bod became his unofficial name. He has played many parts—Cupid, Santa, Augie grad—and Ole himself. *Ole* is a campus gathering place. He is a central figure in each school day. *Ole* is the Viking.

Another sculpture depicting Moses—the campus has two!—was embroiled in controversy in the 1970s. The second *Moses* sculpture is a bronze copy of the original marble sculpture of Moses by Michelangelo Buonarroti carved between 1513 and 1515. The bronze *Moses*—together with a copy of Michelangelo's *David* sculpture—was presented to the city and the college by Thomas Fawick, a prolific inventor and native son who returned to Sioux Falls to receive an honorary Doctor of Arts degree from Augustana.[1] Augustana's second *Moses* commands the most popular entrance to the campus, the Commons Drive cul-de-sac off Grange Avenue. Cast between 1967 and 1969 in Rome by famous sculptor Felix W. DeWeldon, and specifically commissioned by Fawick, it is thought to be a singular piece. The September 16, 1976, *Mirror* reported on the controversy:

---

1 Campus Beautification Program brochure, 1974–1977.

> Moses, head still held high with pride after "living" through the two-year battle over his permanent location and the "copy of a copy" issue, has finally come out of seclusion in a downtown warehouse to overlook the Augustana campus from the hill west of the Commons.[2]

Fawick's terms were that *Moses* be placed in an aesthetic location with public access. A gift from the Augustana Fellows and friends of the college paid for the location ($35,000). Augustana President Charles Balcer dedicated *Moses* on Founder's Day, September 29, 1976.[3] Today Michelangelo's *Moses* is settled at Augie. Students are casual in his presence. They study and picnic on the surrounding brick plaza. Classes and meetings are held at his feet and under his intense gaze. He dominates the walk to the Commons. John Peters points out the chisel marks on the casting and marvels at Michelangelo's handiwork.

The *Mammoth*, another large campus sculpture, stands at the corner of Twenty-Ninth Street and Grange Avenue, adjacent to Archeology Laboratory I. It is an actual, life-sized replica of the mammoth excavated in the White River Badlands of South Dakota by Augustana archeology professor Adrien Hannus and his archeological team in 1980 and 1981. Hannus says, tongue-in-cheek, that students get an idea of what it is to face a mammoth with only a spear point. The inscription on a glacial boulder next to the *Mammoth* informs readers it is "the largest land mammal that existed world-wide during the last ice age" standing "at the front shoulder 14 feet and weighing approximately 9 tons." The sculpture itself, erected in June 1991 by Eugene Anderson and Hannus, weighs four thousand pounds and is made of COR-TEN steel, an alloy whose surface corrodes to rust and then stabilizes. Rust is the color of a mammoth's fur. *Mammoth* lights up the Augustana Christmas season: 100 sets of lights produce, Hannus observes, 10,000 twinkles. Hannus says the question "Who will hang the lights?" begins circling in the lab at the end of October.

The story behind the *Mammoth* is the death of an adult and a juvenile mammoth at the edge of an ancient pond some 13,000 years ago.[4] Hannus became involved in the story with the discovery in 1980 of a Clovis-era event—two mammoths being butchered using tools "made from their bones and the bones from other animals."[5] Hannus says the

2 Kathy Rang, news editor.

3 Campus Beautification Program brochure, 1974–1977.

4 "The long-awaited report on a rare Covis-era mammoth site," ***Peopling of the Americas Publications.*** College Station: Texas A&M University Press.

5 "A Clovis Mammoth Butchery Site in the South Dakota Badlands," ***Mammoth Trumpet.*** Volume 36, Number 2, April 2021, 1.

Lange/Ferguson archeological site where the discovery was made is the most important excavation he has participated in. It is noted for being "the earliest dated archaeological site in South Dakota and one of the few North American sites."[6] "Serendipity" is the word Hannus uses to describe his involvement and the discovery at the site.

These and other sculptures define the Augustana campus experience. They reflect Augustana's values as well as inspire and delight. All are part of the company we keep and the ground we walk.

---

6 "The long-awaited report on a rare Covis-era mammoth site."

Kilian Community College

CHARLES ROGERS

Students chose to attend Kilian for a variety of reasons. The following stories are an insight into some of those reasons.

Lyla Moore and Her Daughter, Joyce Rooks

Lyla Moore and her son, Marlowe, traveled to Sioux Falls every summer to visit the School for the Deaf because Marlowe had been born deaf. They stayed at the Holiday Inn downtown when they came to Sioux Falls. One day, Lyla stepped out onto the balcony of the hotel to get some fresh air, and as she peered over at a big window on Phillips Avenue, she noticed a reflection that read Kilian Community College. Moore wondered if that was where she was going to start college. In the fall of 2006, that wonder became a reality. Moore was the first one in her family to graduate from college.

Joyce said that she never planned on going to college. Her plans were to complete high school and go to work. She wrote, "It took a lot of convincing from my mom, Lyla, and I'm thankful she was persistent." Joyce was scared because most of what she had heard about college was that it was hard. But her mom said, "There's a lot of help at Kilian. They have a Success Center with great tutors. You'll love it there."

Joyce applied and was accepted. For the first time, she was excited to be in school. She made great friends and has many fond memories of Kilian. "I will always remember the semester when my mom, Lyla, and I were in the same class. My mom is outspoken while I'm usually quiet," Joyce said. "I gained confidence while attending Kilian because the professors helped me realize my potential." Although Joyce changed her major a couple of times, it was at Kilian that she made decisions about her future. This wasn't something Joyce thought about before starting college. She realized that she wanted to do something with her life. She appreciates the professors who helped prepare her to continue her schooling.

Another Kilian student, Le Anne VanRegenmorter, had sold Avon products and loaded boxes on trucks for a local employer. She was injured on the job and was approaching the age of forty. These factors prompted her to search for a new career and this led her to Kilian Community College in 1985. She started taking classes when her youngest was a senior in high school. By 1987, she had completed her AAS degree in executive secretary. She also earned a certificate in word processing and a diploma in legal secretary. A desire to learn had been ignited and she wanted to continue learning. VanRegenmorter enrolled at the University of Sioux Falls and completed her bachelor's degree. A week after graduation, she became Kilian's first full-time registrar. She also managed the bookstore. Her love of learning led to a master's degree in business administration from the University of South Dakota in 1998. Her next position was at Louisiana State University in Shreveport. Her duties included overseeing the bookstore, food and vending services, and the print center.

Origins

In 1969, Augustana College and Sioux Falls College established the Sioux Falls Continuing Education Center (CEC). The North American Baptist Seminary joined the partnership two years later. Dr. Stanford Stenson was the first director. The mission of the CEC was to be a college-level adult education program for the Sioux Falls community. Surveys were conducted that supported the concept of the CEC. In the early 1970s, South Dakota was the only state that did not have a community college system.

Tom Kilian became the director of the CEC in 1973. His experience in education included serving as secretary of education in South Dakota and as executive vice president at Augustana College. His vision was to create a school for nontraditional students. The North Central University Center (NCUC) was incorporated in 1974 to administer the joint academic and administrative programs of the CEC. In 1976, the CEC became the Community Education Center (Com/Ed) and operated as a division of the Community College of the NCUC. An important step in the history of what would become Kilian Community College took place in April of 1977, when the NCUC board of directors voted to "adopt a schedule that would provide for the opening of a community college in September of 1977" (Sneen 3).

Getting Started

Tom Kilian faced several challenges. He had from April to September to find a location for the school, create a school catalog, as well as hire administrators and teachers. Two World War II barracks from the air base were part of the Sioux Falls College campus on South Menlo Avenue. They were rented and became the location of the school. The buildings had been used as a warehouse. Old tires and trunks of abandoned student clothing had to be removed. Carpentry, painting, wallpaper, and new moldings followed. Because the state stored its surplus property in an office in Huron, Tom and others returned from Huron with old desks, file cases, chairs, and an assortment of other items needed for a school.

The Community College of the NCUC opened its doors in September of 1977. It was described as a school "without walls." Most of the classes were held at Augustana College, Sioux Falls College, North American Baptist Seminary, and public rooms in the community. Administrative offices were located at 1600 South Menlo Avenue. The official title for the location was Burton Hall, aka "the Barracks."

Original Administrators

The paths of Jim Schmidt and Tom Kilian first crossed at Augustana. Schmidt was a student and Kilian was an administrator. Kilian contacted Schmidt, who had taken a position as a teacher and principal in Wisconsin. The new position sounded intriguing, and Schmidt answered the call.

Schmidt helped Kilian and others clean out the barracks. A hole in the roof needed immediate attention. Schmidt remembers that there was a picture of Don Quixote, *Tilting at Windmills*. "That picture was a perfect description of their situation," he said (interview 2016).

Schmidt became director of admissions and visited area high schools during their career days for seniors. He spoke at regular meetings of service organizations such as Lions, Kiwanis, and Rotarians, to promote the school. The community was not receptive to a new school for nontraditional students. To promote the school, marketing stands were set up in surrounding communities to advertise class schedules for the next term and general information about the school.

One of the biggest challenges was creating courses and course descriptions. One of the early challenges was in the area of finances. Grants kept the school going in the early years, and Augustana contributed paper as well as the use of copy machines. Schmidt's position at the school changed when he became director of the college. One of his responsibilities was to hire teachers. He always tried to hire teachers who were willing to give people a second chance.

Schmidt developed programs in cooperation with Stewart's School of Hairstyling. Upon completion of cosmetology classes, the students were awarded an associate's degree from Kilian. He also developed classes for the Sioux Falls Fire Department. These courses increased enrollment and helped the school gain recognition and credibility in the community. Kilian also had the distinction of being the first school in Sioux Falls to offer a paralegal program.

Schmidt left the school in 1981 to pursue other interests. The next step for him was to become president of the school, and his first action was to appoint a naming committee. Tom Kilian's name was suggested because of his dream and efforts in founding the institution. The committee agreed and the school officially became Kilian Community College.

Schmidt had three goals for the school, and the first was to pay off debt. Agreements were worked out with Augustana, Sioux Falls College, and North American Baptist Seminary. Each institution was gracious enough not to demand full payment of the money they were owed. Schedules were set up, and over a period of time, the debts were paid. The second goal was to expand the curriculum. One technique that was used to achieve this goal was to contact business leaders and find out what types of courses would be helpful to their employees. After assessing these needs, courses were developed and then taught at businesses. Computers were just beginning to appear in 1979, and Kilian's first computer was purchased by Kilian and Schmidt at Radio Shack. It was a TRS-80. Not really knowing what to do with it, they hired Stan Pickard to teach a computer class. It was a challenge for him, as twenty students had signed up to take the class with only one computer. The final goal was to gain approval of North Central for the transfer of credits. Two obstacles faced the college: 1) North Central was objecting to the fact that some of the teachers had not taken teacher preparation/education courses at a four-year institution, and 2) Kilian hired teachers who were practitioners in a given field.

An example was that lawyers were hired to teach the paralegal courses, but they had not taken education courses in college. To overcome this obstacle, Kilian applied for and was awarded a grant from the Bush Foundation. The grant was used to provide in-service for those teachers who had not taken the required courses. The second obstacle was that Kilian did not have a dean with a PhD, so one was hired. Having overcome these two obstacles, North Central approved the transfer of Kilian credits.

A number of changes took place during Schmidt's tenure as president. A new board of directors was needed to oversee changes in the curriculum, changes in credit hours, and a change to the quarter system. The board was made up of members from the business community and representatives from the three founding institutions. A student center was set up so that students would have a place to relax, and the formation of a student council gave the students a voice at the school. When Citibank started a program of tuition reimbursement, Kilian was one of the first schools to participate.

Schmidt's parents died of cancer, so when the position of vice president of the American Cancer Society of South Dakota was offered to him in 1992, he accepted the job and resigned as president.

Original Employees

Sue Kiner has the distinction of being the original employee of KCC. Her teaching career started at O'Gorman High School, and with the approaching arrival of her and her husband's first child, they decided she could be a stay-at-home mom. After being at home for a year, Kiner got a call from Sue Dunmire, head of the Business Education Department at Augustana.

Dunmire asked Kiner if she would be interested in teaching typing at KCC. The class would be held one night a week. This was in 1977. The class was held in a barracks building on the Augustana campus, and one night a week turned into two. By 1983, Kiner was teaching full-time, and from 1986 to 1999, she served as division chairman of the Office Skills Department, later known as Office Technology.

Shirley Garry was the coordinator of the capital campaign for the new location on Phillips Avenue. Her duties included arranging appointments with donors and keeping track of the pledges that were made over a three-year period. She served as academic director from 1994 to 1997. Hiring adjunct faculty and scheduling classes were the main responsibilities of her position.

Between them, Kiner and Garry were members of an advisory council that was made up of local employers. They had to make all the arrangements for meetings, including coffee and treats. Council members would tell the school what their employment needs were, and then programs were developed to meet those needs. Another council activity was bringing employers together with students who were seeking employment. Kiner and Garry described their years at Burton Hall as exciting. This manifested in several ways: small classes enabled teachers and students to develop personal relationships, and the women enjoyed seeing nontraditional students recapture the joy of learning as well as the satisfaction of helping students find jobs. Kiner and Garry saw KCC's strengths in being able to develop and implement new programs in a shorter period of time than was possible at larger institutions. They also appreciated the flexible scheduling to meet the needs of nontraditional students.

Their last project was helping to pack and make the move to the new location on Phillips Avenue. They both left KCC and returned to positions in high schools in Sioux Falls.

In Conclusion

Through his experience in higher education, Tom Kilian became aware of the fact that nontraditional students did not have educational opportunities in the Sioux Falls area. It became his mission to create a school that would provide nontraditional students an opportunity to return to school. He recruited others to help him fulfill his mission and, in time, Kilian Community College became a reality. The school's history is a testament to the impact it had on the lives of students and teachers. There are many personal stories from teachers that we don't have room to share in this publication. Due to several factors, the school closed in 2016.

Sources

Rogers, Charles. Interview with Jim Schmidt. 2006.

Sneen, Donald. *Through Trials and Triumphs: A History of Augustana College*. Sioux Falls: Center for Western Studies, 1985.

Divorce Capital, USA

GRANT WENTZEL

By 1890, the word was out. If you were looking to wrangle a divorce and snub the banns that bound your wayward heart, there was only one place that would do: Sioux Falls, South Dakota, Divorce Capital USA.

Sioux Falls—yes, God-fearing, upright Sioux Falls, that new boomtown settled by the straight-backed sons of prairie pioneers, that sprout of civilization saddling the last wisps of tall-grass prairie and the wide-open west—offered it all to the potential divorcee: plush accommodations, plentiful lawyers, and most importantly, a ninety-day term-of-stay to establish residency. Set up house for three months and you could plead your case before the light laws of the new-formed state.

And so they came by the hundreds—over a thousand before the boom was through—from back East and abroad, as United States citizenship was not a prerequisite before the courts: a DuPont, a Woolworth, an Astor; the forlorn wives of stage stars, athletes, and politicians. The freedom-seekers in Sioux Falls were soon so plentiful that they became known as the Divorce Colony, a separate social sphere, a satellite with a gravity all its own.

Orbiting the corner of Ninth and Phillips Avenue, the glittering menagerie grew—befurred and bejeweled—to be gawked at, envied, profited from, yet scorned by starstruck polite society. One had to be of some means to secure a Dakota divorce. Travel, accommodations, and lawyer fees added up: $3 a day for the hotel, starting rates of $250 to $500 for attorneys, plus expenses—extra for discretion. The outlay could rise to tens of thousands of turn-of-the-century dollars.

While many unfaithful husbands slunk west seeking dissolution, the typical Dakota divorcee was an unhappy wife traveling surreptitiously, lacking other options to escape intolerable, interminable domestic circumstances. Despite the desire to avoid scrutiny, the possession of independent wealth—enough to slip away for a scandalous season—was not hard to spot amongst the hardscrabble pioneers.

A well-healed hierarchy soon evolved, the new arrivals ranked by the number of pampered pets in tow: one dog, two dogs, three dogs. While the three-dog owners might purchase a house for the duration of their campaign, the best of the rest—and their pups—awaited their marital ablutions at the Cataract House Hotel, so named for the cleansing quartzite gurgle a mile to the north.

There, with little to do but wait and seek out distractions, the divorcees luxuriated their days away. At the Cataract, one could find any pleasure feared missing in the rude territory, from champagne to caviar to another flirtatious dalliance. They were all there for the same thing, after all.

Originally built in 1871, the Cataract (motto: "We Strive to Please!") boasted the finest accommodations between east and west, awing and humbling haggard travelers who approached the front desk. The wood-framed Cataract burned down in a fury of fireworks in 1900, but it was quickly resurrected with grander ambitions. The rebuilt hotel soon scaled five fireproof stories, replete with *en suite* accommodations, bars, restaurants, electric lights, a ballroom, an elevator, steam heat, and room-service signaling bells. It was a hedonistic oasis on the plains.

At the Cataract, the seasonal balls and parties were the talk of the town. A rite of passage for the newly freed was the Divorce Dinner, a bacchanal of freedom thrown upon the procuring of one's decree. All fellow sojourners would be invited for an evening's balm to ease the suffering of their shared plight. Wine from France, steaks shipped from New York, oysters from the coasts—what the Cataract didn't have on hand, the new railways could provide. The unshackled spared no expense.

It wasn't supposed to be this way.

The ninety-day threshold for residency was short by necessity. Settlers came and went in those days, staking claims on untested land, following rumors of golden opportunity. Failure was as common as success. To mold something of a constituency out of the migratory chancers wandering west—trying one spot after another, driven by peripatetic desire—the bar had best be set low.

The city itself was newborn. The founding fathers hurriedly sketched out gridded streets across bison-shat soil that offered no resistance to their linear imaginations, plumb lines broken only by the rambling falls—"*rivalling Niagara!*" they fibbed—as they bilked millmen in search of investment opportunities.

Everyone here was from somewhere. The population of Sioux Falls jumped from 600 residents in 1876 to over 10,000 by 1890. All of the major players in the divorce drama were new arrivals themselves:

from Maine, Henry Corson, builder of the Cataract; from Ontario and Rochester, Edmison and Jameson, erectors of the eponymous structure across the street, home of thirty-eight sharp-penciled law firms; from Vermont, Governor Charles Sheldon and the esteemed Senator Pettigrew; from New York, the sympathetic presiding Judge Frank Aiken; and from Philadelphia, the dubious Episcopal Bishop Hare.

Ninety days was the standard set in Dakota Territory and so it remained on the books as North and South were split into states in 1889. Fargo had a good run of its own with divorcee-seeking strangers from the East Coast. Edith Wharton made use of one in her novel *The Custom of The Country*, modelling her New York ingénue, Undine Spragg, after the annulment-seeking heiress Medora de Vallombrosa (*née* Von Hoffman.) But North Dakota made the mistake of tightening things up, requiring a full year of residency by 1899. The divorce trade, like water, flowed south along the path of least resistance.

Yankton, the river town eighty miles to the south, also did its best to cash in on the windfall, but the shiny new tracks of the locomotive converged on Sioux Falls, ushering in efficient escape—both to Sioux Falls and then to spirit away once the gavel was struck and the prairie charms had worn thin.

Although the catchy term "quickie divorce" is often thrown about to describe the aspirations of those who sought refuge in Sioux Falls, like anything in those pre-jet plane days, life was more arduous at the time. Doing your ninety days (and later six months, after the law was changed in 1893) was just the first step. Not that anyone looked too closely. A three-month receipt from a hotel or a properly dated lease might work just fine. Only after that would you have the opportunity to plead your case.

Contested suits could be argued for months, though many were settled in as little as fifteen minutes. ("We rarely fail to make a case!" as one lawyer put it.) The thousand-mile shroud of secrecy between Sioux Falls and the Atlantic was usually enough to avoid an unexpected challenge. Divorce notices needed only to be published in South Dakota papers and thus were unlikely to be read by spurned spouses back home. And there were numerous reports of plaintiffs left empty-handed. Those looking to brazenly flout the law—to wag wealth at unscrupulous attorneys and secure divorce by correspondence—found their petitions dismissed. As reported in the *Brooklyn Daily Eagle*:

> The popular conception of a Dakota divorce court is that all one has to do is drop an affidavit in the slot and take out your decree.

> There is no denying the fact that the laws here are very lax, and their interpretation is very liberal . . . but it is by no means true that an application for a divorce is equivalent to securing a decree. Not all who call are chosen. Not long since an attorney received a letter from Louisiana. The writer said he wanted a divorce, but could not spare the time to come to Sioux Falls for it. "Fix up the papers," he wrote cheerfully, "and I will sign them. Allege anything and I will swear to it." It is needless to say that his case had not yet been commenced.

Yes, even in Sioux Falls one couldn't escape the prying eyes of the press if news of your status proved tattle-rag worthy. Case in point: the Baroness Margaret Laura De Stuers, or more simply, Maggie, the niece of John Jacob Astor III. After a midnight Parisian escape and a clandestine year abroad hiding from her husband, the overbearing and (en)titled Dutch diplomat Baron Alphonse Lambert Eugene Ridder De Stuers, the Baroness eventually materialized in Sioux Falls. Here, she faced five months of well-covered proceedings before the judge ruled in her favor.

While the grounds for divorce in South Dakota were not dissimilar to those in other states (adultery, imprisonment, habitual drunkenness, extreme cruelty, abandonment, willful neglect, bigamy—and indeed—impotence) the burden of proof was logistically low. It was his word against hers, or more likely hers against his. And he was nowhere to be found.

The abundance of competing lawyers in Sioux Falls also proved advantageous. If one attorney's scruples got in the way, another could always be retained, with some willing to accept exorbitant fees, jewels, and gifts to assuage a conflicted conscience. Enterprising lawyers would scout arriving trains for new clients or collude with law firms from Chicago to New York who recommended Dakota colleagues eager for new business.

Need a witness? There was always a local resident ready to hustle a few bucks, swearing to whatever indiscretions were needed to make the case. Many suits were argued on the grounds of cruelty and neglect, sufficiently vague terms covering a multitude of supposed sins. However, petitioners had to sign an affidavit that they were indeed residents of South Dakota, did not come with the express purpose of securing a divorce, and intended to reside in South Dakota after the divorce was granted. Eventually, all had to sit before the gaze of Judge Frank Aiken, a man known to tread a careful line between the letter and spirit of the law. Kindhearted and "just [at] that ardent and susceptible age when woman's distress appeals to man most strongly," Judge Aiken could only rule with the facts at hand. The bereft before him had sworn their tales of woe and intentions were true, and that was enough. Should a newly divorced party have a change of heart and decamp Sioux Falls within days of their decree, what could be done?

Like all booms, the divorce industry would eventually go bust. While celebrated by far-flung progressives as a mighty strike for the liberation of women, most of the townsfolk were wary. The Divorce Mill, as the industry was also known, was seen in many circles as an affront to Christian decency. Sioux Falls had acquired a new reputation. Once a frontier town of sod-breaking settlers and hardworking agricultural opportunity, Sioux Falls found a new louche infamy as a city that flaunts the law, rife with the licentious behavior rumored to surround the Divorce Colony: gambling, drunkenness, gluttony, and most horribly, promiscuity. The good name of Sioux Falls was at stake, and something had to be done.

The organized backlash began with the return of Bishop William Hobart Hare, the Episcopal authority for the state of South Dakota. Coming home in 1892 after a stint of missionary work in China and Japan, he was shocked by the growing scandal of the Divorce Colony. Alas, even his own congregation had been corrupted! Here, in his newly built quartzite cathedral—a gift of the great John Jacob Astor III, who allocated funds and oversaw the design in honor of his saintly wife, Charlotte Augusta—knelt throngs of guileless divorcees. Among them was the Baroness Margaret Laura De Stuers, niece of John Jacob himself, innocently accepting the host from his very hands.

Finding sanctuary in the congregation before the return of Bishop Hare, the Baroness showed her appreciation by donating three gleaming stained-glass windows to the church. Keen to avoid further desecration, the Bishop refused to have them hung, angrily stashing the jewel-toned panes away in the basement, where they languished for years.

Bishop Hare soon took his indignation public and immediately began to push for tighter laws. With hopes of lengthening the residency requirement to a full year, he saw through the passage of an extension to six months. This left the divorce industry wounded, yet viable, as six months was still in line with the minimum offered by other western states such as Texas and Nebraska. Not one to be defeated, the bishop eventually got his wish, leading the charge to require a full year of residency in 1909. This put an effective end to those looking for efficient divorce in Sioux Falls. A race-to-the-bottom competition ensued, with Reno, Nevada, declaring repeated victories as the go-to destination for the spurned and spurning: six months, to three months, to an easy six weeks-of-stay by 1931.

While the divorce industry of Sioux Falls has been put asunder, the practice of exploiting loopholes for lucre lives on.

Bulldozed in a fit of misguided 1970s urban renewal, the physical evidence of the Divorce Colony has been swept away, architectural relics interred in another shortsighted lustration. Gone is the Cataract House Hotel and its competitors. Gone is the Edmison-Jameson Building where the lawyers plied their trade. Gone are the department stores and taverns that catered to big spenders. Today, on the corner of Ninth and Phillips Avenue, banks tower overhead.

The credit card industry now fills the void: plastic convenience, instant access, erasing the fear of last-dollar destitution from the acquisitive masses. South Dakota abolished all caps on interest rates in 1981, usurping the usury laws set in place during Roosevelt's New Deal. Citibank arrived days later, starting a trend that has brought trillions of bank deposits to the state.

Unsatisfied with one windfall, South Dakota eliminated rules against perpetuities in 1983, creating a chance to establish eternal trusts—private, secure, personal bolt-holes to stash gain of unknown provenance—no questions asked. Scattered around today's downtown in nondescript office blocks, behind smoked-glass windows, the servants of the law persevere at their task, minting gold from grievance, spinning silver from sin, eschewing prudence for the printing of paper profits. By now over $300 billion has been locked up in South Dakota, making Sioux Falls the new Zurich, the prairie-flat pinnacle of the world's shady wealth.

But walk onward, a few blocks to the south. Knock and enter the apse of the Episcopal Cathedral and lift your eyes to heaven. Three stained-glass windows greet your gaze: Christ crucified, Christ in ascension, Christ who brings comfort to the little children. Our Lord in three ways.

The Baroness's dedications on each frame have been scratched out—scratched out like the sight-unseen claims of westward pioneers, scratched out like sod houses and first crops from antediluvian dirt, scratched out like gold nuggets from Black Hills creeks, scratched out like the marital vows of gilded travelers who yearned for reprieve in the open arms of the courts of Sioux Falls.

The gifts of the divorcee have been redeemed. Raised up from cellar storage, they now hang restored, beaming down wryly on the penitent, a backlit testament to the past and to the enduring spirit—Sioux Falls's strange pride—of ignoble enterprise.

Sister Cities

ANDREW ERICKSON

Imagine snacking on pretzels and drinking a foamy beer under the late summer sun and then chasing the experience with *kuchen* as the evening's polka music gets underway.[1] This describes the scene at Germanfest, which every year transforms Falls Park West into a site of German and American exchange.[2] In doing so, the annual event highlights the city's past as a center of activity for German immigrants and its present and future as a "sister city" to Potsdam, Germany.

Sioux Falls became the first US city to partner with a city in the former East German Republic (GDR) when it began its formal relationship with Potsdam in 1990 ("Germany"; "Straßenbahn"). What might seem like an odd pairing at first glance reveals more similarity than difference. Potsdam traces its history back more than a thousand years to roots in Slavic settlement, while Sioux Falls occupies the lands of the Osceti Sakowin, who have held an ancestral relationship to the land for at least as long. Long histories and the complicated mixing of peoples and political struggles have led both cities toward complex, sometimes violently shifting identities and a contemporary era of rapid growth and further diversification, with current populations that are approaching 200,000.[3] In both communities, the presence of German and American (and German American) influences can be observed. Areas of parallel, if considerably different, past and present development identify the pairing as one of commensurable opportunity for personal exchange and ongoing education. This further indicates the ways in which the Sioux Falls-Potsdam partnership invigorates the Sister Cities model.

Sister Cities International (the parent organization of the Sister Cities Association of Sioux Falls) grew out of a postwar-era desire to foreground individual and community partnerships across perceived divides. Its mission to "create global relationships based on cultural, educational, information and trade exchanges" provided the impetus to situate already

1 For an overview of how the German American kuchen became South Dakota's state dessert, see Huber.

2 Germanfest did not take place in 2020 due to the COVID-19 pandemic. This is the only documented interruption of which I am aware.

3 While comparisons of population are always fraught, depending on definitions of metropolitan areas, etc., here I elect to use figures from the US Census Bureau for Sioux Falls and Eurostat for Potsdam, respectively. For further reference to increasing population and diversification of Sioux Falls, see Mitchell.

existing connections between Americans and the wider world at the front of its "citizen diplomacy" efforts. In Sioux Falls, the Sister Cities mission has manifested in cultural events that celebrate food and language and also in the exchange of educational development.

Sister Schools, Sister Universities

Between Potsdam and Sioux Falls, students of different ages benefit from the exchange of ideas as they move between their cities. Students from Lincoln High School and the Humboldt Gymnasium in Potsdam swap places each spring to better understand how education functions across cultures; students from O'Gorman share experiences as pen pals (Sneve). Groups of students and researchers from Potsdam's *Brandenburgisches Bildungswerk für Medizin und Soziales* (Brandenburg School for Medical and Social Work, or BBW) make regular trips to Sioux Falls, and students from Augustana University, in turn, have conducted internships organized by BBW in Potsdam and Berlin (see Buschena; "Straßenbahn"). Further exchange is facilitated by a formal partnership between Augustana University and the University of Potsdam—another product of the Sister Cities affiliation—with students regularly studying abroad from each location at the partner university. Some students further take on teaching assistantships facilitated by the relationship. Graduate and postgraduate education are another product of the affiliation and partnerships between cities and universities. In this regard, I can personally attest to the success of the mission.

Attending college and traveling abroad were not on my radar when I was a kid. Like many South Dakotans, I grew up in the rural farmland that comprises the outer orbit of Sioux Falls. I felt rooted in place yet open to—and even hungry for—new experiences. And because of the meaningful intervention of the Sister Cities relationship and its manifestation of study abroad programs, my world expanded into what has since become more than a decade of involvement between two places. While completing studies at Augie, I was twice hosted by the Sister Cities association in Potsdam, both as a student on a travel abroad experience and later as a teaching assistant. After graduating, having enjoyed meaningful experiences facilitated by the Sister Cities organizations in both locations, I moved from Sioux Falls to attend graduate school at the University of Potsdam. During this time, I participated in welcoming another generation of students abroad. As a result, I can personally attest that the partnership between Sister Cities and their universities is strong and growing.

The Sister Cities relationship between Sioux Falls and Potsdam is directly responsible for my vocational success. Because of the early insights that I developed during research internships at Augustana about the history of Sioux Falls, and also during study abroad and host stays in Potsdam, my understanding of these cities and the importance of their interrelatedness has increased. As a postgraduate lecturer and doctoral candidate of American Studies in Germany, I regularly contribute to and engage with the discourse of how perspectives and narratives of the United States, the Midwest, and even of my own hometown near Sioux Falls influence domestic and international thinking and diplomacy. The clear guidance of the Sister Cities mission has helped me clarify and further explore this dynamic, shifting space, and I can tell you that this "citizen diplomacy" frequently happens in classrooms and lecture halls but also in coffeehouses and living rooms in Sioux Falls and in Potsdam.

Mission Success

Take it from me, connections between Sioux Falls and Potsdam abound. The partnership between parallel cities—both growing in population and regional influence—continues to produce important innovations. "Germanfest" continues to provide a popular platform from which to drive awareness and understanding of the ongoing history of German American participation and of the Sister Cities affiliation. It evidences the success of the mission to facilitate cross-cultural awareness and exchange, all the while maintaining a sense of humor. But the ties that bind go deeper than watching dachshunds race and enjoying *Bier und Brez'l.* It was more than one hundred years earlier that South Dakota gained statehood in a community center built by German-speaking American immigrants (Renshaw). That site is now occupied by City Hall, where in 1990, a new stage in diplomacy and international exchange came into being.

The Sioux Falls-Potsdam Sister Cities affiliation in 2017 was recognized by the Steuben-Schurz-Gesellschaft as "the most successful German-American City/Community partnership[s]" ("Preis"; Sneve). This can be attributed to active, meaningful engagement across educational opportunities and cultural events and also to the commitment of senior municipal officials to the relationship. Several delegations from Potsdam City Hall have visited Sioux Falls over the years (Buschena), culminating in a visit in 2017 by Potsdam's lord mayor to "tour the city and attend the annual Germanfest celebration downtown" (Sneve). Sioux Falls Mayor

Mike Huether visited Potsdam in 2014 to attend the christening of a streetcar there; it was named "Sioux Falls" in honor of the relationship ("Straßenbahn"; "Sioux Falls mayor"). Strong educational connections between high schools and universities, reciprocal visits by city officials and groups of interested citizens and "friends circles" of the Sister Cities affiliation, as well as prizes won, all indicate the strength of the relationship and provide reason to believe it will continue to develop and thrive for years to come.

I did not seek to write an exhaustive or official cultural history of the Sioux Falls-Potsdam connection here. Instead, my goal was to introduce the topic for a general audience and to share my own experience of the ways in which the Sister Cities have shaped my personal and professional journey. I look forward to more scholarship in this area, as there exists much more to this exciting story of Sioux Falls as a site of international exchange, and of the Sister Cities relationship in facilitating meaningful opportunities for South Dakotans of all ages.

Sources

Buschena, Alyson. "Delegation from Germany visits Pioneer Village." *The Globe* (Worthington, MN). The Globe and Forum Communications Company, 28 Mar. 2013.

"Germany." Sister Cities Association of Sioux Falls, 2020.

Huber, Makenzie. "What is kuchen? Why this dessert became a South Dakota food favorite." *Sioux Falls Argus Leader*. Gannett, 22 Aug. 2019.

Landeshauptstadt Potsdam. *Eine Straßenbahn namens Sioux Falls*. 12 Jun. 2014. Web. 6 Oct. 2021.

Mitchell, Trevor J. "Census 2020 data shows Sioux Falls' population is growing—and becoming more diverse." *Sioux Falls Argus Leader*. Gannett, 12 Aug. 2021.

"People-to-People Initiative." Sister Cities Association of Sioux Falls, 2020.

"Potsdam Teaching Assistantship." Augustana University, 2021.

"Preis für die aktivste deutsch-amerikanische Städtepartnerschaft." Steuben-Schurz-Gesellschaft e. V., n. dat.

Renshaw, Eric. "Looking Back: Germania Hall celebrated German heritage in Sioux Falls until WWI broke out." *Sioux Falls Argus Leader*. 31 Jul. 2021.

Sneve, Joe. "German sister city sending dignitaries to Sioux Falls." *Sioux Falls Argus Leader*. 13 Apr. 2017.

The Lost Boys

DAVID WAL JAL

My name is David Wal Jal. I was born in Dunyal Village in Nasir County, South Sudan, in Northeast Africa. I lived there for the first ten years of my life, and it was very difficult due to the civil war in my home country. The marginalization of our people by the Islamic government of Sudan caused the rise of the Southern Sudanese to fight for their freedom.

The Sudan People's Liberation Army, or the SPLA/SPM, was a guerrilla army fighting against the government of Sudan with a vision to unify Sudan as a whole. The SPLA began to forcefully recruit young boys to serve in the military. I was one of those child soldiers who were forced to serve in the military from the age of seven to the age of fourteen. None of us were given a choice whether we wanted to serve or not. However, every one of us was motivated to serve because we were told that the enemy would kill our families, and anyone who served would be defending their family and providing strong protection.

Today, I have no doubt in my mind that many people, including myself, would think this was a horrible idea, but who in this world would refuse to provide protection for their loved ones? We all came to understand that it was better to fight than to tell others that our people were all slaughtered because we could not protect them.

During the military conflict, many child soldiers sustained serious injuries, and many lost their lives. A large number of children in South Sudan, including children in Dunyal village, fled their home due to the civil war in Sudan.

Most of us, known today as "the Lost Boys" of Sudan, were living in various refugee camps in Ethiopia, but we were forced to leave that country when the camps were closed and dismantled. We had to travel for two months, crossing dangerous rivers and walking about 1,000 miles barefoot and without food in search of safety. We spent the next ten to fifteen years in Kakuma refugee camp in Kenya, Africa.

In 1994, I received a message from the United Nations High Commissioner for Refugees (UNHCR) that my cousin in the US was willing to sponsor me. I went through an interview with Homeland Security, formerly known as INS, completed a medical screening, and was finally approved to travel to South Dakota. On June 20, 1995, I was resettled as a refugee in Sioux Falls, which I still call my home today. In South Dakota, I found many compassionate people who helped me to become who I am today. With the help of Lutheran Social Services, church volunteers, Mennonite volunteers across the US and Canada, and the entire community of the city, I was able to pursue and complete my bachelor's degree in social work at the University of South Dakota in Vermillion. I have been blessed with four wonderful children. With the help of a Bush Foundation fellowship, I was able to obtain a master's degree in social work from the University of North Dakota, Grand Forks, as well as a diploma in international restorative justice from Queen's Theological College in Kingston, Ontario, Canada.

Even though there were challenges and many unusual circumstances during this journey, it provided us, the Lost Boys, with the perfect conditions and opportunities for a new kind of growth. This journey was special because of the people with whom we shared our new home and their big hearts willing to share their blessings with us. From our life experiences in refugee camps, we have learned the importance of cherishing each moment and especially appreciating the people with whom we spend those moments.

We all felt very lucky to be settled in the Sioux Falls area. It made our assimilation so easy because all the agencies, including the Sioux Falls School District, were involved in our adjustment to the community. Some of the boys were adopted by local families, and they were well cared for. Those of us who were still under the age of eighteen were able to attend school, which would not have been possible without the district's leadership.

After we arrived in Sioux Falls, we built great friendships and fell in love with the community that opened its doors to us. We were eager to work and support ourselves. It was exciting to see what could be accomplished with a group of young boys who have been separated from their families for such a long time. Having said this, I have to admit that the loss of family, separation from family, and having no place to call home still haunts us, regardless of the calm and peaceful environment in which we now live. Sioux Falls became one of the largest communities of Lost Boys in the nation.

I believe that God has preserved our lives for a purpose. It is a miracle that some of us are still alive. I believe that part of God's purpose in keeping us alive was made clear to me, after seeing the overwhelming support from the Sioux Falls community when I returned to my home village in 2010. I was shocked to see that little had changed. I was especially surprised to see the effects of the civil war on children. Children were still walking around with AK-47s as toys. Girls still did not go to school and instead were staying home to grind corn for their family meal. Everyone in the village still got their drinking water from the Khor Wakow River. There were still no medical services for the sick. As a result, I founded a nonprofit organization—the Khor Wakow Project—to provide a school and safe drinking water in this village in South Sudan.

In 2012, with support from the Sioux Falls community, we dug a well in the Dunyal village. We also delivered corn grinders so the girls could attend school. The recent fighting in South Sudan brought the construction of a permanent school in Khor Wakow to a halt. In January 2014, the construction of our school was to begin; however, civil war broke out on December 15, 2013, and all those plans were put on hold. It is now exciting to see the completion of Khor Wakow Christian Academy become reality in 2021, but I am still disheartened about the lack of progress in South Sudan.

I dream that we will return to Khor Wakow with a heightened sense of God's presence and of the mission He wants to accomplish through us. Hearing countless stories of hearts and lives forever changed brings me joy and confidence. I can rest knowing that God is with the villagers, students, and everyone with whom we came in contact. I can trust Him that their futures are in God's plans and that He will provide. I have found myself holding on to the memories of working with and teaching the children during my visits to South Sudan. It is difficult to let go, not knowing what will happen to them once I leave, but I have learned to give all my concerns to God, knowing He will take care of them.

If we were to start over and decide for ourselves where to be settled, Sioux Falls, South Dakota, would still be the place. We will always remember the welcoming reception and the assistance we received upon our arrival in Sioux Falls, and we are always willing to return this courtesy to other people in the city.

A Kiss beneath the Clock: A Short Story

STEVEN WINGATE

Reed Hankinson didn't want the whole thing about the clock to be about in-staters vs. out-of-staters, but Eriksen Grenier made that impossible. Everything about Grenier screamed Northern California carpetbagger. His Tesla, his wine snobbery, his open marriage, his cannabis advocacy, his house (bought with cash) tucked away among the doctors and the moguls near Twenty-Second and Kiwanis. Though Reed had grown up a mile west of there and now lived a mile south, he'd never felt the need to defend Sioux Falls values or South Dakota values—whatever they were—until Grenier stepped into his life. Or *onto* his life. Reed couldn't decide which.

They worked together at Cameron Associates, a public relations firm where Reed ran the graphic design department and Grenier was the hotshot sales rep everybody envied. Man, could Grenier turn on the charm. When he gave presentations about how Cameron Associates would transform your enterprise, he electrified everybody. Reed had to acknowledge that if it weren't for Grenier's slickness, he'd have a much less glamorous job. He wouldn't be going fantasy home and furniture shopping with his fiancée Katrina, wouldn't be thinking about buying a BMW, wouldn't have signed the petition to get legal pot on the ballot, wouldn't have bought a pair of shoes for client meetings that cost fifty dollars more than his first suit.

So it was complicated, this Reed/Grenier relationship. Reed, who was genuinely Norwegian and had actually been over twice to visit relatives in Stavanger, couldn't stand that Grenier's parents—without a single drop of Norwegian blood!—had named their son after the country's most famous explorer. Reed had to buck up and take it, because when you owe somebody as much as he owed Grenier, accepting condescension almost always came with the territory. But he couldn't simply accept his own subservience and move on, couldn't roll with that particular punch. How hard was it to acknowledge that Grenier was an asshole he simply had to tolerate so he could build his own career?

Very, Reed realized the longer he worked with the man. Some part of him—spleen, appendix, radius, ulna—dug in its heels to say, *No, I'm a South Dakota man, and Eriksen Grenier is a corrupting influence who represents everything wrong with the modern world.* That part of Reed would fight to preserve who he was. A native son of the open prairies, with grandparents who could still drive him to the small pit in the ground outside Pierpoint where their own grandparents had built a sod house in 1887. He wasn't a man of the soil himself, and in fact had never wielded a farm implement beyond the rototiller his father rented when it was time to turn over the garden. But dammit, he wouldn't let some philandering fop with a fake Norwegian name change what Sioux Falls meant, what South Dakota meant.

Here's what Reed couldn't understand about himself, though. Before he met Eriksen Grenier, he desperately wanted to change what Sioux Falls and South Dakota meant. He turned down college scholarships out of state and jobs out of state to stay home and turn Sioux Falls into the city he believed it could become—a destination city that people from all over the world visited because it offered everything you needed, every kind of person you wanted to meet. By any logic, Eriksen Grenier was exactly the kind of import who could help him do the job. Yet somehow, the man had boxed Reed into an emotional corner and turned him into a defender of a set of values he'd never believed in, and in fact spent most of his life trying to rip to pieces.

Reed's internal conflict kicked into high gear because of the damn clock. It was March of 2020, in the early days of COVID-19 when people disinfected cereal boxes from the grocery store and masks weren't a political issue yet. The little clock tower at the strip mall on Forty-First and Marion had stopped working. It was stuck at 9:45, and a rumor started that if you kissed your beloved there at exactly 9:45 at night, it guaranteed your love would last. Bullshit, of course, and *rumor* wasn't the right word. It was more of a ritual fueled by rumor that went viral through Reed's socioeconomic class—the yuppie types who wanted a more progressive Sioux Falls, who didn't hate gays and immigrants, who knew that authoritarianism started at home and vowed not to raise their kids the way their parents had raised them.

Katrina had heard about the clock at Quince—the public relations firm where she wrote copy and ran social media campaigns—and they were among the first couples to make it a habit. By the third time they kissed beneath the clock, the ritual had gotten so popular that they had to take the very last spot in the lot. It was eighteen degrees and windy, so they stayed in the car, feeling each other up and not smooching so they could save their kiss for the big moment. Neither of them were particularly superstitious, but they didn't want to bring themselves bad luck by kissing too early. Especially when the country looked ready to hurl itself into a plague half by mistake, half by blind stupidity. But Reed couldn't stand touching Katrina without kissing her, and he went for her lips. She pulled back, shook her head, and wagged a finger at him.

"Timing is *muy importante*," she said, and her Spanish wasn't bad because she liked to watch *telenovelas* on YouTube whenever she got into a cooking frenzy.

"Fine." Reed sat back in the driver's seat of the Audi he dreamed of replacing and looked at the other cars in the lot. Almost all of them foreign sedans, not a pickup truck in sight. This suited Reed just fine, because he didn't believe in trucks or people who always wanted a bigger one. He preferred people like himself who always wanted fancier sedans—unless Eriksen Grenier was around, in which case he believed in trucks so much that he felt like blasting country music and waving around an American flag twice as big as he was.

When 9:43 came, people got out of their cars and waddled closer to the tower on the lightly iced asphalt. They gathered in a two-layer semicircle, took out their phones, wrapped their arms around their loved ones, and waited for the right minute to come. Reed wondered how this would have worked out back in the days of wristwatches, when everybody had their own time. Who could have agreed on the right moment to kiss? Finally, people's phones flipped over to 9:45 Apple time—most of the crowd had iPhones—and two dozen pairs of lips came together and brought the nightly ritual to life.

Reed and Katrina didn't count the seconds of their kiss, but both felt it was shorter than the last time. Was the novelty wearing off already? Were they flirting with bad luck by being too greedy for good luck? When they straightened out their necks and looked around, they found a different crowd than last time, with one Central American couple and one looking vaguely Somali. For one delicious second, Sioux Falls seemed to be tipping toward the real, diverse city Reed believed it could be. A mini-Minneapolis, a Chicago in the cornfields. Then he heard Grenier's voice.

"That you, Hankster?" came his brash, ass-like bray from across the semicircle. Reed loathed that nickname, which reminded him too much of *hamster*. But at the job, things worked out better if Grenier had a nickname for you.

"Yeah, it's me." Reed flashed the most Grenier-like smile he could muster. Katrina, who'd grown up in Mitchell and knew the customs of Minnesota Nice exquisitely, flashed him one too. "Nice night."

"Always," Grenier told him, and then he kissed the woman next to him. At first, Reed hadn't noticed that it wasn't Grenier's wife, Sylvia, because both women were the same height. But this woman had a sharper face and wore redder lipstick than Sylvia ever would.

"Where's Sylvia?" Reed asked, and beneath his arm Katrina flinched.

"Off doing her thing," Grenier told Reed with a laugh. "It's the twenty-first century, Hankster. Time to update your relationship paradigms."

Then the men went their separate ways, waving like they hadn't just had a miniature but potentially devastating blowout. Katrina went to the driver's side, which was never good news.

"What was that?" she asked Reed once she settled into the passenger seat. "Are you *trying* to piss off your meal ticket?"

"He cheapens everything," Reed told her, making sure to drain every milligram of irony and sarcasm from his face. "We kiss here because we love each other and we want it to last. He kisses here because—" The words didn't want to come out. "I don't know, entertainment value or something."

"It's just a clock." Katrina furrowed her brow at him, then she kissed his forehead like a mother would. "It's just a kiss. I don't know why you let him bother you so much."

But it wasn't just a clock, and it wasn't just a kiss. Reed could never explain it because Katrina could never understand. She didn't know what Grenier stood for, what he *meant*. For the first time since they got engaged, Reed felt sure their relationship was doomed.

The next day at work, Grenier acted chilly even though Reed didn't say anything about the woman at the clock tower. Twice in a meeting, he used the name "Reed" instead of "Hankster." The morning after that, things boiled over when he attacked Reed in front of Jake Cameron—the younger and more vindictive of the firm's founding brothers—for daring to correct the misspellings in the copy a potential client had provided.

"Reed here is essentially telling the client they're imbeciles," Grenier said. "I can't go out there with this presentation as it stands, because then

I'm telling them they're imbeciles."

Jake took Reed's side, saying the errors were so bad that letting it go would reflect poorly on the firm's reputation. Grenier actually sneered at Reed later that morning, but after that, his smiles got twice as smarmy as usual. Reed, deciding to fight fire with fire, learned how to do it himself. He flared his nostrils slightly and pulled the corners of his mouth straight back as far as they'd go while flashing his eyes wide for half a second.

He even practiced it in his rearview mirror on the drive home, finally feeling like his own man—like he might actually get somewhere at work without having to kiss Grenier's ass constantly. Reed felt full of himself and jumped on Katrina as soon as she got home, and they cooked dinner naked. They didn't talk about work like they usually did, since Katrina had a rule about not doing that after sex. They did it again after dinner, agreeing that they should enjoy their libidos while they were still young, and they fell asleep until 9:15.

A kiss beneath the clock? They had the time, so why not? They had to park on the other side of the building, by the bank, and they scrambled to the tower just as everybody's phone said 9:45. A few people even had alarms. Reed and Katrina went with the flow, kissing when everybody else did and getting all wet and sloppy about it. They kissed longer than usual, too, as if trying for a personal best.

"Now *that* was a kiss," Katrina told him when it ended. By then, a lot of couples were walking away, but one other couple kept on kissing even longer. It was Grenier with yet another woman, this time blonde and almost his height. Reed's whole body trembled with the unreasonable prudishness that Grenier inspired within him. Katrina saw Grenier and hooked her elbow into Reed's. She tried to lead him away, but he wouldn't budge. Soon the parking lot cleared, and it was just the four of them—it reminded Reed of the rumble scene in *West Side Story*. He and Grenier both turned to gaze up at the clock, checking to see who'd make eye contact first. It was Grenier, and Reed felt triumphant about it.

"Nice night," Reed told him. He stepped closer and flashed his smarmy, imitation Grenier smile. It earned him one right back.

"You used that line last night," Grenier said. "When all else fails, talk about the weather, right? Isn't that what South Dakota people do?"

"Isn't that what *humans* do? What do people in Marin County talk about when there's nothing else to talk about?"

"Buddhism and retirement accounts," Grenier said, and the blonde laughed. "Aren't you going to ask me any judgmental little questions tonight, Hankster? Like why Sylvia isn't with me?"

"No," Reed said. The tone of his voice rattled Katrina, who yanked him by the elbow. "But it sounds like you want to talk about it."

"I do." Grenier pecked the blonde's cheek, and she let her forehead rest against his shoulder. "This is Simone, and we're having our goodbye kiss tonight. We had a nice run together. Four years. We were together longer than you and Katrina. She and Sylvia really respected each other."

"I see." But Reed used the wrong tone again. Katrina told him so with another yank of his elbow.

"No, Hankster, I don't think you see at all." Grenier's voice turned colder. "You think you're the future of this place, but you're the past. You act like you want Sioux Falls to be a real city—don't bullshit me on that, I've heard you talk about it—but when you come face to face with the way city people think, you dig in your heels like you're back on the farm."

"I didn't come from a farm." Reed unhooked his elbow from Katrina's so she wouldn't yank him again—and maybe so he could clock Grenier in the face if it came to that. "And not all city people think marriage is a team sport."

"But more and more of us do," Grenier said. Then he looked into Simone's eyes.

"More and more," she said, pecking his cheek. Grenier stood up taller and lifted his chin a little, like he always did before he gave the kind of speech that made him such a star at work.

"The thing is, Hankster, you're really not moving this city forward at all. I can't speak for your fiancée, but *you* personally aren't doing anything but changing the shade of its conservatism. You're adding a few drops of white to the red and you're proud as shit of that, which is a totally masturbatory self-con job. You're congratulating yourself for being part of the natural evolution of a place over time. You want praise for putting your two drops of white into the red, but you could be pouring in two buckets."

"What do you recommend, *Eriksen*? Should I start with campaigning to legalize pot or with open marriage?"

"What a prude!" Grenier laughed and guided Simone back to his Tesla, and as they hopped in, Reed lost all desire to buy a BMW. He needed a truck that told the world he was a fifth-generation South Dakotan, not some pretentious wannabe Californian. Reed stood there in the parking lot, watching Grenier drive off without looking back at him once.

"I'm cold," Katrina said. "Why are we standing here?"

Reed still didn't move. He looked up at the clock and thought about kissing Katrina again, but it wasn't 9:45 anymore. Kissing her at the wrong time might reverse all the good luck they'd built up—if his squabble with Grenier hadn't pissed it all away already. In the time he hesitated, Katrina pulled his keys out of his coat pocket and stomped to the driver's seat. Even as cold as she was, she didn't start the engine when he got in.

"You know what's wrong with you?" she said. "You get into meaningless fights for fun. There wasn't any reason in the world to call him out for who he kisses."

"And you know what's wrong with you?" Reed said back. "You're so worried about *not* getting into fights that you won't stand up for what's right."

Katrina put her fingers on the key but didn't turn it. Would she ever? Reed waited and waited, and every second he didn't hear the grind of the ignition, he worried more that everything between them was over.

Prude. Grenier's word hurt, and he heard it over and over inside his head with fifty different intonations. But what really got Reed was what he imagined doing with the gallon can of white paint Grenier talked about, the bucket that could change Sioux Falls if he poured in all of it, not just the two measly drops he congratulated himself for. All he could think of doing with that can of white paint was pouring it over his own damn head. Then somebody—Katrina, Grenier, one of the women Grenier had kissed?—handed him another can, and he poured that one over his head too. Poured it and opened his eyes and saw exactly who he was.

The Nordic Hall

ELINOR NAUEN

When you walked into the Nordic Hall in the 1950s, what you saw on the floor was a huge wooden medallion with the initials NH. When you left, you (naturally) beheld those letters upside down: HN. My dad, Hans Nauen, an accountant, was the Nordic Hall's first tenant, and as a kid, it seemed fitting that they honored him by displaying his initials so large and lordly. (He did nothing to set me straight.)

Built by the Sioux Falls lodge of Sons of Norway, a fraternal society for people of Norwegian descent or affiliation, the Nordic Hall was financed by stock subscriptions at $10 per share, "together with some outright contributions," the *Hutchinson Herald* of Menno (SD) announced on February 12, 1953. There were members in twenty-two South Dakota counties, and the Nordic Hall Association (NHA) was seeking more in the state's forty-three other counties, according to Ralph O. Hillgren, NHA finance chairman (whose devotion to the hall once involved him in New Year's Eve fisticuffs. See *Stene vs. Hillgren*, SD Supreme Court, 1959).

The NHA did its best to keep the project in the public's mind with benefit dances and celebrations. State Rep and soon-to-be Governor Joe Foss, head of the "Building Bee" committee, contributed in June 1952, saying, "Nordic Hall, with a museum of pioneer relics, a library, and proper decorations recalling the inspiring story of the pioneers, should do more than anything imaginable to perpetuate the fine character and traditions of the first settlers." Ricki Sogge Lauritsen, one of several Washington High classmates who told me of Nordic Hall connections at our recent reunion, sent me a clip from the *Argus* about the Norwegian rosemaling her mother won for naming a new women's organization—the "Nordettes"—who were to assist in developing the Nordic Hall.

"The Sons of Norway had the resources to build that building and they still own it," the late Howard Paulson, a local attorney who served on the board of directors for thirty years, told me last summer. "They also donated the land where it was built."

The Nordic Hall Association was nothing if not frugal. Much of the labor and materials were donated. The steel used to hold up the roof was salvaged from an abandoned construction project in Flandreau. On

November 7, 1954, the museum room on the first floor was dedicated, marking the official opening of the building.

"Giants in the Earth"

The Nordic Hall was conceived as a memorial to the Scandinavian pioneers of the area, according to "The Significance of Nordic Hall," a talk delivered by Ralph O. Hillgren to the South Dakota State Historical Society in January 1953 and placed in the congressional record by then-Senator Karl Mundt:

> On the walls will be linear murals depicting the story of the giants in the earth who came by ox-drawn covered wagons and lived in sod huts, in poverty of pocketbook but not of spirit, and laid the foundations for the future life of South Dakotans. . . . Through its museums and mural art, new generations may learn something of the sacrifices of their forebears and catch some of the vision of the pioneers in striving for something better than they had ever known. . . . It is safe to predict that . . . Nordic Hall will be a source of inspiration, and the scene of many significant events as tens of thousands visit its museum, banquet hall, and auditorium in years to come.

The small brick building at 218 West Thirteenth Street, a block from the Washington Pavilion, does not suggest a "source of inspiration" as much as the ordinary office building it is. Over the years, it has been home to a psychiatrist, Junior Achievement, beauty/barber shops, the IRS, a lady selling wigs to women with cancer, goods from Guatemala, a photography studio, and more. The wood floor is now linoleum, and the museum is long gone. "When I joined in the late sixties, they were disbanding it," Howard Paulson told me. "A big skeleton of a ship was one of the last things I remember seeing them carry out."

My siblings and I remember the polished natural wood walls, the old-fashioned bathrooms, the cool and dim interior. Dad had an air-conditioner, and in the hot summer, we would sometimes have a picnic dinner there. "His office had a musty business smell," my brother, Charlie, recalled. "A guy who smoked cigars in his office, that's what it smelled like."

"He liked the location," my sister Lindsay said. "He could walk to clients and the bank, which mattered as he didn't drive." A refugee from

Nazi Germany, Dad kept the books for several local businesses: clothing and appliance stores, the Indian School in Flandreau, the Arts Council, and other nonprofits. He bartered his services at times, "like for Earl the Barber," Lindsay said, "who gave Charlie awful haircuts until he finally refused to go there again."

"My early memories are of the annual Sons of Norway lutefisk dinners in the basement social hall," Howard Paulson said. "Lutefisk is a staple. Torsk is cod, the poor man's lobster, boiled and served in chunks, swimming in butter. Torsk is not so much an acquired taste as lutefisk."

Like me, Michael Paulson (Howard's son), a Sioux Falls attorney, "grew up at the Nordic Hall. I've been a Sons of Norway member since I was born." The youngest of four, he and his siblings would work the lutefisk and torsk dinners. "Our hair and clothes smelled like lutefisk for weeks from cooking it all day. After every fish dinner, we were always the last ones there, mopping the floor." These days, the Torsk and Meatball Dinner and Bake Sale is a fundraiser that provides scholarships for young people to attend heritage summer camps or colleges. Along with Joe Foss, among the luminaries honored at these dinners were Lawrence Welk and Myron Floren (Welk's accordion player and son of immigrant Norwegians). I remember meeting Floren there when I was very young and being prodded to ask for his autograph.

"Everything at the Nordic Hall was a celebration of Norwegian heritage," Michael Paulson said. "You were Norwegian, you were Lutheran, you were at the Nordic Hall."

While Scandinavian presence in the Americas began with Leif Erikson a thousand years ago, the largest numbers came roughly from 1825 to 1925, largely ending with the Immigration Act of 1924. All it took to have a farm was the price of passage and a lot of hard work. Howard Paulson was honorary consul for the state of South Dakota to the Royal Norwegian Embassy from 1986 to 2009, followed by his son Michael. These branch consuls served as liaisons for immigrants, helping with correspondence, distributing funds between countries, and these days, managing estate planning and probate.

"When I was a kid, we didn't have activities four nights a week," Michael Paulson told me. "Being Norwegian doesn't resonate as much now. As generations go by, where one's ancestors came from becomes less compelling." He paused, then added, "Boy, I'd like to ask Dad about what our parents went through to get to where they were. How hard they worked! It's respect for what they did that gives you pride in wanting to maintain that heritage. They scraped everything together to make it, and we benefit."

His father said something similar about mine. "People who came to America really welcomed the opportunity to be here, to work hard, to appreciate the opportunities and freedoms we have in this country."

"A Lot of Life, Though It Might Not Seem Like It"

I see now that it isn't the building itself, no architectural marvel, that makes the Nordic Hall vital but the seven decades of memories that stretch back to the earliest Scandinavian presence in the area.

Among those memories, surprising to me, were a few years in the nineties when the hall hosted liquor-free punk concerts, drawing some not-yet-big bands like Green Day. "Going to Nordic Hall for concerts in the basement was a really neat way to spend time," says Catherine Dekkenga, now an architect in Sioux Falls. "The Nordic Hall was *the* place to go. It would be packed! There were always people coming in and out of Nordic Hall. It had a lot of life, though it might not seem like it."

What lies ahead for this piece of local history that's been around half as long as the state itself? "People have made offers," Howard Paulson said. "The big stairway is a barrier for older people, and renters are reluctant. They might knock it down and build low-cost housing. Meanwhile, there's talk about building a new facility down by Falls Park."

Aundre Myles, who's had a recording studio at the Nordic Hall for three years, has his own ideas. "I really want to revive the Nordic traditions here," he said. "People don't know I love the Nordic Hall as much as I do." His dream is to buy the building and provide services to homeless people.

And so the Nordic Hall, understated as Norwegians traditionally are, quietly lopes on. Not quite central, not quite beloved, but the secret heart of many lives.

Sioux Falls Railroads

H. ROGER GRANT

Following the Civil War as the Railway Age matured, Sioux Falls scored victories and experienced disappointments. By the close of the 1880s, this growing city of approximately 20,000 inhabitants proudly claimed five railroads. These were not woebegone short lines. Rather, they were interregional carriers that operated in large portions of the Midwest and Great Plains. Unfortunately, none of these iconic names offered long-distance routes through the Minnehaha capital. Southern Dakota Territory was not a "natural" path from Midwest population centers to the Rocky Mountain West or the Pacific Coast.

Sioux Falls citizens realized early on that if they were to prosper, they must have a railroad, ideally two or more. Completion of the Dakota Southern Railroad, which in 1873 linked Sioux City, Iowa, with Yankton, offered encouragement to the several hundred inhabitants of this gestating community along the Big Sioux River.

In 1874, agitation for rails to Sioux Falls began, and soon it paid dividends. Although there were initial setbacks, the first passenger train steamed into town on August 1, 1878. At last, residents gained rail access to the outside world. "Their ears could hear the whistle of a locomotive," related an ecstatic commentator, "and their eyes see a train of cars in Sioux Falls." It would be the Chicago, St. Paul, Minneapolis and Omaha Railway (Omaha Road) that claimed this honor. This sixty-two-mile line connected at Worthington, Minnesota (Sioux Falls Junction), with the Omaha Road's main stem between the Twin Cities, Sioux City, and Omaha gateways. Later, this Sioux Falls trackage extended west to Mitchell.

Railroad euphoria continued. As 1879 ended, the Chicago, Milwaukee, and St. Paul Railway (Milwaukee), which had absorbed the neighboring Dakota Southern and Sioux City and Pembina Railroads, built the twenty-one miles from Canton north to Sioux Falls. As with the Omaha Road, the public contributed to construction costs, providing in this case right-of-way from Canton and station grounds in Sioux Falls.

The 1880s witnessed a railroad boom in Dakota Territory, and Sioux Falls did not escape the frenzy. The Chicago and North Western Railway (North Western), which controlled the Omaha Road, and the Milwaukee dominated construction during these halcyon years. The former installed

1,096 miles and the latter 744 miles. Neither company, however, considered this mileage to be a springboard to the West. The state ultimately sported a 4,420-mile network.

More railroads came to Sioux Falls between 1886 and 1888. The first was the Burlington, Cedar Rapids, and Northern Railway (BCR&N), a company controlled jointly by the Chicago, Rock Island and Pacific (Rock Island) and the Chicago, Burlington, and Quincy (Burlington) Railroads, but after 1902, it was a wholly Rock Island property. It entered the town from Ellsworth, Minnesota, a distance of forty-two miles. Service, which commenced on November 1, 1886, cost local taxpayers $60,000 in bond subsidies. This line fed the company's Cedar Rapids, Iowa, to Watertown core, one projected (but never built) to a Northern Pacific (NP) connection in Bismarck.

The Illinois Central Railroad (IC) was the fourth to arrive; December 19, 1887, was the official date of entry. This trackage extended the ninety-six miles from Cherokee, Iowa, and provided an attractive route to the East. "The whole city was soon made aware that Sioux Falls had an air line [direct] railroad connection with Chicago." Once again, the local citizenry aided financially, providing right-of-way within the city limits and real estate for the station and support facilities.

The final railroad during the 1880s to reach Sioux Falls was the Willmar and Sioux Falls Railway (W&SF). Its arrival occurred on October 25, 1888. The W&SF was not an independent carrier but controlled by James J. Hill's St. Paul, Minneapolis and Manitoba Railway, which was soon to be renamed the Great Northern Railway (GN). This construction can be considered more than a branch, extending 148 miles to Sioux Falls from Willmar, Minnesota, and forging a direct link to the Twin Cities. At Garretson, Minnesota, the company pushed the Willmar line ninety-seven miles south to Sioux City. Later, in 1893, the GN extended the Sioux Falls trackage to Yankton. Hill expected financial support, and Sioux Falls responded with a $50,000 bond commitment and rights-of-way within the city and county.

Even though Sioux Falls boasted multiple carriers, it was no railroad center. The city never had a union station; each carrier constructed its own depot. Passenger service lacked stellar qualities. Four of the five roads provided only a daily passenger train, and the Omaha Road dispatched two. These were locals—no limited or named trains paid calls. Travelers to Sioux City, including those who attended the Populist Party national convention in 1900 or who wished to take advantage of the state's "quickie" divorce law, may not have been pleased. Freight service, too, was hardly exceptional. There were no through runs to distant terminals; rather, local or "way" freights handled the traffic. Inbound movements included lumber, manufactured products, and consumer goods. The outbound business involved agricultural-related shipments, granite, bricks, and aggregates.

Happily for Sioux Falls, its railroad map had not jelled in 1893. Although the depression of 1893–1897 stymied construction, the homegrown South Dakota Central Railway (SDC) appeared during the twilight years of railroad building. Launched in 1904 and spearheaded by Iowa industrialist F. L. Maytag, it soon reached Watertown. This 101-mile short line served as a feeder to Sioux Falls businesses, especially those engaged in grain and meatpacking, and as an outlet for jobbers, quarry operators, and others. But the SDC struggled, failing in 1908 and emerging eight years later as the Watertown & Sioux Falls Railway. In 1922, the property entered the orbit of the GN.

Railroads continued to be the transportation lifeline of Sioux Falls. For passengers, this extended into the 1920s with double-daily service having become the norm. At various times, sleepers served the city; the Milwaukee, for example, offered such accommodations to and from Chicago. Freight traffic remained active. Just as automobiles, buses, and the good roads movement cut heavily into local passenger traffic, trucks took a greater share of the less-than-carload (LCL) and livestock business. What evolved into the best known of Sioux Falls-originated freight movements were packing house products from John Morrell & Company. The plant, which opened in 1909, grew into one of the nation's leading processors of pork. The IC and Milwaukee dominated these expedited meat shipments.

Sioux Falls travelers surely envied comparable midwestern and Great Plains cities that received excellent passenger service. The city, though, had named trains before a major upgrade occurred in 1940. During the post-World War I era, the IC operated the *Hawkeye Limited.* Yet this Chicago train was merely a poky local between Cherokee and Sioux Falls. During the 1920s, the Milwaukee operated two named trains. The first was the *Sioux*, which ran from Chicago through southern Wisconsin and northern Iowa via Prairie du Chien and Mason City. The railroad subsequently introduced the Chicago *Arrow*, which ran over its busier trans-Hawkeye State line via Manilla, Iowa. Both trains, which provided sleeper and dining options, were never fast movers.

On the eve of World War II, Sioux Falls citizens rejoiced when they experienced a sea change in passenger service. They now enjoyed improved access to and from the Windy City. The Milwaukee would be the operator, and the train would be the *Midwest Hiawatha*. This sleek streamliner, initially steam but diesel-powered after the war, provided all the desired amenities, including dining and sleeper equipment. The route would be that of the former *Arrow*; the Sioux Falls section connected with the Chicago-Omaha mainline at Manilla. The first run of this double-destination train (Chicago-Omaha, Chicago-Sioux Falls) left Sioux Falls via Canton and Sioux City on December 7, 1940. Patronage was strong and soon surged with wartime traffic. Following the conflict, the *Midwest Hi*, as it was often called, remained popular, explaining why the company in 1948 added replacement coaches, drawing-room parlors, and diner-lounge cars. But when a radical restructuring of passenger service took place on the Omaha mainline in the mid-1950s, prompted by Union Pacific (UP) switching its Chicago-bound *Cities* streamliners to the Milwaukee from the North Western, the *Midwest Hi* disappeared. The not-so-glamorous *Arrow* returned and operated on a slower schedule. Within a decade, the Milwaukee became the last carrier to provide Sioux Falls with passenger service.

While railroads nationally enjoyed a postwar Indian summer, increasing modal competition and better roads, especially interstate highways after 1956, hurt passenger ridership. By the early 1960s, South Dakota had only two trains. One operated through Aberdeen and Lemmon on the Pacific Coast extension of the Milwaukee, and the other ran over the Burlington between Alliance, Nebraska, and Billings, Montana, stopping only at Edgemont. Both disappeared before the Amtrak era.

In the 1960s, railroads nationwide encountered serious financial problems. The response: mergers and acquisitions. The most notable one was the uniting of the New York Central and Pennsylvania Railroads to become the Penn Central Transportation Company in 1968. Yet after only twenty-eight months, this 19,000-mile carrier collapsed, becoming the largest business failure in American history. A combination of excessive federal regulation, modal competition, poor (even dishonest) management, and limited premerger planning led to its demise. In 1976, additional bankruptcies in the Northeast culminated in the formation of the quasi-public Consolidated Rail Corporation (Conrail). Other carriers failed or teetered on insolvency, but partial rate deregulation in 1980 helped to revive the industry.

The Sioux Falls railroad scene was not immune to monumental changes. The North Western expanded through acquisitions in 1960 and 1968, and federal aid in the 1970s kept it solvent. The Milwaukee and IC struggled, and in 1975, the Rock Island spiraled toward its third bankruptcy. The GN did reasonably well and in 1970 merged with the Burlington, NP, and Spokane, Portland, and Seattle Railroads to create Burlington Northern (BN). Mergers continued. BN became Burlington Northern Santa Fe (BNSF) following its union with the Atchison, Topeka, and Santa Fe in 1995. That same year, the UP absorbed the North Western. After a prolonged and failed merger attempt with the UP, the bankrupt Rock Island underwent a court-ordered liquidation in 1981. The Milwaukee entered bankruptcy in 1977 and led to greatly retrenched mileage, including the abandonment of its transcontinental line. In 1985, much of the remaining core joined the Soo Line Railroad (later part of the Canadian Pacific Railway).

What did the dramatic redrawing of the railroad map mean for Sioux Falls? Its leading shippers never became stranded, although there were concerns. In 1972, the Rock Island pulled up its Sioux Falls line, and eight years later, the IC left the city. Fortunately, South Dakota government and the private sector helped to stabilize rail transportation. With the demise of the Milwaukee, the state in 1980 purchased 533 miles of threatened lines that were considered essential but not sold privately. Soon, the state, in conjunction with the Sioux Valley Regional Rail Authority, inked a lease arrangement with a startup short line D&I. (The D and I were only letters.) Based in Sioux Falls and operated by aggregate producer L. G. Everist, Inc., it began service in 1982 on 138 miles of ex-Milwaukee trackage between Dell Rapids and Sioux City. Five years later, another short line emerged, the Ellis and Eastern, also headquartered in Sioux Falls. Owned by Sweetman Construction Company, it took over the former North Western line between Brandon and Ellis and is mainly a hauler of aggregates. BNSF operates the former GN to Willmar and portions of the old South Dakota Central and Milwaukee between Sioux Falls and Madison. Thus, Sioux Falls claims two short lines and a Class I road, being a far cry from the multiple railroads that once served the city. Although South Dakota's 1,997 route miles might contract, it is unlikely that Sioux Falls will become an "inland" city, lacking flanged wheel connections to the national rail network.

Sources

Bailey, Dana R. *History of Minnehaha County, South Dakota*. Sioux Falls, 1899.

Lustig, David, et al. "Railroads Where You Least Expect Them." *Trains* 80 (October 2020):14–15.

Scribbens, Jim. *The Hawatha Story*. Milwaukee, 1970.

Smith, Charles A. *A Comprehensive History of Minnehaha County, South Dakota*. Mitchell, 1949.

The Missing Amidons

JOHN ANDREWS

High atop a bluff along busy Cliff Avenue in northern Sioux Falls stands the Pioneer Memorial, a tall quartzite obelisk built to honor the area's first homesteaders: settlers who trickled onto the tallgrass prairie along the Big Sioux River starting in the 1850s. Visit the monument today and you can see 150 years of progress in every direction. Plumes of steam shoot incessantly from the stacks of the Smithfield meatpacking plant at the base of the hill. Handsome pink quartzite buildings that comprise the state penitentiary sit to the west. Cars whiz past on Cliff and Interstate 229 just a bit farther east.

A century and a half ago, this was a quiet hayfield, and no more than a few hundred people lived in Minnehaha County. It's where Judge Joseph B. Amidon and his son Willie were working on August 25, 1862, when gunshots pierced the still summer day's air. The judge and his son were found dead nearby the next day. It was quickly deduced that Indians killed the Amidons, and they were laid to rest. But anyone wishing to pay respects will have no luck finding them in any local cemetery. The Amidons have gone missing.

Bruce Blake first learned about the Amidons through his tireless work of preserving local history. The Wisconsin native was fourteen when he moved to Sioux Falls with his family in 1945. He earned a law degree from the University of South Dakota in 1958 and spent nearly forty years practicing law in Sioux Falls. He joined the Minnehaha County Historical Society in 1962, and in 1988, he created its historical marker program. Under Blake's leadership, more than 200 historical markers have been erected around Minnehaha County.

He placed the original marker on the site of the Amidon murders in 1991 and spent the remainder of his life trying to figure out what happened to them. The story of the Amidons' venture to Dakota and their tragic deaths came together through documents Blake obtained from Amidon descendants scattered around the country. Amidon was born in Hartford, Connecticut, on September 29, 1800. He married Emma Morse in Vermont on Christmas Day in the late 1820s. They had ten children, but only four survived to adulthood.

Emma Amidon died sometime in the early 1850s, and Joseph and his two youngest children—William and Eliza—moved to St. Paul, Minnesota. Amidon married Mahala St. John Drake there in 1855. The Amidons moved to the fledgling village of Sioux Falls in the fall of 1858 and received an inauspicious welcome. On their first night in Dakota, the Indian warrior Inkpaduta allegedly stole two horses that Amidon had stabled in town.

Amidon worked as a stonecutter, and he built a small quartzite house for his family on the left bank of the Big Sioux River near today's Fawick Park. When Minnehaha County was organized in 1862, the Dakota Territorial Legislature approved Governor William Jayne's nomination of Amidon to be a probate judge, treasurer, and commissioner.

On the morning of August 25, 1862, Amidon and his son William left their home to cut hay on William's homestead claim about a mile north. Mahala packed their dinner pails since they expected to be gone all day. They gathered their cart and oxen and departed. It was the last time anyone saw them alive.

Mahala grew worried as day turned into night and the men still hadn't returned. To help ensure the safety of settlers, the federal government had stationed a detachment of federal troops in Sioux Falls, along with men from Company A of the Dakota Cavalry. At 10:00 p.m., Mahala ran to the soldiers' encampment about a quarter of a mile away and begged the men to form a search party.

The men immediately suspected an Indian attack and did not want to get caught in a night ambush. Several soldiers proceeded cautiously to the Amidon claim. When they arrived, they found the oxen tied in a shed, the wagon, and the empty dinner pails. They returned to headquarters and resolved to continue the search at first light.

A few soldiers accompanied Mahala home and stood guard outside through the night. Mrs. Amidon paced her floor until sunrise, which is when the soldiers resumed their search. Shortly after the party disappeared over the bluff, a single rider returned to tell Mahala they had found her husband and stepson lying dead in a cornfield.

It's believed that as the Amidons worked late in the afternoon, William, the son, noticed a large flock of blackbirds in his cornfield. Armed with his shotgun, he intended to fire a few shots to scare them away. But as he approached, he stumbled upon an Indian war party obscured in the corn, planning an ambush on the city during the night or at dawn. With their position discovered, the Indians shot William repeatedly with arrows. When his body was found the next morning, it had nearly a dozen wounds. William had removed several arrows and placed them beside his body before he died.

Amidon noticed his son's absence and went to find him. He entered the cornfield almost exactly where William had but didn't get far enough to see his son's body before he was shot in the chest, likely with his son's shotgun. He was found with his right hand resting inside his vest, a common position according to surviving family members.

Two witnesses reportedly heard the fatal gunshots. Lieutenant James Bacon of Company A was fishing in the Big Sioux River but thought the shots were from his men hunting ducks in a nearby slough. The Amidons' neighbor, B. C. Fowler, heard the blasts and saw the birds take flight. "I wish Willie Amidon would not send the blackbirds down into my corn," he later recalled saying to himself.

George Trumbo, a hired man working for another Amidon neighbor, placed the bodies in his wagon and brought them to the Amidon home. According to a note in the Amidon family Bible, "They received Christian burials August 27th."

The Amidon murders marked a turning point in the settlement of Sioux Falls. When competing land companies arrived at the falls of the Big Sioux River in 1856 to stake out the town, they were treading on land that had been home to various Indian tribes for centuries. Mound builders lived in the area between 500 and 800 AD. Evidence of their existence lies in several burial mounds along the river and in Sherman Park.

The Lakota moved into the region during the eighteenth century, and in 1851, they signed the Treaty of Traverse des Sioux, in which they ceded all land east of the Big Sioux River. That development lured speculators from St. Paul and Dubuque, Iowa, who considered the falls a prime location for a town site, provided they stayed on the east side of the river. Settlement opened on the other side following the Yankton Treaty of 1858, which ceded land between the Big Sioux and Missouri Rivers.

But not all Lakota felt bound by the treaties, and their desire to retain their homeland led to several skirmishes. Medary, one of the first settlements in Brookings County, was abandoned in June 1858 following an Indian attack. A threat to Sioux Falls that year prompted city leaders to construct a sod fort for protection. Violence escalated, especially in southwestern Minnesota in the early 1860s, as the federal government's attention turned to fighting the Civil War.

John Renville and Joseph Laframboise, longtime area fur traders, believed members of White Lodge's band had killed the Amidons. White Lodge was under orders from Dakota Chief Little Crow to drive settlers out of the Big Sioux River valley. The day after the murders, White Lodge's Indians reappeared on the outskirts of town and fired upon the soldiers' encampment. A detachment pursued the band, but they escaped across the prairie.

That small scuffle was the only Indian attack upon the city of Sioux Falls. But word of the Sioux Uprising underway in Minnesota finally trickled into Dakota. The news, combined with the Amidon murders, led Governor William Jayne to issue an evacuation order for Sioux Falls. Families packed what they could and departed for Yankton. The city on the falls was abandoned.

Mahala Amidon returned to St. Paul, where she grieved her loss. "I have felt alone in my great sorrow, and it seems to me sometimes greater than I can bear," she wrote to Amidon's daughter Martha in October 1862.

> I am almost crushed to the earth. I have nothing to live for. Your father always had so much pity for the Indians and used to give them so much and feed them too, and then to have them murder him without the least provocation. It is hard to feel it is right. If he had died by sickness, and I could have had the privilege of taking care of him, and talking with him, I believe I could bear it better. Why did they kill him? His death was no benefit to them. He was one of their best friends. It was the hardest thing for me to leave your father there. I can't bear to think he lies in that desolate place, with no friend to even visit his grave.

The Amidon graves were apparently unmarked, and over the decades, their exact location became a mystery. Sioux Falls historians believed that the Amidons were buried beneath a mound near where they died. In 1927, the Minnehaha County Historical Society marked the location with a quartzite hitching post. Charles Lacey later gave the historical society the title to the two-acre plot of land containing the supposed burial spot.

But Bruce Blake wanted a concrete answer. In 1991, he convinced the historical society to hire renowned archeologist L. Adrien Hannus from the Augustana University Archeology Lab to excavate the site. "I took a lot of flak from local historians for digging into that mound, but I wanted to find out," Blake said. "Some people thought it was better to be a mystery, but I wanted to prove it. Why have the locals believing in something that really is not true?"

Archeologists extracted nine soil samples and four one-meter-square pieces of earth, and they cut a trench twenty-one feet long. It revealed only trash discarded by local farmers for nearly a century.

Blake continued the search and found an account of the murders by Sergeant Jesse Watson, a member of Company A who reportedly accompanied George Trumbo to the scene of the crime. Watson said they collected the bodies and buried them in a cemetery on North Duluth Avenue.

Blake believed the cemetery was located near the intersection of Seventh Street and Duluth Avenue, today part of the Sioux Falls Cathedral Historic District, a neighborhood of 220 homes and other buildings constructed mostly in the late 1800s. Watson reported that the Amidons were buried next to Henry Masters, leader of the provisional government established before the creation of Dakota Territory in 1861. Masters had been the first resident of Sioux Falls to die in 1859.

But the Amidons apparently did not stay in that cemetery. Sometime before 1882, Amidon's granddaughter Chloe Selleck Rider wrote a letter to the Sioux Falls postmaster, A. T. Fleetwood, asking about her grandfather's gravesite. Fleetwood referred her to Josiah Phillips, a founding father of Sioux Falls and the city's first physician. Then he told her the bodies "were removed from their former graves to the cemetery here, the expense being borne by the citizens."

There is no date on the postmaster's reply, but in 1881, four men buried in the city's military cemetery adjacent to the Amidon burial site were moved to Mount Pleasant, Sioux Falls's oldest active cemetery. Blake said he believed that whoever did that would also have moved the Amidons.

Blake and Hannus located the military gravesites and conducted soil testing around them in an effort to find other graves. They came up empty, and Mount Pleasant records contain no mention of the Amidons. "That's where the trail went cold," Blake said.

Blake's passion for the subject never waned. He continued the investigation until his death in 2017 at age eighty-five. The story of his work on the Amidons—as well as hundreds of other people, places, and events that have shaped Minnehaha County—is wonderfully told in the book *Twelve Thousand Years of Human History*, a collection of every historic marker Blake helped to create.

For now, the search for the Amidons has reached a dead end. Perhaps the answer lies in a faded slip of paper in someone's attic, a misplaced cemetery record, or a bundle of correspondence boxed away in the city's archives. But until it surfaces, South Dakotans can honor the Amidons—and the hardy homesteaders who helped tame Dakota—atop that windswept hill on the edge of Sioux Falls.

Yankton Trail Bridge

STU WHITNEY

About once a week, Kameron Carlson sneaks out of his office, grabs an ice cream cone, and heads to the Yankton Trail Bridge, an unheralded Sioux Falls landmark that crosses the Big Sioux River near Fifty-Seventh Street and Western Avenue. "Nobody bothers me," says Carlson, who owns a financial planning business nearby. "It's very peaceful."

There's a sense of satisfaction in those words, delivered as Carlson stood on the aging truss bridge on a recent afternoon with his wife and business partner, Nancy. It was their curiosity, having driven past the bridge every day, that sparked renewed interest in a site where Dakota Indians forded the river in the 1700s and settlers made the crossing two centuries later as part of the Old Yankton Trail.

In 2006, Nancy was cruising for Christmas card photos and snapped a picture of the bridge one winter morning before footprints invaded the freshly fallen snow. The image was wondrous enough to inspire more scrutiny of the rusted steel structure, originally built with horse-drawn wagons and buggies in mind. The bridge had no historical marker and was obscured by overgrown vegetation, making it an afterthought despite its proximity to the Yankton Trail Park soccer complex and bike trail.

Nancy reached out to Bruce Blake, late director of the Minnehaha County Historical Society, about raising funds to create a plaque for the site. The success of that effort led to a story in the *Argus Leader*, setting off a chain of other positive developments. Mayor Dave Munson instructed city crews to clear out vegetation and debris, improving on efforts that Kameron had made in his spare time. In 2010, the city was granted more than $250,000 in federal stimulus money to upgrade the bridge's foundation while also reinforcing guardrails and wood planking.

Even with the improvements, the historical stature of Yankton Trail Bridge seems hidden in plain sight. Growing cities prefer to look longingly at the future rather than dwell on the past.

Its utilitarian purpose lessened, the bridge finds itself in a recreation-based role, surrounded by weekend cyclists and wedding photos, with a story that yearns to be told.

Center of Conflict

It was the Big Sioux River and the power and promise of its falls that lured white settlers to town, with competing trading companies laying claims in 1856. Their presence was gravely noted by Native American tribes, who had farmed and formed villages in the area for centuries.

Tensions in the newly christened Dakota Territory were high six years later, when Joseph Amidon was named probate judge, treasurer, and commissioner of Minnehaha County. On August 25, 1862, Amidon and his son, William, were cutting hay on the family homestead north of Sioux Falls when William stumbled upon a Santee Dakota Sioux war party. His body was found riddled with arrows, and Judge Amidon was later shot in the chest, likely with William's rifle, in the same cornfield where his son met his fate.

Soon after, with the Dakota Conflict that started in Minnesota sparking fears of more violence, an evacuation order was issued for Sioux Falls. Hundreds of settlers packed their belongings and headed for Yankton with a cavalry escort, crossing the Big Sioux River at the point where the historic bridge stands today.

Learning the Land

As the establishment of Fort Dakota spurred a new wave of settlement, a ferry was placed at the Big Sioux crossing in 1880. That was followed by a primitive wooden bridge and eventually the Yankton Trail Bridge in 1895 to accommodate wagon trains and stagecoaches. About two decades later, an agriculturally savvy German immigrant named F. X. Wallner purchased fifty acres of land at Thirty-Third and Minnesota to start his own produce farm, which grew from a roadside stand and nursery to a flourishing wholesale business. The Wallner's Garden operation later expanded to more than 500 acres, encompassing land that is now Yankton Trail Park and Empire East Mall. During World War II, F. X. Wallner's sons—Robert and Paul—ran the business and provided produce for soldiers at the airport army base.

Rob Wallner Jr., a 1969 O'Gorman graduate, started working in the family business in seventh grade and recalls hauling truckloads of potatoes across the Yankton Trail Bridge to a warehouse just south of Fifty-Seventh Street, where an office park now resides. "Everything went back and forth across that bridge," says Wallner. "It was a vital artery for us."

As one of ten children, he fondly recalls working summers alongside cousins and other teen laborers, with "potato fights" among the favorite activities on the bridge and elsewhere.

"The only way I learned how to throw a baseball was by throwing a potato," says Wallner. "We threw every vegetable imaginable. The nuclear option was cabbage; you could knock a man clean over. When we'd see my dad coming across the bridge, we knew it was time to get back to work."

Increased competition and the federal construction of Interstate 229—which cut the Wallners' land in half—made business more difficult as the city grew southward. The business closed in 1979, leaving behind nearly seven decades of productivity along the Big Sioux.

"In all that time," says Wallner, "that bridge never failed us."

Pieces of the Past

It's early afternoon on a weekday, providing some of the peace that Kameron Carlson craves on his ice cream excursions. At the entryway to the bridge, a runner stops to tie his shoes, holding the beams for support. When renovations occurred in 2010, the structure was sandblasted down to its rusted steel, with plans to paint the exterior. "But it looked nice the way it was," says Parks and Recreation Director Don Kearney. "We put a clear sealant on it and left it alone."

That nod to the past adds to the bridge's anachronistic feel, especially in this part of town. With new restaurants and boutiques crowding spaces across Fifty-Seventh Street and I-229 roaring nearby, is the wood-planked expanse holding things back or propelling us forward? For cyclists crossing the Big Sioux on their bike path journey, and kayakers appearing from below, the slightest recognition of things that came before us is enough to brighten a day. That's really all Nancy Carlson wanted when she pulled out her camera on a splendid winter morning twelve years ago. In a city surrounded by progress and restless thoughts of the future, appreciating the past seems like a reasonable thing to ask.

The Center for Western Studies

HARRY F. THOMPSON

Herbert Krause Has an Idea

The police car pulled alongside of the man as he was lowering his field glasses. "Sir," said the officer, "We've had a report of someone using binoculars to look in the windows of those buildings over there." The buildings were Augustana University's twin tower dormitories, recently constructed on Twenty-Eighth Street. The gentleman with the binoculars was the noted ornithologist and cofounder of the South Dakota Ornithologists' Union, Herbert Krause, who was known in town for his peripatetic birdwatching. He was often seen on or near the campus or in Woodlawn Cemetery—or in northern Minnesota, his home state, or the Black Hills—tracking the birds he knew so well. But it was Krause's interest in the historical novel as a professor of English and Writer in Residence at Augustana that led him to the idea of a research center in Sioux Falls.

Writing and Collecting Books

When he came to Augustana in 1938 from the famed Iowa Writers' Workshop, Herbert Krause was first and foremost a poet, but shortly after beginning his teaching duties, he became nationally known, not for his poetry, but for his novel, *Wind Without Rain*, which won the prestigious "Friends of American Writers Award" in 1939. He based the novel largely on his own experience as a farm boy near Fergus Falls, Minnesota, and so did not need to consult other sources. But for his next two novels, *The Thresher* (1946) and *The Oxcart Trail* (1954), he realized that he needed to conduct extensive historical research. He began building his own book collection, which at his death in 1976 numbered over 9,000 volumes. The collection's focus was the American West, by which Krause meant South Dakota and the six contiguous states, comprising much of original Dakota Territory.

Krause understood the West as a crossroads of Indigenous and European powers, a geographical location at the center of the United States, traversed by Plains Indians, Spanish explorers, French traders, and English, German, and Scandinavian settlers. He believed the student of the Great Plains should know Spanish explorer Cabaza de Vaca's account of his journey through the Southwest in the 1530s, as well as O. E. Rölvaag's novels of Norwegian settlement in the Northern Plains in the 1870s.

To learn more about this region, in the 1960s, Krause conceived of a project to survey attitudes about settlement among second- and third-generation Euromericans. With the assistance of a young member of the Augustana history department, William R. "Bill" Wyatt, he obtained funding under the name "The Center for Western Studies" (CWS) from the Rockefeller Foundation, comparing an urban with a rural county on either side of the Missouri River. An inveterate lecturer, Krause also received a Rockefeller Foundation lectureship and so was off to the Philippines, leaving Wyatt to conduct field research. As Eric Bennett observes in *Workshops of Empire*, the Rockefeller Foundation, established by the Standard Oil Company, was interested at that time in promoting American capitalistic democracy as a bulwark against communism through funding writers and teachers.[1] The survey that Wyatt completed in 1967 was followed by another project, this one funded by the nascent National Endowment for the Humanities, to gauge the influence of television viewing habits on residents of three rural counties in western South Dakota. When, after three years, Krause returned from abroad, he recruited another history department faculty member, Gary D. Olson, to manage the growing activities of the center.

Publishing Books

The materials generated by these two projects—oral history recordings and transcripts, letters, and a copy of the minutes of the South Dakota Constitutional Convention of 1885—were the beginnings of the archives of the Center for Western Studies, which was first housed in an office in Augustana's administration building. With his death in 1976, Krause's personal library was merged with the Mikkelsen Library's Dakota Collection, and the center was relocated to Mikkelsen Library. With the doubling of space to the library in 1980, the center was offered additional room for its collections, offices, and exhibits. In 2001, it moved into a new two-story, brick-and-limestone building designed by Sioux Falls

1 Eric Bennett, *Workshops of Empire: Stegner, Engle, and American Creative Writing during the Cold War* (Iowa City: U of Iowa P, 2015).

architect Jeff Hazard, featuring a distinctive tipi-shaped glass-and-steel rotunda, funded by friends of the center, with the naming gift from Sally Fantle, owner of the Fantle Department Store in downtown Sioux Falls.

The third program area to develop—after library and archives—was book publishing. This was a dimension of the center's interpretative mission, begun in 1978 with *Sundancing on the Rosebud and Pine Ridge*, by author Thomas Mails, a friend of Lakota elder and Sundance officiant Fools Crow. A monumental undertaking by an emerging publishing house, *Sundancing* brought instantaneous recognition and financial difficulty to the center. Unlike today, CWS was at this time struggling to cover the costs of staff salaries and benefits in addition to printing costs for a clothbound, full-color, oversize book of nearly 400 pages. The first 5,000 copies sold well, but the second 5,000 did not, and the book was eventually remaindered. The center did not recover its production costs for several years. From that point forward, throughout its forty-three-year history as the longest continuously operating university-affiliated publisher in the state, the center has covered all production costs in advance.

Over the years, the subject matter of the center's books has ranged widely. *Sundancing* was followed immediately by a best-seller, *Natural History of the Black Hills*, by Sven Froiland, executive director at the time. Other books from the first decade of publishing (1978–1988) include an account of the Allen Issue Station on the Pine Ridge Reservation, a memoir by Frederick Manfred, a collection of short stories by O. E. Rölvaag, a 125th anniversary history of Augustana, a biography of sculptor Gutzon Borglum, an account of the surveying and marking of the North Dakota-South Dakota border, a biography of Cheyenne spiritual leader Wesley Whiteman (Black Bear), and a reprint of a popular history of country railroad stations, another best-seller.

The second decade (1989–1999) began with the publication of *An Illustrated History of the Arts in South Dakota*, by Arthur R. Huseboe, who was executive director at the time, with a section on Lakota arts by Arthur Amiotte, and funded by both the South Dakota Humanities Council and Arts Council. This was followed by a collection of Krause's poems and essays, watercolors of Yanktonai Sioux artist John Saul, an account of the marketing of the West by the Northern Pacific Railroad (inaugural volume in the Center's Prairie Plains Series), a collection of essays by—and a collection of critical essays about—novelist Frederick Manfred, essays on the Germans from Russia, World War II home-front columns in the *Argus Leader* by Marie Christopherson, a geography of South Dakota, a history of Fort Sisseton, a memoir by President Eisenhower's speechwriter from Sioux Falls, Arthur Larson, a fiftieth anniversary history of USGS EROS Data Center, an exhibit catalog of *Echoes from the Little Big Horn*, and new and selected poems by South Dakota Poet Laureate David Allan Evans. Of special note from this period are two publications in partnership with other organizations: a reprint of Martha Coleman Bray's biography of explorer and cartographer of the Upper Mississippi River Joseph Nicollet, through the auspices of the American Philosophical Society, and poems by Sicangu Lakota writer Lydia Whirlwind Soldier, in conjunction with the Oak Lake Writers' Society.

South Dakota entered the twentieth century without a new history of the state in forty years. The center sought to rectify this by publishing a history by leading South Dakota historians. In 2005, it brought out *A New South Dakota History* under the general editorship of the center's director of research collections and publishing, Harry Thompson. With twenty-seven chapters by sixteen authors, three of whom were Native American, including nationally recognized Lakota author Vine Deloria Jr., the book represented a generation of South Dakota historians, led by Herbert T. Hoover (USD), John E. Miller (SDSU), and David Wolff (BHSU). Winner of an Award of Merit from the American Association for State and Local History, and funded by foundations and private gifts, the book made thousands of dollars for CWS before a single copy was sold. Other books from this third decade (2000–2010) were a collection of Civil War letters by two Wisconsin brothers, a history of Fort Ridgely during the US-Dakota War of 1862, two volumes of newspaper columns by journalist Anson Yeager, longtime editor of the *Argus Leader*, two books on the Corps of Discovery during the Lewis and Clark Bicentennial, and a history of the South Dakota Farmers Union. The decade ended with a collection of contemporary South Dakota poetry by fourteen writers, including three South Dakota poet laureates, edited by Augustana Writer in Residence Patrick Hicks.

In conjunction with the Eide/Dalrymple Gallery of Augustana University, during the fourth decade of publishing (2011–2021) the center published the exhibition catalog for the Carl Grupp retrospective on display in both the Eide/Dalrymple Gallery and the Madsen/Nelson/Elmen Galleries at CWS. This was followed by a history of the Army Air Forces Technical School in Sioux Falls, an economic history of South Dakota, an account of the cases tried by Dakota frontier judge Peter C. Shannon, a reprint of Krause's most popular novel, *The Thresher*, with an introduction by Patrick Hicks, and a collection of essays on Northern Plains conservation (the inaugural volume in the Public Affairs Series). The second volume in this series, a collection of essays on regional identity in the Midwest and Great Plains, *The Interior Borderlands*, edited by historian Jon Lauck, won the 2020 Midwest Book Award for history. A second history of the state of South Dakota, also by several historians, was published in 2022, edited by Jon Lauck.

Improving Cultural Life

Preserving and interpreting historical and cultural materials is the core of the center's mission, but so is improving the quality of social and cultural life in the Northern Plains and stimulating interest in the solution to regional problems. The center attempts to do this through its signature public events: the Artists of the Plains Show and Sale, Dakota Conference, and the Boe Forum on Public Affairs. The Artists of the Plains celebrated its fortieth anniversary in 2021 and is the longest-running fine art event in South Dakota. Held in downtown Sioux Falls annually, the juried show invites twenty-five artists from the region, including several Native American artists. A hallmark is the presence of the artists themselves, who are available to talk with prospective buyers or with anyone with interest in the life of an artist or the state of art today. The show is free and open to the public, and the center takes no commissions from the artists' sales.

The Dakota Conference, inherited in 1989 from Dakota State University, provides a unique opportunity to share research or perspectives from both academics and amateurs on topics unique to the Northern Plains. As the largest annual humanities and (in more recent years) public affairs conference in the region, the event has tackled a range of topics, from cultural reconciliation, exploration, education, land and water issues, rural and urban identities, transportation, to the Civil War, World Wars, Korean and Vietnam Wars, Wounded Knee 1899 and 1973, the Spanish plains, religion and spirituality, health care and policy, women's vote, immigration, and sustainable agriculture. The conference theme often takes its cue from the centennial of a major historical or cultural event and challenges presenters to interpret that topic for the present.

Through its publishing program, specifically a book about Dakota Territory and South Dakota governors, the center came to the attention of Sioux Falls resident Governor Nils Boe. Desirous of bringing national and world leaders to his home state after a term on the US Customs

Court, in New York City, Boe established a lecture series in the Center for Western Studies under the direction of its university-community board of directors and assisted by a national advisory council. He and his sisters donated over $2 million to endow the series, which began in 1995 with General Colin Powell, who had recently retired as the first Black chairman of the joint chief of staffs. The forum has continued its groundbreaking emphasis on diversity and inclusion in the community by inviting women leaders—Queen Noor of Jordan, the first woman Supreme Court Justice Sandra Day O'Connor, Ireland President Mary Robinson, and the first woman Secretary of State Madeleine Albright—and Black leaders—Desmond Tutu, Neil deGrasse Tyson, and Condoleezza Rice. Other speakers have included President George H. W. Bush, Soviet President Mikhail Gorbachev, Mexico President Vicente Fox, Pakistan President Pervez Musharraf, and iconic journalists Bob Woodward and Carl Bernstein.

Keeping It Going

CWS is unique at Augustana in being officially established by the board of trustees, in 1970, yet responsible for staff and program costs. Although challenging for the first forty years, this ultimately served the center well. Self-reliance led to innovation and entrepreneurial initiative as the center continued to apply for and win many grants, notably from the Mary Chilton DAR Foundation, the South Dakota Humanities Council, and the National Endowment for the Humanities.

The most recent NEH grant, completed in 2013, aided the center in doubling its endowment at Augustana. Other endowments benefiting the center reside at the Sioux Falls Area Community Foundation and First National Bank in Sioux Falls. A recent endowment push, honoring those who helped Krause create the center, raised $500,000—all of it through private donations—bringing the total endowment to over $10 million. With this substantial financial undergirding, the CWS has been able to help support allied cultural institutions, such as South Dakota Public Broadcasting, Minnesota Public Radio, South Dakota News Watch, twenty scholarly journal publications, and twelve professional associations, historical societies, and museums.

The Future

One of the advantages of being blessed with a large endowment, committed membership base, and mutually beneficial relationship with Augustana is the freedom to manage and grow its programs. As it celebrated in 2019–2020—fifty-five years since Krause conceived of the center and fifty years since its official establishment—the board and council discussed several ways to strengthen its resources and expand its outreach, especially westward, in keeping with its name. Ideas that the center resolved to pursue in the next five years include growing its membership base and endowment, refreshing its signature programs, introducing a writers' workshop in keeping with its literary heritage, and emphasizing public (current) affairs in its programming.[2]

2 For a history of the Center for Western Studies, see Harry F. Thompson, *"Clear, Bright Sky Over a Plains So Wide": The Center for Western Studies, 1964–2020* (Sioux Falls: Center for Western Studies, 2021).

The Urbanization of Sioux Falls

JON C. TEAFORD

In 2017, a *Wall Street Journal* article bore the headline "As Many Midwest Cities Slump, Sioux Falls Soars." It was only one of many tributes to the dynamic South Dakota city. Since 1992, when *Money Magazine* declared Sioux Falls as the best place to live in America, national media had repeatedly reported on the new boom town and placed it at the top of lists of the best places to live, do business, find a job, or do anything else one could imagine. A *Huffington Post* contributor noted that Sioux Falls not only shared the same initials as San Francisco but with considerable hyperbole proclaimed that "all those things that everyone loves about the famous, jaded, sea-beaten" San Francisco "can also be found in a fresh, friendly, affordable midwestern" Sioux Falls. The South Dakota city was the wunderkind of the Midwest, an emerging metropolis of promise whose fast-paced urbanization stood out from the generally sluggish norm of America's heartland. Its trajectory of urbanization made it one of the few exceptions to the regional rule, a fact that commanded the attention of the national media.

Yet this was not always the case. Throughout most of its history, Sioux Falls's pattern of development paralleled that of its heartland peers. Its emerging urbanization conformed to the norm for a minor regional center in the western tier of the Midwest and was not notably different from similarly sized cities to the east in Iowa. During the late nineteenth and early and mid-twentieth centuries, it appeared to follow a standard heartland pattern.

Founded in the late 1850s, but temporarily abandoned owing to the perceived threat from hostile Native Americans, Sioux Falls established itself as a permanent settlement in the late 1860s and 1870s. Land speculators initially chose the town site largely because of its location adjacent to the falls of the Big Sioux River. As potential sources of waterpower necessary for industrial development, falls and rapids attracted investors not only in frontier South Dakota but also to other midwestern communities such as Grand Rapids, Cedar Rapids, and Minneapolis. Though the falls of the Big Sioux River never transformed the South Dakota settlement into a manufacturing dynamo comparable to Minneapolis, anticipation of future industrial growth was enough to draw settlers to the nascent community.

The arrival of the railroads in the late 1870s and 1880s connected Sioux Falls to the rest of the world and ensured that it would be a trade center for its rich agricultural hinterland. By 1890, one year after South Dakota statehood, Sioux Falls could claim 10,000 inhabitants, ranking as the largest city in the new state. It never lost that distinction, though this rank was less lustrous than it seemed. In the early twentieth century, South Dakota remained overwhelmingly rural, so large-scale urbanization was not necessary for a community to retain first place. By comparison, in 1890, Iowa, also largely rural, had eleven cities with populations over 10,000, and Sioux Falls's Iowa neighbor, Sioux City, could boast 37,000 inhabitants. At the close of the nineteenth century, Sioux Falls was one of many small regional centers that served the farmers of the trans-Mississippi Midwest.

During the early and mid-twentieth century, Sioux Falls grew at a steady pace, increasing in population and prosperity but never acquiring national attention as a booming metropolis promising to rival Omaha or the Twin Cities. In 1909, the John Morrell meatpacking plant opened and remained the community's chief business for the first eight decades of the century. Like the Iowa cities of Sioux City, Waterloo, Ottumwa, and Dubuque, Sioux Falls was a meatpacking town, one of a number of midwestern communities whose prosperity depended on the nation's burgeoning appetite. Like much of the Midwest, Sioux Falls was the scene of labor conflict, most notably in the mid-1930s when Morrell workers went on strike. South Dakota's governor called in the National Guard, complete with tear gas and machine guns, and the workers responded by burning the governor in effigy. Management denounced the strikes as communist-inspired, and the conflict grew violent on "Bloody Friday" with tire slashing, rock throwing, and fisticuffs, a scene repeated in industrial cities throughout the Midwest. Sioux Falls was not then distinguished for an inordinately favorable business climate. During the first decades of the twentieth century, it was no more business-friendly than any number of minor midwestern regional centers. Capital could not be assured of a safe haven in South Dakota's largest city.

By 1950, Sioux Falls had grown in population but remained pretty much what it had been during the early decades of the twentieth century: a minor regional center with meatpacking as its economic mainstay. Ranking 217th among the nation's cities, it had 53,000 residents and was in the same class as slightly larger Waterloo and slightly smaller Dubuque. It lived in the shadow of its larger sister Sioux City, which could boast a population of 84,000. Rural depopulation rendered South Dakota perennially stagnant, the state having two thousand fewer residents in 1980 than it had in 1930. Sioux Falls was, then, the largest city of a shrinking empire. Though it continued to attract newcomers, Sioux Falls's rate of growth slowed during the 1960s and 1970s, auguring a future of limited hope.

All this changed in the 1980s. Prior to 1980, purists might have insisted that "urbanization" was a misnomer for anything happening in Sioux Falls. To a New Yorker or even a resident of Omaha or Kansas City it did not seem to be approaching truly urban status. Yet from 1980 to 2020, the city's population soared, reaching an estimated 190,000 by the latter date. This was especially remarkable given the slowing of the nation's population growth and the stagnation of many comparable midwestern cities. In 1980, Sioux City was slightly more populous than Sioux Falls; forty years later, the Iowa city's population remained virtually unchanged, and Sioux Falls was more than twice the size of its like-named neighbor. By 2020, Sioux Falls had approximately three times the population of its once peer cities of Waterloo and Dubuque. Sioux Falls boasted the highest growth rate of any midwestern city with a population over 150,000. Fargo, North Dakota, was one of the few heartland communities that could claim a comparable, though not quite as dramatic, growth trajectory. By the dawn of the twenty-first century, marked urbanization was finally reaching the northwestern fringe of the Midwest. Both North and South Dakota were belatedly becoming urban.

According to US Census Bureau estimates in 2020, Sioux Falls had risen to the rank of the 138th largest city in the nation. In other words, it remained a minor presence on the national urban scene. But its growth set it apart. It was no longer stereotypically midwestern in its urban development, and it had advanced into a different class from Sioux City and its ilk.

Underlying this accelerated urbanization was a change in the city's economic base. In 1980, South Dakota's legislature voted to remove a cap on interest rates. Unlike states that retained anti-usury laws, South Dakota now granted a carte blanche to the expanding credit card lending industry. Taking advantage of South Dakota's leniency, in 1981, banking behemoth Citicorp moved its credit card operations to Sioux Falls and during the 1980s and 1990s, brought thousands of jobs to the city. Financial giant Wells Fargo followed suit, adding thousands of additional white-collar employees to the workforce. Then in 1986, Denny Sanford founded the First Premier Bank in Sioux Falls, an institution specializing in high-interest credit cards issued to individuals with poor credit ratings. Though critics attacked First Premier for "loan sharking," the business proved highly lucrative to the city, offering employment to yet more financial service workers. Meatpacking remained a major employer in Sioux Falls, but by the 1990s, it was overshadowed by financial services. Within a decade, Sioux Falls had emerged as a credit card capital.

Aiding in the city's growth was the fact that South Dakota was one of the few states that did not levy either a personal or corporate income tax. Given the immunity of income from taxation, it is little wonder that the likes of *Money Magazine* and the *Wall Street Journal* were to extol the business climate of Sioux Falls. In the late twentieth and early twenty-first centuries, Sioux Falls was a model business-friendly community. Entrepreneurs could expect to make money in the city and could also expect to keep it.

One Sioux Falls entrepreneur who chose not to keep it was Denny Sanford. Having made a fortune from First Premier, he decided to give it away. Through his generosity, he was a factor in the growth of a second pillar of the contemporary Sioux Falls economy—the health care industry. By the close of the second decade of the twenty-first century, Sanford had donated nearly one billion dollars to the Sioux Falls Hospital, which had appropriately been rechristened Sanford Health and had thereby created a massive health care and medical research complex. Together with the expanding Avera Health system headquartered in Sioux Falls, Sanford Health established the city as a major player in patient care and research. In the early twenty-first century, Sanford Health and Avera were by far the largest employers in the city with an estimated 17,000 people on their payrolls. Hospitals were major employers in other midwestern cities, often ranking as the biggest businesses in town, but in few places were they as significant or well-endowed as in Sioux Falls. Like the Mayo Clinic in Rochester, Minnesota, Sanford and Avera were highly lucrative assets. Just as health care boosted Rochester's fortunes and spared that city from the Midwest's economic doldrums, hospitals were paying off for fortunate Sioux Falls.

By the early twenty-first century, financial services and health care were not only accelerating the urbanization of Sioux Falls but were also fueling a wave of metropolitanization. The city was sprawling over an expanding metropolitan region and developing a ring of suburbs. Sioux Falls was the emerging core city of a metropolitan area with fast-growing satellite municipalities benefiting from the core city's prosperity. During the period between 1980 and 2020, Sioux Falls expanded beyond the boundaries of Minnehaha County and spread into northern Lincoln

County. Throughout the early and mid-twentieth century, Lincoln County had been a rural backwater of declining fortunes. Its population in 1970 was 11,761, four hundred less than the count in 1900. The county seemed to be going nowhere. Between 2000 and 2010, however, it was the fourth fastest growing county in the nation, its population rising 84 percent.

The Lincoln County municipalities of Tea and Harrisburg were feeling the impact as their populations soared, straining local sewer services and the public school systems. Prior to 2002, the Harrisburg school district had one building; by 2016, it had nine school buildings and more were needed in the next few years. Families with children were moving from the core city to the suburbs of Harrisburg and Tea and to the Minnehaha County satellite municipality of Brandon. Sioux Falls was not simply a rising city but the center of an expanding metropolis with places like Tea and Harrisburg outpacing the growth rate of the core municipality. Like a "real" big city, Sioux Falls was engulfing the countryside and exporting thousands of residents to communities beyond its boundaries.

The urbanization of Sioux Falls is, then, a remarkable tale of a movement from midwestern norm to midwestern exception. From the 1870s to 1980, there was nothing extraordinary about the city's history. By the mid-twentieth century, Sioux Falls was pretty much what one would expect for a minor regional center in the western tier of the Midwest. It was like Sioux City only smaller. By 2020, it was one of the few exceptions to the midwestern regional rule of a sluggishness bordering on stagnation. It was a midwestern city with Sunbelt-style growth. Without balmy January temperatures, coastal beaches, or majestic mountains, it seemed to have little future in an America enamored with warm climates, outdoor leisure, and dramatic scenery. Flat and frigid Sioux Falls did not fit the bill for rapid urban growth. Yet defying the odds, it emerged from the dilatory ranks of Sioux City, Waterloo, and Dubuque to become a booming capital of credit and health care. It did not have the preferred climate or scenery, but it exploited the insurance-subsidized demand for medical treatment and the propensity of Americans to spend more than they earned. As a consequence, Sioux Falls became a nationally acclaimed boomtown in the heartland.

The Syrian Muslim Community

EDWARD E. CURTIS IV

By the late 1800s, there was a vibrant community of Syrians in Sioux Falls. One of the reasons we know of their success was because the community lost $18,000 when the First National Bank of Sioux Falls went belly up in 1896. The *Argus Leader* reported that one man alone had $9,000 "on deposit."

Part of an immigration of half a million people from Ottoman Syria, which today includes Lebanon, Syria, Jordan, and Palestine, Syrians came to Sioux Falls for the same reason many other working-class immigrants did. The growth of Sioux Falls as an agricultural, business, and transportation center created opportunities for employment and small business.

Syrians were not always welcome at the time. For example, there were complaints about Syrian peddlers, who were seen as bothersome hawkers of useless charms. Some Syrian Christians blamed Syrian Muslims for the problem, but Syrian Christians were just as good at the trade. It was not an easy life. In 1900, a Sioux Falls judge fined a boy $5 and court costs for using "profane language" against a Syrian peddler on North Phillips Avenue.

In addition to meeting their Syrian neighbors on the street through peddling, many citizens of Sioux Falls first came to learn about Syrians at church or in the theater. Before the Olympia Theater (1909) and the Colonial Theater (1915) brought motion pictures to town, live performances such as vaudeville, lectures, melodramas, and musical recitals were the city's most popular entertainments. Across the United States, there was an appetite for "oriental" and exotic performers. The Columbian Exposition of 1893, also called the Chicago World's Fair, hired Syrians, Egyptians, and other Arabic-speaking people to recreate Middle Eastern street life, perform Islamic prayers, and entertain fairgoers. Many of the world's "less civilized" cultures were put on display at the Midway Plaisance very much in the same way that animals were kept in zoos—in 1904, the St. Louis World's Fair featured Filipinos who were literally put in cages. Even if it was demeaning, immigrants (or those pretending to be immigrants) needed the jobs.

The Syrian lecture and entertainment circuit was aided by white Christian missionaries who had lived and proselytized in the Middle East. In 1896, Dr. D. R. Johnson of Sioux Falls's First Methodist Church and former president of the Missionary Training College in Asyut, Egypt, invited Sioux Falls residents to see a "unique oriental entertainment" featuring

Phares Anton Benhannesy. Dr. Johnson testified to the "genuineness of his costumes and the correctness of his representations of Syrian and Egyptian life and customs," according to a November 7 article in the *Argus Leader*. Apparently, Benhannesy was a hit because he came back for another performance in 1899. Tickets to the show at the New Theater cost twenty-five, thirty-five, and fifty cents. It was said to be something that people in Sioux Falls had never seen before, and it did not disappoint. Benhannesy portrayed forty living characters with forty different costumes; he "gives the Mohammedan prayer, Oriental salutation, wedding ceremony and feast, so that there is nothing dry about the entertainment."

Whatever challenges there were in being different, Syrian immigrants managed to create a real life in the city. This applied to Muslims as well as Christians. One of the hallmarks of South Dakota's Syrian community was its religious diversity. The majority of Syrians were Christian, mainly Orthodox and Greek Catholic, but by 1915, more than one third of the 670 Syrians counted in the state census were Muslim. This was a much higher percentage than on the East Coast. The Muslims represented both of the major communities or sects of Islam—they were Sunni and Shi'a Muslims.

Sioux Falls is only now receiving the attention it deserves from scholars as one of the major sites of Muslim life in the United States before 1920. One of the reasons why no one has researched this topic is because of the power of the stereotype of Sioux Falls as almost entirely white and Christian. In truth, not only were there Muslims in town before World War I, but they were among the very few Muslim communities in the United States to organize and charter their own Muslim organization.

It happened in 1916, when there was a lot of talk about whether the United States would enter World War I. The stakes were high for all immigrants who were not yet citizens. If the United States entered the war on the side of the British and French, would alien enemies, including citizens of Germany and the Ottoman Empire, be deported or jailed? Because so many people in Sioux Falls were ethnically German, it was especially tense. And their fears were eventually realized as Germans, including pacifist religious communities, were interned during the war and newspaper editor Conrad Kornmann was convicted by a jury of his peers for writing personal letters that criticized the attempts of the US government to drum up support of Americans against the Germans.

The Syrian Muslim community of Sioux Falls—who were incorrectly called Turks—wanted to make sure that this did not happen to them. Yes, they were from the Ottoman Empire, but most of them were in favor of Arab independence from the Ottomans. So, they supported the British and French forces in World War I, hoping it would lead to freedom for their homelands. They wanted to say loudly and unambiguously to their American neighbors that they were loyal to the United States.

They organized themselves as a civic group called Bedr-El-Moneer, or "The Full Moon." They applied for a state charter from the government in Pierre. Members pledged to "wear an emblem showing the clasped hands of fraternity surmounted by the crossed flags of the Syrian and American people." They were very explicit in their charter about their goal of integrating Syrians into American culture. The group's purpose was to make Syrians "desirable, intelligent and law-abiding citizens of the United States of America." The lodge would educate Syrians "in American ways," and make them "competent to exercise the right of ballot." They did not want to segregate themselves in their own parochial schools (perhaps referring to Roman Catholics): "the children of our countrymen to attend the public schools, to the end that they may be educated as American children are educated, in order that they may become intelligent and useful citizens of our adopted country." They would also "promote acts of charity and benevolence."

Perhaps very few people in Sioux Falls would have known about the group if it had not been for the July 4, 1916, parade. Their participation in that day's civic rituals was, according to the *Argus Leader*, "probably the most novel parade and celebration ever seen on the streets of Sioux Falls." About sixty "Mohammedan Syrians" displayed two flags as they "marched through the business district of the city." One was the Stars and Stripes; the other was the "Syrian" flag, perhaps referring to the flag of the Arab revolt of Sharif Husayn, who was the ally of the British in the fight against the Ottoman Empire.

The group was led by [M]hammed Yusif and Deeb Hossine, also likely known as Charles H. Deeb, who lived on Weber Street and worked as a crusher at Wisconsin Granite Company. Both Yusif and Hossine were sword fighters, "gladiators" who "gave a remarkable exhibition of sword fighting." What they did was more complex than typical fencing. As a reporter who observed Syrian sword-fighting in Cedar Rapids, Iowa, wrote, "the contestants struck savagely at each other from all directions, but each thrust, no matter whether aimed at the head or the feet, in front or behind, was skillfully parried in regular order."

But that was not all Syrian Muslims did in the parade. Spectators also marveled at the music and the dancing. There were drums and instruments that people in Sioux Falls had not seen very much, if ever. The Syrians marchers played music as the swordsmen dueled their way toward Minnehaha County Courthouse. That same year, the well-known three-story Romanesque landmark (with a six-story clock tower built out of quartzite stone) was being transformed. Norwegian American artist Ole Running was painting sixteen large murals inside the building. The Syrian Muslim community stopped in front of the now fabled courthouse, performed more music, and then treated what the newspapers described as a large crowd to some "old country dances."

In 1916, on the eve of America's entry into World War I, the Syrian Muslim community of Sioux Falls claimed the attention of the public so that they could profess their loyalty to the United States and perform obviously foreign styles of music, dance, and sword-fighting. They knew people in Sioux Falls would like it since these "oriental" entertainments had been popular among Americans for decades. Perhaps some Syrian Muslims resented having to sing and dance to reduce their neighbors' anxieties about them. Even so, surely they had a lot of fun as the crowds cheered them on.

They also left us an important legacy: whatever the intentions of the performers, whatever pressures they were under, whatever spectators thought of them, today we can celebrate the fact that Arab culture has been part of—rather than foreign to—Sioux Falls for more than a century.

Fenn's Bros.

DAREN ANDERSON

The Fenn's Bros. story begins in the late 1800s, when two unrelated businesses came together—an existing candy company called Sioux Falls Candy (located at 315–317 North Main Avenue) and Fenn's Bros Shoes (Eighth and Phillips). Although the Sioux Falls Candy Company was thriving at one point, financial troubles caused the business to close in 1889. C. H. Ransom and James W. Fenn purchased the defunct candy company—renaming it Ransom and Fenn. The newly formed partnership sold candy, cigars, crackers, cider, pickles, and vinegar. The Fenn's Bros. shoe store/stock was later sold to Fantle's Department Store in downtown Sioux Falls. After Mr. Ransom died in 1901, Henry C. Fenn, James's younger brother, who was an assistant cashier at First National Bank, joined the company and the name was changed to Fenn's Bros.

In the early years, Fenn's stayed with their staple products, but it later added old style lager beer and more candy choices. During this time, the company moved into a 3,000-square-foot building at 114–128 East Tenth Street. In 1936, Henry C. Fenn passed away after battling tuberculosis. His son, Henry G. Fenn (also called Bill), left college to help run the business. Henry G. Fenn's younger brother, Jim, joined him to keep the "brothers" in the name. In 1939, a major decision was made to move away from their general line of goods/candy to one specializing exclusively in candy bars. Henry G. (Bill) was thought to be the major contributor for this idea. The 1940s were a very transitional time with the introduction and trademarking of many candy bars, as well as ice cream flavors and a variety of flavorings.

In early 1950, a decision was made to purchase an existing candy company (Mannes Candy) in Los Angeles, California. The reasoning behind this decision was simple—as the company continued to grow, shipping costs also increased. Fenn's always tried to use all-natural ingredients in their products and ones that were purchased locally, whenever possible. However, some things, like walnuts and Brazil nuts had to be brought in by ship at seaports on the West Coast. With the raw materials needed, Fenn's went national and started shipping products from the Midwest to the West and East Coasts. In 1952, James W. Fenn, forty-three, passed away and a few years later in 1958, Henry G. Fenn (Bill) died at the age of fifty-four.

The 1950s marked a growth spurt in the company, which included an expansion to 80,000 square feet and hiring more staff. According to reports in the 1950s, Fenn's Bros was the third largest employer in Sioux Falls with anywhere between 175 and 200 employees. In 1954, it was stated that the ice cream department was one of the larger independents in the United States. According to some published articles, Fenn's Bros went national in 1953, though others contradict this with notes of it happening up to fifteen years earlier.

The 1960s proved to be another very critical time in the expansion of Fenn's Bros as a company. First, in 1961 and 1962, the Fenn's Guernsey Dairy was purchased in eastern Sioux Falls, which was in the area of the current Washington High School. Second, up to this point, all Fenn's products had been sold through the wholesale market; this was the first time they would start selling products retail. This venture proved very expensive because of the additional new trucks, equipment, new employees, and the necessary marketing and advertising. Along with these added expenses, Fenn's Bros was facing many other hurdles, including outdated facilities and machinery, rising costs to ship ingredients and products from and to the West and East Coasts, along with many labor issues. The downtown Sioux Falls location was not ideal for a manufacturing company of this size because the rail lines, which went by the loading docks, could be blocked for up to two days. In looking forward, the company purchased two blocks of space in the industrial park to rebuild the factory and use it as warehouse space.

In the end, due to all of the issues, it was decided to sell the company in the late 1960s. In 1968 and 1969, the ice cream and dairy divisions were sold to Marigold Foods. The ice cream flavorings were sold to other ice cream manufacturers nationally and internationally. In February of 1971, the company and all Fenn's stock were sold to George A. Fox Products Company in Kansas City, Missouri. The purchase price was said to be more than one million dollars and included the plant in California. As with many buyouts, it was stated the Sioux Falls facility would continue to operate without any change in personnel. However, in December of 1971, the Fenn's Bros. facility was closed after being in the city for seventy-three years. It was reported there were many copper kettles still filled with Butter Brickle when the lights were turned off for the last time.

Shortly after the sale, the building was razed and replaced with a parking lot, which later became a new parking ramp. All the registered trademarks and recipes were sold to Heath Candy in Missouri. Heath attempted to produce the Walnut Crush bar, but that effort was discontinued when the only way they could turn a profit was to use artificial ingredients, which drastically changed the flavor and was met with no sales. Hershey Candy purchased Heath in 1996 so they now own all the recipes. Many people have tried to imitate (and failed) the candy bars produced by Fenn's, but since all real ingredients were used, it was difficult. Most of the trademarks that were registered in the late 1940s and early 1950s expired in the 1990s.

Although the Walnut Crush candy bar was the most popular treat among many, the Butter Brickle candy bar/ice cream flavoring was the top seller for Fenn's. In the 1920s, Butter Brickle was introduced to the world at the Blackstone Hotel in Omaha, Nebraska, and Fenn's registered one Butter Brickle trademark in 1927. A second Butter Brickle trademark was registered in 1947, and in 1955, the final one came for English Toffee Chocolate Covered chips. This is the only remnant left of Fenn's today—it is sold and branded by Heath/Hershey.

The original Butter Brickle candy bar was a toffee-centered chocolate-covered sensation. As some recall, the bar was made by laying the centers on cookie sheets and drying for three days, giving them the "snap." This was time consuming and not a very profitable process. A popular marketing slogan for the candy bar was "Got a Nickel—Butter Brickle Candy Bar." In the 1950s, Fenn's provided the Butter Brickle ice cream flavoring to General Mills, who introduced it in their cake and frosting mix up until the 1990s, when it was discontinued.

The Walnut Crush candy bar was very popular and is brought up many times when Fenn's is discussed. The candy bar was like a Three Musketeers or Milky Way, except the filling was a bright, white, fluffy nougat with crushed walnuts covered in dark chocolate. The early candy bars were in brown wrappers and cost a nickel, whereas in the later years, the wrapper was orange and cost ten cents.

The Big Bogie candy bar was created in four-by-eight sheets, then cut down into smaller pieces and put in a yellow wrapper. The ingredients included sugar, corn syrup, nuts, honey, vegetable oil, egg whites, and salt—something not commonly found in today's candy bars. The Big Bogie name was short lived and was later changed to Big Nougat in the 1950s due to racial overtures in the South.

The Royal Brazil candy bar consisted of Brazil nuts with a milk chocolate coating. In 1954, it was reported that Fenn's was the largest user of shelled Brazil nuts in the United States; this candy bar was the main reason. Other candy bars manufactured by Fenn's included Red Bird, Blue

Seal, Pecan Crush, Horehound Sticks, and many others. The research and development team were always on the outlook to try to create new and different flavors.

The ice cream and flavorings could have almost been considered a company all its own. Many people remember the popular slogan: "Fenn's—That Good Ice Cream." As with their candy bars, their ice cream only used real cream, milk, and sugar. They offered many different flavors including Butter Brickle, Sherbet, Orange Lime, Vanilla, Chocolate, Strawberry, Cherry Nut, Peppermint, Mint Bon-Bon, along with many others. During the holidays, they always offered different combinations—for instance July Fourth was celebrated with Yankee Doodle ice cream, a combination of fresh strawberry and juicy blueberry and vanilla for a tasty treat.

Products and services can make or break a company but just as valuable are the employees—a company and community asset. Fenn's Bros offered a community room where up to seventy-five people could meet and have all the ice cream, pop, candy bars, and dairy products they could eat for free. This was very popular for church groups and/or students who were on a field trip.

Fenn's Bros. had a long and profitable history not only in Sioux Falls but all over the United States as well. When gathered in a group and discussing the company, you will almost always be guaranteed to hear words like Walnut Crush candy bar, Butter Brickle, and you can never forget "Fenn's—That Good Ice Cream."

The Banquet

ERIC SCHULTE

Inside the Banquet Hall
everyone has a need.
Some come to be fed,
some come to feed.

—Ray Feller, poet and guest of the Banquet

In 1985, Bishop Paul Dudley of the Sioux Falls Catholic Diocese had an idea. He was concerned about rising hunger in Sioux Falls and wanted to do something about it. He called together a group of people from diverse backgrounds to come up with a plan for opening a kitchen and gathering space where all those who were hungry could be fed. This new ministry would be ecumenical. It would be open to all. It would feed both the body and the soul. It would also be funded exclusively by private donations, and meals would be served by volunteers. His idea, which culminated in the opening of the Banquet, now serves roughly 200,000 meals per year. Among many other things, it provides school supplies to over 6,000 students each year and changes countless lives for the better every single day. The history of the Banquet is remarkable. It is a story of community coming together to address a problem. Born out of ingenuity, faith, and hard work, it is a story that needs to be told.

The Beginning

Paul Dudley was the Bishop of the Sioux Falls Catholic Diocese from 1978 until 1995. Bishop Dudley is fondly remembered for being kind and personable. He was also committed to serving the poor and the underprivileged. In 1985, he called together a group of people from the community to think about how to address the rising problem of hunger in Sioux Falls. This group included Lutheran Pastor David Holm, Father James Michael Doyle, former Governor Richard Kneip, local lawyer Jeremiah Murphy, local businessman David Billion, John Wenande, Sister Veronica Haig, Vada Thomas, Joan Weber, Les Wills, and Jo Vaughn Gross. What happened next is eloquently and thoroughly explained in

Jo Gross's book, *The Welcome Table: Reflections on the Banquet.*[1] During their first meeting, the group toured the Good Shepherd Center located at 300 North Main Avenue. This building had been generously donated by the Billion family to the Catholic Diocese. A space in the building was set aside to create a kitchen and dining hall.

While the group came away from their initial meeting knowing that hunger was a pressing issue, they had little to no experience in running a feeding ministry. A trip was scheduled to Milwaukee, Wisconsin, because churches there of all denominations operated large feeding programs. The group hoped lessons could be learned they could then take back to Sioux Falls. Fortunately, the group learned many important lessons in Milwaukee. These lessons culminated in certain fundamental tenets about how the Banquet would be operated. First, the ministry needed to be as important to the volunteer serving the meal as it was to the guest receiving the meal. It was critically important that the volunteer and guest interact with each other. The goal was to "build a bridge between the powerless, lonely and impoverished people and those with influence, resources and strength."[2] The poor would not be treated poorly at the Banquet. It would be a place of fellowship where everyone belonged and interacted with each other.

Moreover, it was critically important that the Banquet was ecumenical. It could not become just the "Catholic" or "Protestant" feeding ministry. Instead, it needed to be supported by people of all faiths throughout the community, just like the feeding program in Milwaukee. Everyone needed to be involved and welcomed. Along these lines, it was decided early on that the Banquet would be privately funded. The volunteer groups serving the meal would also pay for it. This served the critical need of the volunteer interacting with the guest not just with a financial donation but also by breaking bread with the guest to create a greater sense of community.

It was also necessary for the dining hall to have a family atmosphere. Art would be on the walls. Fresh flowers would be placed on the tables. It needed to be welcoming. This all stemmed from the core idea that the Banquet was premised upon love for each other. The group learned in its research that without love as the main ingredient, most feeding programs fall flat. As Jo Gross explains, "Impoverished people really don't care how much you know or even how much you do, until they know how much you care."[3]

---

1 Sadly, this beautiful book is out of print. For years it was given out to new Banquet board members as a useful guide explaining why it functioned as it did. It also serves as an eloquent history capturing the founding of the Banquet. Hopefully this book can be published once again.

2 Jo Vaughn Gross, *The Welcome Table—Reflections on the Banquet*, 10.

3 Ibid., 47.

With all of these ideas in mind, the Banquet was formed.[4] A board of directors was named, and Jo Gross was hired as the organization's first executive director. Opening night was June 17, 1985, at 300 North Main Avenue. Members of the First Presbyterian Church and the founding board members prepared the first meal. When the doors opened at 5:30 p.m., however, not many people showed up. Les Wills, one of the founders, was not deterred. As explained by Jo Gross: suddenly, he left and went out on the street. He walked the area, past the dumpsters, into the bars, into the cheap hotels to find people. He invited them to the meal, pointed the way, and walked beside them to the door. By the time he returned, the dining room was full.[5]

The Banquet was on its way.

Into the Future

Carolyn Downs joined the Banquet in 1988 as an administrative assistant to Jo Gross. She became executive director in 1990 and served in this position until her retirement in 2008. During this time, she became a pillar in the Sioux Falls community known for her strength and tireless devotion to the poor and underprivileged. Carolyn ran a tight ship: the food served needed to be nutritious and of high quality, the dining room spotless, and chairs at the dining tables needed to be perfectly aligned when guests entered the room. Most importantly, she continued requiring that compassion be shown. Those served were "guests" and needed to be treated accordingly with love and respect.

During Carolyn's time at the Banquet, the ministry transformed from serving meals two nights a week to serving evening meals every Monday through Friday with lunch on Saturday. Breakfast meals were also served three days a week later in Carolyn's tenure.[6] All of these meals were prepared and paid for by volunteers from the local community. Furthermore, and incredibly, by the time she retired in 2008, the Banquet was serving over 135,000 meals per year. During an interview for this essay, Carolyn recalled her early days. She told me, "When I started, Jo taught me everything I needed to know, and Father Doyle gave me all the courage I needed." She

4 The Banquet's name is based on a parable in the Gospel of Luke in which Jesus said, "A man once gave a great banquet, and invited many . . . go out quickly to the streets and lanes of the city and bring in the poor and maimed and blind and lame," Luke 14:16–24, New Revised Standard Version. As explained by Jo Gross, there was 'no intention of being an ordinary feeding program, the "soup kitchen" was called THE BANQUET." *The Welcome Table—Reflections on the Banquet*, 11.

5 *The Welcome Table*, 63–64.

6 Breakfast started being served five days a week, from Monday through Friday, in 2013.

also worked closely with Bishop Dudley. When she assumed the duties of executive director, she was nervous and wondered if she was the right person for the job. Bishop Dudley told her, “Don’t worry about what you don’t know.” He also blessed her, saying, “All you need to do is listen to the Holy Spirit. Please remember that and go forth and do the work of the Lord.”

In the late 1990s, Carolyn went on a work retreat to San Francisco and volunteered at a food ministry in the city’s Tenderloin District. She was surprised to learn that this ministry forbade any interaction between the guests and the volunteers. She was specifically instructed to not look at the people being fed as they went through the serving line. When asked why she wanted to interact with the people being served, Carolyn told them, “Because they have so much to offer.” They ultimately relented and let her sit with the guests where she, incredibly, met and talked with someone she had previously met through the Banquet in Sioux Falls. This experience only reinforced her strong belief that the Banquet’s model of having volunteers and guests interact is critical for its success.

Marvella Shatter

Shatter worked as the Food Service Director for the Banquet from 1999 through 2019. In this position she was in charge of ordering food and planning menus. She also helped coordinate the volunteer groups serving and preparing meals and would work with them when it came time for service. She was a favorite of the guests and knew many of them by name. In reflecting on her time at the Banquet, Marvella fondly recalls the people she was able to meet. Marvella told me, “Imagine a job where you get to meet people from every walk of life every single day—from the most affluent people in our community to people that are struggling to live. It was quite an experience.” It was not uncommon for people to just drop in and visit with her, which resulted in people leaving a donation or sometimes just sharing a cup of coffee. Her door was always open.

When I asked Marvella to pick out her favorite stories, she vividly recalled a meal shortly after Christmas when she asked two young children about how their holiday went. These children, a brother and sister, came from a family of limited means. When she asked how Christmas went, the young girl said it was the best Christmas ever. The reason was that she got to spend time with her cousins, including another young girl. The girl went on to tell Marvella that her cousins did not have any Christmas gifts at all, so she decided to give the girl cousin one of her gifts. Her cousin opened it, and it was a doll she had wanted, which momentarily made her sad. But when she saw how happy her cousin was, "it didn't matter anymore." To Marvella, this beautiful story is the real lesson of the Banquet: the beauty and joy of serving others.

Time to Grow

It became clear that the location on 300 North Main Avenue was too small. The Banquet had expanded by leaps and bounds since 1985, and it simply could not fit everyone that needed to be served into its original location. As a result, a committee was formed to raise money for a new Banquet building. This committee was chaired by Bill Baker, the CEO of First National Bank in Sioux Falls and a longtime supporter of the Banquet. Through the efforts of many, $1.2M was raised for a new building on the corner of Eighth Street and Indiana Avenue. It opened to guests in 2006.

The need for even more services, however, continued. It became clear that hunger was a pressing concern on the west side of Sioux Falls. As a result, a temporary Banquet location was opened at the fairgrounds in 2014. The Banquet rented a building at the fairgrounds two nights a week. Meals would be prepared downtown and then delivered and served at this temporary location. Although the location was not convenient for guests, or for the staff that prepared and delivered the food, between 2014 and 2018, over 50,000 meals were served there.

Because the need for a permanent and more convenient location was so clear, plans were made for a new building to serve residents on the west side of Sioux Falls. The Delbridge family generously donated two acres of land for a new building to be built on the corner of Fifth Street and Marion Road. Once again, Bill Baker answered the call to chair a committee to raise funds. Through the efforts of many people in the community, $1.9M was raised. The west side location opened in March of 2020 and has served thousands of meals since.

The Banquet's Ministry during the Pandemic

The Banquet has been under the steady guidance of Tamera Jerke-Liesinger since 2008, when she was hired to replace Carolyn Downs as executive director. Tamera has continued the tradition of the Banquet demonstrating love in action. She helped oversee the growth of the Banquet to the city's west side and managed the increasing demands on the Banquet's services. Nonetheless, when the pandemic gripped the world in 2020, the Banquet faced challenges unlike anything ever faced before. Volunteer groups were down due to the risk of disease, and the guests feared getting sick by eating in the dining room. As a result, meals were made to go, and the dining room was closed for sixteen months. Remarkably, the Banquet never missed serving a meal even when the pandemic was at its peak.

To put all of this in perspective, when the Banquet opened in 1985, it served one meal per week. In 2020, when COVID upended the world, the Banquet served 189,687 meals. All of these meals continued being prepared and served by volunteers and funded by private donations.

During the pandemic, critical work was accomplished largely due to a group of dedicated people known accurately as the "Angels." The Angels are a group of roughly 1,800 people that have volunteered to receive a text message if a group that was scheduled to serve cancels, or if for any reason, additional volunteers are needed to help. During the pandemic, this group was called on more than ever before, and they responded. A core group of thirty to forty Angels worked at the Banquet tirelessly and made sure people were fed. These quiet and humble servants are owed a debt of gratitude from everyone in the Sioux Falls community.

Project SOS

One of the most significant ways the Banquet helps families in need is through Project Supply Our Students or, as it is more commonly known, Project SOS. Every August, the Banquet organizes a distribution of backpacks and school supplies to students in Sioux Falls and surrounding communities. This program's goal is to ensure that all students have the supplies they need for the coming school year. No questions are asked about a parent's ability to pay for supplies. New backpacks filled with school supplies are given to students from kindergarten through college. Currently, students in over thirty school districts in the area are helped through Project SOS each year

Like so many things connected with the Banquet, Project SOS. started as a small idea, which transformed into a defining community program demonstrating love in action. In 1989, a working mother with various health problems told Carolyn Downs she needed to work a second job just to pay for her children's school supplies. Carolyn agreed to help the mother, but she also realized that many students were going to school without supplies. No organizations in Sioux Falls were helping families that could not afford school supplies, and the students were disadvantaged because of it.

Seeing this clear need, Carolyn decided the Banquet needed to do something. The result was a plea to the community for donations to help children in need. In the fall of 1989—the first year of Project SOS—school supplies were handed out randomly to children as they arrived at the Banquet for a meal. On one night, pencils were handed out, on the next night, glue, and the next, scissors. This initial year resulted in eighty students being given school supplies for the year.

Since 2010, the Banquet has handed out over 6,000 backpacks filled with supplies for students. The highest number in a single year occurred in 2014, when 6,776 backpacks filled with supplies were distributed. Organizing such a massive program is a monumental task. Hundreds of volunteers are needed to both collect and fill the backpacks. Care must be given to make sure each school district's supply lists are complied with. This need became so great that the Banquet hired a special events coordinator to assist with Project SOS and other special projects. From 2005 through 2016, Madeline Shields worked for the Banquet in this role. Under her tenure, local high school sports teams were recruited to pack and fill backpacks. Multiple local organizations, business, churches, and the young and old all pitched in either through donating supplies or helping pack the supplies for their distribution. This hard work all culminated in distribution day at Whittier Middle School, where literally thousands of schoolchildren and their parents would line up in the morning to receive supplies. Volunteers working in shifts would arrive early in the morning to help. Distribution day was always well organized and left a strong sense of satisfaction with both the volunteer and the child receiving supplies. In true Banquet style, the volunteer was left with a sense of joy in helping a student find just the right backpack for the coming year, while the child left with a sense of joy and excitement for the coming school year.

Project SOS continues to be a defining event in Sioux Falls, demonstrating the community's compassion and willingness to address an important need. Jo Gross eloquently wrote as follows about the organization's dedication to children: "There are few answers to most of the questions raised at the Banquet. But this I know: the children who come experience a moment of caring, they are welcomed and loved, and somewhere down their rough journey of life, they will remember. This is one race we have not run in vain."[7]

Amen to that.

Father James Doyle said the Banquet "is not only a story to be told, but one to behold." The remarkable growth of the Banquet since 1985 is nothing short of amazing. But like all things worth fighting for, supporting the Banquet requires constant diligence and effort. The Banquet is nothing less than the community coming together to make sure hungry people have food to eat and can experience true love in action. With continued faith, hard work, and community involvement, the Banquet will continue for years supporting all those in the Sioux Falls area who need help.

---

7 Jo Vaughn Gross, *The Welcome Table—Reflections on the Banquet*, 59.

Joe Foss

RANDY BROWN

Joe Foss was a "World's Most Interesting Man" before there was even an internet. Foss was born in Sioux Falls. He was a farmer, a business owner, a fighter pilot, and a war hero Marine. A cowboy in both spirit and in hat, he was the youngest-elected governor of the state of South Dakota and helped found the South Dakota Air National Guard. He became a globe-trotting celebrity sportsman but always made sure to return to hunt and fish the lands of his youth. He made the cover of *Life* magazine at age twenty-eight and the cover of *Time* magazine at age seventy-five.

He also played the saxophone. And invented the Super Bowl.

His legacies still permeate the South Dakota firmament and the skies above Sioux Falls in particular. He is a legend, but also the Real Deal. "The most notable thing about Foss," wrote the *Argus Leader*'s Peter Harriman in Foss's 2003 obituary, "is that there are so few unanswered questions about him. What you saw is what you got."

In 1915, Joe Foss was born in an unelectrified farmhouse east of Sioux Falls. He was a first child—a brother and sister would come later. "As a youngster I wasn't much help around the farm. I was there, acting like a busy little man, but that was about all. I wanted to go fishing and hunting—things like that," he said in a 1943 biography, an "as told to" book written with *Chicago Tribune* war correspondent Walter Simmons. "Farm work was always interfering with my extracurricular activities."

In 1927, an overexcited twelve-year-old Foss climbed up onto a platform at Renner Field, five miles north of Sioux Falls, in an attempt to shake hands with his hero, Charles A. Lindbergh, who was the first pilot to fly solo across the Atlantic. By his own report, Foss was tossed off the stage. He didn't get to meet Lindbergh that day.

In 1930, Foss attended a Sioux Falls "air fair" that featured a formation flight of US Marine Corps F4B4 biplanes commanded by Captain Clayton C. "Jerry" Jerome. "The roar of those old egg beaters, the dust and excitement, the skill of the flyers—all those things drove me wild." He took his first ride in an airplane in 1934. It cost him $1.50. In 1937, he learned it cost $65 to learn to solo as a pilot. That was a whole month's pay working at Tollefson's filling station, but he made extra income playing alto saxophone in a municipal band. He spent the $65.

Joe Foss served as the president of the National Rifle Association in 1988 and 1989. Later, he wrote that hunting was a way he'd helped his family survive economically during his youth and coincidentally sharpened himself for war. "A pheasant brought from the field meant one more chicken to sell at the market rather than having to eat it for our daily provisions. Similarly, fishing in the Splitrock or Sioux Rivers, four or five miles away, was an economic activity, not a sport."

In 1936—Joe Foss's senior year of high school—his father was killed when he stepped on a downed roadside powerline during a nighttime electrical storm. Foss enrolled at Augustana College but only lasted a few months while juggling studies with working the family farm. "A college education seemed totally unnecessary, and I quit." Making a living as a farmer proved difficult, however. After working a few nonfarm jobs, he enrolled at Sioux Falls College, which is now the University of Sioux Falls. Foss got an on-campus job as a janitor while attending classes there. He also played football, ran distance events in track, and went out for boxing.

In 1939, Foss transferred as a junior to the University of South Dakota, Vermillion. He worked at a meat market, and waited tables and washed dishes at the Sigma Alpha Epsilon fraternity house for room and board. During his senior year, he and some fellow students started a Civil Aeronautics Administration course. The course was comprised of seventy-two hours of ground school and fifty-eight hours of flying at Rickenbacker Field near Sioux City, Iowa. The field was named after another of Foss's heroes, World War I pilot Eddie Rickenbacker, a fighter "ace" who had downed a record twenty-six enemy planes.

In February 1940, with five dollars in his pocket, Foss hitchhiked with a friend to travel 300 miles to Minneapolis, Minnesota, where they each hoped to enlist as US Marine aviators. Twenty-eight men applied, but Foss and his friend were the only ones who made the cut. He graduated with a business degree in June and was commissioned as a second lieutenant.

To his disappointment, after pinning his Marine aviator's wings, Foss was sent to photo-reconnaissance school. "I wanted to fight, and reconnaissance planes have no guns in them." When he complained, he was told that he was too old for fighter planes. He was twenty-seven years old.

"I think Joe has always lived in a different kind of world than most of us mortals," his second wife Donna "Didi" Wild Foss later wrote. "He lives in the present tense. Whatever is happening right now is the most important thing."

"In the past, when there was something he couldn't cope with, he just left—he went hunting or fishing," she also wrote. "But through the years Joe's relationship with God has changed all that, and as far as I'm concerned, it's nothing short of a miracle."

In World War II, Joe Foss eventually landed himself an assignment flying a Grumman-manufactured F4F fighter plane called the "Wildcat." Foss's fighter-pilot peers variously nicknamed him "Smokey Joe" (due to his cigar habit) and, as well as "Old Joe" and "Old Foos." The Wildcat mounted six belt-fed, .50-caliber machine guns. A single .50-caliber round is the shape of a good-sized carrot, and the single-prop plane carried 450 rounds per gun. In order to conserve ammunition—on at least four engagements, Foss came back empty of all rounds—he disabled two of his six guns. With a top speed of 318 miles per hour, the Wildcat was a little slower and less maneuverable than the adversary's Mitsubishi A6M "Zero" fighters, but it was more armored and more survivable.

Foss compared dogfighting to jousting. "My style was to head straight at the target until the very last minute, when I either had to turn or collide," he wrote. "Then I'd pour on the lead just before I swerved away, using the same trigger-finger action I'd used back home to target a pheasant."

As a US Marine aviator who flew and fought over the Pacific during World War II—most famously, during the Battle of Guadalcanal in the Solomon Islands—Foss at one point held the highest number of confirmed aircraft kills in the US armed forces. In military jargon, that made him the "Ace of Aces." Between October 1942 and May 1943, while serving as the executive officer of US Marine fighter squadron VMF-121, Foss downed a career total of twenty-six Japanese fighters, bombers, and other aircraft. In that, he tied Eddie Rickenbacker's World War I record. His self-named "Flying Circus"—a subgroup of eight pilots led directly by Foss—was credited with another forty-six.

At one point during the battle, Admiral William "Bull" Halsey Jr. pinned a Distinguished Flying Cross (DFC) on Foss and some other aviators. The awardees wore their combat gear during the ceremony. Following the event, Foss and his fellow pilots immediately took off on yet another mission.

In 1955, the Sioux Falls Municipal Airport was rededicated in honor of Joe Foss. "When it was advertised that [retired] Admiral Halsey would be there, soldiers and sailors and Marines from all over the Midwest came up to see him," Foss wrote. Now Sioux Falls Regional Airport (airport code: KFSD), the facility is still proudly called "Joe Foss Field." Even the entrance sign bears his name. Co-located with the civilian airport, the South Dakota National Guard's 114th Fighter Wing is headquartered at "Joe Foss Air National Guard Station."

As passengers arrive in the airport terminal's lobby, twenty-first-century travelers pass by an eight-foot-tall statue of Foss, depicted in his World War II flying gear and helmet. When the statue was originally installed in 1995, airport officials placed it somewhat out of the way. After the terrorist attacks of 2001, however, activists successfully petitioned to move the statue to a more honored location.

The local volunteer squadron of the Commemorative Air Force (CAF)—a national nonprofit network of historic aircraft preservationists—is also named after Joe Foss. The organization's distinctive patch features an ace of spades, an F4F Wildcat, and the nickname of a US Marine fighter squadron Foss commanded after Guadalcanal, VMF-115: "Joe's Jokers."

After the war, Foss and his buddy Duane L. "Duke" Corning spent a year hunting and fishing. They opened a small company called "Joe Foss Flying Service" and offered executive charters and pilot training. Later, they added crop-spraying to their business mix.

In 1946, Foss resigned his commission as a major in the Marine Corps reserve, and the next day, he was appointed as a lieutenant colonel in the newly commissioned South Dakota Air National Guard. Comprised of volunteers from Sioux Falls, the 175th Fighter Squadron was issued P-51 "Mustang" fighters—but no manuals and limited budget. Pilots reportedly bought their own parachutes.

According to a unit history maintained by Sioux Fall's modern-day 114th Fighter Wing, Foss mounted external fuel tanks on the squadron's planes so they could "borrow" gas from the active-duty US Air Force. Once, upon landing at what is the present-day Ellsworth Air Base near Rapid City, Foss and Corning were quickly surrounded by military police, who had no idea who they were. Corning was wearing his old US Navy flight suit. Foss was wearing blue jeans.

In 2003, eighty-six-year-old Joe Foss made headlines at Phoenix, Arizona's Sky Harbor Airport. There, overzealous security personnel threatened to confiscate and destroy his Congressional Medal of Honor, as well as a commemorative souvenir keychain once presented to him by National Rifle Association (NRA) President Charlton Heston, a former movie actor. Foss himself was a former president of the organization.

The security personnel thought that the medal was ninja throwing star and that the keychain looked like a bullet. Foss was patted down and three times made to remove his hat, bolo tie, and cowboy boots.

"I wasn't upset for me," he told *Chicago Tribune* columnist Bob Greene. "I was upset for the Medal of Honor, that they just didn't know what it even was."

In 1944, Joe Foss flew combat missions over the Pacific, accompanied by Charles Lindbergh. Foss was then the commander of VMF-115, a US Marine Corps squadron of Vought-manufactured F4U "Corsair" fighter planes. Lindbergh was an unpaid civilian contractor, who had lost his commission as a military reservist over a political difference with US President Franklin Delano Roosevelt. Foss bent the rules on behalf of his childhood hero. After *Parade* magazine ran a captioned photo of Foss and Lindbergh outside a military dining facility, however, Lindburgh's combat flights came to a quick end.

It wasn't Foss's first brush with insubordination. Only his Distinguished Flying Cross and his reputation, he would later write, saved him being relieved of duty during the later days of Guadalcanal. Foss and his commanding officer, Colonel Sam Jack, were convinced the enemy retained the capacity to counterattack. Their superior, Brigadier General Francis P. Mulcahy, disagreed. When Mulcahy learned Foss had disobeyed his orders to put everything in the air, and had instead held eight planes as a reserve force, he told Foss to expect a transfer.

On the day that Foss was due to be shipped out, however, an enemy attack validated his hunch. Not only that, but Foss was able to scramble a defense with his "extra" fighters. In the air, they found a number of enemy aircraft circling high over the US airfield, which Foss correctly guessed was actually a decoy away from the primary attack. He held his fighters back, declining to take the bait.

"By refusing to run away when the odds were clearly and overwhelming against us, we instilled the deep suspicion that we must have many more planes in the air," Foss wrote in his autobiography. "Hundreds of poker games I'd won during the long hours of military waiting were nothing compared to the extraordinary bluff I'd just pulled off—without firing a shot. Old Foos had played the greatest empty hand of his life."

In a ceremony attended by his mother, President Franklin Delano Roosevelt awarded Foss the Medal of Honor, the highest award in the US military. By tradition, even the highest-ranking general officers are the first to salute those who wear the medal. The citation reads, in part, "His remarkable flying skill, inspiring leadership, and indomitable fighting spirit were distinctive factors in the defense of strategic American positions on Guadalcanal."

Foss would say that having his Democrat mother witness the presentation was the proudest moment of his life.

There is another statue of Foss wearing a military flight suit, this one located in the South Dakota state capitol of Pierre, part of a "Trail of Governors." Elected in 1954, at the age of thirty-nine, Foss was the youngest person to become governor of the State of Dakota. He served two terms, from 1955 to 1959.

The Republican loved hand-shaking retail politics and hated debates. A man of the people, one of his first executive decisions was to do away with formal invitations to his inaugural ball—anyone could come, whether they wore tuxedoes or overalls. In his daily business, he similarly maintained an "open door" policy. His staff learned to buffer his continual tardiness, often caused by overlong conversations with constituents. "The governor," they would say, "is *en route*."

An inveterate cigar-chomper, Foss installed throughout the capitol building some old spittoons he and Secretary of Employment Henry Tunge had found stored in the capitol. Foss carried a duck call in his pocket because there was a pond on the two-block walks between the governor's mansion and his office.

More than once, thinking he was John Wayne, people asked Joe Foss for his autograph. Maybe it was his signature Stetson, midwestern drawl, or even a physical resemblance to the movie star. Coincidentally, in the mid-1950s, Hollywood producer Hall Barlett wanted to make a movie about Joe Foss's life, in which John Wayne was to be the featured lead. The movie was never made, however. Foss balked at the script's depiction of his fellow Marine pilots as insecure or resentful, as well as the insertion of a fictitious romance. "I've never been one to stake my life on baloney," Foss wrote of the incident.

Wayne and Foss, however, remained friends. They even went dove-hunting together.

Joe Foss—who as governor, had established an annual South Dakota pheasant hunt to promote economic development and tourism—was also one of the very first stars of sports-focused reality TV programming. First as host of ABC Television's *The American Sportsman* (1964–1967) and then of his own syndicated show, *The Outdoorsman* (1967–1972), Foss was seen hunting and fishing while traveling around the world, accompanied by celebrity guests such as military aviation heroes Chuck Yeager and Jimmy Doolittle, as well as movie stars Charlton Heston and Roy Rogers.

Foss almost died in the production of "The Outdoorsman" TV show. During a shoot in a Nebraska cornfield, he'd revisited a youthful habit of chewing on cornstalks. The production crew didn't realize the crops had recently been sprayed with an arsenic-based pesticide. "When the grim reaper finally caught up with me, it wasn't a Zero, or a plane crash, or even a charging elephant. It was a cornstalk, like the kind I used to plant and cultivate and harvest back in South Dakota."

Joe Foss invented the Super Bowl. He also invented players wearing names on their football jerseys, locker room interviews, and the Miami Dolphins. Starting in 1959, as the first commissioner of the upstart American Football League (AFL), Foss shrewdly maneuvered the teams and their owners toward financial stability and success—mostly through media attention and lucrative network television negotiations. When team owners resisted allowing sportswriters access to players immediately following games, Foss notably recalled his wartime experiences. "I gave the war correspondents permission to climb up on the airplane wings after we flew back from a mission because I wanted the news to be hot and just exactly what it was."

Foss stepped down as commissioner in 1966, two months before the AFL merged with the National Football League (NFL). In his letter of resignation, he wrote, "Professional football should be operated with one commissioner and two league presidents as is major league baseball. Those in pro football owe it to the general public to present it with an annual world series and an all-star classic."

The first Super Bowl was played in January 1967.

Later in life, according to his autobiography, written with help from his second wife, Didi, Foss found God and variously gave up gambling, smoking, and drinking hard liquor.

Together, they also founded the Joe Foss Institute, an organization that promoted good citizenship and patriotic values, via presentations made to school children by Foss and other military veterans.

"For years when the press interviewed me, they would ask, 'Joe, out of all the things that have happened to you, what do you rate number one?' And I would always say, 'It hasn't happened yet,'" Foss wrote.

"All the medals in the world wouldn't solve my dilemma with God. That only happened when I stepped out of the cockpit and turned the controls over to Him."

Sources

Appearance on CBS Television Network game show *What's My Line?* aired May 1, 1955.

Jack Cafferty interview with Joe Foss, "Decorated WWII veteran detained, searched at airport," CNN posted Feb. 27, 2002.

Carol Fader, "Fact Check: Was 86-year-old stopped from boarding plane because of his Medal of Honor?" *The Times-Union*, June 13, 2014.

Joe Foss with Donna Wild Foss, *A Proud American: The Autobiography of Joe Foss*. Pocket Books /Simon & Shuster Inc., New York 1992.

Joe Foss Squadron, Commemorative Air Force (CAF) website.

Peter Harriman, "State's youngest governor, WWII pilot dies at 87," *Argus Leader*, January 2, 2003.

Magazine cover photo "Captain Foss, U.S.M.C., America's No. 1 Ace" *Life*, June 7, 1943.

Magazine cover photo "NRA President Joe Foss," *Time*, January 29, 1990.

Walter Simmons, *Joe Foss, Flying Marine: The Story of His Flying Circus as told to Walter Simmons*. Books, Inc. / E.P. Dutton & Co, Inc. New York 1943.

Sioux Fall Regional Airport History website.

Rob Swenson, "6-year battle over spot for airport artwork ends," *The Argus Leader*, Sept. 28, 2001.

Unit history, 114th Fighter Wing, South Dakota Air National Guard, document dated Sept. 22, 2017.

Latinx Comunidad

MARCELLA PROKOP

On the day I meet Marvella Mercado to talk about her growing party supply business, she tells me that, like her vivid handcrafted piñatas, no two Hispanic people are the same. "I think a lot of times, people look at us and don't know we're different, that we have different cultures," she says. "They don't know about our foods or traditions, the special things we're all proud of."

While this might be true for many people unfamiliar with Marvella's Mexican culture, in a city like Sioux Falls, where nearly 10,000 residents identified as Hispanic or Latino in the recent census, it's becoming easier and easier to connect with the various Latinx cultures flourishing here. As a hyphenated Hispanic—a Colombian-American—I'm grateful for the variety of communities and traditions that foster understanding for myself and others.

When I moved to Sioux Falls as a college freshman in the fall of 2001, I was looking for a way to understand the liminal existence of my mixed heritage. In rural Nebraska, where I grew up, my mom and I were the only people I knew with naturally tan skin. I believed being in a city would help me connect not only with other Hispanics but also with some part of me I couldn't understand. Because I had always believed the essence of my maternal culture came from a distant place, Colombia, in my new home, I turned to other venues, including a church, a grocery store, and a panadería, or bakery, for connections to a culture I'd known all my life only through travel.

First, Our Lady of Guadalupe beckoned to me. I did not feel a strong pull to religion, but in Colombia, everyone I knew went to church on Sunday. And often Monday, and sometimes on Tuesday, and Wednesday if it was a Holy Day. Basically, on any day, church was the place to connect with others in flesh and blood and spirit. But the contemporary music and overwhelming clouds of incense were nothing like the services I celebrated with my family in Colombia. And knowing no one, I felt too clunky in my stilted Spanish to spark a conversation. Throughout college, I attended mass at Guadalupe off and on, but I did not cultivate the connection I wanted.

At Nicki's La Mexicana grocery store and adjoining restaurant, just down the road from Guadalupe's brick walls, the shelves and smells and bright colors reminded me of the bodegas in mi tía's barrio in Bogotá. But we eat arepas, not tortillas, in Colombia, and the Carlos V chocolate bar I once bought didn't taste like the Jet bars I grew up eating with cousins in abuelita's kitchen. Like the church and Nicki's, Manna, the panadería provided a pop of Hispanic culture. Walking into the bumpy trill of the double "r" and thick, guttural Spanish exchanged faster than I could understand it made me feel like I was walking around the plaza with mi tío. But aside from the brazo de reina (a fat, pink, sugar-coated cake roll), none of the pastries or breads were familiar to me. These places did not hold the connection to culture I thought I was seeking.

In an informal poll of friends, I found these locations represent "Hispanic culture" to many in Sioux Falls. While they certainly are anchors of the Latino community, this assemblage of well-known Sioux Falls spots didn't give me the roadmap to my heritage and myself that I wanted. At eighteen and nineteen and even into my early twenties, I thought if I could just find the right place, here in the US, I could go there and embrace and be embraced by this culture that was partially mine. Sioux Falls surely gave me a "place" to grasp that understanding. But it took me many years to recognize that my own rigid interpretations of what it means "to be" Hispanic held me back. As I recognized this reality, I also realized that another word for "place" is "community."

Today, I occasionally attend mass at Guadalupe, and my son has enjoyed a fresh brazo de reina from Manna but not yet Colombia. I served tongue tacos—the first meal I bought all those years ago at Nicki's—at my wedding. There are now so many places to get this dish in Sioux Falls that the food is hardly a novelty, and my wedding feast came from Giliberto's, not Nicki's.

As the Latinx community in Sioux Falls continues to grow, I've found that at the heart of what I have in common with other Latinos is that no matter what food is shared, what dialect is spoken, or if we identify as Hispanic, Latino, Latinx, Latin@, or something more specific, we rely on community to make any space feel like ours. I can't speak for others with my broken Spanish and the boundaries of my own unique experience, but I know when I spend time with friends from El Salvador or Honduras or Mexico, I feel a sense of unity even in our differences.

In the two decades since I moved to Sioux Falls, I have seen Latino community hubs spread from traditional places like the Eighth and Cliff corridor hosting Guadalupe and Nicki's to Falls Park for an annual celebration of Hispanic culture. I've watched Latinidad come into its own on the airwaves, with broadcasts from Mundo Latino Network, a news source for Spanish speakers in Iowa, Nebraska, and South Dakota. I read news from *¿Que Pasa?*, a Sioux Falls news and community resource and nod in solidarity with their tagline: "Unidos hacemos la diferencia," or, "together, we make a difference." And in these venues, I see more and more places for people to connect with their heritage and each other while sharing their culture beyond real or digital structures.

Although in my youth I felt out of place while trying to connect with my background, almost daily I see that people with much deeper ties to a Hispanic homeland have made Sioux Falls theirs. I see the future of Latinx comunidad in Sioux Falls continue to grow in places like the school district, where 13 percent of students in kindergarten through twelfth grade are Hispanic or Latino. Although the Chamber of Commerce doesn't have hard data on the number of Hispanic business owners in the city, every day I see new posts from multiple business owners in the Sioux Falls Latinos or Hispanic Business Network forums. And on a warm Saturday in the summer of 2021, I watched as the mobile Guatemalan consulate filed hundreds of people through the community center at Our Lady of Guadalupe. More than 600 Guatemalans from South Dakota and the surrounding area had appointments with the Denver-based consulate for the once-a-year visit.

Whether all this growth is considered a "boom" by others, I don't know. But what I do know is that booms often cycle the other way, to bust, to ghost towns, to shuttered windows and locked doors. In a Latino community as strong as the one growing in Sioux Falls, where requests for piñatas and cake toppers and party favors keep Marvella busy, I don't see a slowdown of this trend.

As Marvella finishes showing me her latest piñata—a number six that's half as tall as we are—she tells me she spends hours sketching out her designs before fabricating the actual piñata. I've read of the piñata as a metaphor for Mexican American existence, and here, now, surely it is life and art coming together. As I watch Marvella's piñatas take on depth when they come to life layer by layer, I see there is no single experience or place or word that can contain the sweet vibrancy of Latinx culture—in Sioux Falls, or anywhere around the world.

The Schools

LINDA HALLSTROM

Establishing a school system in a pioneer community required three essentials: a teacher and students, a school building, and funding. In 1873, Sioux Falls had just one of the three.

Clara Ledyard, the first teacher hired by the Sioux Falls School Board, enrolled forty-four boys and thirty-three girls for a three-month term in the fall of 1873. They gathered in a room in Libby's Hall near what is now Eighth and Phillips. The Libby building was a sixteen-foot-by-thirty-two-foot frame. The front part of the first floor was partitioned off and used as a meat market. The rear part was used as a school room and, occasionally on Sundays, for church.

Members of the school board had been working for several months to provide a school building for the village, but progress had not been smooth. The school board minutes of 1873 contained this reflection: "A meeting was held on the 29th of April and a school board was chosen; a tax was ordered levied to support the school and a committee appointed to secure a site for a schoolhouse. The selection thus ordered was made and then the difficulties began."

"Difficulties" referred to uncertainty about the board's authority to levy taxes.

On April 29, 1873, the people of Sioux Falls elected the first school board president, Artemus Gale. He had moved to Sioux Falls from St. Paul in 1870. One of the original members of the Dakota Land Company, Gale claimed 400 acres of land in what is now central Sioux Falls. With Gale leading the three-member board, the officers started conducting business . . . or tried to. At the time, Sioux Falls had 593 residents, which is the average enrollment of one of today's elementary schools. Not all village residents were in agreement with the actions of the board.

At the second board meeting on May 12, 1873, board members voted a 1 percent tax for the purpose of building a schoolhouse and a 1 percent tax for school furniture. By June 2, both taxes had been rescinded because nobody was sure whether the board had legal authority to levy taxes. With no way to raise money, the idea of a public school was, in the words of district clerk R. F. Pettigrew, "necessarily abandoned."

The board waited until September to convene again, but when they came together, they were ready to take action. At the September 6 meeting, they voted to provide a three-month school term before the end of the year, collect a tax of three quarters of 1 percent on all taxable property in the district, advertise for the construction of a schoolhouse (to cost not more than $1,000) and to provide a six-month school in 1874.

Advertising in those days meant posting the notice in "prominent places" in the town.

Board minutes reflect their determination, stating that board members "committed themselves one to the other that every possible effort should be made that it might no longer be said that Sioux Falls was without a public school."

At the next meeting, the Board accepted a bid from Edwin Sharpe, who said he would build the school for $985. The building was to be completed by November and financed "when there is money in the treasury to pay with."

Raising the funds to pay for the schoolhouse met with opposition. When Treasurer Homer Whipple tried to collect the taxes, many residents refused. By November, Whipple had collected only $50.15. Meantime, citizens had petitioned Judge P. C. Shannon for an injunction restraining the treasurer from making any more attempts to collect taxes.

Fortunately, the judge refused; property taxes were pronounced legal, and the Sioux Falls School District was on its way.

During November and December 1873—while Clara Ledyard was teaching in the back half of the meat market—Edwin Sharpe was hard at work, building the first school building in Sioux Falls. The schoolhouse was finished and turned over to the board December 5, 1873, less than three months from the time the board was elected.

Located on the site of the present-day Washington Pavilion, the building was a twenty-two-foot-by-forty-four-foot wooden structure with a rock foundation, six twelve-foot windows, and two six-foot-by-ten-foot cloakrooms.

As 1873 drew to a close, the board voted to offer at least six months of school when the new year arrived. They estimated that they would need $420 for teachers' salaries. Excerpts from the 1874 financial report show the following custodial expenses: pail and broom, $1.00; painting schoolhouse, $35.00; wood and hauling, $8.50; fixing up stove, $5.70; hauling seats, $7.12; cleaning schoolhouse, $3.00; hauling water to clean schoolhouse; $0.50.

Reading school board minutes from the 1870s and 1880s is like reading today's news reports. The population of the town was mushrooming, and the schools were scrambling to keep up.

Sioux Falls outgrew its first school building very quickly. Students had moved into the building in the spring of 1874. By the fall of 1875, the district found it necessary to rent a room from the Methodist Church at Eleventh and Main.

But parents were no longer content with makeshift classrooms. Thomas H. Brown, a member of the school board at that time, recalled in his memoirs:

> The Board was criticized because of the cheap, inferior appearance and inadequacy of the house. At a subsequent school election the board was changed by the election of Thos. H. Brown, chairman; Cyrus Walts, treasurer; and C. W. McDonald, clerk. The new board, aided by a few optimistic citizens, in the face of a storm of opposition and some threats, took the necessary steps for the erection of the present schoolhouse which was completed in 1878.

Brown was referring to Central School—later commonly called "Old Central." Constructed where the Washington Pavilion now stands, Central was sixty feet square with two stories and a basement. There were eight rooms for both grade and high school students.

In 1877, L. D. Henry had been hired as principal of the high school for the spring term. In 1881, Sutton Young was elected principal of the high school. By then, Sioux Falls also had two elementary schools—the North School, or Hawthorne, with Mila Tupper as principal and the East School, or Whittier, with Louisa Kinney as principal. Both women were teachers, and each was paid an extra $10 a month for taking on the additional duties of principal.

A growing school system with three school principals, Sioux Falls needed a superintendent of schools, so the board retained Sutton Young as both superintendent of schools and principal of Central School at the sum of $120 a month.

Historian Dana Bailey said of Sioux Falls's first superintendent: "He was not always successful in what he attempted to do, but he was always adroit, energetic and persistent in carrying out his plans. He is a man of fine appearance and a good public speaker."

By the early 1890s, the need for repair and upgrading of Central was frequently mentioned in the board minutes. Flooding along Twelfth

Street threatened the building; pipes were sometimes frozen, and possible condemnation was feared.

In 1895, the district rented a building at Eleventh and Spring that had been a Catholic boarding school. They renamed the school McKinley High. McKinley was Sioux Falls's high school until 1908 when the first part—the north wing—of Washington High School was completed.

The central part of Sioux Falls, from the block where the Washington Pavilion now stands, to the corner of Eleventh and Spring, is the genesis for today's public schools. In that setting, the Sioux Falls schools first grappled with growing pains and began the transition from pioneer schoolhouse to today's citywide system of schools and services.

One hundred and fifty years after Clara Ledyard taught seventy-seven students in the back of a meat market, the school district enrolled some 24,000 students. The district comprised more than thirty-five facilities.

In the fall of 2021, doors opened at Sioux Falls's newest high school—Jefferson High School. With an enrollment of 1,500–1,700 students, Jefferson joined Washington, Lincoln, Roosevelt, and the Career and Tech Ed Academy.

Sioux Falls also opened a sixth traditional middle school for the 2021–2022 school year—Ben Reifel Middle School—with a projected enrollment of 900 students.

Along with the high schools and middle schools, Sioux Falls has twenty-three elementary schools as well as options for early childhood programs including preschool and junior kindergarten.

In addition to growth in enrollment and buildings, over the years, the Sioux Falls School District expanded programming to meet the needs of students. Services included support for students with disabilities, a K–12 Spanish immersion program, and an A+ (arts plus academics) school. Students for whom English was a second language received instruction in an immersion program and had continued support as they transitioned into regular classrooms.

When the COVID-19 epidemic closed schools in March of 2020, the district implemented a Virtual Academy and continued the option in subsequent school years.

From its early days as a pioneer settlement until today, Sioux Falls has been committed to providing excellent schools. As district clerk C. W. McDonald wrote in 1876, "the question of the education of the children being the one of the greatest importance among the many coming before our people it seems to us that we should keep a little in advance of the actual needs of the village both as regards rooms and appliances."

Sources

Sioux Falls School Board Minutes, 1871–1895.

Sioux Falls Public Schools 1873–1989, Sioux Falls School District publication.

A Century of Progress: Sioux Falls Public School 1872–1973, Sioux Falls School District publication.

Pandemic: You Are Here

DESTINY PINDER-BUCKLEY

I proposed this essay when the pandemic was new and when I didn't quite believe it would go on this long. I'm writing this toward the end of 2021, and you'll be reading this in 2022 or 2023 or 2057, and I don't know if COVID-19 will still be a relevant battle or a distant memory or a bullet point in a history book when you get around to reading this. But in any case, right now, you are here.

It took me a long time to get "here," to get to this point of acceptance—and even more, adoration—for South Dakota. College was the only thing that kept me in the state at first. I had dreams of going to a big city, a metropolis like Chicago or New York, which I knew reeked of piss but also promise. I couldn't afford the glamour of skyscrapers and student loans of equal size, so I begrudgingly submitted my deposit to a local college, Augustana University, on the day of the deadline.

The proximity to my childhood home felt like a ball and chain. An hour wasn't enough. I wanted a different universe, somewhere new to escape to. I believed the tropes of the Midwest: that we were behind on current trends, surrounded by cornfields, said "ope" nonstop, never left our hometowns, and that almost everyone here, myself included, could be traced back to some Scandinavian or German hard-working immigrant from over a century ago. Back then, I would call Sioux Falls small and boring. If I had paid any attention, I would've seen Sioux Falls's growth—since my birth in 1997 to today, the population has grown by over 50 percent.

I began travelling as a way to escape South Dakota. I thought my personal growth would be measured in miles, a distance from my upbringing and my new life. At the beginning, it felt like the stereotypes were painfully true—people from my hometown couldn't fathom why I wanted to travel to places like India and Russia. But the world loves to remind you how small it is. While in India, at a hotel in the beach town of Puri, I ran into an older couple who were also from my hometown. They knew my grandmother, even though I didn't recognize their name. That's expected of small towns—everyone knows everyone, especially grandmas. I had never once met these people in my town of 15,000, but there we were, worlds apart, staying at the same hotel in India. We disagreed over the grace of the Corn Palace; I argued it paled in comparison to "real" palaces, like the *Taj Mahal*, but they stayed loyal to their opinion that it has a certain charm you don't find elsewhere.

And that was just the first encounter. In Vienna, I met a man who heard of Sioux Falls because of the show *Fargo*. Over the years, I've run across bucketfuls of Australians who say they drove through on an American road trip. My favorite was the bus driver in Iceland who told me he's visited Sturgis six times for the infamous motorcycle rally and then proceeded to sing me a song he wrote about his girlfriend in the eighties, who was also named Destiny. A professor from New Zealand visited the Corn Palace in the late nineties and bought a ceramic souvenir model, which she showed me proudly at dinner the next night. She confessed her love of Laura Ingalls Wilder and recalled her visit to the museum in De Smet, which was a special trip she made from Iowa City where she was staying for work. I couldn't fathom why a woman from across the world would be obsessed with Little House on the Prairie, a series I have never read myself.

I was from nowhere, yet everywhere I went I could find a connection. These strangers, from different continents, countries, and consciousnesses, had fond memories of South Dakota. Not until years later did I realize that I had used South Dakota as a scapegoat for my insecurities, a black hole to toss all blame.

South Dakota actually gave me the world on a silver platter. Because I stayed, I went to Augustana, where I went overboard with the study abroad opportunities. And the more people I met, the more places I got lost, the more I came to love South Dakota. It wasn't about the state itself; it was about my state of mind. When all I allowed myself to know about South Dakota was the torture of high school, local politics, frayed family ties, the view of the Corn Palace from my bedroom window, and the cold winters and hot summers, I turned blind to all the good. It was easier to believe that fate had trapped me here. South Dakota had been my birthplace, a place I left and returned to, a place where I stayed for good scholarships. I had never considered South Dakota home until it was almost too late.

As my senior year rolled around, I still had no idea what I was headed for after graduation. I left for spring break on a girl's trip to Boston, expecting to return and enjoy the last few months of my undergraduate career and worry about job prospects later. I hadn't expected the world to shut down overnight, that a random Friday in March would be the last time I sat in a class. I went from loving my small, in-person classes to seeing everyone on a screen.

I had almost forgotten that in October 2019, I applied for a year-long English teacher position in France. I heard back in May, as I scrambled to complete my degree via Google Docs and Zoom. I'd been accepted to my top location choice: Corsica, a beautiful island off the south of France, surrounded by clear blue waters and Mediterranean architecture. I could've ferried to Italy on the weekends and spent my mornings eating *pain au chocolat*.

I surprised myself when I declined. Wasn't it everything I wanted? A new world, a new adventure, a paying gig to get out of South Dakota? To add not just hours, but almost *days*' worth of travel between me and my hometown? I looked down at the three neatly typed words tattooed on my left wrist: *you are here*. I got the phrase permanently inked on my twentieth birthday after a particularly hard semester. I had a slew of bad luck, some untreated depression, and I had overloaded myself with responsibilities and a major I didn't like. I contemplated dropping out. I cried a lot. I still harbored the anger that I could be somewhere else. The tattoo reminded me to be present, to stop dwelling on the past and daydreaming about the future. Be here and go from there.

It took a global pandemic, but I realized for the first time in my life that I was actively living through history. The things I was living through would be talked about for years and would become the anecdotes I'll tell the youngsters in 2057. I had a history to reckon with, and I wanted to do it in the place I had history.

I don't know where I'll be in 2022, 2023, or 2057. I might be in South Dakota. Maybe I'll finally visit Corsica or end up somewhere new. After being out in the world, I realized how lucky I have it in Sioux Falls. I don't have an hour-and-a-half commute through traffic jams, I can leave my valuables unattended at a coffee shop without fear of theft, the rent is so cheap compared to the big cities that people's jaws hit the floor when I tell them what I pay (utilities included), I get to know people in my community, and I can ask a stranger for help and genuinely expect to receive it. I remember foreign exchange students in high school being amazed at snow for the first time. All of these are small joys I overlooked. I hope one day you visit Sioux Falls, if you haven't already, and you learn to love it. Just sit on a bench somewhere, let the wind rattle you and fling the pages of this book around, and remember: you are here.

Contributors

Daren Anderson is a native of Hartford, South Dakota, and currently resides on the family farm where he was raised. He has over thirty-three years' experience in the IT field. His entrepreneurial ventures include Big D Technology Solutions, Inc. and Memorials First, Inc, where he is President/CEO—both are located in Sioux Falls. He is most proud of his involvement with LSS School-Based Mentoring and being Diplomat of the Year four times for the Sioux Falls Area Chamber. His interest in Fenn's Bros. started when his dad, Delmer "Andy" Anderson, worked for the company from 1948 until their closure in 1971. A book titled *Fenn's Remembered*, which covers the complete history and products of the company, is in the works.

John Andrews is the managing editor of *South Dakota Magazine*, a bimonthly publication based in Yankton that explores the arts, history, and culture of South Dakota. A Lake Norden native, he earned degrees in journalism and history from South Dakota State University in Brookings and a master's degree in history from the University of South Dakota in Vermillion. He lives in Yankton with his wife, Michelle, and two children, Joseph and Elizabeth.

Randy Brown traveled the world as part of an active-duty US Air Force family in the 1970s, then landed happily in the American Midwest. He embedded with his former Iowa Army National Guard unit as a civilian journalist in Afghanistan, May–June 2011. A twenty-year veteran with one overseas deployment, he authored the 2015 collection *Welcome to FOB Haiku: War Poems from Inside the Wire*. His writing about Iowa highway rest areas appeared in Belt Publishing's *Midwest Architecture Journeys* (2019). A chapbook of prose and poetry, *Twelve O'Clock Haiku*, is forthcoming, and he coedited the anthology *Why We Write: Craft Essays on Writing War* (2019). Find him on Twitter: @FOB_haiku.

John Kennedy Claussen Sr., is a lifelong resident of Sioux Falls and still resides in the neighborhood he wrote about in his "Forty-First Street" essay. John has studied at the University of South Dakota, Georgetown University, Augustana University, and the USD School of Law. While in college, he interned on Capitol Hill and also for a member of the UK parliament in London. He received two national first-place sales and one second-place sales awards from JCPenney, where he worked for twenty-seven years. He is married with two adult children and a first grandchild that is on its way. He enjoys current events, history, blogging, cycling, canoeing, travel, and carpentry.

Mara W. Cohen Ioannides, born and raised in Central New Jersey, lives in Springfield, Missouri, where she has been teaching in the English Department at Missouri State University for the last twenty-five years. She is president of the Midwest Jewish Studies Association and the Ozarks Studies Association. The focus of her research is American Judaism, specifically the American Midwest. Her book publications, both fiction and nonfiction, include *The Evolution of the Non-Liturgical Parts of the Central Conference of American Rabbis Haggadah*, *We Are in Exile*, *A Shout in the Sunshine*, and forthcoming books on the history of the Jews of Missouri and the city of Springfield.

Mike Cooper grew up in Sioux Falls and graduated from Lincoln High School in 1971. After receiving a BS degree in landscape design from South Dakota State University, he worked in the Aberdeen, South Dakota, city planning office. He returned to Sioux Falls in 1978 and began his career with the city in 1986 as a senior planner. In 1999, Mike became director of Parks and Recreation, and he retired from the city in 2019. Since retirement, Mike has worked as a consultant with Landscape Garden Centers in Sioux Falls and volunteered as a member of the Mary Jo Wegner Arboretum Society board of directors. He recently has been serving as interim executive director of the arboretum.

Edward E. Curtis IV traces his midwestern Syrian heritage to the Hamaway and Samaha families who first settled in the region during the late 1800s. He is the author or editor of over a dozen books, including *Muslims of the Heartland: How Syrian Immigrants Made a Home in the American Midwest* and *Arab Indianapolis*. His *Muslims in America: A Short History* was named one of the *Publishers Weekly* Hundred Best Books of 2009. He has contributed interviews and articles to the *New York Times*, the *Wall Street Journal*, the *Washington Post*, National Public Radio, and the Associated Press, among other media outlets. Dr. Curtis is William M. and Gail M. Plater Chair of Liberal Arts and Professor of Religious Studies at the Indiana University School of Liberal Arts at IUPUI.

Jeff Danz is the co-owner of Zandbroz Variety, which has been a downtown institution for over three decades.

Tom Dempster is a director of IFAM Capital and a native of Sioux Falls. He served in the South Dakota Senate and the Minnehaha County Commission. He is a USD graduate with a BA in economics. He and his wife Patti have three daughters, each married to a man they admire and love. They relish their nine grandchildren. Tom is the photographer of *Behold* and the author of *North of Twelfth* Street, a finalist for *Foreward Book Review*'s book-of-the-year. His work has appeared in international, national, and local media and in solo gallery exhibitions. He hosted *South Dakota Heroes*, a SDPR documentary earning a national Edward R. Murrow Award. Tom has served as chair of the Avera-McKennan Board along with many other nonprofits. He is one of the founders of the Levitt at the Falls.

Jonathan Ellis started his career in journalism in 1998. He joined the *Argus Leader* in 2005, where he covered city, state, and federal politics before becoming a columnist and investigative reporter. He also spent five years as a correspondent for *USA Today*. He has climbed most of Colorado's 14,000-foot mountains, enjoys coaching and watching soccer, and he served in the infantry in the US Army Reserve. He is married to a Sioux Falls native, Amy, and together they have two children, Grace and Thomas.

Andrew Erickson is doctoral researcher and instructor in American Studies at the Europa-Universität Flensburg (Germany) and editorial assistant for *Amerikastudien / American Studies*. Recent publications focus on anti-intellectualism and counterfactual history, and on the critical posthumanism of Black American disaster fiction. His current book project understands speculative fiction by Black and Indigenous makers through the lens of the postapocalypses of American enslavement and settler colonialism. During consecutive undergraduate research internships at the Center for Western Studies, he compiled an annotated bibliography of Sioux Falls theatre history.

Larry Fuller is a former publisher of the *Argus Leader* and was involved in many community activities in Sioux Falls between 1978 and 1993. In Honolulu, where he moved in 1993, he was publisher of the *Honolulu Advertiser*, a daily newspaper, and later of *Pacific Business News*. He and his wife, Suzanne, returned permanently in December 2009. Over the last thirty years, Larry observed Sioux Falls and South Dakota "grow up" and in some cases, played a role in helping make that happen. He was part of the start-up for Forward Sioux Falls, Downtown Development Corp., Children's Inn, and other initiatives. He was also consulted on marketing and strategic facilitation for organizations and companies. Larry and Suzanne have a daughter, Beth Jensen, and her family in Sioux Falls, and a son, Mike, and his family in Minneapolis.

Daniel Max Gerling is a mild-mannered English professor at Augustana University with a background in American studies. His research ranges from the cultural history of US sanitation practices to ideological elements in writing instruction. Hunter S. Thompson initially inspired him to become a writer at a young age, and he has long admired George McGovern's integrity and commitment to public service. He finds it rather serendipitous and fortunate that he landed in Sioux Falls.

H. Roger Grant, a native of Albia, Iowa, is the Kathryn and Calhoun Lemon Professor of History at Clemson University in Clemson, South Carolina. Of his more than thirty-five academic book publications, four have been corporate studies of midwestern carriers, including the *Chicago & North Western*; *Chicago Great Western*; *Chicago, Rock Island & Pacific, and Wabash Railroads*. He has also written *Twilight Rails: The Final Era of Railroad Building in the Midwest* (University of Minnesota Press, 2010). Between 2012 and 2019, Indiana University Press published Grant's trilogy, *Railroads and the American People, Electric Interurbans and the American People*, and *Transportation and the American People*. He lives on Lake Hartwell outside Clemson.

Tom Greco chose Sioux Falls as his home after retiring from a twenty-year career as an officer in the active US Army. Born and raised in New York, he graduated from the US Military Academy at West Point and holds masters degrees from Georgetown University and the University of Missouri-Rolla. He is married to Jennifer (from Madison, South Dakota) and they have three children. Tom currently works for the city of Sioux Falls.

Douglas J. Hajek is a lawyer with Davenport, Evans, Hurwitz & Smith. He is a native of Tyndall, South Dakota. After graduating from South Dakota State University in 1972, he began a ten-year career in banking. Somewhat by accident, he had a front-row seat in the passage of legislation that led to the historic move of Citibank's credit card business to South Dakota in 1981. After finishing law school in 1985, Doug began a practice in banking, corporate and public finance law, and lobbying. He has served on numerous local and statewide boards and currently serves as chair of the board of directors of Meta Financial Group, Inc. Doug and his wife, Anne, live in Sioux Falls.

Linda Hallstrom was born in Sioux Falls and has lived there most of her life. Over the years, she has been employed in a variety of writing positions, including editor/reporter at the *Freeman Courier*, columnist for *Sioux Falls This Week* and the *Tri-State Neighbor*, and community relations supervisor for the Sioux Falls School District. Now semiretired, she finds time to enjoy freelance assignments, fiction/short stories, and poetry. She is proud that several poems have been selected for publication in recent issues of *Pasque Petals*.

Mary Hartnett is a veteran journalist born in Sioux City, Iowa. She has worked mainly in public radio and television as a reporter, producer, host, and news director. Mary's career has given her a chance to live in some interesting places, like Chicago; Iowa City; Toledo, Ohio; Chapel Hill, North Carolina; and Indianapolis. She is now the news director at Siouxland Public Media in Sioux City. Mary lives with her daughter, Katie, and two perpetually hungry guinea pigs in Sioux City.

Patrick Hicks is the author of *The Commandant of Lubizec*, *In the Shadow of Dora*, *Adoptable*, *This London*, and *The Collector of Names*, among others. His work has appeared on NPR, the *PBS NewsHour*, *American Life in Poetry*, and his first novel was selected for National Reading Group Month. A former Visiting Fellow at Oxford, he is the Writer-in-Residence at Augustana University as well as a faculty member in the MFA Program at Sierra Nevada University. He was recently a finalist for an Emmy and hosts the popular radio show, *Poetry from Studio 47*.

Stephen Jackson is an associate professor of history at the University of Sioux Falls. He is a historian of the British Empire with most of his work focusing on the intersection of religion, education, and settler colonialism in the twentieth century. He is the author of two books on these topics, *Constructing National Identity in Canadian and Australia Classrooms* (Palgrave, 2018), and *Religious Education and the Anglo-*

World (Brill, 2020). He can often be found rummaging through the USF campus archives, laughing or crying at stories told by faculty, students, and administrators from the more than 135-year history of the institution.

David Wal Jal was born and raised in South Sudan until the civil war forced his family to flee. After growing up in various refugee camps in east Africa, he was resettled as a refugee in Sioux Falls on June 21, 1995. Jal holds bachelor and master's degrees in social work and a diploma in international restorative justice. He worked for several years at LSS Refugee and Immigration Center as a case manager and is currently employed as a court services officer in Sioux Falls. Jal has maintained close ties with the local and national refugee population.

Beth Jensen is a Sioux Falls native who began working at KELO Television in 1996. Beth spent time as a reporter and then a producer before becoming the executive producer in 2001. She was named news director in 2008. She has produced stories, newscasts, and specials that have received national Edward R. Murrow awards and regional Emmys. She is a graduate of Boston University, where she studied broadcast journalism and political science. Beth developed a love of news thanks to her journalist parents, Larry and Suzanne Fuller.

Carolyn Johnson grew up in Goodhue, Minnesota, before moving to Sioux Falls for college. She was part of the final graduating class of Augustana College before the institution's name change in 2015. After graduation, she chose to stay in Sioux Falls, where she has worked for Siouxland Heritage Museums, Siouxland Libraries, LifeScape, and Mikkelsen Library at Augustana University. She is currently the volunteer coordinator and museum interpreter at Siouxland Heritage Museums.

Avery M. Jones is a Kapoja, *Travels-Light,* of the Bdewakantunwan, *People of the Mysterious Lake*, of the Oceti 'Sakowin, *The Seven Council Fires.* He teaches Dakodiapi in the Wakpa Ipak'san community, where he was born and raised. He hopes to see his thirty-first winter this year. He has an Eminent Scholar Dakota Language and Culture Educator Permit from the state of South Dakota, but the words of encouragement and call to action from his elders carry more weight. He has one single poem published.

Duane Jundt is a native of western North Dakota now living in Orange City, Iowa. He taught American and European history at Notre Dame and Northwestern College in Iowa for twenty years. A member of the advisory board of the Theodore Roosevelt Association, he is a frequent contributor to the *TRA Journal.* His review essays and articles on Roosevelt have appeared in journals including *Orion*, *Middle West Review*, and the *Journal of the Wild West History Association*. He is one of the authors of *Theodore Roosevelt, Naturalist in the Arena* (University of Nebraska Press, 2020).

Patrick Lalley is a Sioux Falls native and veteran journalist. He graduated from O'Gorman High School and the University of South Dakota. Lalley was cofounder of *Tempest Magazine*, a reporter in Sioux City and Des Moines, then copy editor, night editor, state editor, managing editor, and news director of the *Argus Leader*. Lalley is the author of seven nonfiction children's books including *9.11.01: Terrorist Attack the US*. He writes for *FiveFour* and *Pigeon605.com* and occasionally contributes to the *Washington Post*.

Austin Lammers grew up in Rapid City, South Dakota, and graduated from Rapid City Central High School in 2016. He earned a media and journalism degree at the University of South Dakota in 2021, where he served as editor in chief of the *Volante* in 2019. He's written for the *Argus Leader*, *605 Magazine*, and as a marketing intern with Fernson Brewing Co. in Sioux Falls. He now lives in Fort Collins, Colorado, where he covered the 2020 general election for the Colorado News Collaborative and now serves as marketing director for a startup food hub called ReKaivery.

Jon K. Lauck is a native of rural Madison, South Dakota. He is the author of *The Lost Region: Toward a Revival of Midwestern History* (University of Iowa Press, 2013) and *From Warm Center to Ragged Edge: The Erosion of Midwestern Regionalism, 1920-1965* (University of Iowa Press, 2017). Lauck has worked for several years as a lawyer, professor, and political advisor and is currently serving as an adjunct professor of history and political science at the University of South Dakota and as editor-in-chief of *Middle West Review*. He earned his PhD in history from the University of Iowa and his law degree from the University of Minnesota.

Sandra C. Looney is from Worthington, Minnesota. Her doctorate in English is from the University of Arkansas. She began teaching at Augustana in 1964, retiring in 2018. In 1974, she received an AACTE Grant (American Association of Colleges for Teacher Education) for study in India with a focus on modernization and Indian writers. She co-led January Study Abroad Seminars to Northern India, and her passion for travel led her to offer other study-abroad seminars in England, Ireland, and Scotland. Looney values the small liberal arts institution for promoting a multidisciplinary approach to learning and the liberal arts for framing a life of enduring worth.

Chris Madsen, a 1993 graduate of the USD School of Law, is general counsel and director of operations for Claims Associates, Inc. With nearly twenty-five years of experience with litigation, he brings a wealth of knowledge to bear on claims work. Madsen practices law as the primary means of funding a chronic cooking habit and his ongoing quest for tasty experiences with family and friends.

Cheyenne Marco holds a PhD in literary studies with an emphasis on creative writing, and she enjoys writing about the complexities of life on the Northern Plains. She grew up on a poultry farm in southwest Minnesota, and her rural upbringing has greatly influenced her writing. Her works have appeared in *South Dakota in Poems: An Anthology*, *Turk's Head Review*, *Prairie Winds*, and other venues. In 2017, she won the Western Literature Association's Frederick Manfred Award for Creative Writing. Marco currently teaches undergraduate English at the University of South Dakota-Community College for Sioux Falls campus.

Marty McGoey grew up in Anoka, Minnesota, though he considers himself more of a midwesterner rather than a Minnesotan, having lived also in Nebraska, Iowa, North Dakota, and South Dakota. He has taught college composition courses for many years at various institutions. Prior to working as a college instructor, he taught high school English for three years at a small, private school in Minnesota. His work has appeared in *Vermillion Literary Project*. In 2012, he was awarded the Lakeside Lab Writing Fellowship at Lakeside Lab in Okoboji, Iowa. He lives in Vermillion, South Dakota, with his wife, a dog, and a cat.

Michael J. Mullin is a professor of history at Augustana University, where he teaches American, regional, and American Indian history. He is currently the University's NEH Chair in Regional Heritage; he is a two-time recipient of the Vernon and Mildred Niebuhr Faculty Excellence Award. His writing currently focuses on various aspects of South Dakota and Sioux Falls history. He has had articles appear in *South Dakota History*, the *American Indian and Culture Journal*, the *American Indian Quarterly*, and *Mid-America: A Historical Review*. In addition, he has six book chapters in various compilations. He has one published manuscript, with another currently under review at a university press.

Elinor Nauen was born and raised in Sioux Falls, graduated from (the old) Washington High School, and currently lives in New York City. Her books include *Now That I Know Where I'm Going*, *So Late into the Night*, *My Marriage A to Z: A Big-City Romance*, *American Guys*, *CARS & Other Poems*, and, as editor, *Ladies, Start Your Engines: Women Writers on Cars and the Road* and *Diamonds Are a Girl's Best Friend: Women Writers on Baseball.* Her poem "The History of Western Philosophy" was recently selected for the *Best American Poetry* blog. As a journalist, she has written about health, automobiles, sports, travel, and much more for many national magazines. She also maintains a six-day-a-week blog at ElinorNauen.com.

Evan Nolte moved with his parents to Sioux Falls from Iowa. He graduated from Augustana University with a BA in political science and business administration. In 1992, he was named president/CEO of the Sioux Falls Chamber, retiring in February 2017. During his career, he held a number of community leadership positions, including serving as co-president of Forward Sioux Falls, the community's premier economic development and quality of life program initiative, and a joint venture of the Chamber and the Sioux Falls Development Foundation. In retirement, he is a board member of Sioux Falls Thrive, a new "Cradle to Career" community coalition designed to enhance the alignment of pre-K, K–12 and postsecondary education and community resources.

Virginia Olson is a Sioux Falls native. Currently, she is the editor and content coordinator for the monthly magazine, *Southside Living*, and also regularly writes local features for *Sioux Falls Woman* and *Sioux Valley News* in Canton. Before shifting her passion to writing, she was a teacher at

Lincoln High School. There, she taught creative writing and journalism and was adviser for the school newspaper, the *Statesman.*

Destiny Pinder-Buckley is a recent Augustana University alumna (depending on how long "recent" entails) who has lived in many places, but mostly in South Dakota. She double majored in English and French because she loves words and languages and bad accents. She spent a semester in St. Petersburg, Russia, and it became a personality trait for her, along with enforcing her wanderlust addiction. But when she returns from wherever the heck she's been, she's always happy to land back in Sioux Falls.

Margaret Preston grew up in New Orleans and received her BA from Loyola University. She has lived in Sioux Falls since 2001. Preston is a professor of history and teaches at Augustana University, where she is currently the Stanley L. Olsen Chair of Moral Values. On the board at the Center for Western Studies at Augustana, Preston is the author and co-editor of a number of books and articles, including *Charitable Words: Gentlewomen, Social Control, and the Language of Charity in Nineteenth-Century Dublin* (2004). In 2011, for the hospital's centennial, she authored *A Journey of Faith a Destination of Excellence: Avera McKennan Hospital's First Century of Caring.*

Marcella Prokop is a writer, educator, and vagabond at heart. Neither wholly Colombian nor American, her dual identity shapes her writing and her place in the world. Marcella's work has been published online or in print by *Ploughshares, Pank*, the *Brooklyn Review*, and the *Christian Science Monitor*.

Hannah Redder grew up blocks away from the World's Only Corn Palace. She holds an undergraduate degree from Augustana College (not University!) in Sioux Falls and recently graduated from NYU's creative writing MFA program. She currently lives in New York, where she is finishing her first novel.

Charles Rogers is a lifelong resident of South Dakota who became interested in history while attending Wessington High School. After earning a masters of education in school administration with a minor in history from South Dakota State University, he taught American history and American government at Scotland High School and Washington High

School. He served as an adjunct professor at Kilian Community College for twenty years. An active member of the Washington High Historic Committee, he was involved in the placement of historic markers around the school. He has authored two books on South Dakota history: *South Dakota's Challenges Since 1960* (2011) and *South Dakota Stories from WW II* (2020).

Eric Schulte was born and raised in Sioux Falls. After graduating law school at USD in 1999, he worked as a law clerk for one year in Sioux Falls for the judges of the Second Judicial Circuit. Since 2000, he has practiced law in Sioux Falls at Davenport, Evans, Hurwitz & Smith, LLP. From 2015 through 2016, he served as president of the South Dakota State Bar Association. He also served for several years on the executive board of the Banquet, including a one-year term as president in 2017. Eric also writes poetry, with some of his poems being published in *Pasque Petals*, the magazine for the South Dakota State Poetry Society, and *South Dakota Magazine*.

George W. Shurr was born in Rock Rapids, Iowa, and raised on the family farm about thirty miles east of Sioux Falls. After graduating from geology programs at the University of South Dakota, Northwestern University, and the University of Montana, he taught at St. Cloud State University in Minnesota for thirty years. When he moved back to the family farm about twenty years ago, he became interested in local archaeology. As a part of his interest in Blood Run archaeology, George met Dr. Dale R. Henning who has done the foundational professional excavation on the site. Dr. Henning's extensive publications are the main basis for our understanding of the people who once lived in the Blood Run National Historic Landmark.

Jon C. Teaford was born and raised in Columbus, Ohio, and now lives in West Lafayette, Indiana. He received his PhD from the University of Wisconsin. In 2011–2012, he served as president of the Urban History Association. At present, he is professor emeritus of history at Purdue University. He is the author of a number of books on urban history including *Cities of the Heartland: The Rise and Fall of the Industrial Midwest*. He also served as a senior consulting editor to *The American Midwest: An Interpretive Encyclopedia*.

Harry F. Thompson holds a PhD in English with a concentration in historical fiction. His own research activities have included publications about the history of American literary publishing houses, the intersection of history and literature in the novels of Willa Cather and Frederick Manfred, and radicalism among contemporary western authors. Previous to his appointment as executive director of the Center for Western Studies in 2009, he managed the center's research collections and book publishing programs and directed the annual Dakota Conference. Thompson directed the History of the Arts in South Dakota project, cosponsored by the state's arts and humanities councils, and is the editor and publisher of over sixty books for the center.

Christopher Vondracek grew up in Kiester and Wells, Minnesota, and currently lives in Washington, DC. He taught college English for a decade before pivoting to journalism, and he is now the South Dakota correspondent for Forum News Service. His poetry collection, *Rattlesnake Summer* (Badger Clark Publishing), assigns a poem for each of the sixty-six counties in the state, while tracking local news, family history, and a drought.

Bob Wendland is the artistic director and cofounder of the Good Night Theatre Collective and serves as the assistant director of performances and events at the Washington Pavilion. A graduate of Augustana College, Wendland has performed, directed, and collaborated with numerous theatre groups, visual artists, dance companies, and musicians. He received the Mayor's Award for Individual Excellence in the Arts, Innovative Project Award from the Sioux Falls Arts Council, Best Pivot of the Year Award from Hey Sioux Falls, and Best Actor Award from Sioux Falls Stage.

Grant Wentzel is an incidental transplant from Columbus, Ohio, and he can be found all over town performing music as Link West, covering local arts and culture at fyisiouxfalls.com and publishing creative work at ouchthatshot.com

April White is an award-winning writer, editor, and researcher. She is the author of *The Divorce Colony* (Hachette Books, 2022), the stunning true story of the socialites who pioneered modern marriage and divorce in Sioux Falls. She has also written numerous other historical tales—including the story of a Hollywood makeup artist who taught World War II spies how to hide in plain sight and the harrowing saga of a 1930s search for a summit higher than Everest—for publications such as the *Washington Post, Smithsonian Magazine, WWII Magazine, Atlas Obsurca, JSTOR Daily*, and the *Atavist Magazine*. White previously served as an editor at *Smithsonian Magazine*. She is based in Washington, DC.

Stu Whitney is a native of Grosse Pointe, Michigan, who graduated with a journalism degree from Michigan State University in 1989. He worked at the *Lansing State Journal* before embarking on a thirty-year career at the *Argus Leader*, where his roles included sports editor, news columnist, content coach, and editorial board member. Whitney was a three-time South Dakota sportswriter of the year who also won awards for his reporting on Native American student-athletes and ethics abuses in South Dakota politics. He and his wife, Lisa, have a daughter (Emily) and son (Elliot).

Steven Wingate is the author of the novels *The Leave-Takers* (2021) and *Of Fathers and Fire* (2019), both part of the Flyover Fiction Series from the University of Nebraska Press. His short story collection, *Wifeshopping* (Houghton Mifflin Harcourt, 2008), won the Bakeless Prize in Fiction from the Bread Loaf Writers' Conference. He is associate editor at *Fiction Writers Review* and associate professor at South Dakota State University.

Publication Credits

Andrews, John. "The Missing Amidons." *South Dakota Magazine*. November/December 2014.

Hallstrom, Linda. "Sioux Falls Public Schools: 1873-1989" Brochure.

Whitney, Stu. "Yankton Trail Bridge." *Argus Leader*. 10 August 2018.

Belt Publishing

beltpublishing.com